Defective Premises:
Law and Practice

William Hanbury

SWEET & MAXWELL

 **THOMSON REUTERS**

First Edition 2009

Published in 2009 by
Thomson Reuters (Legal) Limited
(Registered in England & Wales, Company No 1679046.
Registered office and address for service: 100 Avenue Road, London, NW3 3PF)
trading as Sweet & Maxwell.
For further information on our products and services, visit
http://www.sweetandmaxwell.co.uk
Typeset by Matthew Marley, Devon
Printed and bound in Great Britain by TJ International, Padstow, Cornwall

No natural forests were destroyed to make this product;
only farmed timber was used and re-planted.

British Library Cataloguing in Publication Data

A CIP catalogue record for this book
is available from the British Library

ISBN 978-1-84703-126-6

Dedication

To Ra and to weekends.

Preface

This book is intended to fill a surprising gap in the market. As landlords, both residential and commercial, face ever greater regulation there is a strange lack of material to help them.

The function of this book is therefore to provide landlords, tenants and all those involved with the legal side of property management with a starting point if not the complete answer to their legal problems.

The subject is by its broad nature difficult to define precisely and there will undoubtedly be detail which has been left out of a practitioner's text. However, I aim to cover as comprehensively as possible an area which straddles many boundaries. In practice, problems concerning defective premises do not fall neatly, for example, into the law of landlord and tenant or construction law, but include elements of both these and other areas.

In summary, my aim is to simplify and explain a complex area of the law, without which the practitioner would have to rely on those overworked practitioner's texts on landlord and tenant, dilapidations and construction law.

Thanks go to my colleagues Gordon Exall, Simon Read and Christopher Dodd for the help they gave on the precedents section of this work and to Robert Goldie, for his help with the proofs.

William Hanbury
November 2008

Contents

Dedication	v
Preface	vii
Table of Cases	xxi
Table of Statutes	xlv
Table to Statutory Instruments	li
Introduction	lv
Background	lv
What is meant by "Defective Premises"?	lvi

Part 1: Contractual Liability

Chapter 1: Principles of Contractual Liability	3
The privity rule	3
Agreements or assurances before a lease	5
Collateral contracts and warranties	6
Avoiding the Formality Requirements	7
Equitable Intervention	8
Liability under leases following assignment or subletting	9
Effect of the Contracts (Rights of Third Parties) Act 1999	9
Effect of the Landlord and Tenant (Covenants) Act 1995	10
Pre-January 1996 tenancies	11
Position of T's assignee A	12
Post-January 1996 tenancies	13
Original tenant	13
Original landlord's position	13
L's assignee R	14
Original landlord's position following assignment by the tenant	14
T's assignee A	14
Operation of the 1995 Act in Practice	14
Chapter 2: Express obligations on landlords and tenants to repair and maintain	17
The repairing covenant—the concept of disrepair	18
The decision in *Quick v Taff-Ely*	18
The application of the concept of disrepair to later cases	18
Problems with the decision in Quick	20
Repair versus improvement	20
Construing the repairing covenant	24
The general approach to construction	24

Examples of particular covenants 25
When the obligation to repair arises—the notice requirement 26
 What constitutes notice? 26
 Exceptions to the notice requirement 27
 Notice clauses 28
 Who does notice have to be given to? 28
Applying to court under section 35 of the Landlord and Tenant
Act 1987 to vary express terms in long leases 29
Proposals for reform 30
Chapter 3: Unfair terms in leases 31
 The Unfair Contract Terms Act 1977 31
 The Unfair Terms in Consumer Contracts Regulations 1999 32
  Scope of the regulations 33
  What the regulations say 33
  What terms will be judged unreasonable 34
  Possible future challenges 35
Chapter 4: Terms implied into leases at common law relevant to
repair and maintenance 37
 When a term will be implied 38
  The business efficacy test 39
 Implied terms in practice 39
 When a term will not be implied 43
 Furnished lets 44
 Negotiations for termination/terminal dilapidations 44
 Implied rights of access to effect repairs 45
Chapter 5: Obligations on Landlords to repair and maintain
implied by statute 47
 The historic background—legislative interference with freedom
 of contract 48
 Section 8 of the Landlord and Tenant Act 1985 48
 Repairing obligations in short leases under section 11 of the
 Landlord and Tenant Act 1985 49
  Contracting out 49
  Additional obligations 49
  The extent of section 11 50
  Cases to which section 11 will not apply 52
  Common parts 53
  Standard of repair 54
  Installations 54
   Keeping installations in "proper working order" 55
 The statutory rights of access under the Landlord and Tenant
 Act 1985 55
Other provisions relevant to long leaseholders 56
 Terms implied at the end of long leases 56
 Proposals for reform 56

Chapter 6: Other express and implied obligations on landlords
relevant to the repair or maintenance of the premises 57
  Not to derogate from the grant 57
    Examples of cases where the covenant has been held to apply 58
    Consequences of establishing derogation from grant—can the
    tenant repudiate? 59
  For quiet enjoyment 60
  Nature of the covenant at common law 60
  Absolute and qualified covenants 61
  When the covenant against quiet enjoyment is relevant to
  defective premises claims 61
  Relying on the covenant as a defence 63
Chapter 7: Implied obligations on tenants relevant to the repair or
maintenance of the premises 65
  To occupy in a "tenant-like manner" 66
    When the obligation is relevant 66
    What is expected of the tenant 66
    Consequences of breach 67
    Limitation 68
  Not to commit waste 69
  Voluntary waste 70
    Examples of voluntary waste 70
    Reasonable wear and tear 71
    Remedies for breach 71
  Permissive waste 71
    Remedies for breach 72
  To keep the premises wind and watertight 73
  To permit the landlord to view the state of repair and carry
  out repairs 73
  Proposals for reform 74

Part II: Non-contractual liability

Chapter 8: Negligence, nuisance and the rule in Rylands v Fletcher 77
  Negligence 78
    Rights and liabilities between adjoining occupiers 78
    Liability of landlords to adjoining occupiers 78
    Rights of support between neighbours 79
    Negligence of occupiers arising out of unlawful acts
    of third parties 79
    Landlord's right to sue adjoining occupiers 80
    Tenant's liability to adjoining occupiers 80
    The tenant's right to sue adjoining occupiers 81
    Builder's and builder-landlord's liability to the tenant 81
    Examples 82
  Nuisance 83

Nature of the tort of nuisance 83
When liability arises 83
Liability and rights of the tenant 83
Liability and rights of landlord 84
Common categories of nuisance by landlords 85
Nuisance in common or retained parts affecting
demised premises 85
Nuisance at the date of the lease—liability to third parties 87
Nuisance arising after the commencement of the lease 87
Liability of landlords for acts of tenants towards other
tenants or neighbours 88
Entry to abate nuisance 89
Rylands v Fletcher 90
Cases where Rylands v Fletcher liability does not arise 90
Examples 91
Chapter 9: Tortious liability of builders and landlords under the
Defective Premises Act 1972 and other statutes 93
Liability of the builder to the purchaser in negligence at
common law 94
Liability of the landlord-builder at common law 95
The statutory duty to build dwellings properly 96
Who does the duty apply to? 96
What type of work is covered? 96
Which premises are excluded? 96
Nature and scope of the duty 97
What is the limitation period? 98
Can the employer or purchaser recover from economic loss? 99
The Supply of Goods and Services Act 1982 100
The seller / builder 100
Goods 100
Liability of landlords under the Defective Premises Act 1972 101
The duty to tenants and third parties 101
The nature of the duty under section 4 101
Key points 103
"let under a tenancy" 103
"which puts on the landlord the obligation for the
maintenance or repair of the premises ..." 103
"a duty to take such care as is reasonable in all the
circumstances" 104
"to see that they are reasonably safe from personal
injury or from damage to their property" 104
"caused by a relevant defect" 104
"The said duty is owed if the landlord knows (whether
by being notified by the tenant or otherwise) or ought in
all the circumstances to have known ..." 104

Liability where there is a right to enter to carry out
any repair or maintenance as well as duty to repair 105
Remedies 106
Secure and assured tenancies 107
Position of licensees 107
Chapter 10: The Occupiers' Liability Act 1957-1984 109
The duty to visitors 110
The 1957 Act 110
What premises are covered? 110
Who is the "occupier"? 111
Trustees and unincorporated associations 112
Who is a "visitor"? 113
Visitors exercising rights of way or other legal rights 113
The nature of the duty and standard of care to visitors 114
Defences 116
Obvious dangers 116
Volenti non-fit injuria (voluntary assumption of risk) 116
Contributory negligence 116
Can the occupier exclude or restrict liability? 117
Guests 117
Liability of the occupier for his independent contractors 117
The duty to trespassers 118
Intentions of trespasser 118
Nature of duty under 1984 Act and the standard of care 119
Defences 120
Warnings and exclusions 120
Volenti non-fit injuria 121
Chapter 11: Obligations under miscellaneous statutes and regulations 123
The Building Act 1984 123
The building regulations 124
Liability in negligence or breach of duty following a
breach of the building regulations 125
Establishing civil liability for a breach of the regulations
and the economic loss problem 125
Liability under miscellaneous health and safety legislation 126
Health and Safety at Work Act 1974 127
Liability for Asbestos 127
Fire Regulations 129
Liability for gas installations 129
Miscellaneous technical regulations about gas installations 130
Construction and design of gas appliances 130
Duties on landlords and others under the 1988 Gas Safety
Regulations 130
Who the regulations apply to 131
What the regulations say 131

Carbon-monoxide poisoning 131
Notice 131
Access 132
Liability for electrical installations 132
Energy efficiency standards 133
Legislation applying to particular types of premises 134
Offices Shops and Railway premises Act 1963 134
Disability Discrimination Act 1995 and 2005 135
Chapter 12: Local authority control of defective premises 137
Powers and duties under housing, building and public health
legislation 138
Background 138
The Public Health Act 1936 138
The Building Act 1984 and regulations made
thereunder 139
The Housing Act 1985 139
The Environmental Protection Act 1990 139
The Housing Grants Construction and Regeneration
Act 1996 140
The new system for assessing housing conditions in the
Housing Act 2004 140
Structure of the legislation in outline 140
The new housing health and safety-rating regime in outline 141
Hazards covered by the legislation 142
Enforcement Errors 143
Application of the new scheme 143
Duties and powers with respect to houses in multiple
occupation 143
The power to control statutory nuisances 144
The statutory nuisance power in outline 145
What constitutes a statutory nuisance? 145
What powers are there to deal with statutory nuisances? 146
Local authority powers to enforce energy efficiency standards 146
The "Decent Homes Standard" 147
Proposals for reform 149
Part III: Remedies
Chapter 13: Use of the Human Rights Act 1998 153
The relevant convention rights 154
Who is liable under the Human Rights Act? 154
How a challenge may be made 155
The challenges so far 155
Decisions relevant to defective premises legislation 157
Possible future challenges 158
Chapter 14: Self help 159
Freehold owners' access to adjoining land 160

Common law rights between neighbours 160
Establishing an easement 160
Common law right to abate a nuisance 161
Statutory intervention in relation to access rights 161
The tenant's right to self-help 161
Carrying out the works 162
Defects to the common parts 162
Withholding repair costs against rent 163
Setting off the repair costs in subsequent proceedings 164
Set-off following assignment 164
Attempts to limit the right to set-off 166
The position of licensees 166
The rights of tenants of local authorities to compel the landlord
to carry out repairs 166
The right to carry out improvements 167
The rights of long leaseholders 168
Chapter 15: Forfeiture 169
When the right to forfeit arises 169
What method of forfeiture should be chosen? 170
When will the landlord be taken to have waived the cause for
forfeiture? 171
What constitutes waiver? 171
What procedural steps must the landlord take before forfeiture? 172
Restrictions on the landlord's right to forfeit 172
The section 146 notice 172
What breaches are capable of remedy? 173
The effect of the Leasehold Property Repair Act 1938 173
The requirements of the Act in overview 174
The requirements of the court's leave 174
How the 1938 Act works in practice 175
Can the 1938 Act be avoided? 176
Relief against forfeiture 176
The statutory jurisdiction 176
Terms on which relief should be granted 177
Effect of the grant on relief 178
Sub-tenant's position 178
Costs 179
The particular case of decorative repairs 179
How and when to apply for relief 180
Whether the landlord should forfeit? 181
Tactical considerations 181
Proposals for reform 182
Chapter 16: Specific performance and mandatory injunctions 183
General principles 184
When specific performance will be refused 185

CONTENTS

Delay	185
Lack of particularity	185
The statutory basis for the award	186
Interim relief	186
Claims under section 4 of the Defective Premises Act 1972	187
Which court?	187
How is the order or undertaking enforced?	188
Damages in lieu of an injunction/specific performance	188
Chapter 17: Damages	191
Liability for those responsible for the safety of premises	192
Inconvenience and discomfort	193
When these damages are recoverable	193
The correct method of assessment	193
Residential leases at a ground rent	194
Repair costs	196
Consequential losses	196
Damages for disrepair in commercial leases	197
The landlord's claim	197
The Landlord and Tenant Act 1927	197
When does section 18 apply?	198
The first limb	199
When repair costs will be awarded and when the diminution in value	199
How the diminution in value figure is identified in practice	200
When the landlord is likely to carry out or has carried out the repairs	200
Where there is little likelihood of the landlord doing the repairs	201
Where it may be assumed the premises will be redeveloped	201
Where there is a sub-tenancy	201
Where an arrangement as to the completion of the repairs is reached with the new tenant	202
What is meant by diminution in the value of the reversion?	203
The second limb	204
The tenant's damages claim	204
Damages in tort	206
Landlords who design and build premises	206
Exceptional cases—aggravated or exemplary damages	207
Liability for personal injury and death	207
Carbon monoxide poisoning	208
Asthma	209
Other conditions relating to damp housing conditions	210
Future employment prospects	211

Limitations on the damages award	211
Contributory negligence	211
Examples	212
Causation, remoteness and the failure to mitigate	212
Causation	213
Remoteness	214
Loss of profit	215
Mitigation of loss	215
The betterment problem	216
Interest	217
Contractual claims	217
Personal injury claims	218
The judgment rate	218

Part IV: Practice and Procedure

Chapter 18: Bringing a court claim	221
Limitation	222
When the cause of action accrues	223
Contractual claims	223
Tortious claims	224
Some particular cases	225
Parties	226
Instructing an expert	226
Joint statements	228
What type of expert should be instructed?	228
Complying with pre-action protocols	230
Dilapidations claims	230
The Pre-Action Protocol—Terminal Dilapidations Claims for Damages	230
The landlord's claim	231
Certification of the dilapidations schedule by the landlord's surveyor	232
Timing of the dilapidations schedule	232
The tenant's response	232
Other procedural steps before issue	233
Housing claims	233
Scope	233
Aims	234
Steps under the protocol	234
Expert evidence under the Housing Disrepairs Protocol	235
Costs	236
Consequences of non-compliance with the protocol	236
Pleadings	236
Rules on statements of case—the basics	237
Amendments	237

Scott schedules	238
Claims for contribution and indemnity	238
Further information	238
Statements of truth	239
Case management	239
Track allocation	239
Unless orders	240
T&CC practice	240
Background	240
Features of litigation in the T&CC	241
Basic procedure	241
Transfer to the county court	242
Summary judgment	242
Costs	243
Part 36 offers	243
Other offers to settle and conduct	243
Chapter 19: Other methods of dispute resolution	245
ADR schemes	246
Mediation generally	246
Government sponsored and court based schemes	246
Non-government or non-court-based schemes	247
Choice of mediator	248
Conduct of mediator	248
Without prejudice nature of mediation	248
Costs of mediation	249
Early neutral evaluation—ENE	249
Arbitration	250
Statutory rules governing arbitration	250
Scope of the reference	251
Who is to arbitrate?	251
Challenge	251
Appeal	251
The award	251
Expert determination	252
Challenging the determination	252
Part V: Appendices	
Appendix A—Statutes and Statutory Instruments	
Appendix A1: Landlord and Tenant Act 1927 c.36	255
Appendix A2: Leasehold Property (Repairs) Act 1938 c.34	257
Appendix A3: Occupiers' Liability Act 1957 c.31	259
Appendix A4: Defective Premises Act 1972 c.35	261
Appendix A5: Occupiers' Liability Act 1984 c.3	266
Appendix A6: Building Act 1984 c.55	268
Appendix A7: Landlord and Tenant Act 1985 c.70	277
Appendix A8: Landlord and Tenant Act 1987 c.31	282

Appendix A9: Environmental Protection Act 1990 c.43   284
Appendix A10: Gas Safety (Installation and Use) Regulations
(SI 1998/2451)   302
Appendix A11: Housing Act 2004 c.34   307
Appendix B—Precedents
    Appendix B1   315
    Appendix B2   317
    Appendix B3   319
    Appendix B4   323
    Appendix B5   326
    Appendix B6   328
    Appendix B7   329
    Appendix B8   331
    Appendix B9   333
    Appendix B10   336
    Appendix B11   341
    Appendix B12   344
Appendix C—Useful websites   349
Index   351

Table of Cases

A v Hoare; X v Wandsworth LBC; H v Suffolk CC; C v Middlesbrough Council; Young v Catholic Care (Diocese of Leeds) [2008] UKHL 6; [2008] 2 W.L.R. 311; [2008] 2 All E.R. 1; [2008] 1 F.L.R. 771; [2008] 1 F.C.R. 507; (2008) 11 C.C.L. Rep. 249; (2008) 100 B.M.L.R. 1; [2008] Fam. Law 402; (2008) 105(6) L.S.G. 27; (2008) 158 N.L.J. 218; (2008) 152(6) S.J.L.B. 28, HL 18–02

ABP v CH Bailey. *See* Associated British Ports v CH Bailey Plc ....

Abbahall Ltd v Smee [2002] EWCA Civ 1831; [2003] 1 W.L.R. 1472; [2003] 1 All E.R. 465; [2003] H.L.R. 40; [2003] 2 E.G.L.R. 66; [2003] 28 E.G. 114; [2003] 2 E.G. 103 (C.S.); (2003) 100(10) L.S.G. 28; (2003) 147 S.J.L.B. 58; [2002] N.P.C. 168, CA (Civ Div) 8–21, 14–05

Adami v Lincoln Grange Management Ltd (1998) 30 H.L.R. 982; [1998] 1 E.G.L.R. 58; [1998] 17 E.G. 148; [1997] E.G. 182 (C.S.); (1998) 95(3) L.S.G. 25; (1998) 142 S.J.L.B. 37; [1997] N.P.C. 180, CA (Civ Div) 4–05

Aird v Prime Meridian Ltd [2006] EWCA Civ 1866; [2007] C.P. Rep. 18; [2007] B.L.R. 105; 111 Con. L.R. 209; (2007) 104(2) L.S.G. 31; (2007) 151 S.J.L.B. 60, CA (Civ Div) 18–08

Alderson v Beetham Organisation Ltd [2003] EWCA Civ 408; [2003] 1 W.L.R. 1686; [2003] B.L.R. 217; [2003] H.L.R. 60; (2003) 100(23) L.S.G. 39; (2003) 147 S.J.L.B. 418; [2003] N.P.C. 47, CA (Civ Div) 9–08

Alexander v Mercouris [1979] 1 W.L.R. 1270; [1979] 3 All E.R. 305; (1979) 252 E.G. 911; (1979) 123 S.J. 604, CA (Civ Div) 9–08

Alfred McAlpine Construction Ltd v Panatown Ltd (No.1); sub nom Panatown Ltd v Alfred McAlpine Construction Ltd [2001] 1 A.C. 518; [2000] 3 W.L.R. 946; [2000] 4 All E.R. 97; [2000] C.L.C. 1604; [2000] B.L.R. 331; (2000) 2 T.C.L.R. 547; 71 Con. L.R. 1; [2000] E.G. 102 (C.S.); (2000) 97(38) L.S.G. 43; (2000) 150 N.L.J. 1299; (2000) 144 S.J.L.B. 240; [2000] N.P.C. 89, HL ... 1–02

Alker v Collingwood Housing Association [2007] EWCA Civ 343; [2007] 1 W.L.R. 2230; [2007] H.L.R. 29; [2007] L. & T.R. 23; [2007] 2 E.G.L.R. 43; [2007] 25 E.G. 184, CA (Civ Div) 4–04, 9–21, 9–23

Allied London Investments Ltd v Hambro Life Assurance Plc (1985) 50 P. & C.R. 207; [1985] 1 E.G.L.R. 45; (1985) 274 E.G. 81; (1985) 135 N.L.J. 184, CA (Civ Div) 1–09

American Cyanamid Co v Ethicon Ltd (No.1) [1975] A.C. 396;

[1975] 2 W.L.R. 316; [1975] 1 All E.R. 504; [1975] F.S.R. 101;
    [1975] R.P.C. 513; (1975) 119 S.J. 136, HL 16–07
Andrews v Schooling [1991] 1 W.L.R. 783; [1991] 3 All E.R. 723;
    53 B.L.R. 68; 26 Con. L.R. 33; (1991) 23 H.L.R. 316; (1991)
    135 S.J. 446, CA (Civ Div) 9–07
Anns v Merton LBC; sub nom: ....
    Anns v Walcroft Property Co Ltd [1978] A.C. 728; [1977] 2
    W.L.R. 1024; [1977] 2 All E.R. 492; 75 L.G.R. 555; (1977) 243
    E.G. 523; (1988) 4 Const. L.J. 100; [1977] J.P.L. 514; (1987) 84
    L.S.G. 319; (1987) 137 N.L.J. 794; (1977) 121 S.J. 377, HL 9–02
Anstruther Gough Calthorpe v McOscar; sub nom Calthorpe v
    McOscar [1924] 1 K.B. 716, CA 2–10
Appleton v Garrett [1996] P.I.Q.R. P1; [1997] 8 Med. L.R. 75;
    (1997) 34 B.M.L.R. 23, QBD 17–22
Asco Developments v Gordon (1978) 248 E.G. 683 14–09
Associated British Ports v CH Bailey Plc; ABP v CH Bailey [1990]
    2 A.C. 703; [1990] 2 W.L.R. 812; [1990] 1 All E.R. 929; (1990)
    60 P. & C.R. 211; [1990] 16 E.G. 65; [1990] E.G. 41 (C.S.);
    (1990) 87(17) L.S.G. 35; (1990) 140 N.L.J. 441, HL 15–16
Auto Scooters (Newcastle) v Chambers (1966) 197 E.G. 457; 116
    N.L.J. 388, CA 8–10
Auworth v Johnson, 172 E.R. 955; (1832) 5 Car. & P. 239, KB 7–14
Avonridge Property Co Ltd v Mashru; sub nom Mashru v Avonridge
    Property Co Ltd; Avonridge Property Co Ltd v London Diocesan
    Fund; London Diocesan Fund v Avonridge Property Co Ltd;
    London Diocesan Fund v Phithwa [2005] UKHL 70; [2005] 1
    W.L.R. 3956; [2006] 1 All E.R. 127; [2006] 1 P. & C.R. 25;
    [2006] L. & T.R. 4; [2006] 1 E.G.L.R. 15; [2006] 01 E.G. 100;
    [2005] 49 E.G. 88 (C.S.); (2006) 103(1) L.S.G. 16; (2006) 150
    S.J.L.B. 28; [2005] N.P.C. 138, HL 1–16
Avraamides v Colwill [2006] EWCA Civ 1533; [2007] B.L.R. 76;
    (2006) 103(46) L.S.G. 31; [2006] N.P.C. 120, CA (Civ Div) 1–02
Ball v Plummer, *The Times*, June 17, 1970 5–08
Barnes v City of London Real Property Co Webster v City of
    London Real Property Co; Sollas v City of London Real
    Property Co; Kersey & Co v City of London Real Property Co;
    Oakley Sollas & Co v City of London Real Property Co [1918] 2
    Ch. 18, Ch D 4–04
Barrett v Lounova (1982) Ltd [1990] 1 Q.B. 348; [1989] 2 W.L.R.
    137; [1989] 1 All E.R. 351; (1988) 20 H.L.R. 584; (1989) 57 P.
    & C.R. 216; [1988] 36 E.G. 184; [1988] E.G. 95 (C.S.); (1989)
    86(15) L.S.G. 39; (1989) 133 S.J. 121, CA (Civ Div) ....
    4–03, 4–05, 4–06, 4–07, 16–08
Bateman v British Gas Plc, unreported, March 23, 1998, QBD 17–24

Baxter v Camden LBC (No.2) [2001] Q.B. 1; [1999] 2 W.L.R. 566;
  [1999] 1 All E.R. 237; [1999] Env. L.R. 561; (1999) 31 H.L.R.
  356; [1999] B.L.G.R. 239; [1999] L. & T.R. 136; [1998] E.G.
  157 (C.S.); (1998) 95(45) L.S.G. 41; (1999) 143 S.J.L.B. 11;
  [1998] N.P.C. 147; [1999] E.H.L.R. Dig. 205, CA (Civ Div)..........8–16
Baybut v Eccle Riggs Country Park Ltd, *The Times*, November 13,
  2006, Ch D..3–04
Beegas Nominees v British Gas Plc (1994) 11 E.G. 151.....................17–20
Beswick v Beswick [1968] A.C. 58; [1967] 3 W.L.R. 932; [1967] 2
  All E.R. 1197; (1967) 111 S.J. 540, HL 1–02
Biguzzi v Rank Leisure Plc [1999] 1 W.L.R. 1926; [1999] 4 All E.R.
  934; [2000] C.P. Rep. 6; [1999] C.P.L.R. 675; [2000] 1 Costs
  L.R. 67, CA (Civ Div) 18–33
Billson v Residential Apartments Ltd (No.1); sub nom Residential
  Apartments Ltd v Billson (No.1) [1992] 1 A.C. 494; [1992] 2
  W.L.R. 15; [1992] 1 All E.R. 141; (1992) 24 H.L.R. 218; (1992)
  63 P. & C.R. 122; [1992] 1 E.G.L.R. 43; [1992] 01 E.G. 91;
  (1992) 89(2) L.S.G. 31; (1992) 136 S.J.L.B. 10, HL.....................15–15
Birmingham City Council v Oakley. *See* Oakley v Birmingham City
  Council...
Bishop v Consolidated London Properties Ltd [1933] All E.R. Rep.
  963, KBD..8–24
Blamire v South Cumbria HA [1993] P.I.Q.R. Q1, CA (Civ Div).......17–27
Bluestorm Ltd v Portvale Holdings Ltd [2004] EWCA Civ 289; [2004]
  H.L.R. 49; [2004] L. & T.R. 23; [2004] 2 E.G.L.R. 38; [2004] 22
  E.G. 142; (2004) 101(8) L.S.G. 31, CA (Civ Div).................. 14–09, 14–11
Boyd v Galloway, 1923 S.C. 758 10–10
Bradburn v Lindsay [1983] 2 All E.R. 408; (1983) 268 E.G. 152, Ch D 8–04
Brew Bros Ltd v Snax (Ross) Ltd [1970] 1 Q.B. 612; [1969] 3 W.L.R.
  657; [1970] 1 All E.R. 587; (1969) 20 P. & C.R. 829; (1969) 113
  S.J. 795, CA (Civ Div)..2–09, 8–14, 8–17
Brikom Investments Ltd v Carr; Brikom Investments Ltd v Roddy;
  Brikom Investments Ltd v Hickey [1979] Q.B. 467; [1979] 2
  W.L.R. 737; [1979] 2 All E.R. 753; (1979) 38 P. & C.R. 326;
  (1979) 251 E.G. 359, CA (Civ Div) 1–04
— v Seaford [1981] 1 W.L.R. 863; [1981] 2 All E.R. 783; (1981-82)
  1 H.L.R. 21; (1981) 42 P. & C.R. 190; (1981) 258 E.G. 750;
  (1981) 125 S.J. 240, CA (Civ Div) 1–06
Brioland Ltd v Searson. *See* Searson v Brioland Ltd.............................
British Anzani (Felixstowe) Ltd v International Marine Management
  (UK) Ltd [1980] Q.B. 137; [1979] 3 W.L.R. 451; [1979] 2 All
  E.R. 1063; (1980) 39 P. & C.R. 189; (1978) 250 E.G. 1183;
  (1979) 123 S.J. 64, QBD..14–10

British Telecommunications Plc v Sun Life Assurance Society Plc
    [1996] Ch. 69; [1995] 3 W.L.R. 622; [1995] 4 All E.R. 44;
    (1997) 73 P. & C.R. 475; [1995] 2 E.G.L.R. 44; [1995] 45 E.G.
    133; (1995) 145 N.L.J. 1366; (1995) 139 S.J.L.B. 203; [1995]
    N.P.C. 140, CA (Civ Div) 2–13, 2–15, 5–11
Brown v Liverpool Corp [1969] 3 All E.R. 1345; (1984) 13 H.L.R.
    1, CA (Civ Div) 5–08, 5–09
— v Mansouri, unreported, October 3, 1996, CC (Uxbridge).............17–22
Burchell v Bullard [2005] EWCA Civ 358; [2005] C.P. Rep. 36;
    [2005] B.L.R. 330; [2005] 3 Costs L.R. 507; (2005) 155 N.L.J.
    593, CA (Civ Div) 18–41
Burkeman v GE Capital Europe Ltd [2002] EWHC 2863, QBD........17–35
Burrows v Brent LBC [1996] 1 W.L.R. 1448; [1996] 4 All E.R. 577;
    [1997] 1 F.L.R. 178; [1997] 2 F.C.R. 43; (1997) 29 H.L.R. 167;
    [1997] 1 E.G.L.R. 32; [1997] 11 E.G. 150; [1997] Fam. Law
    246; (1996) 93(43) L.S.G. 26; (1996) 146 N.L.J. 1616; (1996)
    140 S.J.L.B. 239; [1996] N.P.C. 149, HL.....................................9–25
Business Environment Bow Lane Ltd v Deanwater Estates Ltd
    [2007] EWCA Civ 622; [2007] L. & T.R. 26; [2007] 2 E.G.L.R.
    51; [2007] 32 E.G. 90; [2007] 27 E.G. 303 (C.S.); [2007] N.P.C.
    79, CA (Civ Div) 1–04, 18–14
Butland v Powys CC [2007] EWCA Civ 1298; [2008] Env. L.R. 16,
    CA (Civ Div) 12–18
Calabar Properties Ltd v Stitcher [1984] 1 W.L.R. 287; [1983] 3 All
    E.R. 759; (1984) 11 H.L.R. 20; (1984) 47 P. & C.R. 285; (1983)
    268 E.G. 697; (1983) 80 L.S.G. 3163; (1983) 127 S.J. 785, CA
    (Civ Div)...17–02, 17–05
Cambridge Water Co Ltd v Eastern Counties Leather Plc; Cambridge
    Water Co Ltd v Hutchings & Harding Ltd [1994] 2 A.C. 264;
    [1994] 2 W.L.R. 53; [1994] 1 All E.R. 53; [1994] 1 Lloyd's Rep.
    261; [1994] Env. L.R. 105; [1993] E.G. 211 (C.S.); (1994) 144
    N.L.J. 15; (1994) 138 S.J.L.B. 24, HL 8–07, 8–24
Campden Hill Towers Ltd v Gardner [1977] Q.B. 823; [1977] 2 W.L.R.
    159; [1977] 1 All E.R. 739; (1984) 13 H.L.R. 64; (1977) 34 P. &
    C.R. 175; (1976) 242 E.G. 375; (1977) 121 S.J. 86, CA (Civ Div).......5–11
Caparo Industries Plc v Dickman [1990] 2 A.C. 605; [1990] 2 W.L.R.
    358; [1990] 1 All E.R. 568; [1990] B.C.C. 164; [1990] B.C.L.C.
    273; [1990] E.C.C. 313; [1955-95] P.N.L.R. 523; (1990) 87(12)
    L.S.G. 42; (1990) 140 N.L.J. 248; (1990) 134 S.J. 494, HL...........8–20
Carleton (Earl of Malmesbury) v Strutt & Parker (A Partnership)
    [2008] EWHC 424 (QB); (2008) 105(15) L.S.G. 24; (2008) 158
    N.L.J. 480; (2008) 152(14) S.J.L.B. 29, QBD 19–07
Carmel Southend Ltd v Strachan & Henshaw Ltd [2007] EWHC
    1289 (TCC); [2007] 3 E.G.L.R. 15; [2007] 35 E.G. 136; [2007]
    24 E.G. 168 (C.S.), QBD (TCC) 2–07, 17–19

Cartledge v E Jopling & Sons Ltd [1963] A.C. 758; [1963] 2 W.L.R. 210; [1963] 1 All E.R. 341; [1963] 1 Lloyd's Rep. 1; (1963) 107 S.J. 73, HL 18–04

Cartwright v GKN Sankey (1973) 14 K.I.R. 349, CA (Civ Div) 18–04

Catlin Estates Ltd v Carter Jonas (A Firm) [2005] EWHC 2315 (TCC); [2006] P.N.L.R. 15; [2006] 2 E.G.L.R. 139, QBD (TCC) 9–06, 9–07, 9–08

Cavalier v Pope; sub nom Cavalier and Wife v Pope [1906] A.C. 428, HL 4–07, 8–01, 8–09, 9–13

Chandler v Goodman, unreported, October 16, 2000, QBD 17–24

Chartered Trust Plc v Davies (1998) 76 P. & C.R. 396; [1997] 2 E.G.L.R. 83; [1997] 49 E.G. 135; [1997] N.P.C. 125; (1998) 75 P. & C.R. D6, CA (Civ Div) 6–04

Chiodi v Marney [1988] 2 E.G.L.R. 64 17–26

Clarke (Executor of the Will of Francis Bacon) v Marlborough Fine Art (London) Ltd [2002] EWHC 11 (Ch); [2003] C.P. Rep. 30, Ch D 18–30

Cole v Davis-Gilbert [2007] EWCA Civ 396; (2007) 151 S.J.L.B. 335, CA (Civ Div) 10–02, 10–09

Coleman v British Gas, unreported, February 17, 2002 17–32

Collins v Drumgold [2008] EWHC 584 (TCC); [2008] T.C.L.R. 5; [2008] C.I.L.L. 2585; (2008) 158 N.L.J. 521, QBD (TCC) 18–37

Connaught Restaurants Ltd v Indoor Leisure Ltd [1994] 1 W.L.R. 501; [1994] 4 All E.R. 834; [1993] 46 E.G. 184; [1993] E.G. 143 (C.S.); (1993) 143 N.L.J. 1188; [1993] N.P.C. 118, CA (Civ Div) 14–12

Conquest v Ebbetts; sub nom Ebbetts v Conquest [1896] A.C. 490, HL 17–07

Conroy v Hire Token Ltd, unreported, May 29, 2001, CC (Manchester) 17–25

Costain Property Developments Ltd v Finlay & Co Ltd (1989) 57 P. & C.R. 345; [1989] 1 E.G.L.R. 237, QBD 17–07

Craig v Strathclyde RC, 1998 Hous. L.R. 104, Sh Ct 17–29

Craven (Builders) Ltd v Secretary of State for Health [2000] 1 E.G.L.R. 128; [1999] E.G. 126 (C.S.), Ch D 17–37

Creska Ltd v Hammersmith and Fulham LBC (No.2); sub nom Hammersmith and Fulham LBC v Creska Ltd (No.2) [2000] L. & T.R. 288; (1999) 78 P. & C.R. D46, Ch D 16–11

Crewe Services & Investment Corp v Silk (2000) 79 P. & C.R. 500; [1998] 2 E.G.L.R. 1; [1998] 35 E.G. 81; [1997] E.G. 170 (C.S.); [1997] N.P.C. 170, CA (Civ Div) 17–14

Culworth Estates v Society of Licensed Victuallers (1991) 62 P. & C.R. 211; [1991] 2 E.G.L.R. 54; [1991] 39 E.G. 132; [1991] E.G. 16 (C.S.), CA (Civ Div) 17–08, 17–11, 17–14

D&C Builders Ltd v Rees [1966] 2 Q.B. 617; [1966] 2 W.L.R. 288; [1965] 3 All E.R. 837; (1965) 109 S.J. 971, CA 11–05

Dame Margaret Hungerford Charity Trustees v Beazeley; sub nom
  Hungerford Charity (Trs of) v Beazeley (1994) 26 H.L.R. 269;
  [1993] 29 E.G. 100; [1993] E.G. 90 (C.S.); [1993] N.P.C. 71, CA
  (Civ Div)..5–12
Dayani v Bromley LBC (No.1) [1999] 3 E.G.L.R. 144; [1999] E.G.
  135 (C.S.); (1999) 96(45) L.S.G. 35, QBD (TCC)...............7–12, 7–13
De Lassalle v Guildford [1901] 2 K.B. 215, CA 1–04
De Meza v Ve Ri Best Manufacturing Co, 160 E.G. 364; [1952]
  C.P.L. 733, CA..4–06
Defries v Milne [1913] 1 Ch. 98, CA 7–07
Demetriou v Poolaction Ltd; sub nom Demetriou v Robert Andrews
  (Estate Agencies) Ltd (1991) 62 P. & C.R. 536; [1991] 25 E.G.
  113; [1990] E.G. 127 (C.S.), CA (Civ Div).........................4–07, 5–09
— v Robert Andrews (Estate Agencies) Ltd. See Demetriou v
  Poolaction Ltd...
Department of the Environment v Thomas Bates & Sons Ltd [1991]
  1 A.C. 499; [1990] 3 W.L.R. 457; [1990] 2 All E.R. 943; 50
  B.L.R. 61; 21 Con. L.R. 54; [1990] 46 E.G. 115; [1990] E.G.
  104 (C.S.); (1990) 134 S.J. 1077, HL...............................17–21
Devine (A Minor) v Northern Ireland Housing Executive [1992] N.I.
  74, CA (NI)...17–29
Director General of Fair Trading v First National Bank Plc [2001]
  UKHL 52; [2002] 1 A.C. 481; [2001] 3 W.L.R. 1297; [2002] 1
  All E.R. 97; [2001] 2 All E.R. (Comm) 1000; [2002] 1 Lloyd's
  Rep. 489; [2002] E.C.C. 22; (2001) 151 N.L.J. 1610, HL.....3–05, 3–06
Doe d. Rankin v Brindley (1832) 4 B. & Ad. 84 15–05
Doe d. Morecraft v Meux (1825) 4 B. & C. 606................................15–05
Doe d. Worcester School Trs v Rowland (1841) 9 C. & P. 734..........17–07
Doherty v Birmingham City Council [2008] UKHL 57; [2008] 31 E.G.
  89 (C.S.); (2008) 152(31) S.J.L.B. 30; [2008] N.P.C. 91, HL..........13–06
Donoghue v Folkestone Properties Ltd [2003] EWCA Civ 231;
  [2003] Q.B. 1008; [2003] 2 W.L.R. 1138; [2003] 3 All E.R.
  1101; (2003) 100(17) L.S.G. 29; (2003) 147 S.J.L.B. 265; [2003]
  N.P.C. 28, CA (Civ Div) 10–03
— v Poplar Housing & Regeneration Community Association Ltd.
  See Poplar Housing & Regeneration Community Association
  Ltd v Donoghue ....
— v Stevenson; sub nom McAlister v Stevenson [1932] A.C. 562; 1932
  S.C. (H.L.) 31; 1932 S.L.T. 317; [1932] W.N. 139, HL.........8–09, 10–02
Doughty Hanson & Co Ltd v Roe [2007] EWHC 2212 (Ch); [2008]
  1 B.C.L.C. 404, Ch D 19–18
Drake v Harbour [2008] EWCA Civ 25; [2008] N.P.C. 11, CA (Civ
  Div 17–31

Dunnett v Railtrack Plc [2002] EWCA Civ 303; [2002] 1 W.L.R.
2434; [2002] 2 All E.R. 850; [2002] C.P. Rep. 35; [2002]
C.P.L.R. 309; (2002) 99(16) L.S.G. 37, CA (Civ Div) 18–41
Eames London Estates Ltd v North Hertfordshire DC, 18 B.L.R. 50;
(1981) 259 E.G. 491, QBD 11-005
Earle v Charalambous (Addendum to Judgment); sub nom
Charalambous v Earle [2006] EWCA Civ 1090; [2007] H.L.R.
8; [2006] 42 E.G. 245 (C.S.); (2006) 150 S.J.L.B. 1396; [2006]
N.P.C. 109, CA (Civ Div) 2–13, 17–05, 17–20
Ebbetts v Conquest. *See* Conquest v Ebbetts ....
Edlington Properties Ltd v JH Fenner & Co Ltd [2006] EWCA Civ
403; [2006] 1 W.L.R. 1583; [2006] 3 All E.R. 1200; [2006] L.
& T.R. 19; [2006] 2 E.G.L.R. 18; [2006] 22 E.G. 178; [2006] 13
E.G. 141 (C.S.), CA (Civ Div) 1–16, 14–11
Edmonton Corp v WM Knowles & Son, 60 L.G.R. 124 4–10
Electricity Supply Nominees Ltd v IAF Group Ltd ....
[1993] 1 W.L.R. 1059; [1993] 3 All E.R. 372; (1994) 67 P. &
C.R. 28; [1993] 2 E.G.L.R. 95; [1993] 37 E.G. 155; [1992] E.G.
145 (C.S.), QBD 3–02
— v National Magazine Co Ltd (2000) 2 T.C.L.R. 169; [1999] 1
E.G.L.R. 130; [1998] E.G. 162 (C.S.), QBD (TCC) 17–20
Elmcroft Developments Ltd v Tankersley-Sawyer; Elmcroft
Developments Ltd v IAB; Elmcroft Developments Ltd v Rogers
(1984) 15 H.L.R. 63; (1984) 270 E.G. 140, CA (Civ Div) 2–07
English Churches Housing Group v Shine; sub nom English Churches
Housing Group v Shrine; Shine v English Churches Housing
Group [2004] EWCA Civ 434; [2004] H.L.R. 42; [2005] L.
& T.R. 7; (2004) 101(20) L.S.G. 35; (2004) 148 S.J.L.B. 476;
[2004] N.P.C. 61, CA (Civ Div) 17–04, 17–26
Espir v Basil Street Hotel Ltd [1936] 3 All E.R. 91, CA 17–14
Esso Petroleum Co Ltd v Milton [1997] 1 W.L.R. 1060; [1997] 1
W.L.R. 938; [1997] 2 All E.R. 593; [1997] C.L.C. 634; (1997)
16 Tr. L.R. 250, CA (Civ Div) 14–12
Fairchild v Glenhaven Funeral Services Ltd (t/a GH Dovener & Son);
Pendleton v Stone & Webster Engineering Ltd; Dyson v Leeds
City Council (No.2); Matthews v Associated Portland Cement
Manufacturers (1978) Ltd; Fox v Spousal (Midlands) Ltd;
Babcock International Ltd v National Grid Co Plc; Matthews v
British Uralite Plc [2002] UKHL 22; [2003] 1 A.C. 32; [2002]
3 W.L.R. 89; [2002] 3 All E.R. 305; [2002] I.C.R. 798; [2002]
I.R.L.R. 533; [2002] P.I.Q.R. P28; [2002] Lloyd's Rep. Med.
361; (2002) 67 B.M.L.R. 90; (2002) 152 N.L.J. 998, HL 17–31
Fairman v Perpetual Investment Building Society [1923] A.C. 74,
HL 10–05, 10–08

Ferguson v Welsh [1987] 1 W.L.R. 1553; [1987] 3 All E.R. 777;
    [1988] I.R.L.R. 112; 86 L.G.R. 153; (1987) 137 N.L.J. 1037;
    (1987) 131 S.J. 1552, HL..10–05
Field v Leeds City Council [1999] C.P.L.R. 833; [2001] C.P.L.R.
    129; (2000) 32 H.L.R. 618; [2000] 1 E.G.L.R. 54; [2000] 17
    E.G. 165, CA (Civ Div)..18–07
Firstcross Ltd v Teasdale (1983) 8 H.L.R. 112; (1984) 47 P. & C.R.
    228; (1983) 265 E.G. 305, QBD................................2–09, 2–10, 7–04
Forsikringsaktieselskapet Vesta v Butcher [1989] A.C. 852; [1989] 2
    W.L.R. 290; [1989] 1 All E.R. 402; [1989] 1 Lloyd's Rep. 331;
    [1989] Fin. L.R. 223; (1989) 133 S.J. 184, HL..............................17–28
GS Fashions v B&Q Plc [1995] 1 W.L.R. 1088; [1995] 4 All E.R.
    899; [1995] 1 E.G.L.R. 62; [1995] 09 E.G. 324; [1994] E.G. 161
    (C.S.); [1994] N.P.C. 128; (1994) 68 P. & C.R. D24, Ch D..........15–22
Gianfrancesco v Haughton (2008) W.L. 576896 (Lands Tr)..................2–16
Gibson Investments Ltd v Chesterton Plc (No.1) [2002] EWHC
    19 (Ch); [2002] 2 P. & C.R. 32; [2002] L. & T.R. 32; [2003] 1
    E.G.L.R. 142, Ch D..2–07
Goldmile Properties Ltd v Lechouritis; sub nom Lechouritis v
    Goldmile Properties Ltd [2003] EWCA Civ 49; [2003] 2 P. &
    C.R. 1; [2003] L. & T.R. 25; [2003] 1 E.G.L.R. 60; [2003] 15
    E.G. 143; [2003] 14 E.G. 121 (C.S.); (2003) 100(13) L.S.G. 31;
    (2003) 147 S.J.L.B. 144; [2003] N.P.C. 10; [2003] 1 P. & C.R.
    DG23, CA (Civ Div)...6–08
Gordon v Selico Ltd (1986) 18 H.L.R. 219; [1986] 1 E.G.L.R. 71;
    (1986) 278 E.G. 53, CA (Civ Div) 4–06
Goss v Lord Nugent (1833) 5 B. & Ad. 58..1–04
Governors of the Peabody Donation Fund v Sir Lindsay Parkinson &
    Co Ltd [1985] A.C. 210; [1984] 3 W.L.R. 953; [1984] 3 All E.R.
    529; 28 B.L.R. 1; 83 L.G.R. 1; [1984] C.I.L.L. 128; (1984) 81
    L.S.G. 3179; (1984) 128 S.J. 753, HL...11-05
Granby Village (Manchester) Management Co Ltd v Unchained
    Growth III Plc. See Unchained Growth III Plc v Granby Village
    (Manchester) Management Co Ltd..
Greenwood v WEF. See Greenwood Reversions Ltd v World
    Environment Foundation Ltd..
Greenwood Reversions Ltd v World Environment Foundation Ltd;
    sub nom Greenwood v WEF [2008] EWCA Civ 47; [2008]
    H.L.R. 31, CA (Civ Div) 15–05, 15–15
Gurney Consulting Engineers v Gleeds Health & Safety Ltd [2006]
    EWHC 536 (TCC); 108 Con. L.R. 58, QBD (TCC) 18–08
Hackney LBC v Mullen. See Mullen v Hackney LBC.................................
— v Rottenberg. See R. (on the application of Hackney LBC) v Rottenberg
Hadley v Baxendale (1854) 9 Exch. 341 17–32

Halsey v Milton Keynes General NHS Trust; Steel v Joy [2004]
    EWCA Civ 576; [2004] 1 W.L.R. 3002; [2004] 4 All E.R.
    920; [2004] C.P. Rep. 34; [2004] 3 Costs L.R. 393; (2005) 81
    B.M.L.R. 108; (2004) 101(22) L.S.G. 31; (2004) 154 N.L.J. 769;
    (2004) 148 S.J.L.B. 629, CA (Civ Div) 18–41
Hammersmith and Fulham LBC v Creska Ltd (No.2). *See* Creska
    Ltd v Hammersmith and Fulham LBC (No.2) ....
Hancock v BW Brazier (Anerley) Ltd [1966] 1 W.L.R. 1317; [1966]
    2 All E.R. 901, CA.. 9–11
Harbutt's Plasticine Ltd v Wayne Tank & Pump Co Ltd; sub nom
    Harbutts Plasticine v Wayne Tank & Pump Co Ltd [1970] 1
    Q.B. 447; [1970] 2 W.L.R. 198; [1970] 1 All E.R. 225; [1970] 1
    Lloyd's Rep. 15; (1969) 119 N.L.J. 1164; (1970) 114 S.J. 29, CA
    (Civ Div).. 717–35
Harmer v Jumbil (Nigeria) Tin Areas Ltd [1921] 1 Ch. 200, CA.......... 6–02
Harris v Shah, unreported, February 22, 2002...................................... 18–26
Harry v Sykes [2001] 17 EWCA Civ 221 17–28
Harvey v Fairscope, unreported, September 3, 1997, CC (Kingston
    on Thames) 17–24
Hatton v United Kingdom (36022/97) (2003) 37 E.H.R.R. 28; 15
    B.H.R.C. 259, ECHR (Grand Chamber) 13–05
Haviland v Long [1952] 2 Q.B. 80; [1952] 1 All E.R. 463; [1952] 1
    T.L.R. 576; (1952) 96 S.J. 180, CA 17–17
Hawkins v Dhawan (1987) 19 H.L.R. 232; (1987) 283 E.G. 1388,
    CA (Civ Div) 8–07
— v Woodhall [2008] EWCA Civ 932, CA (Civ Div) 17–33
Hedley Byrne & Co Ltd v Heller & Partners Ltd [1964] A.C. 465;
    [1963] 3 W.L.R. 101; [1963] 2 All E.R. 575; [1963] 1 Lloyd's
    Rep. 485; (1963) 107 S.J. 454, HL 9–09
Hewitson v Reynolds [1924] 93 L.J.K.B. 1080 17–05
Hickman v Blake Lapthorn (Costs) [2006] EWHC 12 (QB); [2006]
    3 Costs L.R. 452, QB... D18–41
Hi-Lift Elevator Services v Temple (1996) 28 H.L.R. 1; (1995) 70 P.
    & C.R. 620, CA (Civ Div)... 16–07
Homespace v Sita South East Ltd [2008] EWCA Civ 1 19–18
Hone v Benson (1978) 248 E.G. 1013.. 9–02
Hopwood v Cannock Chase DC; sub nom Hopwood v Rugeley
    Urban DC [1975] 1 W.L.R. 373; [1975] 1 All E.R. 796; (1984)
    13 H.L.R. 31; 73 L.G.R. 137; (1975) 29 P. & C.R. 256; (1975)
    119 S.J. 186, CA (Civ Div)... 5–08
Howard v Walker [1947] K.B. 860; [1947] 2 All E.R. 197; 63 T.L.R.
    518; [1947] L.J.R. 1366; 177 L.T. 326; (1947) 91 S.J. 494, KBD... 8–18
Hungerford Charity (Trs of) v Beazeley. *See* Dame Margaret
    Hungerford Charity Trustees v Beazeley...

Hunter v Canary Wharf Ltd; sub nom Hunter v London Docklands
    Development Corp [1997] A.C. 655; [1997] 2 W.L.R. 684;
    [1997] 2 All E.R. 426; [1997] C.L.C. 1045; 84 B.L.R. 1; 54 Con.
    L.R. 12; [1997] Env. L.R. 488; [1997] 2 F.L.R. 342; (1998) 30
    H.L.R. 409; [1997] Fam. Law 601; [1997] E.G. 59 (C.S.); (1997)
    94(19) L.S.G. 25; (1997) 147 N.L.J. 634; (1997) 141 S.J.L.B.
    108; [1997] N.P.C. 64, HL 8–13, 17–23
Hussain v Lancaster City Council [2000] Q.B. 1; [1999] 2 W.L.R.
    1142; [1999] 4 All E.R. 125; [1998] E.H.L.R. 166; (1999) 31
    H.L.R. 164; (1999) 1 L.G.L.R. 37; (1999) 77 P. & C.R. 89;
    [1998] E.G. 86 (C.S.); (1998) 95(23) L.S.G. 27; (1998) 142
    S.J.L.B. 173; [1998] N.P.C. 85; (1998) 76 P. & C.R. D31, CA
    (Civ Div) 8–20
Hussein v Mehlman [1992] 2 E.G.L.R. 287; [1992] 32 E.G. 59 . 5–08, 6–04
Hyman v Rose; sub nom Rose v Hyman, Rose v Spicer [1912] A.C.
    623, HL 7–09, 15–16
ICI Chemicals & Polymers Ltd v TTE Training Ltd [2007] EWCA
    Civ 725, CA (Civ Div) 18–39
Ibrahim v Dovecorn Reversions Ltd (2001) 82 P. & C.R. 28; [2001]
    2 E.G.L.R. 46; [2001] 30 E.G. 116; [2001] 12 E.G. 165 (C.S.),
    Ch D 5–08
Inntrepreneur Pub Co Ltd v East Crown Ltd; sub nom Inntrepreneur
    Pub Co (GL) v East Crown Ltd [2000] 2 Lloyd's Rep. 611;
    [2000] 3 E.G.L.R. 31; [2000] 41 E.G. 209; [2000] N.P.C. 93, Ch
    D 1–02, 1–04
Investors Compensation Scheme Ltd v West Bromwich Building
    Society (No.1); Investors Compensation Scheme Ltd v Hopkin
    & Sons; Alford v West Bromwich Building Society; Armitage v
    West Bromwich Building Society ....
    [1998] 1 W.L.R. 896; [1998] 1 All E.R. 98; [1998] 1 B.C.L.C.
    531; [1997] C.L.C. 1243; [1997] P.N.L.R. 541; (1997) 147 N.L.J.
    989, HL 2–09
Irvine v Moran [1991] E.G.L.R. 261 .... 5–05, 5–08
JA Pye (Oxford) Ltd v Graham [2002] UKHL 30; [2003] 1 A.C. 419;
    [2002] 3 W.L.R. 221; [2002] 3 All E.R. 865; [2002] H.R.L.R.
    34; [2003] 1 P. & C.R. 10; [2002] 28 E.G. 129 (C.S.); [2002]
    N.P.C. 92; [2002] 2 P. & C.R. DG22, HL 13–01, 13–05
Jackson v JH Watson Property Investment Ltd [2008] EWHC 14
    (Ch); [2008] Env. L.R. 30; [2008] 11 E.G. 94; [2008] 2 E.G. 147
    (C.S.); [2008] N.P.C. 1; [2008] 1 P. & C.R. DG17, Ch D 8–16
— v MOD [2006] All E.R. (D) 14 18–41
Jacobs v Morton and Partners (1994) 72 B.L.R. 92 9–05
Jaggard v Sawyer [1995] 1 W.L.R. 269; [1995] 2 All E.R. 189;
    [1995] 1 E.G.L.R. 146; [1995] 13 E.G. 132; [1994] E.G. 139
    (C.S.); [1994] N.P.C. 116, CA (Civ Div) 16–11

Janet Reger International Ltd v Tiree Ltd [2006] EWHC 1743 (Ch);
    [2007] 1 P. & C.R. 24; [2006] 3 E.G.L.R. 131; [2006] 30 E.G.
    102 (C.S.), Ch D 2–04
Jervis v Harris [1996] Ch. 195; [1996] 2 W.L.R. 220; [1996] 1 All
    E.R. 303; [1996] 1 E.G.L.R. 78; [1996] 10 E.G. 159; [1995]
    E.G. 177 (C.S.); (1996) 93(3) L.S.G. 30; (1996) 140 S.J.L.B. 13;
    [1995] N.P.C. 171, CA (Civ Div)........................... 15–09, 15–13, 16–11
Jeune v Queen's Cross Properties Ltd [1974] Ch. 97; [1973] 3 W.L.R.
    378; [1973] 3 All E.R. 97; (1973) 26 P. & C.R. 98; (1973) 117
    S.J. 680, Ch D 16–01
Johnson v Sheffield City Council, unreported, August 1994, Legal
    Action 2–10
Johnston v NEI International Combustion Ltd [2007] UKHL 39 17–25
Joyner v Weeks [1891] 2 Q.B. 31, CA 17–11
Keown v Coventry Healthcare NHS Trust [2006] EWCA Civ 39;
    [2006] 1 W.L.R. 953; [2006] P.I.Q.R. P19; (2006) 103(8) L.S.G.
    23; (2006) 150 S.J.L.B. 164; [2006] N.P.C. 18, CA (Civ Div) 10–18
Khar v Delbounty Ltd (1998) 75 P. & C.R. 232; [1996] E.G. 183
    (C.S.); [1996] N.P.C. 163, CA (Civ Div) 15–15
Kinane v Mackie-Conteh; Kinane v Almack Marketing Services Ltd
    [2005] EWCA Civ 45; [2005] W.T.L.R. 345; [2005] 6 E.G. 140
    (C.S.); (2005) 149 S.J.L.B. 177; [2005] 2 P. & C.R. DG3, CA
    (Civ Div) 1–06
King v Liverpool City Council [1986] 1 W.L.R. 890; [1986] 3
    All E.R. 544; (1986) 18 H.L.R. 307; 84 L.G.R. 871; [1986] 1
    E.G.L.R. 181; (1986) 278 E.G. 278; (1986) 83 L.S.G. 2492;
    (1986) 136 N.L.J. 334; (1986) 130 S.J. 505, CA (Civ Div) 8–05
Kingston upon Thames RLBC v Marlow ....
    (1996) 160 J.P. 502; [1996] 1 E.G.L.R. 101; [1996] 17 E.G. 187;
    [1996] R.A. 87; (1996) 160 L.G. Rev. 181; [1995] E.G. 161
    (C.S.); [1995] N.P.C. 160, DC 15–22
Knowsley Housing Trust v White; sub nom White v Knowsley
    Housing Trust ....
    [2007] EWCA Civ 404; [2007] 1 W.L.R. 2897; [2007] 4 All E.R.
    800; [2007] H.L.R. 41; [2007] L. & T.R. 31; [2007] 2 E.G.L.R.
    61; [2007] 30 E.G. 134; [2007] 20 E.G. 294 (C.S.); (2007)
    104(20) L.S.G. 27; (2005) 151 S.J.L.B. 611, CA (Civ Div) 9–25
L (a child) v Empire Estates (2002) 6 Q.R. 13 17–25
LMS International Ltd v Styrene Packaging & Insulation Ltd [2005]
    EWHC 2065 (TCC); [2006] T.C.L.R. 6, QBD (TCC) 8–22
Lambeth LBC v O'Kane; Helena Housing Ltd v Pinder [2005]
    EWCA Civ 1010; [2006] H.L.R. 2; [2005] 32 E.G. 67 (C.S.);
    [2005] N.P.C. 110, CA (Civ Div) 9–25

Landmaster Properties Ltd v Thackeray Property Services Ltd [2003] EWHC 959; [2004] L. & T.R. 4; [2003] 2 E.G.L.R. 30; [2003] 35 E.G. 83, QBD...15–12
Larksworth Investments Ltd v Temple House Ltd (No.2) [1999] B.L.R. 297, CA (Civ Div)..17–20
Latimer v Carney [2006] EWCA Civ 1417; [2007] 1 P. & C.R. 13; [2007] L. & T.R. 5; [2006] 3 E.G.L.R. 13; [2006] 50 E.G. 86; [2006] 45 E.G. 191 (C.S.); (2006) 103(44) L.S.G. 31; [2006] N.P.C. 117, CA (Civ Div) 17–18
Lawson v Hartley-Brown (1996) 71 P. & C.R. 242, CA (Civ Div) 6–03
Lee v Leeds City Council [2002] L.G.R. 305.......................................2–04
— v Leeds Crown Court. See R. (on the application of Lee) v Leeds Crown Court ....
Leeds City Council v Price; sub nom Price v Leeds City Council [2005] EWCA Civ 289; [2005] 1 W.L.R. 1825; [2005] 3 All E.R. 573; [2005] U.K.H.R.R. 413; [2005] H.L.R. 31; [2005] B.L.G.R. 782; [2005] 2 P. & C.R. 26; [2005] J.P.L. 1241; [2005] 12 E.G. 218 (C.S.); (2005) 102(19) L.S.G. 33; (2005) 149 S.J.L.B. 359; [2005] N.P.C. 41, CA (Civ Div)......................................13–01, 13–06
Legal & General Assurance Society Ltd v Expeditors International (UK) Ltd [2007] EWCA Civ 7; [2007] 2 P. & C.R. 10; [2007] L. & T.R. 16; [2007] 5 E.G. 307 (C.S.); (2007) 104(6) L.S.G. 32; (2007) 151 S.J.L.B. 163; [2007] N.P.C. 10, CA (Civ Div) 4–01, 4–09
Lewisham v Fenner (1995) ENDS 44...12–17
Lewisham LBC v Malcolm. See Malcolm v Lewisham LBC ....
Liverpool City Council v Irwin [1977] A.C. 239; [1976] 2 W.L.R. 562; [1976] 2 All E.R. 39; (1984) 13 H.L.R. 38; 74 L.G.R. 392; (1976) 32 P. & C.R. 43; (1976) 238 E.G. 879; [1976] J.P.L. 427; (1976) 120 S.J. 267, HL...4–06, 5–11
Liverpool Properties v Oldbridge Investments [1985] 2 E.G.L.R. 111; (1985) 276 E.G. 1352, CA (Civ Div) 15–17
Livingstone v Rawyards Coal Co (1879–80) L.R. 5 App. Cas. 25, HL.....17–01
Lloyds v Harper (1880) L.R. 16 Ch.D. 290 1–02
Loria v Hammer [1989] 2 E.G.L.R. 249; [1989] E.G. 126 (C.S.), Ch D 14–08
Lough v Intruder Alarm Systems [2008] All E.R. (D) 364 (Jun) 10–05
Lunn Poly Ltd v Liverpool & Lancashire Properties Ltd [2006] EWCA Civ 430; [2007] L. & T.R. 6; [2006] 2 E.G.L.R. 29; [2006] 25 E.G. 210; [2006] 12 E.G. 222 (C.S.), CA (Civ Div).....16–11
Lurcott v Wakeley & Wheeler [1911] 1 K.B. 905; [1911-13] All E.R. Rep. 41, CA 2–09
Lynch v Thorne [1956] 1 W.L.R. 303; [1956] 1 All E.R. 744, CA........9–11
Lyndendown Ltd v Vitamol Ltd [2007] EWCA Civ 826; [2007] 3 E.G.L.R. 11; [2007] 47 E.G. 170; [2007] 29 E.G. 142 (C.S.), CA (Civ Div)..17–16

McAuley v Bristol City Council ....
    [1992] Q.B. 134; [1991] 3 W.L.R. 968; [1992] 1 All E.R. 749;
    (1991) 23 H.L.R. 586; 89 L.G.R. 931; [1991] 2 E.G.L.R. 64;
    [1991] 45 E.G. 155; [1991] E.G. 70 (C.S.); [1991] N.P.C. 81, CA
    (Civ Div) 4–04, 4–10, 9–18, 9–23
McCann v United Kingdom (19009/04) [2008] B.L.G.R. 474; [2008]
    28 E.G. 114; [2008] 20 E.G. 136 (C.S.), ECHR 13–05, 13–06
McCoy & Co v Clark (1984) 13 H.L.R. 87, CA (Civ Div) 17–26
McDougall v Easington DC (1989) 21 H.L.R. 310; 87 L.G.R. 527;
    (1989) 58 P. & C.R. 201; [1989] 25 E.G. 104; [1989] E.G. 11
    (C.S.), CA (Civ Div) 2–07
McGeown v Northern Ireland Housing Executive [1995] 1 A.C. 233;
    [1994] 3 W.L.R. 187; [1994] 3 All E.R. 53; (1994) 26 H.L.R. 711;
    92 L.G.R. 629; (1995) 70 P. & C.R. 10; (1994) 91(30) L.S.G. 32;
    (1994) 144 N.L.J. 901; (1994) 138 S.J.L.B. 156; [1994] N.P.C.
    95, HL (NI) 10–08
McGlinn v Waltham Contractors Ltd [2007] EWHC 698 (TCC);
    [2008] Bus. L.R. 278; 112 Con. L.R. 148, QBD (TCC) 18–41
McGreal v Wake (1984) 13 H.L.R. 107; (1984) 269 E.G. 1254;
    (1984) 81 L.S.G. 739; (1984) 128 S.J. 116, CA (Civ Div) ....
    2–15, 7–16, 17–06, 17–35
McNerny v Lambeth LBC (1989) 21 H.L.R. 188; [1989] 19 E.G. 77;
    (1990) 154 L.G. Rev. 272; [1988] E.G. 169 (C.S.); (1989) 139
    N.L.J. 114, CA (Civ Div) 2–05, 5–01, 9–23
Maguire v Sefton MBC [2006] EWCA Civ 316; [2006] 1 W.L.R.
    2550; [2006] P.I.Q.R. P25; (2006) 103(11) L.S.G. 27, CA (Civ
    Div) 10–03, 10–17
Malcolm v Lewisham LBC; sub nom Lewisham LBC v Malcolm
    [2008] UKHL 43; [2008] 3 W.L.R. 194; [2008] 26 E.G. 117
    (C.S.); (2008) 152(26) S.J.L.B. 29; [2008] N.P.C. 76, HL 11–22
Malmesbury (Earl of) v Maltby. See Carleton (Earl of Malmesbury)
    v Strutt & Parker (A Partnership)
Mancetter Developments v Garmanson and Givertz 1986] Q.B.
    1212; [1986] 2 W.L.R. 871; [1986] 1 All E.R. 449; (1986) 2
    B.C.C. 98924; [1986] 1 E.G.L.R. 240; (1983) 83 L.S.G. 612;
    (1985) 83 L.S.G. 612; (1986) 130 S.J. 129, CA (Civ Div) 7–09
Manchester Bonded Warehouse Co Ltd v Carr (1879–80) L.R. 5
    C.P.D. 507, CPD 7–10
Marcan Marketing v G Kefelas and Candida Corp, unreported, May
    17, 2007 18–33
Marlborough Park Services Ltd v Rowe ....
    [2006] EWCA Civ 436; [2006] H.L.R. 30; [2006] 2 P. & C.R. 8;
    [2006] L. & T.R. 12; [2006] 2 E.G.L.R. 27; [2006] 23 E.G. 166,
    CA (Civ Div) 2–10, 5–08

Marsden v Edward Heyes Ltd [1927] 2 K.B. 1; 53 A.L.R. 42,
    CA...7–06, 7–07, 7–08
Marshall v Rubypoint Ltd (1997) 29 H.L.R. 850; [1997] 1 E.G.L.R.
    69; [1997] 25 E.G. 142; [1997] E.G. 12 (C.S.); (1997) 73 P. &
    C.R. D42, CA (Civ Div) 17–31
Marzari v Italy (Admissibility) (36448/97) (2000) 30 E.H.R.R.
    CD218, ECHR... 13–05
Mather v Barclays Bank Plc [1987] 2 E.G.L.R. 254, DC.................. 17–10
Merrington v Ironbridge Metal Works Ltd [1952] 2 All E.R. 1101;
    (1953) 117 J.P. 23, Assizes (Salop)................................... 10–11
Mersey Docks and Harbour Board v Procter; sub nom Procter v
    Mersey Docks and Harbour Board [1923] A.C. 253; (1923) 14
    Ll. L. Rep. 432, HL 10–07
Mickel v McCoard, 1913 S.C. 1036; 1913 2 S.L.T. 106, IH (2 Div 7–04
Middlegate Properties Ltd v Gidlow-Jackson (1977) 34 P. & C.R. 4,
    CA (Civ Div) 15–09
Minchburn v Peck (1988) 20 H.L.R. 392, CA (Civ Div)...................... 2–13
Mint v Good [1951] 1 K.B. 517; [1950] 2 All E.R. 1159; 49 L.G.R.
    495; (1950) 94 S.J. 822, CA 4–04
Moloney v Lambeth LBC, 64 L.G.R. 440; 198 E.G. 895; (1966) 110
    S.J. 406... 10–10
Molton Builders v Westminster City Council (1975) 30 P. & C.R.
    182; (1975) 238 E.G. 411; (1975) 119 S.J. 627, CA (Civ Div)....... 6–02
Montoya v Hackney LBC, unreported, July 15, 2005, QBD ... 18–07, 18–09
Moorcock, The (1889) L.R. 14 P.D. 64; [1886-90] All E.R. Rep. 530,
    CA... 4–02
Morgan Sindall Plc v Sawston Farms (Cambs) Ltd [1999] 1 E.G.L.R.
    90; [1999] 07 E.G. 135; [1998] E.G. 177 (C.S.); [1998] N.P.C.
    159, CA (Civ Div) 19–18
Mott MacDonald Ltd v Department of Transport [2006] EWCA Civ
    1089; [2006] 1 W.L.R. 3356; [2006] N.P.C. 97, CA (Civ Div)........ 2–04
Mullen v Hackney LBC; sub nom Hackney LBC v Mullen [1997]
    1 W.L.R. 1103; [1997] 2 All E.R. 906; (1997) 29 H.L.R. 592;
    (1997) 9 Admin. L.R. 549; (1997) 161 J.P. Rep. 238; [1996] E.G.
    162 (C.S.); (1996) 93(41) L.S.G. 30; (1996) 140 S.J.L.B. 237,
    CA (Civ Div) 16–10
Murphy v Brentwood DC [1991] 1 A.C. 398; [1990] 3 W.L.R. 414;
    [1990] 2 All E.R. 908; [1990] 2 Lloyd's Rep. 467; 50 B.L.R. 1;
    21 Con. L.R. 1; (1990) 22 H.L.R. 502; 89 L.G.R. 24; (1991) 3
    Admin. L.R. 37; (1990) 6 Const. L.J. 304; (1990) 154 L.G. Rev.
    1010; [1990] E.G. 105 (C.S.); (1990) 87(30) L.S.G. 15; (1990)
    134 S.J. 1076, HL 8–10, 9–02, 9–03, 9–09, 9–26, 11–05, 17–21
Muscat v Smith; sub nom Smith v Muscat ....
    [2003] EWCA Civ 962; [2003] 1 W.L.R. 2853; [2004] H.L.R. 6;
    [2004] L. & T.R. 7; [2003] 3 E.G.L.R. 11; [2003] 40 E.G. 148;

[2003] 30 E.G. 144 (C.S.); (2003) 100(35) L.S.G. 37; (2003)
147 S.J.L.B. 900; [2003] N.P.C. 88, CA (Civ Div) 14–11
National Carriers Ltd v Panalpina (Northern) Ltd [1981] A.C. 675;
[1981] 2 W.L.R. 45; [1981] 1 All E.R. 161; (1982) 43 P. & C.R.
72; (1981) 125 S.J. 46, HL..6–04
National Westminster Bank Plc v King [2008] EWHC 280 (Ch);
[2008] 2 W.L.R. 1279; [2008] C.P. Rep. 23; [2008] 2 P. & C.R.
9; [2008] N.P.C. 22, Ch D 18–38
Niazi Services Ltd v Van der Loo [2004] EWCA Civ 53; [2004] 1
W.L.R. 1254; [2004] H.L.R. 34; [2004] 1 E.G.L.R. 62; [2004]
17 E.G. 130; [2004] 8 E.G. 134 (C.S.); (2004) 148 S.J.L.B. 232;
[2004] N.P.C. 18; [2004] 1 P. & C.R. DG23, CA (Civ Div) 5–11
Nichols v Marsland (1876–77) L.R. 2 Ex. D. 1, CA; affirming 8–23
Norwich Union Life Insurance Society v P&O Property Holdings
Ltd [1993] 1 E.G.L.R. 164; [1993] 13 E.G. 108; [1993] E.G. 69
(C.S.); [1993] N.P.C. 1, CA (Civ Div) 19–18
Nynehead Developments Ltd v RH Fibreboard Containers Ltd
[1999] 1 E.G.L.R. 7; [1999] 02 E.G. 139, Ch D 6–04
Oakley v Birmingham City Council; sub nom Birmingham City
Council v Oakley [2001] 1 A.C. 617; [2000] 3 W.L.R. 1936;
[2001] 1 All E.R. 385; [2001] Env. L.R. 37; [2001] E.H.L.R.
8; (2001) 33 H.L.R. 30; [2001] B.L.G.R. 110; [2000] E.G. 144
(C.S.); (2000) 97(48) L.S.G. 38; (2000) 150 N.L.J. 1824; (2000)
144 S.J.L.B. 290; [2000] N.P.C. 136, HL......................................12–17
O'Brien v Robinson [1973] A.C. 912; [1973] 2 W.L.R. 393; [1973]
1 All E.R. 583; (1984) 13 H.L.R. 7; (1973) 25 P. & C.R. 239;
(1973) 117 S.J. 187, HL....................................2–11, 2–12, 2–13, 2–15
Oceanic Village Ltd v United Attractions Ltd [2000] Ch. 234; [2000]
2 W.L.R. 476; [2000] 1 All E.R. 975; [2000] 1 E.G.L.R. 148;
[1999] E.G. 152 (C.S.); [1999] N.P.C. 156; (2000) 79 P. & C.R.
D42, Ch D..1–08
O'Connor v Old Etonian Housing Association Ltd; sub nom
O'Connor v Old Eton Housing Association; O'Connor v Old
Etonians Housing Association Ltd ....
[2002] EWCA Civ 150; [2002] Ch. 295; [2002] 2 W.L.R. 1133;
[2002] 2 All E.R. 1015; [2002] H.L.R. 37; [2002] L. & T.R. 36;
[2002] 1 E.G.L.R. 38; [2002] 14 E.G. 127; [2002] 9 E.G. 221
(C.S.); (2002) 99(12) L.S.G. 33; (2002) 146 S.J.L.B. 54; [2002]
N.P.C. 27; [2002] 2 P. & C.R. DG8, CA (Civ Div) 5–14
Offer-Hoar v Larkstore Ltd; sub nom Larkstore Ltd v Technotrade
Ltd; Technotrade Ltd v Larkstore Ltd ....
[2006] EWCA Civ 1079; [2006] 1 W.L.R. 2926; [2007] 1 All
E.R. (Comm) 104; [2006] B.L.R. 345; 109 Con. L.R. 92; [2006]
P.N.L.R. 37; [2006] 3 E.G.L.R. 5; [2006] 42 E.G. 246; [2006]
C.I.L.L. 2389; [2006] 31 E.G. 89 (C.S.); (2006) 103(32) L.S.G.

20; [2006] N.P.C. 96, CA (Civ Div)..17–21

Ogefere v Islington LBC, unreported, April 22, 1999, CC
(Clerkenwell) 17–26

Ogwo v Taylor [1988] A.C. 431; [1987] 3 W.L.R. 1145; [1987] 3 All
E.R. 961; (1988) 152 L.G. Rev. 589; (1988) 85(4) L.S.G. 35;
(1987) 137 N.L.J. 110; (1987) 131 S.J. 1628, HL 10–11

O'Rourke v United Kingdom (App.No.390 22/97)............................13–05

Owers v Bailey (2006) 103(39) L.S.G. 34; (2006) 150 S.J.L.B. 1292;
[2007] 1 P. & C.R. DG17, Ch D...17–22

P Perl (Exporters) Ltd v Camden LBC [1984] Q.B. 342; [1983]
3 W.L.R. 769; [1983] 3 All E.R. 161; (1980) 77 L.S.G. 2216;
(1980) 80 L.S.G. 2216; (1983) 127 S.J. 581, CA (Civ Div)...........8–05

Page v Smith [1996] A.C. 155; [1995] 2 W.L.R. 644; [1995] 2 All
E.R. 736; [1995] 2 Lloyd's Rep. 95; [1995] R.T.R. 210; [1995]
P.I.Q.R. P329; (1995) 92(23) L.S.G. 33; (1995) 145 N.L.J. 723;
(1995) 139 S.J.L.B. 173, HL...17–32

Parker v Camden LBC; Newman v Camden LBC ....
[1986] Ch. 162; [1985] 3 W.L.R. 47; [1985] 2 All E.R. 141;
(1985) 17 H.L.R. 380; 84 L.G.R. 16; (1985) 129 S.J. 417, CA
(Civ Div)..16–05, 16–07

Passley v Wandsworth LBC; Prince v Wandsworth LBC (1998) 30
H.L.R. 165, CA (Civ Div) 2–13

Patel v Pirabakaran; sub nom Pirabakaran v Patel ....
[2006] EWCA Civ 685; [2006] 1 W.L.R. 3112; [2006] 4 All E.R.
506; [2006] H.L.R. 39; [2006] 2 P. & C.R. 26; [2006] L. & T.R.
24; [2006] 3 E.G.L.R. 23; [2006] 36 E.G. 260; [2006] 23 E.G.
165 (C.S.); (2006) 103(24) L.S.G. 28; (2006) 150 S.J.L.B. 743;
[2006] N.P.C. 63, CA (Civ Div)..15–03

Pattrick v Marley Estates Management [2007] EWCA Civ 1176;
[2007] N.P.C. 122, CA (Civ Div)...5–08

Payne v John Setchell Ltd [2002] B.L.R. 489; (2001) 3 T.C.L.R. 26;
[2002] P.N.L.R. 7, QBD (TCC) 9–08

Peabody Trust Governors v Reeve [2008] 23 E.G. 116 (C.S.), Ch D....3–06

Pembery v Lamdin [1940] 2 All E.R. 434, CA...................................5–08

Peninsular Maritime v Padseal (1981) 259 E.G. 860, CA (Civ Div)...16–02

Penton v Barnett [1898] 1 Q.B. 276, CA 15–05

Perry v Tendring DC; Thurbon v Tendring DC, 30 B.L.R. 118; 3
Con. L.R. 74; [1985] 1 E.G.L.R. 260; (1984) 1 Const. L.J. 152;
[1985] C.I.L.L. 145, QBD 11–05

Phipps v Rochester Corp [1955] 1 Q.B. 450; [1955] 2 W.L.R. 23;
[1955] 1 All E.R. 129; (1955) 119 J.P. 92; 53 L.G.R. 80; (1955)
99 S.J. 45, QBD 10–10

Pirelli General Cable Works Ltd v Oscar Faber & Partners [1983] 2
A.C. 1; [1983] 2 W.L.R. 6; [1983] 1 All E.R. 65; (1983) 265 E.G.
979, HL...18–05

Poplar Housing & Regeneration Community Association Ltd v
Donoghue; sub nom Donoghue v Poplar Housing & Regeneration
Community Association Ltd; Poplar Housing & Regeneration
Community Association Ltd v Donaghue [2001] EWCA Civ
595; [2002] Q.B. 48; [2001] 3 W.L.R. 183; [2001] 4 All E.R. 604;
[2001] 2 F.L.R. 284; [2001] 3 F.C.R. 74; [2001] U.K.H.R.R. 693;
(2001) 33 H.L.R. 73; (2001) 3 L.G.L.R. 41; [2001] B.L.G.R.
489; [2001] A.C.D. 76; [2001] Fam. Law 588; [2001] 19 E.G.
141 (C.S.); (2001) 98(19) L.S.G. 38; (2001) 98(23) L.S.G. 38;
(2001) 145 S.J.L.B. 122; [2001] N.P.C. 84, CA (Civ Div) 13–03
Post Office v Aquarius Properties Ltd [1987] 1 All E.R. 1055; (1987)
54 P. & C.R. 61; [1987] 1 E.G.L.R. 40; (1987) 281 E.G. 798;
(1987) 84 L.S.G. 820, CA (Civ Div) 2–04
Price v Leeds City Council. See Leeds City Council v Price
Princes House Ltd v Distinctive Clubs Ltd [2007] EWCA Civ 374;
[2007] L. & T.R. 34; [2007] 2 E.G.L.R. 75; [2007] 27 E.G. 304;
[2007] 14 E.G. 104 (C.S.), CA (Civ Div) 2–14
Prole v Allen [1950] 1 All E.R. 476, Assizes (Somerset) 10–06
Proudfoot v Hart (1890) L.R. 25 Q.B.D. 42, CA 2–10
Prudential Assurance Co Ltd v Ayres [2008] EWCA Civ 52; [2008]
1 All E.R. 1266; [2008] 16 E.G. 154, CA (Civ Div) 1–02, 1–07
Quennell v Salaman (1955) 165 E.G. 285 2–10
Quick v Taff Ely BC [1986] Q.B. 809; [1985] 3 W.L.R. 981; [1985] 3
All E.R. 321; (1986) 18 H.L.R. 66; [1985] 2 E.G.L.R. 50; (1985)
276 E.G. 452, CA (Civ Div) 2–03, 2–04, 2–05, 13–01
R. v Associated Octel Co Ltd [1996] 1 W.L.R. 1543; [1996] 4 All
E.R. 846; [1996] I.C.R. 972; [1997] I.R.L.R. 123; [1997] Crim.
L.R. 355; (1996) 146 N.L.J. 1685, HL 11–07
— v Bristol City Council Ex p. Everett [1999] 1 W.L.R. 1170; [1999]
2 All E.R. 193; [1999] Env. L.R. 587; [1999] E.H.L.R. 265;
(1999) 31 H.L.R. 1102; [1999] B.L.G.R. 513; [1999] 3 P.L.R.
14; [1999] E.G. 33 (C.S.); (1999) 96(10) L.S.G. 32; (1999)
96(13) L.S.G. 31; (1999) 149 N.L.J. 370; (1999) 143 S.J.L.B.
104; [1999] N.P.C. 28, CA (Civ Div) 12–17
— v Cardiff City Council Ex p. Cross (1983) 6 H.L.R. 1; 81 L.G.R.
105; [1983] J.P.L. 245, CA (Civ Div) 12–01
R. (on the application of Gilboy) v Liverpool City Council; sub nom
Gilboy v Liverpool City Council [2008] EWCA Civ 751; [2008]
27 E.G. 116 (C.S.); (2008) 152(27) S.J.L.B. 30; [2008] N.P.C.
79, CA (Civ Div) 13–02
R. (on the application of Hackney LBC) v Rottenberg; sub nom
Hackney LBC v Rottenberg [2007] EWHC 166 (Admin); [2007]
Env. L.R. 24; [2008] J.P.L. 177, DC.. 12–17

R. (on the application of Khatun) v Newham LBC; R. (on the
  application of Zeb) v Newham LBC; R. (on the application
  of Iqbal) v Newham LBC; sub nom Newham LBC v Khatun;
  Khatun v Newham LBC [2004] EWCA Civ 55; [2005] Q.B. 37;
  [2004] 3 W.L.R. 417; [2004] Eu. L.R. 628; [2004] H.L.R. 29;
  [2004] B.L.G.R. 696; [2004] L. & T.R. 18; (2004) 148 S.J.L.B.
  268; [2004] N.P.C. 28, CA (Civ Div)..3–04
R. (on the application of Lee) v Leeds Crown Court; sub nom
  Lee v Leeds Crown Court [2006] EWHC 2550 (Admin),
  DC...4–05, 13–01, 13–06
R. (on the application of Weaver) v London & Quadrant Housing
  Trust [2008] EWHC 1377 (Admin); (2008) 158 N.L.J. 969;
  [2008] N.P.C. 74, DC 13–03
R&B Customs Brokers Co Ltd v United Dominions Trust Ltd [1988]
  1 W.L.R. 321; [1988] 1 All E.R. 847; [1988] R.T.R. 134; (1988)
  85(11) L.S.G. 42; (1988) 132 S.J. 300, CA (Civ Div)....................3–02
RHJ Ltd v FT Patten (Holdings) Ltd [2008] EWCA Civ 151; [2008]
  2 W.L.R. 1096; [2008] L. & T.R. 18; [2008] 18 E.G. 128; [2008]
  11 E.G. 93 (C.S.); [2008] N.P.C. 29, CA (Civ Div).......................6–03
Radford v De Froberville [1977] 1 W.L.R. 1262; [1978] 1 All E.R.
  33; 7 B.L.R. 35; (1978) 35 P. & C.R. 316; (1977) 121 S.J. 319,
  Ch D...17–01
Rainbow Estates Ltd v Tokenhold Ltd; sub nom Gaynes Park
  Mansion, Epping, Essex, Re [1999] Ch. 64; [1998] 3 W.L.R. 980;
  [1998] 2 All E.R. 860; [1998] L. & T.R. 116; [1998] 2 E.G.L.R.
  34; [1998] 24 E.G. 123; (1998) 95(15) L.S.G. 30; (1998) 142
  S.J.L.B. 116; [1998] N.P.C. 33, Ch D 16–01
Ratcliff v McConnell [1999] 1 W.L.R. 670; (1999) 1 L.G.L.R. 276;
  [1999] Ed. C.R. 523; [1999] P.I.Q.R. P170; (1999) 96(3) L.S.G.
  32; (1999) 143 S.J.L.B. 53, CA (Civ Div)....................................10–22
Ravengate Estates Ltd v Horizon Housing Group Ltd [2007] EWCA
  Civ 1368; [2008] 1 E.G. 135 (C.S.); (2008) 152(2) S.J.L.B. 32;
  [2007] N.P.C. 140, CA (Civ Div)..17–15
Ravenseft Properties Ltd v Davstone (Holdings) Ltd [1980] Q.B. 12;
  [1979] 2 W.L.R. 897; [1979] 1 All E.R. 929; (1979) 37 P. & C.R.
  502; (1978) 249 E.G. 51; (1979) 129 N.L.J. 839; (1979) 123 S.J.
  320, QBD...2–06, 2–07
Read v J Lyons & Co Ltd [1947] A.C. 156; [1946] 2 All E.R. 471;
  (1947) 80 Ll. L. Rep. 1; (1946) 62 T.L.R. 646; [1947] L.J.R. 39;
  175 L.T. 413, HL 17–23
Record v Bell [1991] 1 W.L.R. 853; [1991] 4 All E.R. 471; (1991) 62
  P. & C.R. 192, Ch D..1–05
Regional Properties Co v City of London Real Property Co;
  Sedgwick Forbes Bland Payne Group v Regional Properties Co
  (1981) 257 E.G. 65 4–09

Regis Property Co Ltd v Dudley [1959] A.C. 370; [1958] 3
W.L.R. 647; [1958] 3 All E.R. 491; (1958) 102 S.J. 844,
HL 7–01, 7–02, 7–03, 7–05
Regus (UK) Ltd v Epcot Solutions Ltd [2008] EWCA Civ 361, CA
(Civ Div) 3–02
Reichman v Beveridge; sub nom Reichman v Gauntlett [2006]
EWCA Civ 1659; [2007] Bus. L.R. 412; [2007] 1 P. & C.R. 20;
[2007] L. & T.R. 18; [2007] 1 E.G.L.R. 37; [2007] 8 E.G. 138;
[2007] 1 E.G. 92 (C.S.); (2007) 104(4) L.S.G. 35; [2006] N.P.C.
132, CA (Civ Div) 17–34
— v Gauntlett. See Reichman v Beveridge ....
Richmond v Kensington and Chelsea RLBC; sub nom Kensington
and Chelsea RLBC v Richmond [2006] EWCA Civ 68; [2006] 1
W.L.R. 1693; [2006] H.L.R. 25; [2006] B.L.G.R. 407; [2006] 8
E.G. 175 (C.S.); (2006) 103(10) L.S.G. 25; (2006) 150 S.J.L.B.
265; [2006] N.P.C. 16; [2006] 2 P. & C.R. DG12, CA (Civ Div) 9–25
Rigby v Bennett (1882) L.R. 21 Ch. D. 559, CA 6–03
Rimmer v Liverpool City Council [1985] Q.B. 1; [1984] 2 W.L.R.
426; [1984] 1 All E.R. 930; (1984) 12 H.L.R. 23; 82 L.G.R. 424;
(1984) 47 P. & C.R. 516; (1984) 269 E.G. 319; (1984) 81 L.S.G.
664, CA (Civ Div) 17–21
— v Pearson (2000) 79 P. & C.R. D21, CA (Civ Div) 9–03
Rogers v Rice [1892] 2 Ch. 170, CA 15–21
Ross v Fedden (1871–72) L.R. 7 Q.B. 661, QB 8–24
Rylands v Fletcher; sub nom Fletcher v Rylands (1868) L.R. 3 H.L.
330, HL 8–01, 8–07, 8–08, 8–22, 8–23, 8–24
Sampson v Hodson-Pressinger [1981] 3 All E.R. 710; (1984) 12
H.L.R. 40; (1982) 261 E.G. 891; (1981) 125 S.J. 623, CA (Civ
Div) 8–14
Sanderson v Berwick upon Tweed Corp (1883–84) L.R. 13 Q.B.D.
547, CA 6–07
Saner v Bilton (No.1) (1877–78) L.R. 7 Ch. D. 815, Ch D 6–08, 7–16
Scala House & District Property Co v Forbes [1974] Q.B. 575;
[1973] 3 W.L.R. 14; [1973] 3 All E.R. 308; (1973) 26 P. & C.R.
164; (1973) 117 S.J. 467, CA (Civ Div) 15–15
Searson v Brioland Ltd; sub nom Brioland Ltd v Searson [2005]
EWCA Civ 55; [2005] 5 E.G. 202 (C.S.); [2005] N.P.C. 12, CA
(Civ Div) 10–09
Secretary of State for Transport v MacDonald. See Mott MacDonald
Ltd v Department of Transport ....
Sedleigh-Denfield v O'Callagan (Trustees for St Joseph's Society for
Foreign Missions) [1940] A.C. 880; [1940] 3 All E.R. 349, HL 8–14
Sharpe v Manchester City Council (1981–82) 5 H.L.R. 71, CA (Civ
Div) 8–16

— v Sweeting (ET) & Son [1963] 1 W.L.R. 665; [1963] 2 All E.R.
455; (1963) 107 S.J. 666, Assizes (York)...8–10
Sheldon v West Bromwich Corp (1984) 13 H.L.R. 23; (1973) 25 P.
& C.R. 360; (1973) 117 S.J. 486, CA (Civ Div)............................2–12
Shelfer v City of London Electric Lighting Co (No.1); Meux's
Brewery Co v City of London Electric Lighting Co [1895] 1
Ch. 287, CA 16–11
Shiloh Spinners Ltd v Harding [1973] A.C. 691; [1973] 2 W.L.R. 28;
[1973] 1 All E.R. 90; (1973) 25 P. & C.R. 48; (1972) 117 S.J. 34,
HL 15–15
Shine v English Churches Housing Group. See English Churches
Housing Group v Shine
Siddorn v Patel [2007] EWHC 1248 (QB), QBD...............................10–20
Sidnell v Wilson [1966] 2 Q.B. 67; [1966] 2 W.L.R. 560; [1966] 1
All E.R. 681; (1966) 110 S.J. 53, CA...15–09
Smith v Bradford Metropolitan Council (1981–82) 4 H.L.R. 86; 80
L.G.R. 713; (1982) 44 P. & C.R. 171; (1982) 79 L.S.G. 1176;
(1982) 126 S.J. 624, CA (Civ Div) 4–04
— v Bradford Metropolitan Council (1981–82) 4 H.L.R. 86; 80
L.G.R. 713; (1982) 44 P. & C.R. 171; (1982) 79 L.S.G. 1176;
(1982) 126 S.J. 624, CA (Civ Div) 5–08, 5–09
— v Marable (1843) 11 M & W. 5..4–08
— v Nottinghamshire CC, The Times, November 13, 1981, CA (Civ
Div)..6–06
Southwark LBC v Long; sub nom Long v Southwark LBC [2002]
EWCA Civ 403; [2002] H.L.R. 56; [2002] B.L.G.R. 530;
[2002] 3 E.G.L.R. 37; [2002] 47 E.G. 150; [2002] 15 E.G.
133 (C.S.); (2002) 99(19) L.S.G. 30; [2002] N.P.C. 48, CA
(Civ Div)...2–10, 6–07, 8–01, 8–12
— v Mills; Baxter v Camden LBC (No.2); sub nom Southwark LBC v
Tanner ....
[2001] 1 A.C. 1; [1999] 3 W.L.R. 939; [1999] 4 All E.R. 449; [2000]
Env. L.R. 112; (2000) 32 H.L.R. 148; [2000] B.L.G.R. 138; [2000]
L. & T.R. 159; [1999] 3 E.G.L.R. 35; [1999] 45 E.G. 179; [1999]
E.G. 122 (C.S.); (1999) 96(42) L.S.G. 41; (1999) 96(42) L.S.G.
45; (1999) 149 N.L.J. 1618; (1999) 143 S.J.L.B. 249; [1999] N.P.C.
123; (2000) 79 P. & C.R. D13, HL...................6–05, 6–07, 8–20, 11–08
— v Tanner. See Southwark LBC v Mills...
Stack v Dowden; sub nom Dowden v Stack [2007] UKHL 17; [2007]
2 A.C. 432; [2007] 2 W.L.R. 831; [2007] 2 All E.R. 929; [2007]
1 F.L.R. 1858; [2007] 2 F.C.R. 280; [2007] B.P.I.R. 913; [2008]
2 P. & C.R. 4; [2007] W.T.L.R. 1053; (2006-07) 9 I.T.E.L.R. 815;
[2007] Fam. Law 593; [2007] 18 E.G. 153 (C.S.); (2007) 157
N.L.J. 634; (2007) 151 S.J.L.B. 575; [2007] N.P.C. 47; [2007] 2
P. & C.R. DG11, HL 1–06

Stallwood v David [2006] EWHC 2600 (QB); [2007] 1 All E.R. 206;
  [2007] R.T.R. 11, QBD...18–07
Standen v Chrismas (1874) 10 Q.B. 135...7–03
Staves v Leeds City Council (1991) 23 H.L.R. 107; [1992] 29 E.G.
  119, CA (Civ Div) 5–08
Stent v Monmouth DC (1987) 19 H.L.R. 269; (1987) 54 P. & C.R.
  193; [1987] 1 E.G.L.R. 59; (1987) 282 E.G. 705, CA (Civ Div)....2–07
Sykes v Harry; Sykes v Trustee of Harry's Estate (A Bankrupt)
  [2001] EWCA Civ 167; [2001] Q.B. 1014; [2001] 3 W.L.R. 62;
  (2001) 33 H.L.R. 80; (2001) 82 P. & C.R. 35; [2001] L. & T.R.
  40; [2001] 1 E.G.L.R. 53; [2001] 17 E.G. 221; (2001) 98(14)
  L.S.G. 39; (2001) 145 S.J.L.B. 61; [2001] N.P.C. 26; (2001) 82
  P. & C.R. DG9, CA (Civ Div)......................2–12, 9–22, 11–10, 11–16
Tailby v Official Receiver; sub nom Official Receiver as Trustee of
  the Estate of Izon (A Bankrupt) v Tailby (1888) L.R. 13 App.
  Cas. 523, HL..1–02
Tanner v Southwark LBC. See Mills v Southwark LBC
Targett v Torfaen BC [1992] 3 All E.R. 27; (1992) 24 H.L.R. 164;
  [1992] P.I.Q.R. P125; [1992] 1 E.G.L.R. 274; [1991] E.G. 125
  (C.S.); (1991) 141 N.L.J. 1698; [1991] N.P.C. 126, CA (Civ
  Div)..9–03, 9–26, 17–21
Tennant Radiant Heat v Warrington Development Corp [1988] 1
  E.G.L.R. 41; [1988] 11 E.G. 71; (1988) 4 Const. L.J. 321, CA
  (Civ Div)...8–14, 17–28
Thomas v British Railways Board [1976] Q.B. 912; [1976] 2 W.L.R.
  761; [1976] 3 All E.R. 15; (1976) 120 S.J. 334, CA (Civ Div) 10–08
Thompson v Clive Alexander & Partners, 59 B.L.R. 77; 28 Con.
  L.R. 49; [1955-95] P.N.L.R. 605; (1992) 8 Const. L.J. 199, QBD
  (OR)...9–07
Thornton v Birmingham City Council, *Legal Action*, November 2004.5–08
Thurrock BC v Secretary of State for the Environment, Transport
  and the Regions; Thurrock BC v Holding; sub nom Secretary
  of State for the Environment, Transport and the Regions v
  Thurrock BC (No.2); Holding v Thurrock BC [2002] EWCA
  Civ 226; [2002] 2 P.L.R. 43; [2002] J.P.L. 1278; [2002] 10 E.G.
  157 (C.S.); (2002) 99(10) L.S.G. 34; [2002] N.P.C. 31, CA (Civ
  Div)..18–26
Tomlinson v Congleton BC [2003] UKHL 47; [2004] 1 A.C. 46;
  [2003] 3 W.L.R. 705; [2003] 3 All E.R. 1122; [2004] P.I.Q.R. P8;
  [2003] 32 E.G. 68 (C.S.); (2003) 100(34) L.S.G. 33; (2003) 153
  N.L.J. 1238; (2003) 147 S.J.L.B. 937; [2003] N.P.C. 102, HL 10–20
Transco Plc v Stockport MBC; Stockport MBC v Reddish Vale Golf
  Club; sub nom: British Gas Plc v Stockport MBC; Stockport
  MBC v British Gas Plc [2003] UKHL 61; [2004] 2 A.C. 1; [2003]
  3 W.L.R. 1467; [2004] 1 All E.R. 589; 91 Con. L.R. 28; [2004]

Env. L.R. 24; [2003] 48 E.G. 127 (C.S.); (2003) 153 N.L.J. 1791;
     (2003) 147 S.J.L.B. 1367; [2003] N.P.C. 143; [2004] 1 P. & C.R.
     DG12, HL 8–24
Unchained Growth III Plc v Granby Village (Manchester) Management
     Co Ltd; Granby Village (Manchester) Management Co Ltd v
     Unchained Growth III Plc [2000] 1 W.L.R. 739; [2000] L. & T.R.
     186; [1999] E.G. 116 (C.S.); (1999) 96(45) L.S.G. 33, CA (Civ Div) 3–02
Voaden v Champion (The Baltic Surveyor and the Timbuktu) [2002]
     EWCA Civ 89; [2002] 1 Lloyd's Rep. 623; [2002] C.L.C. 666,
     CA (Civ Div) 17–12
WG Clark (Properties) Ltd v Dupre Properties Ltd [1992] Ch. 297;
     [1991] 3 W.L.R. 579; [1992] 1 All E.R. 596; (1991) 23 H.L.R.
     544; (1992) 63 P. & C.R. 343; [1991] 2 E.G.L.R. 59; [1991] 42
     E.G. 125; [1991] E.G. 64 (C.S.), Ch D 15–03
Wadsworth v Nagle [2005] EWHC 26 (QB), QBD 9–23
Wallace v Manchester City Council (1998) 30 H.L.R. 1111; [1998]
     L. & T.R. 279; [1998] 3 E.G.L.R. 38; [1998] 41 E.G. 223; [1998]
     E.G. 114 (C.S.); [1998] N.P.C. 115, CA (Civ Div) 17–04, 17–05
Ward v Kirkland [1967] Ch. 194; [1966] 1 W.L.R. 601; [1966] 1 All
     E.R. 609; (1966) 110 S.J. 289, Ch D 14–04
Warner v Basildon Development Corp (1991) 7 Const. L.J. 146, CA
     (Civ Div) 9–08
Warren v Keen [1954] 1 Q.B. 15; [1953] 3 W.L.R. 702; [1953] 2 All
     E.R. 1118; (1953) 97 S.J. 742, CA 7–04, 7–12, 7–14
Watermoor Meat Supply Ltd v Walker [2007] All E.R. (D) 292
     (Oct), QBD 17–33
Welsh v Greenwich LBC (2001) 33 H.L.R. 40; (2001) 81 P. & C.R.
     12; [2001] L. & T.R. 12; [2000] 3 E.G.L.R. 41; [2000] 49 E.G.
     118; [2000] E.G. 84 (C.S.); (2000) 97(27) L.S.G. 40; (2000)
     97(28) L.S.G. 32, CA (Civ Div) 2–09, 2–10, 5–06
Westminster (Duke of) v Guild [1985] Q.B. 688; [1984] 3 W.L.R.
     630; [1984] 3 All E.R. 144; (1984) 48 P. & C.R. 42; (1983) 267
     E.G. 762; (1984) 128 S.J. 581, CA (Civ Div) 4–06, 6–07
Wheat v E Lacon & Co Ltd [1966] A.C. 552; [1966] 2 W.L.R. 581;
     [1966] 1 All E.R. 582; [1966] R.A. 193; [1966] R.V.R. 223;
     (1966) 110 S.J. 149, HL 10–05
Whitam v Kershaw (1886) 16 Q.B.D. 613 7–11
White v Blackmore [1972] 2 Q.B. 651; [1972] 3 W.L.R. 296; [1972]
     3 All E.R. 158; (1972) 116 S.J. 547, CA (Civ Div) 10–13
— v Knowsley Housing Trust. See Knowsley Housing Trust v White
Whitman v Kershaw (1886) 16Q.B.D. 613 7–07
Wilson v Finch-Hatton (1877) 2 Ex. D. 336 4–08
Wrotham Park Estate Co Ltd v Parkside Homes Ltd [1974] 1 W.L.R.
     798; [1974] 2 All E.R. 321; (1974) 27 P. & C.R. 296; (1973) 118
     S.J. 420, Ch D 16–11

Wycombe HA v Barnett (1981–82) 5 H.L.R. 84; (1984) 47 P. & C.R.
    394; (1982) 264 E.G. 619, CA (Civ Div) 7–04
Wynn-Jones v Bickley [2006] EWHC 1991 (Ch), Ch D 16–11
X v Hounslow LBC [2008] EWHC 1168 (QB), QBD 8–20, 13–05
Yaxley v Gotts; sub nom Yaxley v Gott [2000] Ch. 162; [1999] 3
    W.L.R. 1217; [2000] 1 All E.R. 711; [1999] 2 F.L.R. 941; (2000)
    32 H.L.R. 547; (2000) 79 P. & C.R. 91; [1999] 2 E.G.L.R. 181;
    [1999] Fam. Law 700; [1999] E.G. 92 (C.S.); (1999) 96(28)
    L.S.G. 25; (1999) 143 S.J.L.B. 198; [1999] N.P.C. 76; (1999) 78
    P. & C.R. D33, CA (Civ Div) 1–06
Yorkbrook Investments Ltd v Batten (1986) 18 H.L.R. 25; (1986) 52
    P. & C.R. 51; [1985] 2 E.G.L.R. 100; (1985) 276 E.G. 545, CA
    (Civ Div) 4–06, 14–09
Young v Kent CC [2005] EWHC 1342 (QB), QBD 10–18

Table of Statutes

1832 Prescription Act (2 & 3 Will.4 c.71) 8–04
s.3 6–03
1838 Judgments Act (1 & 2 Vict. c.110) 17–39
1852 Common Law Procedure Act (15 & 16 Vict. c.76) s.210 18–03
1858 Chancery Amendment Act (21 & 22 Vict. c.27) (Lord Cairns' Act) 16–11
1875 Artisans and Labourers Dwellings Act (38 & 39 Vict. c.36) 12–01
1885 Housing of the Working Classes Act (48 & 49 Vict. c.72) s.12 5–03
1925 Law of Property Act (15 & 16 Geo.6 c.20) 1–05
s.62 14–04
s.78 1–10
s.79 1–10
s.141 .... 1–09, 14–11
s.142 1–09
s.146. 15–02, 15–05, 15–06, 15–07, 15–10, 15–12, 15–21, B1–01, B2–02, B4–01, B5–02
(2) 15–14, 15–15, 15–16, B4–02
(3) 15–10, 15–19
(4) 15–18
s.147 .... 15–14, 15–20
1927 Landlord and Tenant Act (17 & 18 Geo. 5 c.36) A1–01
s.18 .... 17–08, 17–09, 17–10, 17–11, 17–15, 17–16, 17–18, 17–19, 17–20, 18–09, 18–15, A1–1
(1) ... 17–08, 17–09, 18–12
1934 Law Reform (Miscellaneous Provisions) Act (24 & 25

Geo.5 c.41) 18–05
s.11(3) 18–05
1936 Public Health Act (26 Geo.5 & 1 Edw.8 c.49) 11–02
.... 12–03
1938 Leasehold Property (Repairs) Act (1 & 2 Geo.6 c.34) ....
...... 15–06, 15–09, 15–10, 15–12, 15–13, 15–16, A2–01, B2–01, B2–02
s.1 ....A2–01, B2–02
(1) 15–10
(3) 15–10, 15–13, B2–02
(4) 15–10
(5) 15–10, 15–11, B2–02
s.3 15–09
1945 Law Reform (Contributory Negligence) Act (8 & 9 Geo.6 c.28)
s.1(1) 17–28
1954 Landlord and Tenant Act (2 & 3 Eliz.2 c.56) 17–16
s.1 5–16
s.7 5–16
s.34 17–16
s.51 15–09
(2) (a) A2–01
(b) A2–01
(c) A2–01
(d) A2–01
s.65 17–16
1957 Occupiers' Liability Act (5 & 6 Eliz.2 c.31) ....
.... 8–07, 8–14, 8–18, 10–01, 10–02, 10–03, 10–04, 10–08, 10–15, 10–18, 10–21, 17–21, 17–23, 17–30, 18–06, A3–01, B11–01
s.1(3) 10–15
(a) 10–04
(b) 10–03
(4) 10–08
s.2 .... A3–01

(1)............................. 10–15
(2)............................. 10–03
(3)............................. 10–10
   (b)............................ 10–12
(5)............................. 10–13
(6)............................. 10–07
s.3(1) 10–16
(2)............................. 10–17
1961 Factories Act (9 & 10 Eliz.2
      c.34) 11–20
      Housing Act (9 & 10 Eliz.2
      c.65)
      s.32.. 1–06, 2–1, 4–03, 5–04
1963 Offices, Shops and Railway
      Premises Act (c.41)... 11–21
      s.1................................ 11–21
      s.42.............................. 11–21
      s.43.............................. 11–21
      s.44.............................. 11–21
1972 Defective   Premises   Act
      (c.35)................ 3–06, 9–01,
      9–02, 9–13, 9–22, 9–25, 10–
      01, 11–03, 17–01, 17–02,
      17–21, 17–30, A4–01
      s.1..................... 8–09, 9–01,
      9–04, 9–06, 9–07,   9–08,
      9–09, 9–24, 11–04, 11–05,
      17–21, 17–23, A4–01
         (1)............................. 9–07
         (4)............................. 9–04
         (5)............................. 9–08
      s.2.............................. A4–02
         (2)............................. 9–06
         (3)............................. 9–06
      s.3....................................
      9–07, 9–09, A4–03
         (6)............................. 3–06
      s.4........... 2–12, 4–04, 5–08,
      8–11, 9–01,   9–13, 9–14,
      9–15, 9–16,   9–18, 9–21,
      9–22, 9–23,   9–24, 9–25,
      9–26, 11–10, 11–14, 11–16,
      16–08, 17–01, 17–11, 17–
      21, 17–23, 17– 25, A4–04,
      B8–03, B9–01
         (1)............................. 9–22
         (2)............................. 9–22
         (3)............................. 9–21
         (4)......... 4–04, 9–18, 9–23

s.6.............................. A4–05
   (1)............................. 9–17
Land Charges Act (c.61)......
.... 1–15
1974 Health and Safety at Work
      etc Act (c.37). 11–06, 11–21
      s.3.............................. 11–07
      s.15............................ 11–12
      s.47(1)(a).................. 11–07
         (2)........................... 11–14
1977 Rent Act (c.42).....................
      .... 5–16, 7–16, 14–15
      s.116........................... 7–16
      Protection from Eviction Act
      (c.43)
      s.2.............................. 15–03
      Criminal Law Act (c.45)
      s.6.............................. 15–03
      Unfair Contract Terms Act
      (c.50)................ 3–01, 3–02,
      3–04, 9–10, 10–15, 10–21
      s.3.............................. 10–15
      s.12.................... 3–02, 3–04
      s.14............................ 10–15
1980 Limitation Act (c.58)
      s.2.............................. 18–02
      s.5.............................. 18–02
      s.10............................ 18–05
      s.11............................ 11–04
      s.14............... 18–04, 18–05
      s.14A... 9–08, 18–02, 18–05
      s.14B 18–02, 18–05
      s.15(1) 15–02, 18–03
      s.19............................ 18–03
      s.24............................ 18–05
      s.32............................ 18–05
      s.33............... 18–04, 18–05
      Highways Act (c.66)
      s.41............................ 10–08
1981 Supreme Court Act (c.54)
      s.35A......................B5–02
         (4)........................... 17–37
      s.37............... 16–07, 16–09
      s.50............................ 16–11
1982 Supply of Goods and
      Services Act (c.29)...... 9–10
      s.4(2) 9–12
         (5)............................. 9–12
      s.13.............................. 9–10

s.14.............................. 9–10
s.15.............................. 9–10
s.16.............................. 9–10
1984 Occupiers' Liability Act
(c.3)................ 8–07, 10–01,
10–03, 10–08, 10–18, 10–
19, 10–20, 17–21, A5–01
s.1..................10–20, A5–01
(3)........................... 10–20
(c)............................ 10–21
(3)–(4)................... 10–20
(5)........................... 10–21
(6)............................ 10–2
s.2(1)......................... 10–21
County Courts Act (c.28)
s.38............. 16–07, 16–09
s.40(2)...................... 18–38
s.69 B3–02, B9–03, B10–06
(4)............................. 17–37
Housing Defects Act (c.50) .
.... 12–05
Building Act (c.55)..............
.... 9–01, 11–02,
12–03, 12–04, A6–01
Pt III..................... A6–01
s.36............................ 11–04
s.38............................ 11–04
s.44............................ 11–02
s.45............................ 12–03
s.59............................ 12–04
s.76............................ A6–01
s.77.................12–04, A6–02
s.78............................ A6–03
s.79.................12–04, A6–04
ss.79–80 12–03
s.80............................ A6–05
s.81............................ A6–06
s.82............................ A6–06
s.83.................12–03, A6–07
1985 Housing Act (c.68)..............
.... 12–01, 12–05,
12–10, 12–14
Pt XVIII 12–05, 12–09
s.96............................ 14–13
s.97............................ 14–15
s.352.......................... 11–09
s.528.......................... 12–05
s.604.......................... 12–05
Landlord and Tenant Act

(c.70).............18–16, A7–01
s.8............ 5–01, 5–03, 5–17
s.11................... 1–06, 2–01,
2–03, 2–11, 4–03, 4–04,
5–01, 5–03, 5–04, 5–05,
5–08, 5–09, 5–10, 5–11,5–
12, 5–13, 5–15, 5–17, 7–05,
8–16, 9–23, 11–08, 11–10,
11–16, 16–06, A7–01, B8–
03, B9–01, B10–01, B12–03
(1)............................ 5–07
(a)............................ 5–08
(1A)......................... 5–11
(2)............................ 7–05
(a)............................ 5–10
(3)................ 5–12, 18–07
(3A)......................... 5–11
(6)........ 4–10, 5–15, 7–16
s.12........................... A7–02
(2)............................ 5–05
s.13.................5–04, A7–03
(1)............................ 5–04
s.14........................... A7–04
s.15.................5–07, A7–05
s.16........................... A7–06
s.17................16–06, A7–07
(1)............................ 16–06
Housing (Consequential
Provisions) Act (c.71)
s.2(3)......................... A7–01
s.4.................A6–01, A6–05
s.5(2)............A6–01, A6–05
Sch.2, para.58(2)...... A6–01
(3)........................... A6–05
Sch.4 ....A6–01, A6–05
1986 Agricultural Holdings Act
(c.5)........................ 15–09
s.17............................ 14–12
Latent Damage Act (c.37)....
.... 9–08
Gas Act (c.44)
s.67(1)...................... A6–05
(3).......................... A6–05
Sch.7, para.30 .... A6–05
Sch.8, para.33 .... A6–05
Housing and Planning Act
(c.63)........................ A6–02
s.24(1)...................... A6–05
s.40........................... A6–04

Sch.5, para.11(1)...... A6–05
(2)........................... A6–05
Sch.9, para.6(2)........ A6–04
1987 Landlord and Tenant Act
(c.31)...2–16, 18–16, A8–01
s.21............................ 14–16
s.24............................ 14–16
s.35.................2–16, A8–01
s.37............................ 2–16
s.59(3)........................ 2–16
Consumer Protection Act
(c.43)........................ 11–18
s.11................ 11–11, 11–18
s.41............................ 11–18
1988 Housing Act (c.50)...... 5–11
s.5............................. 15–03
(1)–(2)..................... 15–03
s.16............................ 7–16
s.116.......................... 5–11
(1)........................... A7–01
(2)........................... A7–01
(4)........................... A7–01
s.119.......................... A8–01
Sch.2 15–03
Sch.13, para.5 .... A8–01
1989 Electricity Act (c.29)
s.112(1).................... A6–05
(3)........................... A6–05
Sch.16, para.31 .... A6–05
Sch.17, para.33 .... A6–05
Law of Property
(Miscellaneous Provisions)
Act (c.34)................... 1–05
s.1............................. 18–03
s.2............ 1–04, 1–05, 1–06
(1)........................... 1–06
(5)(c) 1–06
1990 Planning (Consequential
Provisions) Act (c.11)
s.4................A6–02, A6–04
Sch.2, para.67(3)...... A6–02
(4).......................... A6–04
Environmental Protection
Act (c.43) 12–01, 12–06,
12–12, 12–15, ... A9–01
Pt III......................... 12–16
s.79.................12–17, A9–01
(1)........................... 12–16
s.80.................12–18, A9–02

s.80A..............12–18, A9–03
s.81............................ A9–04
s.81A......................... A9–05
s.81B A9–06
s.82............................ A9–07
s.160.......................... 12–18
s.162(1)..................... A6–01
Sch.15, para.24 .... A6–01
1992 Access to Neighbouring
Land Act (c.23)8–03, 14–06
s.8(3)........................ 4–06
1993 Leasehold Reform, Housing
and Urban Development Act
(c.28)
Pt I, Ch.6.................. A8–01
s.86............................ A8–01
s.121.......................... 14–14
1995 Home Energy Conservation
Act (c.10).................. 12–19
Environment Act (c.25)
Sch.17, para.5 .... A9–05
Landlord and Tenant
(Covenants) Act (c.30)........
.... 1–08, 1–09,
1–10, 1–14, 1–15
s.3.................... 1–15, 14–11
(1)............................ 1–13
s.5.............................. 1–11
s.6.............................. 1–12
s.8...................... 1–12, 1–15
(1)............................ 1–12
s.16(4)........................ 1–11
s.18............................ 1–09
s.23(3)........................ 1–14
s.24............................ 1–11
s.25............................ 1–16
Disability Discrimination
Act (c.50).................. 11–22
s.21............................ 11–22
s.27............................ 11–22
1996 Arbitration Act (c.23) 19–11
s.9............................. 19–11
s.34............................ 19–10
s.66............................ 19–16
ss.67–68 19–14
s.69............................ 19–15
s.93............................ 19–13
Party Wall etc. Act (c.40).....
.... 8–03, 14–02, 14–06

Housing Act (c.52)..... 3–07,
.... 19–03
Pt VII 3–04
s.27A(1) 12–09, 12–20
Housing Grants, Construction
and Regeneration Act (c.53)
.... 12–07
s.106........................... 19–01
1998 Human Rights Act (c.42) ....
6–07, 8–01, 13–01, 13–07
s.6............................. 13–03
(a)........................... 13–03
(b)........................... 13–03
s.7(1)(a)..................... 13–04
1999 Contracts (Rights of Third
Parties) Act (c.31) 1–02,
.... 1–07, 10–16
2000 Countryside and Rights of
Way Act (c.37) 10–08
Pt 1, c.1 .... A5–01
s.13........................... 10–08
(2)........................... A5–01
2001 Regulatory Reform Act (c.6)
s.1............................. 11–09
2002 Land Registration Act (c.9) .
.... 1–15
s.27......................................
18–06
Commonhold and Leasehold
Reform Act (c.15)....... 2–16
Pt 2, Ch.5 .... A8–01
s.162........................ A8–01
(2).......................... A8–01
2003 Sustainable Energy Act
(c.30)......................... 12–19

2004 Sustainable and Secure
Buildings Act (c.22).. 11–02
Housing Act (c.34)... 11–09,
12–01, 12–08, 12–10, 12–14
Pt 1 ... 12–08, 12–09, 12–10,
.... 12–11, 12–12
Ch.1..........12–09, A11–01
Ch.2............ 12–09, 12–12
Ch.3......................... 12–09
Ch.4......................... 12–09
Ch.5......................... 12–09
Pt 2 12–09
Pt 3 12–09
Pt 4 12–09
Pt 5 12–09
Pt 6, Ch.5 12–10
Pt 7..............12–14, A11–04
s.1....12–10, 12–13, A11–01
s.2........................... A11–02
(1)........................... 12–10
s.3........................... A11–03
s.61........................... 12–14
s.62........................... 12–14
s.63........................... 12–14
s.217......................... 12–19
s.220.............. 12–09, 12–20
s.254............12–14, A11–04
(3)........................... 12–14
s.266......................... 12–05
s.270(11) 12–08
2005 Disability Discrimination
Act (c.13)................. 11–22
2007 Tribunals, Courts and
Enforcement Act (c.15).......
.... 14–12, 15–23

Table of Statutory Instruments

1965 Rules of the Supreme Court (SI 1965/1776)............18–01
1973 House Building Standards (Approved Scheme etc) Order (SI 1973/1843)..............9–06
1975 House Building Standards (Approved Scheme etc) Order (SI 1975/1402)..............9–06
1977 House Building Standards (Approved Scheme etc) Order (SI 1977/642)................9–06
1981 County Court Rules (SI 1981/1687)..................18–01
1988 Landlord and Tenant Act 1987 (Commencement No.3) Order (SI 1988/1283) art.2 ..A7–01
Sch., para.7.................A7–01
1992 Gas Appliances (Safety) Regulations (SI 1992/711)....
....................................11–11
Manual Handling Operations Regulations (SI 1992/2793)..
....................................11–21
Provision and Use of Work Equipment Regulations (SI 1992/2932)..................11–21
Workplace (Health, Safety and Welfare) Regulations (SI 1992/3004)..................11–21
1994 Secure Tenants of Local Authorities (Right to Repair Scheme) Regulations (SI 1994/133)........14–14, 14–15
reg.4..............................14–14
Plugs and Sockets (Safety) Regulations (SI 1994/1768)..
....................................11–18
Gas Safety (Installation and Use) Regulations (SI 1994/1886)..................11–13
Unfair Terms in Consumer Contracts Regulations (SI

1994/3159)....................3–03
Electrical Equipment (Safety) Regulations (SI 1994/3260)...
....................................11–18
1995 Gas Appliances (Safety) Regulations (SI 1995/1629)..
....................................11–11
1996 Housing Act 1996 (Consequential Provisions) Order (SI 1996/2315) Sch.2, para.16(2)........A7–04
1997 Secure Tenants (Rights to Repair) Regulations (SI 1997/73)......................14–14
1998 Gas Safety (Installation and Use) Regulations (SI 1998/2451)..................11–12, ... 11–13, A10–01
Pt F A10–01
reg.36............ 11–14, A10–01
reg.39............................11–14
Civil Procedure Rules (SI 1998/3132) 15–19, 18–10, 18–11, 18–15, 18–19, 18–24, 18–39
r.1.1 18–26
Pt 3 18–32
r.3.1 18–23
r.3.4................. 18–33, 18–39
r.3.9..............................18–33
Pt 7....15–21, 18–25, B11–01
Pt 8..... 15–12, 15–21, B2–01, ...B2–02
Pt 8 PD 15–12
r.15.2............................15–21
r.15.7............................15–21
Pt 16................. 18–24, 18–25
r.16.4(2)........................18–25
(b) 17–37
r.16.5............................18–25
Pt 16 PD, para.4.3 .....B12–03
para.13.1 18–25

Pt 17.....18–06, 18–26, 18–28
r.18.1............................18–29
(1)(a).............................18–29
Pt 19.............................18–06
r.19.6(1)........................10–06
Pt 20.......8–17, 18–06, 18–28
r.20.4(2)........................15–21
Pt 22.............................18–30
Pt 24.................. 18–01, 18–39
r.25.1............................16–07
Pt 26.............................18–31
r.26.4(1)........................18–31
r.26.6............................18–31
r.27.5............................18–07
Pt 29.............................18–37
r.30.3(2)........................18–37
Pt 35.............................18–07
r.35.1............................18–07
r.35.7............................18–07
r.35.12(4)......................18–08
    (5) 18–08
Pt 36................. 18–40, 19–01
r.36.2............................18–40
r.36.10..........................18–40
r.44.3................ 18–40, 18–41
    (5)(b) 18–23
Pt 55.............................15–21
r.55.2(1)(c) 15–21
r.55.7............................15–21
r.56.1............................15–12
Pt 56 PD, para.2 15–12
Pt 60................. 18–34, 18–37
r.60...............................18–37
r.60.6............................18–37
Pt 60 PD 18–34, 18–37
para.5.1.........................18–37

1999   Unfair Terms in Consumer
        Contracts Regulations (SI
        1999/2083)......... 3–02, 3–03,
        3–04, 3–07, 5–05
        reg.3(1)...........................3–04
        reg.5...............................3–05
        reg.6...............................3–05
        reg.7...............................3–06
        Sch.2...............................3–06

2000   Building Regulations (SI
        2000/2531) 11–02, 12–03, ...
       12–04
        Sch.1, Pt E....................11–03

Pt N.............................11–03
Pt P 11–03, 11–18
reg.1 11–03

2002   Control of Asbestos at Work
        Regulations (SI 2002/2675)..
       11–08

2005   Regulatory Reform (Fire
        Safety) Order (SI 2005/1541)
       11–09
        Sch.2, para.33(7).........A6–06
        Sch.4, para.1................A6–05
        Housing, Health and Safety
        Rating System (England)
        Regulations (SI 2005/3208)..
        12–11
        reg.3 12–10
        Sch.1..............................12–10
        Sch.2..............................12–11

2006   Housing, Health and Safety
        and Rating System (Wales)
        Regulations (SI 2006/1702)..
        .... 12–10, 12–11
        Sch.2.............................12–11
        Control of Asbestos
        Regulations (SI 2006/2739)..
       11–08
        reg.4..............................11–08

2007   Construction Design and
        Management Regulations (SI
        2007/320)........ 11–07, 11–12
        Energy Performance of
        Buildings (Certificates and
        Inspections) (England and
        Wales) Regulations (SI
        2007/991)........ 11–19, 12–19
        reg.38............................12–19
        Home Information Pack
        Regulations (SI 2007/992) ....
       11–19
        Energy Performance of
        Buildings (Certificates
        and Inspections) (England
        and Wales) (Amendment)
        Regulations (SI 2007/1669) ..
       11–19
        Home Information Pack
        (No.2) Regulations (SI
        2007/3301)...................11–19
        CTEAct2007Commencement

Order No.2 (SI 2007/3613)....
....................................15–23
2008 Energy Performance of
Buildings (Certificates
and Inspections) (England
and Wales) (Amendment)
Regulations (SI 2008/647)....
....................................12–19

Introduction

Background

There are various suggestions as to the amount of defective housing accommodation there is in the UK at the present time. According to the English Housing Condition Survey 2006, 40 per cent of private-sector landlords did not meet the Government's Decent Homes Standard (source: Department of Communities and Local Government Website). The worst offenders are supposed to be private-sector landlords but the same private-sector landlords have assumed an ever-greater role in providing rented accommodation after years of decline brought about by the Rent Acts. It is not the function of this book to explain how the state of the housing stock has deteriorated to its present condition other than to observe that it has been a feature of social housing going back to the 19th century that the legislature has attempted to improve the situation.

The same source suggests a high level of ignorance about the ever-increasing web of regulation affecting the provision of private-sector housing accommodation. Unfortunately, it cannot be assumed that all professional advisers are any less ignorant. It is the function of this book to reduce that level of ignorance.

The Government's latest attempt to improve housing standards has been the Decent Homes Standard referred to above. But there has also been a high level of regulation, particularly in the Housing Act 2004, as to a number of other aspects of housing condition. This substantially puts the burden of enforcing higher housing standards on local authorities whilst leaving civil remedies for disrepair and other defects largely untouched. It is surprising that despite a number of Law Commission recommendations in recent years, the Government have chosen not to intervene in the whole field of implied covenants relating to the condition of premises. The legislation on the statute book which implies covenants into certain leases (currently found in the Landlord and Tenant Act 1985) dates back to 1961.

Unfortunately, in trying to address this deficiency in the housing stock the legislature has faced a difficult dichotomy which it has not been able to satisfactorily resolve: the greater the amount of regulation, the higher the standard of that housing stock, but the less incentive there will be for landlords to enter the letting business.

What is meant by "defective premises"?

The term lacks any technical definition either in this work or elsewhere. It covers defects in the fabric of buildings, more commonly called disrepair in the landlord and tenant context, and any number of defects in the condition of those buildings. In order to place additional liability for the physical condition of demised premises on landlords beyond their repairing obligations requires express warranties are required. These are rare in most leases and there has been only limited interference by the legislature with the freedom of landlord and tenant to provide for such limited liability.

In some legislation (e.g. Occupiers' Liability Acts) the term "premises" extends to vehicles as well as to land and not just to land which has been built on, but here generally the term is used in its more commonly-understood sense of a building or buildings.

As has already been commented, the subject of liability for defective buildings crosses many boundaries. Inevitably, there will be subjects that have to be left out of a practitioner's work. In particular there is a greater emphasis on the liability of landlords and tenants for defective and dangerous buildings given the complex issues that the relationship of landlord and tenant often gives rise to. Actions between sellers and purchasers arising out of their defective state are less common and are generally covered by certain well-established principles, particularly the caveat emptor principle.

No distinction will be made in the degree of coverage between commercial and residential premises. The principles of landlord and tenant, particularly as to construction of the repairing obligation, apply equally to both types of premises. However, certain problems special to commercial premises, such as the limit on the level of damages under s.18 of the Landlord and Tenant Act 1927, are covered separately and in some detail.

There is also an emphasis on civil remedies over public law enforcement because this is the principal area of litigation between parties over the defective state of buildings. Generally practitioners are more likely to become involved in civil-law proceedings than public-law proceedings arising out of a failure to comply with, for example, the health and fitness standard. Apart from anything else, the extraordinary complexity of the Government's legislation and the other demands that are made on local-authority finances mean that it is unlikely local authorities will be able to use their new powers as much as they would like. But, again, the importance of the new legislation on the health and fitness standard and on overcrowded dwellings in relation to private rented accommodation should not be overlooked.

The broad nature of the subject means that there has had to be considerable pruning of detail, particularly in relation to such matters as health and safety regulations. There is a danger that a book of this type would become unmanageable and inaccessible if over-detailed coverage of health and safety legislation were included. This is not to say that such legislation is unimportant and where it touches on other areas in practice I include references where necessary.

On the other hand, at the heart of the discussion over tortious liabilities I have included detailed coverage of the Defective Premises Act 1972 and the Occupiers' Liability Acts 1957–1984. These provide the simplest means by which a person injured or suffering loss whilst visiting premises, particularly a person who has no legal interest in the premises, may claim redress. However, it is unfortunately the case that the way the former Act has been interpreted in relation to the duties on landlords, has given rise to some difficult issues of law.

The Law is stated in England and Wales as at 31st August 2008.

PART I

CONTRACTUAL LIABILITY

Chapter 1

Principles of contractual liability

Claims arising out of the need to repair or maintain defective premises   **1–01**
are most likely to be under leases, which, particularly in relation
to non-residential occupiers, often involve different layers of rights
with different tenures. A lease is a contract as well as being, in most
cases, a legal estate in land. At the heart of the topic of attaching
liability for breaches of leasehold covenants is the need for privity
of contract between landlord and tenant. However, where privity
is established, problems also arise where there are a succession of
occupiers and sometimes potential liability of an original contracting
party may arise years after the party has given up possession of the
premises. This problem became acute in relation to the liability of
tenants under leasehold covenants where the lease was assigned. That
problem, along with the associated problem of claiming in contract
against non-contracting parties, needs to be grappled with before
turning in the next chapter to the problems of enforcing repairing
and other obligations.

This chapter also tackles those cases where liability may attach for
non-contractual statements or assurances, for example in relation to
the repair of the premises. Sometimes these promises or assurances
are said to arise as collateral contracts but often they arise in equity
as a form of estoppel in favour of the person who acts in reliance on
the promise or assurance.

The privity rule

It is a basic principle of contract law that a contract may not confer   **1–02**
rights and impose duties other than between the parties to that contract.
However, this apparently simple principle is sometimes overlooked,

particularly in the housing field, so that it is sometimes forgotten that any claim under the terms of the lease should be brought in the name of the tenant and not that of a member of his family.

This principle is subject to a number of modern exceptions:

- There is nothing to prevent a contract between A and B conferring benefits on C but at common law only B could sue, even though the rights were conferred on C. Thus in *Alfred McAlpine v Panatown* [2001] 1 A.C. 518 the House of Lords found that one company in a group of companies could claim in respect of its other group members' loss, even though it was not a party to the contract.

- It has long been held that the promisor may be a trustee of a chose in action, including a promise to perform an obligation to a third party (see *Tailby v Official Receiver* (1888) 13 App. Cas. 523, and, in the context of a guarantee, *Lloyds v Harper* (1880) L.R. 16 Ch.D 290).

- In *Beswick v Beswick* [1968] A.C. 58 the House of Lords used the remedy of specific performance to overcome the privity problem that existed when a widow and executrix of her husband's estate wished to sue for a benefit which she had not contracted for. Her late husband would only have suffered nominal damage but she, however, would have suffered substantial damage in the form of the loss of an annuity the defendant agreed to pay to her late husband. The availability of specific performance reflected the difficult nature of an action for damages on the facts.

- An alternative method of benefiting a third party is by a collateral warranty. This frequently arises in building contracts where a third party (C) is given an express right to enforce rights in contract between A and B, because in the contract between A and B, C's rights are warranted. For example, nominated sub-contractors are generally required to give undertakings to the employer as to design in circumstances where a main contractor may not be liable for that design, e.g. because it becomes insolvent. However, pre-contractual statements will only have contractual effect where the parties intended them to have that effect (see *Inntrepreneur Pub Co v East Crown Ltd* [2000] 2 Lloyds Rep. 611). The topic will be considered further below in the context of pre-lease assurances.

- The Contracts (Rights of Third Parties) Act 1999 allows a party on whom a contract conveys a benefit to sue but the

Act only applies to contracts entered into at least six months after it received Royal Assent on November 11, 1999 (i.e. contracts entered into on or after May 11, 1999). It did not affect the rights of a stranger to the contract but only those expressly benefited by the contract. By using this Act, A may specify that the contract is for the benefit of B and C, or may specify a generic class of persons. Third parties not expressly referred to will not fall within that class unless they form part of that generic class (see *Avraamides v Colwill* [2006] UKHL Civ 1533). Recently the High Court allowed a former tenant to rely on a provision limiting liability, which was contained in a supplemental deed made between the landlord and the then current tenant, by virtue of the Contracts (Rights of Third Parties) Act 1999 *(Prudential Assurance Company v Ayres* [2007] EWHC Ch.775). However, the Court of Appeal disagreed with the judge at first instance (Lindsay J.). Having regard to the background to the supplemental deed they were construing as well as the nature of the landlord and tenant relationship (being to enable the landlord to enforce obligations under the lease), the supplemental deed could not be considered under the 1999 Act. Nevertheless, this case seems to indicate a trend whereby greater reliance is being placed on the Act; indeed, there appears to be an active movement towards greater use of this Act at present, particularly amongst construction lawyers (see for e.g. (2003) 14 10 Cons. Law 6, where the author charts some of the developments up to that time).

Agreements or assurances before a lease

Another important exception to the strict application of the privity   **1–03** rule relates to certain statements made before a lease is entered into. These may consist of promises or assurances that the prospective tenant assumes to be correct and acts on. Although these will often be by the landlord himself this will not necessarily be so. In such cases the party relying on the pre-lease statement or obligation may wish to rely on a collateral contract. There will be many cases in which such statements do not satisfy the formality requirements to be enforceable. Specifically, those statements may not have been incorporated in a written agreement for lease or lease under seal. Therefore, the formality requirements of signed writing or incorporation in a deed will not be met. When these pre-contractual assurances or obligations may be relied on will need to be considered therefore.

Collateral contracts and warranties

1–04 The majority of business leases will be by deed whereas residential leases will usually be written but will sometimes be oral. A lease is both a contract and a conveyance. Sometimes the contract is included in the lease itself and sometimes there is a separate agreement for lease. Where a lease or agreement for lease is reduced to writing, parol evidence (i.e. evidence of oral discussions surrounding its negotiation) is inadmissible to supplement it (*Goss v Lord Nugent* (1833) 5 B& Ad 58). The rule is strictly enforced where one is concerned with a written lease. However, ways have been found of giving assurances that are not reduced to writing contractual effect. Usually this is by arguing that a collateral contract arose. By this means it may be possible to argue that assurances given by the landlord and acted on by the tenant are supported by consideration in the form of the future tenant's agreement to taking the lease (as in *De Lassalle v Guildford* [1901] 2 K.B. 215). In that case, the assurance the landlord gave (that the drains were in good condition) was acted on by the tenant in entering the lease, which contained no reference to the drains being in good condition. Provided the representation is entirely *collateral* to the main agreement it seems that it will probably survive a challenge on the basis that the formalities under s.2 of the Law of Property (Miscellaneous Provisions) Act 1989 have not been complied with (see *Hill and Redman* at HRA 1106).

By way of a more recent example, in *Brikom Investments v Carr* [1979] Q.B. 467 the landlord offered the tenants of a block of flats new leases but promised to repair the roofs of the block at his own expense first. The lease provided for the landlord to do the repairs to the roof but allowed him to recover the cost off the tenants. The landlord carried out the repair but having granted the new leases tried to claim the cost back under the terms of this covenant. The Court of Appeal thought that, although the promises given by the landlord were unsupported by consideration and went beyond the obligations in the lease, they were nevertheless enforceable. Furthermore, they were not only enforceable by the existing tenants but also by their assignees. The majority of the Court of Appeal gave as their reasoning that there was a collateral warranty in relation to the additional obligation or that there had been a waiver by the landlord of the strict position under the lease on which the tenants and their assignees could rely.

Similar arguments have also arisen in the context of negotiations to surrender a tenancy. In *Business Environmental Bow Lane Ltd v Deanwater Estates* [2007] EWCA Civ 622 it was held that in respect of such negotiations any assurance (in that case, assurances during negotiations for surrender that on completion of the new lease the landlord would not serve a schedule of dilapidations) may be enforceable. It was essential, the Court of Appeal said, that all terms were incorporated into the relevant conveyancing documents, be they the contract, transfer, conveyance or lease. In order for the collateral-contract argument to succeed it would be necessary to show it was intended to have contractual effect outside those formal legal documents. On the facts, the tenant failed on that allegation.

In summary, to successfully argue for a collateral warranty, the Court of Appeal in *Deanwater* indicated that the following requirements must be met (these were approved by the judge at first instance in *Deanwater* who quoted Lightman J. in *Inntrepreneur Pub Co Ltd v East Crown Ltd* [2000] 2 Lloyd's Rep 611, 615, [2000] 3 E.G.L.R. 31):

- the intentions of the contracting parties to the main contract must have included giving effect to the collateral obligations;
- the test for the parties' intentions in relation to the collateral contract is the same as the test for the main contract, i.e. those intentions must be judged objectively against the factual background known to the parties;
- if the result of the parties negotiations' was a contract, for example an agreement for lease, which made no reference to the collateral contract or its subject matter then it will be more difficult to establish such a collateral contract;
- it will also be difficult to establish a collateral contract where there is a significant lapse in time between the alleged collateral agreement and the main agreement;
- a statement of *existing fact* is more likely to result in a collateral contract than a statement of *future intent.*

Therefore, arguing for a collateral warranty in order to place an additional obligation on one of the parties will not always be straightforward. However, the practical importance of the discussion is illustrated by the *Brikom* case whereby collateral assurances may have long-term consequences and do not merely operate as temporary waivers of otherwise enforceable contractual terms.

Avoiding the formality requirements

In practice arguments may arise as to whether the formality **1–05** requirements in s.2 of the Law of Property (Miscellaneous Provisions) Act 1989 have been complied with and whether, where those requirements are not satisfied, oral representations or assurances may be given effect.

Section 2 of the 1989 Act provides that all contracts for the sale or disposition of land or an interest in land (including an agreement for lease) must be reduced to writing in one document and, where contracts are exchanged, recorded in each part (i.e. part and counterpart). That document or each of those documents must be signed by the parties. It was held in *Record v Bell* [1991] 1 W.L.R. 853 that because a collateral contract was not itself *the agreement* to dispose of land the provisions of the 1989 Act did not bite. Although that case was a decision at first instance it is generally thought to be correct as it followed decisions under s.40 of the Law of Property Act 1925 and is approved in the current edition of *Woodfall* "The Law of Landlord and Tenant" (at 4.006). However, the contractual obligation must be genuinely collateral to be enforceable in this way.

Equitable intervention

1–06   It is more likely that a party relying on an oral discussion will argue that the discussion should be given effect in equity under s.2(5)(c) which provides that "nothing in this section affects the creation of an implied resulting or constructive trust". Courts exercising an equitable jurisdiction have given a very broad construction to these words so that an interest created by proprietary estoppel may have the effect of defeating the formality requirements in s.2(1).

For example, in *Yaxley v Gotts* [2000] Ch.162, D2 made certain assurances to C in return for which C carried out extensive conversion work to a flat D2 owned. However, in fact, unbeknown to C, title to the flat passed to D1. The facts as found by the trial judge established that the owners of the flat (first D2 and then D1) were estopped from denying C an interest therein. It was held by Robert Walker L.J. in the Court of Appeal that the doctrine of proprietary estoppel had been effectively assimilated with the notion of the constructive trust and therefore C was able to bring himself within s.2(5).

Whilst this assimilation of proprietary estoppel and the constructive trust has since been doubted by the same Robert Walker (in *Stack v Dowden* [2007] Fam. Law 593, by which time he had become Lord Walker of Grestingthorpe) the *Yaxley* case has been extensively followed. It is likely to be relied on in any case where the landlord seeks to rely on the strict terms of an agreement for lease which has been reduced to writing where assurances were given before that agreement was entered into. "Agreements for lease" are referred to because s.2 is concerned with *executory* agreements not *executed* agreements, i.e. where a lease has subsequently been executed or a term of years granted, orally or in writing. Once the lease has been granted s.2 ceases to be relevant.

Therefore, in summary, any understanding reached or promise given which was acted on by the other party to his detriment may potentially found an estoppel. Provided the estoppel relied on overlaps with the concept of the constructive trust (*Kinane v Mackie-Conteh* [2005] EWCA Civ 45 tries to explain what this means) in relation to an executory agreement, the formality requirements of s.2 may be avoided. However, stating with any certainty whether the type of estoppel in question overlaps with a constructive trust is, in practice, very difficult. Furthermore, the cases decided under s.2 have introduced uncertainty into an area of the law in which Parliament desired a greater degree of certainty.

There may also be numerous other circumstances where the conduct of the landlord is such as to give rise to an estoppel argument in favour of the tenant. For example, in *Brikom Investments v Seaford* [1981] 1 E.G.L.R. 30 the landlord granted a lease after an agreement for lease. The agreement for lease taken with the term in the lease made the total duration of the term more than the seven years. On the face of it this would take the lease outside the provisions of s.11 of the Landlord and Tenant Act 1985 (in fact s.32 of the Housing Act 1961, its predecessor). However, the rent had been registered as a fair rent on the assumed basis that s.11 applied.

The Court of Appeal held that s.32 did not apply to the lease. However, it was also held that the landlord was estopped from denying liability under the section which had been assumed by all to apply. The tenant could in the future have a fair rent assessed on the correct basis that the landlord was in fact under no obligation to repair the structure and exterior of the demised premises, whereas in the past the rent had been increased to reflect the fact that the additional obligation existed. The case was one of promissory estoppel which operates as a defence and does not give rise to substantive rights but the court described the "shield" as one with "quite a sharp edge".

Liability under leases following assignment or subletting

Effect of the Contracts (Rights of Third Parties) Act 1999

For practical purposes a claim to enforce repair or maintenance **1–07** obligations in relation to a building is most likely to arise in the context of a lease. A sub-tenant may not sue or be sued on the covenants in the head-lease. However, it is common for the head-lease to provide that any sub-lease is to be on the terms of the head-lease or to provide that on creation of a sub-lease the sub-lessee must enter a direct covenant with the head-lessor. The covenant is normally given in the licence by the head-lessor to sub-let but may also be given by separate deed. The practical relevance of the Contracts (Rights of Third Parties) Act 1999 is that it may enable the head-lessor to enforce covenants directly against a sub-lessee without having to go through the above rigmarole, if the head-lease expressly provides that the head-lessor may do so.

Although the 1999 Act is relatively young it has produced some interesting decisions which help to identify whether it is potentially as far reaching as it appears at first sight to be. However, so far these have not been great in number.

One recent example was *Prudential Insurance v Ayres* [2007] EWHC 775 (Ch.) where Lindsay J. had to consider whether a tenant who had assigned his lease could use the Act to avail himself of a clause in a deed entered into between its assignee and the head landlord to exonerate himself from liability on that assignee's bankruptcy. In particular, the original tenant had assigned to a firm. On the licence to assign being given by the landlord, the original tenant had covenanted that if before assignees had themselves assigned there was any default in its payment of the rent then the original tenant would be liable for the shortfall. The firm to which the lease was assigned entered a supplemental deed with the landlord following assignment whereby the landlord agreed to limit the firm's liability to the partnership but that liability did not extend to the personal assets of its partners. When the assignee firm went bankrupt and therefore defaulted on the payment of its rent the landlord went against the original tenant for the shortfall.

The tenant relied on the clause in the supplemental deed which limited liability to the extent of the partner's personal assets, placing reliance on the 1999 Act. Lindsay J. held that the benefit to the third party, in this case the original tenant, did not have to be the predominant purpose of the term. Although the clause which limited liability had not been particularly well drafted it was clear enough to limit liability of the original tenant and would be given effect.

However, the Court of Appeal ([2008] All E.R. (D) 90 (Feb)) disagreed. It held that cl.2.1 of the relevant deed did not confer a benefit on the partners for the purposes of the 1999 Act. This was largely a matter of the court's interpretation of the relevant clause in its commercial context; the court having concluded that the parties had not intended to limit the partner's liability in that way.

Effect of the Landlord and Tenant (Covenants) Act 1995

1–08   This Act was of great importance in shifting liability for breaches of covenant following assignment onto those currently in a landlord and tenant relationship rather than the original contracting parties. It created a "new code" for the enforcement of covenants following assignment (see Neuberger J. in *Oceanic Village v United Attractions* [2000] Ch.234) in respect of leases granted on or after January 1 1996. It also applies to leases granted after that date pursuant to an agreement before that date. Before turning to these new provisions, and in order to properly understand the new provisions, it is necessary to have some understanding of the historic position.

Pre-January 1996 tenancies

The original tenant
The basic rule is that the original tenant (T) is liable on the covenants **1–09** following assignment for the remainder of the term because of privity of contract between T and the original landlord. Therefore, unless there was some express provision in the lease which released the original tenant from further liability, T would remain liable following an assignment by him for the remainder of the term. T's assignee (A) would also potentially be liable to the landlord (L) by virtue of privity of estate. L would have the option of suing either or both of them provided L gave credit for any sum he recovered. This led to a range of problems. For example, T was potentially liable for a breach by A's assignee, over whom they had no control.

On an assignment of the freehold reversion the original tenant may become liable to that assignee on the basis of privity of estate by virtue of s.141 of the Law of Property Act 1925. This is therefore an exception to the normal rule that a stranger to a contract can neither claim the benefit nor be subject to the burden of a contract. By virtue of the doctrine of privity of estate the landlord upon sale of the reversion assigned the benefit of, for example, the original tenant's covenant to put and keep the demised premises in repair. By that means T could be liable at the end of the term to the landlord's successor in respect of terminal dilapidations. Similarly, by s.142 of the Law of Property Act 1925, the purchaser of the landlord's (L's) reversion, (R), could be liable to both T and A following the assignment of L's reversion to him for R's breaches following that assignment, including breaches that were extant at the date of the assignment.

The original tenant could avoid liability under the original covenant where the original landlord had released the assignee from liability. However, in the following examples (considered in *Allied London Investments Ltd v Hambro Life Assurance* [1984] 1 E.G.L.R. 16) there would be no release of the original tenant:

1.   the landlord had released the original tenant's surety;
2.   a variation of the lease had occurred between landlord and assignee without the consent of the original tenant;
3.   the assignee has passed into a voluntary arrangement.

In one important respect this position has been altered in respect of both "new" and "old" tenancies by the 1995 Act. Where the landlord effects a variation and the assignee of the original tenant did not agree to be liable in respect of the varied obligation, then, unless he guaranteed the obligations of his assignee, the assignor is not liable following assignment (s.18 1995 Act).

However, there were serious flaws in the old law. Apart from the potential liability on the part of the original tenant, sometimes, many years after the assignment took place there were, in practice, significant limitations on the extent to which the original tenant could recover his loss from his assignee. For example, when sued the original tenant had lost possession of the premises so he could not take the step of carrying out any repairs that were outstanding. His principal remedy was to sue his assignee for a contribution or indemnity in respect of a breach of covenant subsequent to the assignment, which was normally specified under the terms of the deed of assignment as between the original tenant and the assignee. This of course would depend on the solvency of the assignee. In the event of insolvency on the part of A, T would rank merely as an unsecured creditor.

Position of T's assignee A

1–10   Successors in title under pre-January 1996 leases are only liable under covenants which touch and concern the land but not covenants which are merely personal. They can only sue on those covenants that touch and concern the land. There would also have to be a valid assignment of the remainder of the term. This would not only have to be by deed but, where title to the land was registered, the estate would need to comply with the registration requirements in order to be vested in the name of the assignee.

Section 78 of the Law of Property Act 1925 provided that where an assignment took place a covenant which touched and concerned the land was deemed to be made on behalf of the party giving the covenant, i.e. the covenantor, and his successors in title and, by s.79 (above), between the covenantee and his successors in title.

Thus a problem that frequently arose under the old law and still arises in relation to leases granted before January 1, 1996 was in establishing that the covenant "touched and concerned" the land. However, covenants to repair the premises were covenants that touched and concerned the land and were therefore enforceable by the original landlord and his successors against the original tenant and his successors in title.

Post-January 1996 tenancies

These are subject to the regime in the new Act. A tenant's covenant creates a much more limited liability on the part of the outgoing tenant. As well as reforming the unsatisfactory parts of the law relating to the transmission of covenants and reducing significantly the extent to which the original parties to a lease would be liable following an assignment, the Act tidied up some parts of the old law. Therefore it is inadvisable to see leases granted before the 1995 Act as being in a wholly different category than those granted after that Act. There are important areas of crossover which will need to be considered.

Original tenant

Provided the tenant assigns in accordance with the lease, he is **1–11** automatically released from further liability under the original lease and ceases to be entitled to the benefit of the landlord's covenants (s.5 1995 Act). The original tenant continues to be liable in respect of any breach occurring before the assignment (s.24). An original tenant who assigns part of the lease in accordance with its provisions (i.e. with the landlord's consent where that is required) will be released from any obligations relating to that part.

In practice the way that the landlord protects himself from an assignee's default in performance of the obligations under the lease, without the benefit of a continuing contractual liability on the part of the original tenant, is by entering an authorised guarantee agreement with the outgoing original tenant. By that means the original tenant guarantees the performance of his assignee. This is secured by making it a requirement of assignment in the covenant dealing with assignment in the lease. However the liability of the original tenant under the authorised guarantee agreement will automatically cease when his assignee assigns to a subsequent assignee of the remainder of the term (s.16(4)).

Original landlord's position

The landlord's own position is protected by s.6 whereby he can apply **1–12** under s.8 of the 1995 Act to be released from a covenant, but that release is not automatic. The effect of successful release will be that the tenant will not be able to enforce landlord's covenants against him following an assignment of the landlord's reversion to R. Those provisions will apply to any part of the premises that the landlord assigns. The tenant must be given notice by the landlord of his intended assignment and subsequent release (s.8(1)). The landlord will be released on assignment to R unless T serves a counter notice objecting to the release, whereupon he may only be released if he applies to the county court on the basis that the release is reasonable or T indicates that he is withdrawing his objection.

L's assignee R

1–13   Generally speaking, the successor to the original landlord, R, becomes liable from the date of assignment of the covenants, except to the extent that they did not bind the assignor at the date of the assignment. The assignee of the landlord's reversion can claim the benefit of those covenants (s.3(1)). Again, merely personal covenants do not pass. The requirements for transmission of the benefit of covenants do not affect any registration requirements which exist for the transaction in question.

Original landlord's position following assignment by the tenant

1–14   The position as to antecedent (i.e. pre-assignment) breaches of covenant by the tenant is slightly more complicated. Following assignment the landlord may enforce a subsequent breach against the assignee but not any antecedent breach. This contrasts with the position which pertained before January 1996. Provided there was privity of estate and the covenant touched and concerned the land he could pursue that breach against the assignee in respect of an antecedent breach. Following the 1995 Act a right to forfeit the lease survives the assignment unless it is expressly or impliedly waived (s.23(3)).

T's assignee A

1–15   The assignee on taking the assignment automatically becomes liable on the covenants in the lease other than those covenants which were personal to the original tenant, and becomes entitled to the benefit of the landlord's non-personal covenants (s.3). The original tenant ceases to be liable from the date of assignment but instead will frequently have to enter into an authorised guarantee agreement.

However, the Act does not affect any requirement to register a covenant under either the Land Registration Act 2002 or Land Charges Act 1972. In other words, any covenant which is unenforceable by virtue of a failure to register will remain unenforceable.

Operation of the 1995 Act in practice

1–16   A number of questions were left unanswered by the new legislation. For example in *Edlington Properties Ltd v JH Fenner and Co Ltd* [2006] EWCA Civ 403 the Court of Appeal had to consider whether the defendant lessee (F) was entitled to set off claims that it had

against its former landlord (W) against rent due to the
assignee of the reversion (E). In particular the court had to
the effect of assignment on a subsequent failure to pay rent. N
L.J. decided that the 1995 Act had not changed the law and it
rights and obligations with the assignor save to the extent t   ---,
were expressly transmitted under the provisions of the 1995 Act.
This case is considered in greater depth in Ch.14 when set-off is
considered in greater detail.

In *Avonbridge Property v Mashru* [2005] 1 E.G.L.R. 15 the Court
of Appeal rejected an attempt by a head-lessee to avoid the provisions
of the Act where it had failed to take the necessary steps in s.8 of the
Act to protects itself by applying to be released from the terms of its
continuing obligation following assignment. The attempt in that case
to avoid the provisions of the Act was void under s.25.

The 1995 Act has been described as "a smudgy parliamentary
compromise" (in Gray, *Elements of Land Law*, 4th edn at 14.228)
and it is excessively complex. Certainly, it creates real challenges
for those drafting authorised guarantee agreements as well as those
engaged in litigating over covenants. However, by and large the new
law works reasonably well and is an improvement on the former
position.

Chapter 2

Express obligations on landlords and tenants to repair and maintain

The duties on property owners may, broadly, be divided into **2–01** contractual, tortious and statutory. This chapter is concerned with the express contractual duties on landlords and tenants which lie at the heart of this subject.

The contractual obligations on landlords need to be seen in the context of an increasing amount of regulation in relation to the physical condition of buildings in general and dwelling houses in particular. For example, the express duties on landlords to repair and maintain the structure and exterior and the installations are supplemented and increased in relation to certain dwellings by s.11 of the Landlord and Tenant Act 1985. There are also a number of important implied contractual obligations. In many cases these implied obligations overlap with the express obligations. Therefore it must be stressed that whereas consideration of the express terms of the lease must be a necessary starting point it will in many cases not be the end of the journey. The implied obligations on landlords and tenants, and some further obligations which are both express and implied such as the covenant for quiet enjoyment, will be considered in Chs 4 to 7.

There are several problems with the repairing covenant in a lease but prime amongst them are the concept of "disrepair" and the construction of the repairing obligation contained in that covenant. Repairing covenants come in many shapes and sizes but a few concepts, for example in relation to residential accommodation, the concept of structural defects as opposed to defects relating to the habitability of that accommodation, are of great practical importance.

The repairing covenant—the concept of disrepair

2–02 The concept of disrepair is fundamental to both commercial and residential leases. Before considering some of the many adjectives inserted into repairing covenants it is essential to understand what is meant by "repair". This is best explained by reference to the case law.

The decision in *Quick v Taff-Ely*

2–03 Amongst the modern cases the case of *Quick v Taff-Ely Council* [1986] Q.B. 809 has become the leading case. In that case the tenant had taken a lease of the dwelling from the Council, which was subject to the obligation on the part of the landlord to repair the structure and exterior in s.11 of the Landlord and Tenant Act 1985. Condensation occurred at the premises which was so bad that it resulted in mould growth. It was caused by the familiar problem of un-insulated windows and the effect of warm internal air coming into contact with them. That warm air condensed on contact with the cold window panes. The central heating system was also inadequate.

In the Court of Appeal Dillon L.J. explained that the concept of disrepair connotes deterioration in the state of the premises from the state they were in *when built*. As he said (at p.818):

> "In my judgment, the key factor in the present case is that disrepair is related to the physical condition of whatever has to be repaired and not to questions of lack of amenity or inefficiency ... Where decorative repair is in question one must look for damage to the decorations, but where, as here, the obligation is merely to keep the structure and exterior of the house in repair, the covenant will only come into operation where there has been damage to the structure and exterior which requires to be made good."

The application of the concept of disrepair to later cases

2–04 *Quick* has been followed in numerous subsequent cases at Court of Appeal level and below. Those cases illustrate clearly the concept of disrepair.

In *Post Office v Aquarius* [1987] 1 All E.R. 1055 Ralph Gibson L.J. summarised the concept of disrepair in this way:

> "the reasoning of the court in *Quick's* case is equally applicable whether the original defect resulted from error in design, or in

workmanship, or from deliberate parsimony or any other cause. If on the letting of premises it were desired by the parties to impose on landlord or tenant an obligation to put the premises into a particular state or condition so as to be fit at all times for some stated purpose, even if it means making the premises better than they were when constructed, there would be no difficulty in finding words apt for that purpose."

In other words the court is not concerned with questions of *utility*, which can, if so desired, be dealt with by appropriate covenants and warranties in the lease, but in the normal repairing situation is concerned with applying the words used to ascertain whether there has been deterioration in the *physical state* of the premises. There is also a distinction between repairing a property and maintaining it. This distinction is well established in the highways cases (see *Secretary of State for Transport v McDonald and others* [2006] EWCA Civ 1089). The former obligation appears not to arise until there is a falling away in the condition of the property from its former state whereas the latter concept appears to require the party enforcing the obligation to inspect to ensure compliance with a certain minimum standard.

The facts of *Lee v Leeds City Council* [2002] L.G.R. 305 also illustrate clearly the concept of disrepair. The tenant complained of extensive damp at the premises. However, the expert evidence suggested the cause of the damp was condensation, not a defect of repair. The Court of Appeal not only upheld *Quick* but also rejected the argument that the tenant's rights under Article 8 of the European Convention on Human Rights (ECHR) (the right to a private and family life and respect for one's home and correspondence) were not adequately protected (see Ch.13).

In terms of the concept of disrepair there is no distinction between commercial and residential leases, nor between accommodation provided by local authorities and private landlords. In *Janet Reger International v Tiree Ltd* [2006] 3 E.G.L.R. 131 the court had to consider a lease of tenant's Knightsbridge shop. The lease required the landlord, Tiree Ltd (D), to use its best endeavours to "maintain, repair or renew" the structure of the premises. The premises suffered damp and other defects. The deputy High Court judge, Terence Mowchenson Q.C., found that the defective damp-proof membrane (DPM) was not connected with the damp-proof course in the walls of the premises but that there was no damage to the structure as such. The issue before the judge was whether that constituted a breach of the particular repairing covenant. He held that it did not.

Problems with the decision in *Quick*

2–05   The Law Commission has drawn attention to the unsatisfactory state of the present law (see LC 238 "Landlord and Tenant: Responsibility for the State and Condition of Property" (1996) and consultation paper 181 "Encouraging Responsible Letting" (2007)). In particular, it was of concern to the Commission that there is no express duty to maintain residential premises that are let so that they are fit to live-in. There would normally be no implied obligation either. The Commission thought the approach adopted by the present law could be regarded as conservative.

However, the courts have repeatedly made it clear that it is for Parliament to intervene and not for the courts. As the higher courts have observed on more than one occasion, there has been a marked reluctance to do so (see *McNerny v Lambeth LBC* (1989) 21 H.L.R. 188 at 193). Therefore the position remains as set out by Dillon L.J. in that case where he said:

> "statutory protection for those in occupation of defective premises is geared to the landlord's obligation to repair the premises".

The attitude of the courts is to strictly construe repairing obligations. However, the principle in *Quick* is easier to state than to apply in practice and difficult questions of law and fact arise, as the examples given above help to demonstrate. Experts often do not provide all the answers to these questions, which become critical when one is considering whether an item of work to demised premises is a repair or an improvement. That topic is now considered in greater depth.

Repair versus improvement

2–06   A problem of key importance in practice is the distinction between repairs and improvements. This often arises in commercial leases where the landlord is entitled to recover the cost of repairs from the tenant in a terminal-dilapidations claim but not to recover the cost of improvements.

In *Ravenseft Properties v Davstone* [1980] Q.B. 12 the court was concerned with a 16-storey block of maisonettes where the external stone cladding needed replacing. The issue before the court was whether its replacement with new cladding incorporating expansion joints, which had not previously been there, was capable of being a repair or whether in fact it was an improvement. The lack of the expansion joints was an inherent design factor and did not constitute a falling away of the condition of the property from its state when built. The failure to tie-in the defective stone cladding was a matter of defective building practice. Forbes J. found nevertheless that:

> "By this time it was proper engineering practice to see that such expansion joints were included, and it would have been dangerous not to include them. In no realistic sense, therefore, could it be said that there was any other possible way of reinstating this cladding than by providing the expansion joints which were, in fact, provided. It seems to me to matter not whether that state of affairs is caused by the necessary sanction of statutory notices or by the realistic fact that as a matter of professional expertise no responsible engineer would have allowed a rebuilding which did not include such expansion joints to be carried out."

In his view the question which needed to be answered was whether the works proposed would result in giving back to the landlord at the end of the term "*a wholly different thing from that which was demised*". In his judgment (which has been extensively followed) the only way the repairing covenant could be performed was by fitting those expansion joints and in the context this did not amount to an improvement.

Ravenseft is generally thought still to be the leading case of repair **2–07** versus improvement but the following later cases also provide some practical illustrations of the application of the *Ravenseft* test:

- In *Elmcroft v Tankersley-Sawyer* (1984) 15 H.L.R. 63, an old slate damp-proof course had been positioned below ground level thus causing the ingress of moisture. This caused damage to the plaster, decorations and woodwork to the demised premises (basement flats in a Victorian purpose-built mansion block). The court held that having established damage to the structure of the premises the tenants were entitled to have the old slate damp proof course replaced with a modern damp-proof course. The question of whether this work was an improvement or a repair was a matter of degree; the answer to that question depended on whether the fitting of the new damp-proof course would involve a change in the nature and character of the building in which the flats were situated.

- In *Stent v Monmouth District Council* (1991) 23 H.L.R. 107 the premises had a rotten door and on that basis the tenant was able to establish actionable disrepair. In the course of giving judgment Stocker L.J. said:

> "The installation of a purpose-built, self-sealing aluminium door was one of the methods which could have been adopted much earlier, and which in my view should have been adopted."

On the facts this was the only practical method of discharging the obligation to repair the structure and exterior of the premises. The door was not performing the function of a door and therefore could not be in repair. However, it is important to emphasise that the court had found the old door to be rotten. Had it not, it would probably not have found there to be actionable disrepair.

- In *McDougall v Easington Council* (1989) 21 H.L.R. 310 the Court of Appeal agreed with the assistant recorder at first instance that the work required to the claimant's house, which amounted to fairly radical remedial work, was not repair but renewal or replacement of significant parts of the house concerned. The case involved badly designed pre-fabricated system houses. In particular the houses had problems with the method for disposing of rainwater. As a result of the works carried out the houses, which were of modest value, would have increased in value from £10,000 to £18,000. The works could not be described as repairs consisting as they did of major re-design, giving the houses in each case "a new life in a different form". Mustill L.J. said:

> "Nor do I think it necessary to attempt a complete reconciliation of the whole body of authority by means of a single statement of principle: for I believe that whatever particular formula one selects from the various judgments, the result in the present instance must be the same. It is sufficient to say that in my opinion three different tests may be discerned, which may be applied separately or concurrently as the circumstances of the individual case may demand, but all to be approached in the light of the nature and age of the premises, their condition when the tenant went into occupation, and the other express terms of the tenancy:
>
> (i)   Whether the alterations went to the whole or substantially the whole of the structure or only to a subsidiary part;
>
> (ii)   Whether the effect of the alterations was to produce a building of a wholly different character than that which had been let;

(iii)   What was the cost of the works in relation to the previous value of the building, and what was their effect on the value and lifespan of the building."

The correct analysis in his view was that the tenants, having consented to the local authority's doing work at the house, had impliedly granted a licence to the local authority to complete that work. They could not recover their redecoration costs which arose as a result, effectively, of an improvement and not as a consequence of the performance by the landlord of its repairing obligation.

- In *Gibson Investments Ltd v Chesterton Plc* [2003] 1 E.G.L.R. 142 the tenant was liable to keep the premises in "good and substantial repair". Rival schemes were put forward for dealing with the defects to the steel framework of the building in question which resulted in cracking to the outer stone-cladding. Neuberger J. looked at current building practices as well as the circumstances at the time the lease was granted. He considered whether the works proposed constituted implementation of a reasonable scheme and decided that the scheme proposed by the tenant was inadequate. He went instead for one of the schemes proposed by the landlord, which involved significant replacement of stonework and other work to the commercial premises concerned.

On the other hand the landlord or tenant as the case may be is not bound to do more than the *minimum* required to ensure that the property is brought into a state of repair. Generally speaking where there are two methods of putting right the defect in question the covenanting party is only bound to adopt the *cheapest* method of achieving the desired result, i.e. putting the defect back into repair. Thus:

- In *Carmel Southend Ltd v Strachan & Henshaw Ltd* [2007] EWHC 1289 (TCC) [2007] 35 E.G. 136 [2007] the court was concerned with industrial premises in which the tenant had covenanted to keep and yield up the premises in repair. The landlord tried to claim the cost of expensive overcladding works from the tenant. It was held that the cheaper patch repairs that the tenant suggested were both possible and a permissible performance of its repairing obligation. Therefore the landlord could not recover the cost of the more expensive overcladding work from the tenant by way of damages for disrepair.

Construing the repairing covenant

2–08 The second problem identified at the start of this chapter is the need to construe the particular repairing obligation. This topic is considered more fully by reference to the case law in Dowding and Reynolds, *Dilapidations: The Modern Law and Pratice* 3rd edn. in Ch.4.

The general approach to construction

2–09 It is well established now that in construing commercial contracts in general and leases in particular the court looks at the underlying commercial purpose of the transaction. The words used will be considered in their context so as to give effect to that underlying commercial purpose (see *Investors Compensation Scheme v West Bromwich Building Society* [1998] 1 All E.R. 98). First and foremost the court will be concerned to ascertain the intentions of the parties from the words they used in their context and will not be concerned with their subjective intentions. Contracts in general and leases in particular will therefore be construed objectively. That is not to say that the courts will ignore the background facts. The court will consider the matrix of fact available to the parties when they contracted by entering the lease or agreement for lease which is to be enforced. Interpretation questions often arise in leases in relation to the repairing obligations and in relation to the rent-review provisions.

Some of the specific difficulties in construing repairing obligations are considered below.

Many leases, particularly older commercial leases, adopt what has been called a "torrential style" in relation to obligations to repair and maintain. Although covenants are strictly construed, whereby every word should count, there is a general presumption against superfluous drafting. Where the torrential style is adopted it makes it difficult to ascribe meaning to every word used (see Walker L.J. in *Walsh v Greenwich LBC* [2000] 3 E.G.L.R. 41 at 43). It may be clear from the context that some of the words used are superfluous. In the context of a repairing obligation, adjectives such as "good" do not add to the extent of the obligation on landlord or tenant, as the case may be (see *Hill and Redman* A 6482).

Caution should therefore be applied when the authorities are considered because the same expression may mean different things in different contexts. Thus in the context of a short furnished tenancy the obligation on the tenant to keep the premises in "good and tenantable condition" meant no more than merely maintaining the premises in a "tenant-like manner" (*Firstcross v Teasdale* (1983) 265 E.G. 305).

However certain words and phrases now have well-established meanings. A covenant to "*keep in repair*" includes an obligation to "*put*" in repair where the premises are not already in that condition at the commencement of the term since the former pre-supposes the latter has first been complied with (see *Brew Bros v Snax* [1970] 1 Q.B. 612). As Fletcher Moulton L.J. said (in *Lurcott v Wakely* [1911] 1 K.B. 905 at 919):

> "It is settled law that when a man undertakes to keep a thing in good condition or in thorough repair, and it is not in that condition when the demise commences, the covenant implies that he is to put it in that state as well as to keep it in that state."

Examples of particular covenants
Having set out the general approach some commonly found covenants **2–10** will be considered. However, it should be remembered that the following are merely examples of how particular covenants have been construed. In practice, even where two very similar covenants are found, their proper construction may vary according to the context (see *Welsh v Greenwich* [2000] 3 E.G.L.R. 41 per Robert Walker L.J. at 43).

The following cases illustrate how the courts have interpreted some of the more commonly found covenants:

- "*Good tenantable repair*" means "such repair as, having regard to the age, character, and locality of the house, would make it reasonably fit for the occupation of a reasonably minded tenant of the class who would be likely to take it" (per Esher M.R. in *Proudfoot v Hart* (1890) 25 QBD 42 at 52).

- "*Habitable repair*", according to the same authority, means much the same thing (see above and Scrutton L.J. in *Anstruther Gough Calthorpe v McOscar* [1924] 1 K.B. 716, but see also the discussion above about *Firstcross v Teasdale* (1983) 265 E.G. 305).

- "*Good condition*" will also constitute a covenant to keep the premises fit for habitation (*Welsh v Greenwich* [2000] 3 E.G.L.R. 41) and this will include eradicating damp.

- "*Take reasonable steps to keep the estate and common parts clean and tidy*" was held to place an obligation on the landlord to maintain a minimum standard of cleanliness at a Council-owned block of flats (in *Southwark LBC v Long* [2002] L.G.R. 530). In that case the Court of Appeal held that the local authority had to have a system in place for cleaning the common parts and could not rely on the fact that they had appointed outside contractors without establishing that they had taken proper steps to ensure that they carried out their obligations to the required standard.

- A covenant to keep the staircases *"well and sufficiently lit"* meant obliged to illuminate it sufficiently for people of normal vision to see where they were going (*Quennell v Salaman* (1955) 165 E.G. 285)!

- *"Fit to live in"*, according to one first-instance decision, means there will be liability for condensation-related damp (*Johnson v Sheffield City Council* August 1994, Legal Action and [1994] CLY 1445).

- *"The main structures of property"* was held to include floor joists supporting the tenant's property as well as parts external to the demised premises (*Marlborough Park v Rowe* [2006] EWCA Civ 436).

When the obligation to repair arises—the notice requirement

2–11 The obligation to repair only arises where the landlord (or tenant, as the case may be) has had both express notice of the defect giving rise to the obligation to repair and a reasonable opportunity to effect the repair in question (*O'Brien v Robinson* [1973] A.C. 912). In that case the common law requirement of notice of defects within the demised premises was held to apply equally to claims under s.32 of the Housing Act 1961 (now s.11 of the Landlord and Tenant Act 1985).

What constitutes notice?

2–12 Generally, express notice will be required. In practice that would be such notice as would put a reasonable landlord "on inquiry" (see *Robinson* at 916 and per Lord Diplock above at 929) but this is not to say that there is any doctrine of constructive notice or reasonable notice, as would be the case, for example, in a claim under s.4 of the Defective Premises Act 1972 (see *Sykes v Harry* [2001] EWCA Civ 167). There must have been some communication with the landlord of the physical state of the premises. Furthermore the landlord must know that the item concerned is defective not merely that the tenant has complained about it. This seems to rule out any latent defect. However, the tenant need not identify the cause of the defect and will normally not possess the technical knowledge to do so.

In *O'Brien* the tenant had complained about noisy neighbours above, who had probably weakened the ceiling above his flat by stamping on it. The tenant and his wife were subsequently injured when the ceiling fell onto them but the House of Lords found that their earlier complaints about the tenants above did not constitute notice that the ceiling was defective. As Lord Diplock said (at 929):

> "(the landlord would not be liable) unless the tenant can show that before the ceiling fell the landlord had information about the existence of a defect in the ceiling such as would put him on inquiry as to whether works of repair to it were needed."

However, it has been held (in *Sheldon v West Bromwich Corp* (1973) 25 P. & C.R. 360) that where the landlord sent a plumber employed by it to inspect a water tank and the tank was corroded but not weeping, it would be taken as having notice that the tank was defective. In that case the tank subsequently burst causing extensive damage. There was corrosion calling for repair and that was sufficient.

Exceptions to the notice requirement

An exception exists to the usual notice requirement in relation to **2–13** properties where the landlord has retained the common parts of the building of which the demised premises form part. This occurred in *BT v Sun Life* [1996] Ch.69. There, the tenant had taken a lease of the sixth and seventh floors of an office building. The landlord agreed to keep the whole of the premises in "complete good and substantial repair and condition". It was held that the landlord was in breach of its repairing obligation as soon as the defect in question arose. That defect was a bulge on the fifth floor of the property forming part of the structure or exterior of the demised premises which did not form part of the demised premises themselves. It was held that the tenant was not required to give notice in relation to disrepair to the common parts. The notice rule applied only to the demised premises not to structural repairs to an external part of the building of which the demised premises formed part.

The exception in *BT v Sun Life* to the rule in *O'Brien v Robinson* has been upheld but distinguished in an addendum to the main judgment in the case of *Earle v Charalambous* [2006] EWCA Civ 1090, [2006] All E.R. (D) 147 (Oct) where counsel for the tenant tried to argue that defects to the roof of the premises concerned fell outside the general notice rule rendering the landlord liable in damages from the date the defect arose, rather than a reasonable time after he had been given notice of the defects. The court rejected that because there had been a concession before the trial judge that the landlord was entitled to a reasonable period to rectify defects to the roof. The court said (at para.9):

> "Once it was accepted that notice was the starting-point, then it seemed to us illogical not to allow the lessor a reasonable time to respond to the notice by practical action. We see no reason to change that view of the case."

Nor will the rule in *O'Brien v Robinson* apply where the landlord has covenanted to repair the structure of premises which they had demised where the defect arises in that part of the structure within his control. This was the case in *Minchburn v Peck* [1988] 1 E.G.L.R. 53. It is also illustrated by *Passley v Wandsworth LBC* (1998) 30 H.L.R. 165, where the defect was to pipes in the roofspace. Although the landlord was unaware of the defect before it arose, it was nevertheless responsible for the damage to the top-floor-flat below as the defect arose in a part of the premises which they had retained control of.

Notice clauses

2–14   Leases, particularly commercial leases, sometimes have clauses which require tenants to give written notice before any liability to repair will arise on the part of the landlord. This was the position in *Princes House Ltd v Distinctive Clubs Ltd* [2007] EWCA Civ 374. The landlord tried to rely on the clause to avoid liability for disrepair which had arisen even though the landlord had actual knowledge of the defect in question. The court held that the landlord manifestly had knowledge of the defect in question and it could not avoid liability on the basis that express written notice had not been given. According to Chadwick L.J., this was on the basis that, based on the facts, the landlord had waived any entitlement to rely on the need for notice. The landlord's indication to the tenant that it intended to do the work to the roof (i.e. the defective area in question) amounted to an indication that it did not intend to rely on the need for notice.

Who does notice have to be given to?

2–15   Notice may be given to the landlord's servant or agent, the landlord being on notice when it learns of the disrepair from whichever source it comes (see *McGreal v Wake* (1984) 13 H.L.R. 107). In that case the landlord learned of the disrepair from a repairs notice served by a local authority. However the Court of Appeal also expressed the view that notice to the landlord's agent would also have sufficed.

Obiter dicta they were critical of the *O'Brien* decision but felt compelled to follow it. In addition it is clear from *BT v Sun Life* that notice was required whether the covenant was to "keep" in repair or simply to "repair".

Applying to court under section 35 of the Landlord and Tenant Act 1987 to vary express terms in long leases

There is the power in s.35 of the Landlord and Tenant Act 1987, as **2–16** amended by the Commonhold and Leasehold Reform Act 2002, for the tenant to apply for an order varying the terms of the lease. This section applies to long leases of flats. Tenants under such leases are able to apply to the Leasehold Valuation Tribunal to vary the terms relating to repair. The 1987 Act also enacted a number of rules for acquiring the landlord's interest in relation to and controlling the management of long leasehold accommodation. For example, the legislation enables a manager to be appointed in certain circumstances.

The application to vary the lease may be made on the basis that the lease makes inadequate provision for the repair or maintenance of the flat in question or the building in which it is situated.

A "long lease" is a term exceeding 21 years (s.59(3)).

In cases where the application to vary the terms is on behalf of leaseholders who own other leases in the building which the landlord is liable to maintain, that application will be under s.37 rather than s.35. Such an application will need to be made on behalf of a majority of the leaseholders. Where the Leasehold Valuation Tribunal is concerned with an application under s.37, it may only make an order which accords with the form of application made. There is also provision in the Act for the other parties to the lease to make a cross application requesting that a variation be made to one or more other leases specified in that cross application.

The section does not seem to have stimulated a rush of litigation and many of those who would be entitled to apply under s.35 will wish to enfranchise instead. There is little by way of recent case law, but one recent case worthy of mention was *Gianfrancesco v Haughton* (2008) W.L. 576896 (Lands Tr). That case came before the Lands Tribunal on appeal from the Leasehold Valuation Tribunal (LVT). There the tenant under a 999-year lease sought to argue that the liability to maintain the exterior of the premises (the cost of which could be recovered from him under the service-charge provision) was excessive. George Bartlett Q.C., the President, said that:

"Although it is right that the question of satisfactory provision should be determined in all the circumstances, the weight to be given to particular matters may need careful consideration. What the landlord or the tenant says that he is willing to do in addition to his obligations may have some relevance as to how, in practice, the provision in question is likely to operate. But it would normally be wrong, it seems to me, to base a decision on such an expression of willingness since the person in question could change his attitude or be replaced as landlord or tenant by another person differently disposed. It is possible for this reason that the LVT placed too much weight on Mr Haughton's expression of willingness to allow the roofing sheets to be removed. But in all other respects, and in their particular conclusions, I am satisfied in the light of the material before me that the LVT's decision was correct."

The tenant's appeal and original challenge before the LVT therefore failed. In fact cases where effective challenges to repair provisions in leases have been made are hard to find. Therefore, it is presently uncertain that the provision is of great practical importance.

Proposals for reform

2–17   The Law Commission has proposed a number of reforms in this area. Its report "Landlord and Tenant: responsibility for the state and condition of property" (Law Com. No.238 (1996)) contains the most thorough examination of the then existing law as well as a key proposal for an implied fitness standard in residential leases. More recently (in Law Com. No.284 "Renting Homes: The Final Report" (2006)) the Commission recommended reform of the law of landlord and tenant so as to simplify leasehold rights and obligations; the object being greater clarity in dealings between landlord and tenant in both the private the public sector. However, until those proposals are implemented it will be left to individual landlords and tenants to agree the extent of the repairing obligations in their leases. This is at the present time supplemented by various statutorily implied obligations which will be considered later.

Chapter 3

Unfair terms in leases

At common law landlords were largely free to negotiate such terms as **3–01**
they thought fit but they have long-sought to exclude or restrict their
liability for the defective state of the premises let by them by inserting
appropriate clauses into their leases. In some cases these included
clauses which excluded or restricted liability for certain types of loss
and damage (see *Halsbury's Laws* "Contract" Vol.9(1) reissue,
para.800). The rules of construction which applied to these exclusion
clauses, including the contra proferentem rule, i.e. the rule that
instruments are construed against the grantor, tended to favour the
party who is trying to establish liability as against the party relying on
an exclusion clause. In addition, Parliament and the courts have long
intervened to protect the party in the weaker negotiating position.

The regulation of freedom of contract generally and terms in
leases in particular, is an increasingly important area. There has been
a steady increase in the number of statutory controls over the ability
of contracting parties to freely negotiate terms which are regarded as
being unduly burdensome or unfair and this has included freedom
of landlord and tenant to agree the terms of their lease. The present
power to control unfair contract terms is largely found in the Unfair
Contract Terms Act 1977 but, as will be seen, that Act does not
apply to leases. It has therefore been left to EU-derived regulations
introduced in the last few years to strike-out those terms which are
judged unduly onerous and, therefore, unenforceable. Nevertheless,
it is neccessary to know something of that Act before considering the
regulations in greater detail.

The Unfair Contract Terms Act 1977

This Act introduced the concept of "reasonableness" into certain **3–02**
types of contract and is of significance in many commercial areas as

well as protecting consumers. Business to business contracts are only covered if the purchaser deals with the seller as a consumer but the onus of showing that the buyer bought or held themselves out as buying in the course of business is on the seller (see s.12 of the Unfair Contract Terms Act 1977 and *R & B Customs Brokers Ltd v United Dominions Ltd* [1988] 1 All E.R. 847).

However, the Act is not generally thought to apply to leases because Sch.1 of that Act provides that it shall not extend to "any contract so far as it relates to the creation or transfer of an interest in land". Thus in *Electricity Supply Nominees v IAF Group* [1993] 2 E.G.L.R. 15 a term providing that the landlord was not to be liable in respect of a defect until it had notice of it was found to be effective and the 1977 Act had no application. More recently, in *Granby Village Management v Unchained Growth* [2000] 1 W.L.R. 739, a term which provided that the maintenance charge could not be setoff in any way whatsoever, was held not to be subject to the test of reasonableness in the Unfair Contract Terms Act 1977.

However, this may leave open an argument that the 1977 Act does apply where the complaint relates to a tenancy between a consumer and his landlord, dealing in the course of business, in relation to, for example, the operation of the repairing obligation. This is because the obligations in the lease relating to repair do not appear on the face of it to relate to the creation or transfer of an interest in land.

In any event, cases under the 1977 Act may be helpful in considering the extent to which terms in leases may be considered "reasonable" under the Unfair Contract Terms Regulations 1999, which now require fuller consideration. For example, in one recent case the judge found a term restricting liability for loss of profits to be "reasonable" in a contract for the supply of air conditioning (*Regus v Epcot* [2007] EWHC 938 (Comm.), per D. Mackie Q.C.). The concept of "reasonableness" under the 1977 Act, as interpreted by the deputy judge in that case, is thought to be the same as the concept of "reasonableness" in relation to leases under the 1999 Regulations, albeit in a different context. Those regulations will now be considered.

The Unfair Terms in Consumer Contracts Regulations 1999

3–03   The Unfair Terms in Consumer Contract Regulations 1994 came into force on July 1, 1995 to give effect to EU Directive 93/13 EEC. The Unfair Terms in Consumer Contract Regulations 1999 (SI 1999/2083), which re-enacted the 1994 Regulations with some modifications, are those currently in force. The Office of Fair Trading, whose latest publication on the subject was in September 2005, gives guidance on the application of the regulations. It also oversees enforcement and has wide powers in that regard, including the power to fine offending landlords.

Scope of the regulations

The Unfair Terms in Consumer Contract Regulations impose limits **3–04** on the written terms in all "consumer contracts". A "consumer" is someone who "contracts outside his trade or business" (reg.3(1) of 1999 Regulations). Just as in the case of contracts covered by the 1977 Act it is only those contracts where at least one of the parties holds itself out as contracting as a consumer that the Act applies (s.12) under the 1999 Regulations, business-to-business transactions would not be covered. The regulations apply to leases as well as to other types of consumer contract. Therefore there is a considerable overlap between the two statutory provisions. The regulations contain various restrictions on the ability of the landlord to place exemption clauses in leases.

The regulations do not apply to contractual terms that are implied at common law (see *Baybut v Eccle Riggs Country Park Limited* (2006), *The Times* 13th November), for example the implied obligation on the part of the tenant to occupy the premises in a tenant-like manner. In that case a judge at first instance (HHJ Pelling Q.C. sitting as a High Court Judge) also found that the regulations applied to licences as well as leases.

The regulations apply to the public sector as well as the private sector. In *R. (On the Application of Khatum) v Newham LBC* [2004] EWCA Civ 55 the Court of Appeal considered the terms on which property was let by a local authority to homeless persons pursuant to its obligations under Pt VII of the Housing Act 1996. However, whilst the Court of Appeal held that the regulations applied, they did not decide the question of fairness, which was left to be resolved in conjunction with the Office of Fair Trading, which oversees the implementation of the regulations.

What the regulations say

Under reg.5, the term must be "fair" and reg.6 provides that the **3–05** language used must be "plain and intelligible" to the tenant. The test of unfairness was explained in *Director General of Fair Trading v First National Bank Plc* [2001] UKHL 52, where Lord Bingham indicated the test to be applied, (at para.17):

"A term falling within the scope of the regulations is unfair if it causes a significant imbalance in the parties' rights and obligations under the contract to the detriment of the consumer in a manner or to an extent which is contrary to the requirement of good faith. The requirement of significant imbalance is met if a term is so weighted in favour of the supplier as to tilt the parties' rights and obligations under the contract significantly in his favour. This may be by the granting to the supplier of a beneficial option or discretion or power, or by the imposing on the consumer of a disadvantageous burden or risk or duty."

What terms will be judged unreasonable

3–06   There is no doubt that any term seeking to restrict liability for death or injury to any person under the Defective Premises Act 1972 would be struck out and be unenforceable just as it would in an ordinary consumer contract, e.g. in an exclusion on a ticket to travel on a bus or train. Such a term is in any event void under s.6(3) of that Act. There are also a number of terms listed in Sch.2 of the 1999 Regulations which are regarded as being unfair, but they are not aimed at the landlord and tenant relationship. However, the OFT cites a number of other terms which are likely to be struck out under the Regulations (see, for example, 3.13 et seq. of the latest guidance). Examples of terms in leases that are likely to offend the regulations and thus be struck out are:

- a term which has not been freely negotiated;
- a term seeking to impose an obligation on the tenant for any item that would otherwise be considered "fair wear and tear";
- out-of-date forfeiture clauses which do not recognise modern levels of statutory protection;
- excessive and inappropriate powers of re-entry;
- a provision which requires the tenant to pay rent without any set-off;
- a provision which requires rent to be paid even though the property becomes uninhabitable.

Landlords and those advising them should avoid those clauses which are ambiguous or unintelligible. Obligations should not be unduly onerous having regard to the length of the term and the level of the rent.

A recent challenge under the Regulations came in *Governors of Peabody Trust v Reeve* (2008), *The Times*, June 2, 2008, where the landlord's power to vary the terms in a lease in favour of a social landlord was considered. There the standard terms of the tenancy agreement relied on by the landlord provided for unilateral variation by the landlord serving a notice. In this case the landlord wished to vary the tenancy by notice so as to recover service charges. The judge, Gabriel Moss Q.C. sitting as a High Court Judge, found the term to be unreasonable under the 1999 Regulations. The judge noted that reg.7 of the 1999 Regulations provided that where there was doubt as to the interpretation of a provision it would be construed in a way that is most favourable to the consumer, which he described as similar in effect to the contra proferentum rule. He noted that the clause which allowed for unilateral variation of the lease terms contradicted another term in the standard terms. The latter term provided that any alteration in the terms of the lease had to be by agreement in writing. The judge decided that the provision requiring agreement of the tenant should prevail over the unilateral variation clause. Otherwise there was no satisfactory way of reconciling the conflict. He noted that this version of the law coincided with the common-law position under the contra proferentum rule. He therefore found that there was no power to vary the lease unilaterally in this case.

Possible future challenges

The regulations seem likely to become of greater importance with   **3–07** time, particularly if Parliament continues to take the view that warranties as to fitness for habitation are a matter for individual negotiation. However, there seems likely to be a large subjective element to the concepts of "unfairness" and lack of "good faith" despite the judicial guidance given by Lord Bingham in *DGFT v First National Bank Plc* (above).

Some of the terms that the OFT considers "unfair" or "unreasonable" are standard lease terms, certainly in commercial leases; for example, the requirement that the tenant should pay the rent without any set-off. Although in most cases commercial tenants would be unlikely to have any effective redress (due to the fact that normally commercial leases will be entered into in the tenant's ordinary course of business), there may be other cases where onerous obligations are imposed where those terms can be declared unenforceable. These may include long leases, where the Regulations seem likely be invoked to attack service-charge and other provisions, and property cases outside the landlord and tenant field. In relation to the latter, occupiers of freehold flats are sometimes subject to onerous covenants similar to long leaseholders.

Of specific relevance to defective premises in the OFT Guidance the possible striking-out of forfeiture clauses and clauses which require rent to be paid when the premises become uninhabitable. It remains to be seen if challenges in these areas are successful. The fact that the 1999 Regulations have been successfully used to challenge the imposition of terms in relation to the provision of emergency housing accommodation under the Housing Act 1996 (in *Khatun* supra) suggests they are likely to be of broad application.

Chapter 4

Terms implied into leases at common law relevant to repair and maintenance

In this chapter the relatively rare cases where it is necessary to imply **4–01** obligations on the part of the landlord to repair and maintain the premises will be considered. Terms are frequently implied into contracts and leases to fill gaps in the express obligations. Sometimes terms are implied by statute. This is partly to ensure a level playing field between landlord and tenant and partly, in the case of residential property, to secure the policy objective of ensuring a viable private-rented sector that is reasonably well-maintained. Those statutorily implied leasehold terms that are relevant in the context of defective premises will be considered in Ch.5. More commonly, terms are implied into leases and agreements for lease at common law, particularly in the residential field, to fill gaps that might otherwise exist and ensure a minimum standard of residential accommodation. Such terms are also implied into settlement negotiations at termination. In practice there are a number of established situations where the law will imply terms. These will be considered in detail below.

In theory the better drafted a lease is the less likely it is that the court will need to imply a term into that lease. However, in practice terms are commonly implied to achieve a particular result. Sometimes the means by which the court achieves that result seems surprising. For example, recently, in *Legal and General v Expeditors* [2007] EWCA Civ 7 the Court of Appeal implied a term into a settlement of a dispute following the exercise of a break clause in a commercial lease. The court made a somewhat strained application of the officious bystander test in order to achieve the result it wished to achieve. However, as Lloyd L.J. pointed out in his dissenting judgement, it was strongly arguable that the officious bystander test was not met. That case is considered more fully below.

Given the importance of implied terms in certain leases it is now necessary to look at the main situations where terms are likely to be implied in practice.

When a term will be implied

4–02   First and foremost where the lease has been reduced to writing the court will have to construe the extent of the express obligations to repair and maintain before it considers any implied obligations. Having said that the circumstances in which a court will imply a term into a commercial or non-commercial contract, including a lease, are now reasonably well-established (see *Chitty on Contracts* 29th edn Ch.13 and *The Moorcock* (1889) 14 PD 64). The court may only imply a term where that is an inference it has been forced to draw from the express terms. The implied term contended for must be "too obvious to need stating" and not merely desirable to improve upon the expressly agreed terms.

Broadly one of the following alternative bases must be satisfied:

1. It must be necessary for the missing term to be inserted to give "business efficacy" to the agreement;
2. it must be a necessary implication from a prior course of dealing;
3. it must be implied by custom or usage.

A term is sometimes implied from a course of dealing in a trade context where the parties have a long history of trading with one another. It may be said there that a later agreement for the same contractual subject matter (e.g. the supply of goods) will be on the same terms as previously. A term is unlikely to be implied from a prior course of dealing in the context of a landlord and tenant relationship.

A term will be implied from custom or usage where there is a local custom or, sometimes, a national trade usage. Again this is unlikely to arise in the landlord and tenant situation.

By far the most important basis for implying terms into leases and agreements for lease is to give business efficacy to the agreement. This category of implied term is now considered in greater detail.

The business efficacy test

There is no universal definition of the term "business efficacy" but   **4–03**
Barrett v Lounova (1982) Ltd [1990] 1 Q.B. 348 is a good illustration
of when a court may imply a term to achieve this. In that case a
periodic tenancy had been entered before s.32 of the Housing Act
1961 came into force (on October 24, 1961). Section 32 of the
Housing Act 1961 (now s.11 of the Landlord and Tenant Act 1985)
placed an obligation on the landlord to repair the structure and
exterior of a dwelling house which he let on certain types of lease.
Specifically, it applied only to short leases including periodic
tenancies. In *Barrett* there was an obligation on the tenant in relation
to the "inside repairs" but the lease said nothing about the structure
and exterior. It was held that the court would imply a "correlative
obligation" on the landlord in order to give effect to the underlying
purpose of the lease and business efficacy to the transaction, for it
was impossible for the tenant to repair the inside of the premises
without the landlord first repairing the outside.

Implied terms in practice

In practice the courts are willing to imply terms to ensure a fair result,   **4–04**
provided the other ingredients necessary to imply a term are present,
as in *McAuley v Bristol City Council* [1992] Q.B. 134. In that case
the court had to consider a case where the tenant suffered injury on a
rear step to the property. Because it had occurred on a rear step,
which provided only a secondary rather than the primary means of
entry to the property, the Council had repudiated liability under s.11
of the Landlord and Tenant Act 1985. However the court was able to
find that the landlord had the *right* to effect the repair for the purposes
of finding a breach of s.4 of the Defective Premises Act 1972 even
though it was not under an *obligation* to do so. Section 4(4) of that
Act provides that there may be liability on a landlord wherever they
have a right to enter to carry out any description of maintenance or
repair by converting that right into a duty (see para.9–23 at p.105).

In that case the lease gave the landlord the right to enter "for any
purpose which may from time to time be required by the Council".
Because the court was able to imply a right to enter the rear garden to
maintain the steps in question it followed that there was an implied
obligation on the council to repair the defect in question, under s.4(4)
of the DPA. Under that subsection there was a duty to put right the
dangerous defect on which the claimant was injured. As will be seen,
the result might have been different when the landlord's entry into
the premises was merely to effect an improvement or maintain the

premises in a particular condition (see *Alker v Collingwood* [2007] 2 E.G.L.R. 43). In *McAuley* the court thought that other cases, such as *Smith v Bradford* (1982) 44 P. & C.R. 171 and *Mint v Good* [1951] 1 K.B. 517, were justified on the same basis. In each of those cases terms had been implied to give business efficacy to the agreements.

In *Barnes v City of London Real Property* [1918] 2 Ch.18 the landlord let various rooms for use as office accommodation. Although not all the leases of those rooms had the benefit of an express obligation on the part of the landlord to provide a housekeeper during business hours, it was argued that as part of the rent reflected this benefit there was an implied term that such a service would be provided. The argument succeeded "in so far as it was necessary to decide that question".

4–05   However, generally the courts have declined to imply obligations into leases in situations other than those well-established ones referred to above. In particular the courts have refused to imply terms in the following cases:

- In *Adami v Lincoln Grange Management Ltd* [1998] 1 E.G.L.R. 58 the tenant tried to argue that the landlord, who covenanted to insure the premises, would not only use insurance money to comply with his repairing obligation under the lease but would also pay for additional work carried out by the tenant, including loss of rental income by him. It was held that there was no necessity to imply a term that the landlord would keep the structure in repair or compensate the tenant for his losses in such circumstances.

- In *Lee v Leeds City Council* [2002] 1 W.L.R. 1488 the Court of Appeal thought the doctrine expounded in *Barrett v Lounova* was confined to its own facts and, in particular, those unusual cases where the parties had omitted a vital term. Chadwick L.J. said (at para.64):

  > "The principle is not, I think, in doubt. But, as Kerr L.J. pointed out in the Barrett case, the question whether the terms and circumstances of the particular lease require or enable such an implication to be made may not be easy. It must be kept in mind, as Stuart-Smith L.J. observed in *Demetriou v Robert Andrews (Estate Agencies) Ltd* (1990) 62 P. & C.R. 536, 545, that there may be circumstances in which there is no repairing obligation imposed either expressly or impliedly on anyone in relation to a lease."

In the following categories of case there is likely to be a need to **4–06** imply terms:

1. Where the lease is silent on a significant item of repair
Difficult issues arise where there is a failure in the lease to deal with an item of structural or interior repair or decoration. In the absence of an implied obligation at common law, for example, the implied obligation on the tenant to occupy the demised premises in a tenant-like manner, the extent to which the common law will impliedly oblige either the landlord or the tenant to repair or maintain an item in the demised premises is limited to circumstances similar to those in *Barrett v Luonova*. It is a necessary pre-condition for the implication of a term that the lease is silent on the point not merely that it is poorly expressed or difficult to construe. Having said that, the paragraphs that follow contain a number of examples of cases where the courts have been prepared to imply terms and demonstrate a willingness to do so.

2. Where there is inequality of bargaining power between landlord and tenant
Cases falling within this broad category probably represent the most important cases where terms will be implied into a residential lease. These cases will include those where there is a plain mismatch between the extent of the burdens on the tenant and those on the landlord, as in *Barrett* above. The injustice of the dominant contracting party (the landlord) having the benefit of extensive obligations on the part of the tenant whilst the tenant has none on behalf of the landlord is obvious. In a number of cases as well as *Barrett* the courts have grappled with this problem. Generally, where there is a burden on a tenant, or indeed any other occupier of land, to comply with a particular covenant, there will be a correlative obligation on the landlord or other owner to achieve a similar standard with regard to areas within his control.

3. Where the tenant occupies unit within a blocks of flats or other shared building which requires terms to be implied
The modern law on implied terms was extensively reviewed and extended in *Liverpool City Council v Irwin* [1977] A.C. 239. In that case the House of Lords by the implication of terms was able to find a solution to the problem that often arises in relation to buildings in multiple occupation when the landlord is under no express obligation to maintain important facilities for the residents. *Liverpool City Council v Irwin* is an important case because it extended the scope for arguing for implied terms and potentially provided a practical remedy to those tenants, particularly residential tenants, who would otherwise have to fall back on the limited repair obligations which

are implied by statute in their favour. It established a means by which obligations in large leasehold blocks, where there is shared access and use of facilities, could be mutually enforceable.

The case involved a block of flats. The defendants were tenants of a maisonette situated on the ninth and tenth floors of a tower block owned by the claimant Council. The maisonette was let under a written tenancy agreement, to which were attached written conditions. Access to the floors on which the maisonette was situated was gained via two lifts and a stairway. The tenant was to dispose of rubbish via a rubbish chute. However, the lifts continually failed to operate, the stairs were inadequately lit and the rubbish chute became blocked. The tenancy agreement placed various obligation and restrictions on the tenant but none, in relation to the defects complained about, on the landlord. There was no dispute that the tenant had an easement to use the stairs, the lift and the rubbish chute, but who was obliged to repair them?

The House of Lords held that it was necessary to imply an obligation on the part of the landlord to maintain and repair those areas. It would be inconsistent with the nature of the relationship to leave the landlord free of obligations in relation to those areas. Such obligations were demanded by the nature of the relationship in a modern tower block setting, with its range of easements in favour of the tenant, many of which are implied if they are not express.

The decision in *Irwin* was not without any precedent. Where a landlord agreed to provide a lift it was held (in *De Meza v Ve-Ri-Best Manufacturing Co* (1952) 160 EG 364) that they must ensure it is in working order.

Invariably a complex range of services is needed to maintain blocks of flats and similar buildings in a useable state such as lifts, rubbish chutes, walkways and landings. In many cases these facilities are essential and (as it was held in *Yorkbrook Investments v Batten* (1985) P. & C.R. 51) the provision of these services is not dependent on the payment of a service charge, although clearly the landlord has the contractual right to sue and take other enforcement measures where these are not paid.

In many cases the court will be able to construe the express covenants in such a way that they create obligations on the tenant which are commensurate with the true intentions of the parties. Thus in *Yorkbrook* the landlord covenanted to "supply good sufficient and constant hot water". The court construed this obligation in such a way that this included an obligation to replacing the original boiler if necessary and the landlord is not able to avoid doing so on the basis that the original boiler was not up the job.

4. Where the landlord retains control of part of the building of which the demised premises form part
This overlaps with the last category. There is also thought to be an obligation to take reasonable care to ensure the condition of all parts of a building, other than those demised to the tenant, are maintained in such condition that no damage is caused either to the tenant or to the premises demised to them. This obligation is separate from the obligation in *Irwin* in relation to shared facilities.

There has been confusion whether it is an implied *contractual* term or an obligation in *tort*. In *Duke of Westminster v Guild* [1985] 1 Q.B. 688 the Court of Appeal found an implied obligation on the landlord to effect a repair to keep the drains, which affected the tenant's demised premises, in repair. But the court thought this could arise at common law under the law of negligence or nuisance as well as an implied contractual obligation in the lease. In *Gordon v Selico* [1985] 2 E.G.L.R. 79, Goulding J. at first instance thought that the better view was that this was a contractually implied term rather than a tortious obligation under the law of negligence or nuisance. That case was appealed to the Court of Appeal on other points (at [1986] 1 E.G.L.R. 71).

As the obligation to maintain retained parts has been treated by some judges as a tortious obligation it will be further considered in that context (see Ch.8 para.8–15 at p.85 et seq., where tortious rights and duties in relation to defective premises are considered in detail). It will also be touched on in relation to the obligation not to derogate from grant in Ch.6.

When a term will not be implied

Strange as it may seem, there remain cases where there is no   **4–07** obligation on either the landlord or the tenant to effect repairs where the court will nevertheless decline to imply a term. Thus in *Demetriou v Robert Andrews (Estate Agencies) Ltd* (1990) 62 P. & C.R. 536 Stuart-Smith L.J. (at 544–545) considered that "it is a phenomenon, certainly known at common law, that there may be situations in which there is no repairing obligation imposed either expressly or impliedly on anyone in relation to a lease". This conclusion was part of the ratio of the case and was reached after consideration of *Barrett v Lounova Ltd (1982)*. However, it would be a most unusual case where there is no obligation on either party to effect a repair and the decision must be based on a consideration of all the terms in the lease to see what may necessarily have been implied.

Furnished lets

4–08   At common law furnished lets provided an exception to the rule in *Cavalier v Pope* that the landlord will not, in the absence of an express obligation, responsible for the physical condition of the premises when let (see *Smith v Marable* (1843) 11 M&W 5). The theory behind this form of liability was that the landlord in providing furniture for the tenant impliedly warranted that the house or other dwelling was reasonably fit for the tenant to live in. Indeed where this minimum standard was not achieved the tenant was within his rights repudiating the contract and walking away from the contract (*Wilson v Finch –Hatton* (1877) 2 Ex. D 336).

However, in modern times cases alleging unfitness of furnished premises are relatively rare. Just as defects in the quality of premises do not necessarily amount to disrepair and must affect the fabric of the building to be actionable, save where the covenant relates to decorative repair only, where unfitness is successfully alleged it does not necessarily follow that the premises are also in disrepair. The two concepts are very different. However, generally speaking any defect which is such as to pose a threat to a person's health would be taken to render the premises unfit for habitation.

Negotiations for termination/terminal dilapidations

4–09   Implied terms may also be important in relation to negotiations at the end of the lease, as in *Legal and General Insurance Society Ltd v Expeditors International (UK) Ltd* [2007] EWCA Civ 7. That case involved a settlement reached in a dilapidations claim not the implication of terms into the lease. The majority of the judges were able to interpret the relevant clause in negotiations to bring about a break in the lease so as to achieve a termination of the tenant's liabilities. Otherwise the tenant would have continued to be liable under the terms of the lease even after the date had passed when he should have yielded up vacant possession pursuant to the settlement. Although the tenant had breached the terms of the settlement, the majority in the Court of Appeal construed the negotiations in such a way as to put an end to the tenant's obligations. The landlord was merely entitled to compensation for the tenant's failure to yield up vacant possession on the date stipulated. However, Lloyd L.J. thought that whilst there was scope for arguing for an implied term to this effect, such an argument did not satisfy the officious bystander test. The case illustrates that the officious bystander test is not always easy to apply.

Arguments similar to those in the *Expeditors* case often arise in practice.

Implied rights of access to effect repairs

The right to enter the premises to view their state and, if necessary,   **4–10**
effect repairs is a right reserved to the landlord in most leases and is
dealt with in a number of statutes. At common law there is no implied
right for the landlord to access a property which he lets for the
purposes of carrying out work which would bring about an
improvement in the property. Nor, in the absence of an express or
implied right to enter to repair the premises in the lease, does a
landlord have a right of access to perform a *repair* to the demised
premises (see *Regional Properties Co v City of London Real Property
Co Ltd* [1981] 1 E.G.L.R. 33). However, this is subject to the
important exception in the case of repairs which the landlord is under
an *obligation* to carry out. There is thought to be an implied right of
access in such circumstances. The implied licence that arises in that
situation continues for as long as is reasonably necessary to effect
the relevant repair (*Edmonton Corporation v. Knowles* (1962) 60
L.G.R. 124).

As Ralph Gibson L.J. pointed out (in *McAuley v Bristol City
Council* [1992] Q.B. 134 at 146), the circumstances in which a court
will imply a right to enter to effect repairs are likely to be the same as
the circumstances in which the court will imply an obligation to repair.
Indeed such an implied contractual right will be "readily" implied
from an express obligation to repair (see *Edmonton Corporation v
W.M. Knowles & Son Ltd* (1961) 60 L.G.R. 124). In short, there will
be a myriad of circumstances where the court will imply rights on
the part of landlords to enter premises to repair or maintain those
premises. Where such rights are implied there is no reason why the
landlord should not be able to obtain an injunction to compel the
tenant to allow his access.

As mentioned above, in addition to the express provision that is
made for this in many leases, certain legislation, for example s.11(6)
of the Landlord and Tenant Act 1985, (considered in Ch.5, para.5–15,
p.55), also gives the landlord this implied right. This must be on 24
hours notice, although where the repair is urgent the landlord would
probably not face any repercussions if he physically re-entered to
effect the repair in question before 24 hours had elapsed.

Chapter 5

Obligations on landlords to repair and maintain implied by statute

There is still relatively little intervention by Parliament to imply **5–01** terms into leases. This is a surprising omission, particularly in relation to residential tenants who enjoy extensive security of tenure. However, it has long been recognised that some minimum standards had to be imposed, in part, to maintain the quality of the housing stock. The following provisions are of varying degrees of practical importance.

The implied obligation under s.8 of the Landlord and Tenant Act 1985, to ensure that a dwelling house within the section will be fit for habitation, has become progressively less important as the upper rent limits of tenancies to which it applied have not been updated for inflation since 1957. More than one judge in the Court of Appeal has noted this and concluded that Parliament deliberately has not increased these limits (see per Dillon L.J. in *McNerny v Lambeth LBC* [1989] 1 E.G.L.R. 81 at p.83).

On the other hand, s.11 of the Landlord and Tenant Act 1985 is of great practical importance. The concept of disrepair and the meaning of the words and phrases used in that Act will already be familiar from the discussion in Ch.2 (where the more important express terms in leases were considered). However, s.11 also contains important obligations relating to installations which have not yet been considered in detail.

The historic background—legislative interference with freedom of contract

5–02 In Ch.3 the relatively recent intervention by the legislature in the freedom of the landlord or licensor to contract, on terms that are considered unfair, was considered. However, at common law freedom of contract has been accorded considerable respect. Whereas in many areas of trade, particularly consumer contracts, considerable statutory and common law intervention has occurred, it is striking that where premises are let which are defective, so far as the civil law is concerned, it is primarily viewed as a matter for the parties. The rule in *Cavalier v Pope* referred to in the last chapter is the classic illustration of this.

However, in modern times, particularly since the Second World War, the maintenance of reasonable quality housing stock has come to be seen as an important social aim as well as an economic necessity. The provisions which follow were therefore introduced during the course of the twentieth century to place additional obligations on landlords. They remain of varying degrees of relevance.

Section 8 of the Landlord and Tenant Act 1985

5–03 This section provides a further statutory exception to the rule in *Cavalier v Pope*. In practice it is of limited practical importance because of the failure to up-date the upper rent limit to which it applied in line with inflation. What is now in s.8 of the Landlord and Tenant Act 1985 first appeared in s.12 of the Housing of the Working Classes Act 1885 and appeared again in 1923. In its current version the section provides that where the landlord lets a house at one of the exceptionally low rent levels to which the section applies there is an implied condition that those premises shall be "fit for human habitation at the commencement of the tenancy" and will be kept fit during the term. The original financial limits, based on the annual rent at the date of making the contract, were £40 in London and £26 elsewhere. On July 6, 1957 these limits were up-rated to £80 in London and £52 elsewhere.

Up-rating the annual rental limit would be a simple way for the legislature to extend the fitness for human habitation requirement to all rented dwellings but, as stated above, hitherto they have declined the opportunity to do so. It is also worth mentioning that in 1996 the Law Commission (in Law Com. No.238: "Responsibility for the State and Condition of Property") recommended extension of s.8 to all short leases to which s.11 applies (terms of less than seven years, which include all periodic terms). But this requirement would be subject to an exception in the case of works that are the responsibility of the tenant. Nor would the standard apply where it was modified by another statute or the work could not be carried out at modest expense. Some have therefore expressed the view that, given the number of caveats there were in the proposed obligation, the new law would not make as much difference as at first sight appears to be the case (see Arden, *Encyclopedia of Housing Law and Practice* looseleaf, at 12–28).

Repairing obligations in short leases under section 11 of the Landlord and Tenant Act 1985

The obligation under s.11 of the Landlord and Tenant Act 1985 **5–04** places a minimum obligation on landlords to repair the structure and exterior of a dwelling house to which the section applies as well as maintain the installations "for the supply of space heating and water, gas and electricity" to those residential premises. The section only applies to "short leases". A short lease is defined in s.13 as a lease of less than 7 years. This includes all periodic terms.

Section 11 of the 1985 Act applies to leases granted on or after October 24, 1961 (s.13(1))—the provision having been first introduced by s.32 of the Housing Act 1961 which came into force on that day.

Contracting out

The parties may not contract out of the Act (s.12(2)) but they may **5–05** adopt a different or more extensive obligation on the landlord, provided the term or terms adopted do not constitute unfair contract terms within the Unfair Contract Terms in Consumer Contracts Regulations 1999 (see Ch.3). Effectively, it will be necessary to consider whether the tenant's residual obligations after the landlord's obligations are taken away are greater than the minimum obligations in s.11. If they are, then those additional obligations will in fact be on the landlord (see *Irvine v Moran* [1991] E.G.L.R. 261).

Additional obligations

Many older leases place additional burdens on the landlord. These **5–06** included the requirement that the landlord shall keep the premises in "good condition and repair". In *Welsh v Greenwich London Borough Council* [2000] 3 E.G.L.R. 41 the Court of Appeal had to consider this covenant. It held that the words "good condition" created a separate concept from that conveyed by the word "repair". It was therefore intended to place an additional burden on the landlord and would render him liable, for example, for condensation-related damp.

The extent of section 11

5–07 Section 11(1) places the landlord under an implied obligation to keep in repair the "structure and exterior" of the dwelling house and to keep in repair and proper working order the installations in the premises for the supply of water, gas, electricity and for sanitation. It also requires the landlord to keep in repair and proper working order the installations in the premises for space heating and heating water.

By s.15 of the Act the county court is given the power to declare whether s.11 applies to a lease or not.

5–08 The following are some of the more important words and phrases used in s.11:

"Keep in repair"

The obligation to "*keep* in repair" includes an obligation to *put* in repair (see Hill & Redman A6482 and see Ch.2 above, where the concept of repair is considered in greater detail). It should also be noted that, strictly, the repairing obligation applies to deterioration in the premises from their state when constructed (see *Hill and Redman* at A6468).

"The structure"

"The structure" is not limited to load bearing walls but includes anything which gives "essential stability and shape" to the dwelling house (*Irvine v Moran* (1992) 24 H.L.R. 1). Therefore decorative items will not be included. In deciding what is meant by the "structure" a court will often look at other case law including structural repairing obligations under commercial leases where such obligations frequently arise. In such cases the structural repairing obligation will need to be considered in the context of the whole lease. Nevertheless these cases are also helpful and will therefore also be considered below.

The following items have been held to be part of the structure:

- The floor joists (*Marlborough Park Services v Rowe* [2006] EWCA Civ 436 and *Thornton v Birmingham City Council*, Legal Action November 2004);
- the front steps but not the rear yard (see *Hopwood v Cannock Chase District Council* [1975] 1 W.L.R. 373 and *Smith v Bradford* [1982] 44 P. & C.R. 171 referred to below), although these may also form part of the exterior of the dwelling (see *Brown v Liverpool Corporation* [1969] 3

All E.R. 1345);

- the internal plaster, provided the deterioration is not merely decorative (see *Staves v Leeds City Council* [1992] 2 E.G.L.R. 37 and *Hussein v Mehlman* (1992) 24 H.L.R. 1);

- external windows and doors and their constituent parts (see *Irvine v Moran* [1991] 1 E.G.L.R. 261) but these may also be part of the exterior (see also *Patrick v Marley Estates* [2007] EWCA Civ 1176);

- a roof terrace other than the surface layer (see *Ibrahim v Dovecorn Reversions Limited* [2001] 2 E.G.L.R. 46);

- a partition wall between two terraced houses (*Pembery v Lamdin* [1940] 2 All E.R. 434, although that case was concerned with the phrase "external part of the demised premises");

- all external drains, gutters and pipes (s.11(1)(a), although these also appear to be part of the exterior).

"The exterior"
This includes: **5–09**

- The essential means of access to the dwellinghouse excluding the rear yard (see *Hopwood v Cannock Chase DC* [1975] 1 W.L.R. 373). This contrasts with the extent of a landlord's liability under s.4 of the Defective Premises Act 1972 which has been held to extend to the rear yard (in *Smith v Bradford* (1982) 44 P. & C.R. 171);

- the external windows and doors and their constituent parts (see *Irvine v Moran* [1991] 1 E.G.L.R. 261 and *Ball v Plummer* 17/6/70 *The Times*);

- a partition wall between two semi-detached/terraced houses where there was a covenant to keep "the external part of the demised premises" in repair (*Pembery v Lamdin* [1940] 3 All E.R. 434);

- drains, gutters and external pipes (s.11(1)(a)).

"The dwelling-house"
The s.11 obligations only apply to a lease of a dwelling house. The "dwelling house" has been held to include the main means of access but not, for example, the rear path or yard (see *Brown v Liverpool Corporation* [1969] 3 All E.R. 1345). This contrasts with s.4 of the Defective Premises Act, which applies to the whole of the demised premises (see *Smith v Bradford* above).

Where a building or part of a building is "let wholly or mainly as a private residence" (s.16(b)), s.11 will apply, but it will not apply to mixed-use business and residential premises. Thus in *Demetriou v Robert Andrews Estate Agencies* (1991) 62 P. & C.R. 536 the court held that a letting of a property in part for sub-letting as residential property did not fall within the Act. Stuart-Smith L.J. said (at p.545):

> "it is common ground that the case was not one to which section 32 of the 1961 Act applied. The reason why that was common ground is because under the provisions of that Act, which are now re-enacted in the Landlord and Tenant Act of 1985 and are to be found in section 11 of that Act (which is the equivalent of s.32 of the Housing Act 1961) and section 16 of the Landlord and Tenant Act 1985 (which is equivalent to s.32(5) of the previous Act), that section only applies to the lease of a dwelling-house (I refer to para.(b)) which means a lease by which a building or part of a building is let wholly or mainly as a private residence. It is plain on the judge's findings that these premises were not let wholly or mainly as a private residence but for the purpose of sub-letting as rooms. Therefore, it was common ground that section 32 of the Housing Act did not apply and, in my judgment, in those circumstances it is not easy to imply a term into a business tenancy such as this in the way the learned judge sought to do."

Cases to which section 11 will not apply

5–10   Section 11 will not apply to:

- cases where the disrepair is as a result of the tenant's own failure to occupy the premises in a tenant-like manner (s.11(2)(a)—see Ch.7);

- destruction or damage that has occurred by inevitable accident, save where this causes actionable disrepair to the structure and exterior (however, see the next bullet);

- disrepair which the landlord has not been given express notice of, or where, having been given notice, the landlord has not had the reasonable opportunity to carry out the repair in question (see Ch.2, para.2–11 at p.26 et seq.). This will be the case where the defect arises within the premises themselves which the landlord is not aware of but will not be the case where the disrepair is to the common or external parts of a building to which the landlord has access.

The extent of the tenant's "tenant-like manner" obligation will be considered in Ch.7 and the nature of the repair obligation and notice has already been considered. However, the repairing and maintaining obligation in relation to common parts requires fuller explanation.

Common parts

Where the lease was granted before January 15, 1989, disrepair or **5–11** failure to maintain installations within the common parts of the building of which the dwelling formed part, as opposed to being within the dwelling house itself, were not within s.11. However now these areas are caught by the provisions of s.11(1A). That sub-section (inserted into the 1985 Act by s.116 of the Housing Act 1988) provides that references to the "dwelling house" include any part of the building in which the landlord has an estate or interest and the same applies to any installation which directly or indirectly serves the dwelling-house. However the landlord has a defence under subs.3A if he made all reasonable endeavours to obtain access to the part of the building concerned but was unable to do so.

It should be noted that prior to the date the Housing Act 1988 came into force, the landlord's repairing obligation did not extend to the common parts (see *Campden Hill Towers Ltd v Gardner* [1977] 1 All E.R. 739) but only applied to the dwelling-house itself . In relation to leases still subsisting from before that date it will still be necessary to establish a defect to the dwelling itself, including the structural supports and divisions of that unit. In such cases it was often necessary to rely on the implied terms discussed in the previous chapter and in particular the implied obligations relating to shared facilities considered by the House of Lords in *Liverpool City Council v Irwin*. Save where the statutory exception created by s.11(1A) applies, or it is possible to rely on an implied obligation, s.11 still only extends to the dwelling-house and not the full extent of the demise.

The extent of the landlord's obligations in respect of the common parts following the amendment of s.11 was considered in *Niazi Services v van der Loo* [2004] 1 W.L.R. 1254. There the landlord, himself the tenant of his own flat and the head tenant of the claimant's flat under a long head lease, let the premises he held on the long lease to the claimant. The claimant therefore became his sub-tenant. Defects arose to the common parts of the building, in which those flats formed part, but which did not form any part of the landlord's head lease. The complaints included poor water pressure emanating from a shared facility and poor lighting in the common parts. It was held that there was no basis for implying any repairing obligation on the landlord in relation to those common parts in favour of another tenant of the same building.

In a case which is not caught by s.11(1A) the lease will need to be considered to see whether, as in *British Telecommunications Plc v Sun Life Assurance Society Plc* [1996] Ch.69 (see Ch.2, para.2–11 at p.26 et seq.), the responsibility for maintaining the common parts rests with the landlord or the tenant. As has already been commented, that case involved an obligation to keep the building of which the demised premises formed part in "good repair and condition". It was held that made the landlord liable from the moment the common parts fell out of repair and no notice was required. But it would be unusual to find such obligations in relation to short leases of flats or other dwellings within buildings.

Standard of repair

5–12 It is important to note that the standard of repair under s.11 is no higher than that which applies at common law, namely it need be no higher than is consistent with the "age, character and prospective life of the dwelling-house and the locality in which it is based" (s.11(3) LTA 1985). This may mean that patch repairs will be sufficient for a modest property whereas for a more expensive property more extensive refurbishment may be required (see for e.g. *Trustees of Hungerford Charity v Beazeley* [1993] 2 E.G.L.R. 143).

In *Montoya v Hackney* [2004] unreported, the single joint expert was requested to visit the property that was the subject of the claim and report on the defects. Having done so he reported that the defects he found were consistent with the age and the type of dwelling in question but the trial judge had nevertheless given judgement for the tenant on these issues. It was held that given that the expert's comments had been read and his evidence was not challenged the judge was not entitled to conclude that there had nevertheless been a breach of the repairing covenant under s.11. In many cases though the assessment that the premises are consistent with their age and location will simply be a matter for the judge and they will often not be assisted by expert evidence on the point.

Installations

5–13 Save in relation to leases granted before January 15, 1989 (see the discussion above in relation to common parts) where the duty in relation to installations only extended to installations *within* the dwelling-house and not outside it, the landlord's duty extends to keeping the utility supply installations *serving* the dwelling in "proper working order". For leases granted before that date (but not leases where the contract was entered into before that date but the lease granted after it) the landlord will only be liable in respect of installations within the dwelling itself.

The "installations" referred to in the implied covenant are effectively fixed installations rather than loose installations that can be removed at the end of the term. Thus if the landlord happens to provide a fridge or cooker for the tenant's use these will not constitute "installations for the supply of water, gas and electricity" all appliances being excluded, save those which may be called "installations for space heating and heating water". However, installations and appliances which are not within s.11 may be subject to other regulation.

Pipes and radiators will be regarded as within the obligation relating to "installations for space heating and heating water", whereas other installations and appliances will not be. In relation to communal boilers, on or after January 15, 1989 these will be within s.11 but in relation to leases entered into before that date they will not be.

Keeping installations in "proper working order"
In relation to installations, it should be noted that in some cases this **5–14** might extend to taking positive steps to improve those installations and the distinction which exists in relation to repair works between repairs and improvements does not exist in relation to installations. Thus, in *O'Connor v Old Etonian HA Limited* [2002] 2 All E.R. 1015 the Court of Appeal decided that the pipes for the conveyance of water to parts of the building would only be in proper working order if they were able to function under the conditions which it could reasonably be anticipated would occur. Therefore, there was a positive obligation on the landlord to improve the pipework in that case.

The statutory rights of access under the Landlord and Tenant Act 1985

Specific provision is made in s.11(6) for the landlord to have access **5–15** to view the state of repair of the premises on 24 hours written notice to the occupier. Although there is no express right to enter the premises to actually carry out the repairs, it follows that if the tenant unreasonably refuses the landlord the opportunity either to view the state of the premises or carry out necessary repairs the landlord would, effectively, have discharged his repairing obligation to the tenant and would be absolved from future liability in respect of past disrepair. However, unless it is necessary to complete the repairs, the tenant need not give his landlord exclusive possession to carry out the repairs. This topic will be considered in greater detail when the implied obligations on the part of the tenant are considered in Ch.7.

Other provisions relevant to long leaseholders

Terms implied at the end of long leases

5–16 Section 1 of the Landlord and Tenant Act 1954 protects tenants of long leases at low rents on the termination of their term. In certain cases such tenants those who do not seek to enfranchise will become statutory tenants under the Rent Act 1977 (see s.6). Section 7 of the 1954 Act provides details of how the terms of those statutory tenancies are to be determined. Importantly, for the purposes of this publication, the tenant's obligation to repair, which would ordinarily come to an end, will need to be agreed or fixed. Section 7 of the Landlord and Tenant Act 1954 enables this to be done by means of a notice. In default of agreement these terms may be fixed by the county court.

Proposals for reform

5–17 If the Law Commission's recommendations (in "Renting Homes: the final report" (2006)) are adopted there will be a reduction in the need to rely on implied terms. All tenants, whether of local authorities, registered social landlords or private landlords, will be entitled to a minimum standard of accommodation and would have a private law remedy if it did not meet that standard. It was also proposed in that report that s.11 should be modernised and apply to licensees as well as tenants so that they better reflected the consumer character of the transaction, rather than being based on traditional property law principles. These, with earlier proposals by the Law Commission (Law Com. No.238: "Responsibility for the State and Condition of Property" 1996) in relation to the extension of s.8 of the Landlord and Tenant Act 1985 to all premises to which s.11 of that Act applies, would constitute a considerable alteration of the present position. That position is best characterised as one of relative freedom of contract between landlord and tenant, subject to meeting the minimum standard required by s.11.

Chapter 6

Other express and implied obligations on landlords relevant to the repair or maintenance of the premises

Most residential leases restrict the landlord's duty to repair and **6–01** maintain to that which is required as a minimum by Parliament. In practice this often means that liability is limited to the essential items to the structure and fabric of the demised premises. For this reason tenants, particularly tenants of residential premises, often try and bring in additional private law claims on the basis that the landlord has derogated from his grant or has interfered with the tenant's quiet enjoyment of the demised premises. The latter will nearly always be an express covenant in the lease but even if it does not appear there, or the lease is oral, it will be implied as is the obligation not to derogate from grant. The obligation not to derogate and the covenant for quiet enjoyment are often pleaded in the alternative and are thus dealt with together in the same chapter.

Although it will be a relatively rare case where liability on the part of the landlord for the physical state will only be based on the obligation not to derogate and/or the covenant for quiet enjoyment, these claims are often raised in addition to allegations of disrepair. It is therefore necessary to have an understanding of the nature of these covenants.

Not to derogate from the grant

This covenant is a form of assurance by the landlord that the tenant **6–02** can use the premises demised for the intended purpose throughout the term. Specifically, the landlord may not take away with one hand what he grants with the other. The covenant has been described as a rule of common honesty" (in *Harmer v Jumbil Nigeria Ltd* [1921] Ch.200). The argument that is sometimes raised is that, by allowing the premises to fall into disrepair, the landlord has taken away from the thing that he granted. Therefore the covenant is sometimes prayed in aid of a disrepair claim.

However, the cases where the covenant may successfully be invoked in support of an allegation of disrepair will be rare. In particular the following points need to be borne in mind:

- The covenant protects the tenant's *physical comfort* during the term but does not guarantee that the premises will have a particular *amenity or quality*.

- To found an action for derogation from grant the interference must be "*substantial*"; it must be such as to prevent the tenant using the premises for the purposes for which they were taken not merely render the premises less comfortable than they should have been.

- It will only be to a very limited extent that the landlord can be held liable for the acts of third parties, for example, a landlord was held not to be liable where a local planning authority chose to take enforcement proceedings against the tenant arising out of an unlawful use for which the premises had been let (*Molton Builders Ltd v City of Westminster LBC (1975)* 30 P. & C.R. 182). The covenant does not provide that sort of assurance at all.

6–03   Examples of cases where the covenant has been held to apply

- Where the landlord retains adjoining land and allows that adjoining land to be used in a way that interferes with the tenant's occupation of the demised premises this may constitute a breach of the covenant (*Rigby v Bennett* (1882) 2 Ch. D 559).

- Where a landlord built over the demised premises by erecting two additional floors this also constituted a breach of the covenant (*Lawson v Hartley-Brown* (1995) 71 P. & C.R. 242, CA.) although on the facts no damage had been proved.

However, many landlords will be able to avoid liability arising even in these limited circumstances by reserving appropriate powers to themselves in their leases, for example, to carry out work to adjoining premises where otherwise that would constitute a breach of the covenant. There seems little doubt that a landlord may effectively limit the scope of his grant by insert appropriate reservations into the lease for this purpose.

This was the case in *RHJ Patten Limited v FT Patten Holdings Ltd* [2008] EWCA Civ 151, in the analogous situation of the implied grant of an easement. Although that case involved rights to light and the ambit of s.3 of the Prescription Act 1832, it contains a contemporary discussion on the extent of the covenant.

The facts were that the landlord granted a lease which purported to limit rights of light for the benefit of the demised premises. In particular, the landlord inserted into the lease a provision to the effect that no estate, right or easement other than those expressly provided for in the lease would be impliedly granted. It was held that this had the effect of preventing the accrual of a right to light by prescription over the landlord's adjoining land.

Consequences of establishing derogation from grant—can the tenant repudiate the lease?

The tenant's main remedy will be in damages or for an injunction to **6–04** prevent a continuance of the behaviour which is said to constitute derogation from grant. In some cases the landlord will have to take positive steps to reinstate the premises into their former state and the tenant will be able to apply for specific performance of the landlord's obligation. However, in recent years, following the case of *National Carriers v Panalpina* [1981] A.C. 675, there has been greater use of the argument that the landlord has been in repudiatory breach of the tenancy by virtue of the alleged derogation. That case is the leading case on frustration of leases but it also contains a discussion on the extent to which a lease may be repudiated. Essentially the argument that has been employed has been that the tenancy has been repudiated by the landlord's acts or omissions which are said to constitute the breach of the obligation. This would have the important consequence that the innocent party may be able to walk away from the lease. The argument has been considered in the case of *Nynehead Developments Ltd v RH Fibreboard Containers Ltd* [1999] 1 E.G.L.R. 7 *and Chartered Trust Plc v Davies* [1997] 2 E.G.L.R. 83. These cases are now considered in greater detail.

In *Nynehead Developments v RH Fibreboard* the landlord let business premises to the tenant. The lease provided for some shared parking and other exclusive parking but unfortunately other occupiers of the units would park vehicles in various places including on the other tenant's own exclusive parking area. The tenant argued that this was derogation from grant by the landlord and that the breach by the landlord was such that the tenant could treat the lease as repudiated.

The High Court agreed that there had been a breach of the covenant but declined to treat the lease as repudiated because they were not such as to substantially deny the tenant the whole benefit of that which they had contracted to take from the landlord.

In *Chartered Trust Plc v Davies* on the other hand the Court of Appeal found that the tenant was entitled to treat the lease as repudiated by the landlord's failure to take action against a pawn broker in the same retail development. The pawnbroker in question was bound by covenants with the same landlord, which he breached to the detriment of the tenant's business. The landlord could be expected to control his other tenant (the pawn broker) by enforcing those covenants, but he had not done so. The lease was repudiated. This follows the comments of Sedley L.J. sitting as an assistant recorder in the first instance case of *Hussein v Mehlman* [1992] 2 E.G.L.R. 87 (a disrepair case) in which he expressed the view that a lease could be repudiated.

However the case of Davies has been subject to a certain amount of criticism (see e.g. *Hill and Redman* A9423.1).

Practically therefore the reliance on the obligation not to derogate from grant may have the profound consequence that the entire lease is treated as repudiated. Obviously it would be for the tenant to raise this argument and it will be a rare case where he could successfully do so.

For quiet enjoyment

Nature of the covenant at common law

6–05   In every lease, oral or written, legal or equitable, the landlord impliedly covenants not to interfere with the tenant's possession of the demised premises during the term. This is crucial to the exclusive possession granted at the commencement of the term. The covenant is important in the context of unlawful eviction but is less so in the context of enforcing obligations to repair and maintain demised premises. Nevertheless, particularly in recent years, attempts have been made to extend the covenant to cover the physical condition of the premises as well as the conduct of the landlord in relation to those premises.

As Lord Hoffmann has observed (in *Southwark LBC v Tanner, Baxter v Camden LBC (No.2)* [2001] 1 A.C. 1 at p.10, also known as *Southwark LBC v Mills*) the covenant is not about keeping the premises "quiet" nor is it concerned about the tenant's "enjoyment" of them. The "quiet" referred to in the covenant appears to be no more than an assurance that the landlord or his agents will not physically interfere with the possession that the lease has granted. Moreover the covenant protects the tenant against *"substantial"* interruption on the part of the landlord and his agents and thus does not prevent *every* interference.

Furthermore the covenant is prospective in character in that it looks forward from the date of the grant and asks what the landlord covenanted to provide at that time, not backwards from the time of breach.

Absolute and qualified covenants

Where the covenant is express rather than implied, the nature of the   6–06
assurance given by the landlord will depend on the words used. The covenant in absolute form is an assurance against interruption by the landlord or those claiming title *paramount* whereas the qualified form of covenant only applies to the acts or those claiming title *under* the landlord (the distinction is explained in *Hill and Redman* at A6805).

The qualified form of the covenant is the form implied into every lease and sometimes into agreements for lease. It may even be implied into residential licences (see *Smith v Nottinghamshire CC* (1981), *The Times*, 13 November). However, there (where there was a contractual licence of a student hall of residence) the obligation was a contractually implied term rather than a covenant in a lease. The extent of the landlord's obligation will depend on the context and it did not necessarily follow that because the term was implied into the contractual licence it was identical to a covenant implied into a lease. Indeed there may be cases where no such term could be implied.

When the covenant against quiet enjoyment is relevant to defective premises claims

This covenant is sometimes invoked to fill a gap in the express   6–07
repairing obligations in a lease. However, like allegations that the landlord has derogated from his grant, it is relatively rare for a tenant to successfully rely on the covenant for quiet enjoyment in a claim arising out of the physical state of the premises. Indeed, in *Duke of Westminster v Guild* [1985] Q.B. 688 (also considered this in the context of implied terms at p.43) the Court of Appeal stated that:

> "the express covenant for quiet enjoyment and the implied covenant not to derogate from grant cannot be invoked to impose obligations to repair." (per Slade L.J. at 703)

Sometimes the failure of a lease to refer to a particular part of the premises which falls into disrepair may be rectified by implying a term, but Slade L.J. declined to imply a term on the facts of that case holding that the test was one of necessity, not one of convenience.

In *Southwark LBC v Tanner*, (also known as *Baxter v Camden LBC [No.2]* [2001] 1 A.C. 1) the tenant failed to establish a breach of the covenant for quiet enjoyment in support of his claim that the flat he had rented from Southwark had inadequate sound insulation. Crucially the House of Lords decided that the covenant was prospective in character, i.e. it looked forward from the date of the lease. The landlord covenanted that he *would not* in the future interfere not that there *was not* any physical impediment to the tenant's enjoyment of the demised premises at the date of grant. The covenant against quiet enjoyment covered any physical interference with the tenant's enjoyment of the premises demised. If there was an inherent defect in design at the date of the demise, which allowed noise to interfere with the tenant's enjoyment, that would not be covered. Nor would the tenant be able to claim for noise emanating from the common parts retained by the landlord where they were part and parcel of the ordinary everyday occupation and use of the premises. Their lordships did not rule out noise nuisance falling within the covenant altogether. However, their lordships found such a noise nuisance did not give rise to a cause of action on the facts of the cases before them.

Lord Hoffmann found that the case of *Sanderson v Berwick upon Tweed Corporation* 13 Q.B.D. 547 was consistent with this principle, which seems at first sight surprising. In that case the Corporation let a farm to Sanderson. The lease was subject to a drainage right they had reserved in favour of another farmer called Cairns, who was also the Corporation's tenant. However they reserved a right to enter Sanderson's land to maintain and repair the drain used by Cairns. That drain was so badly built that it flooded Sanderson's land. Sanderson sued the Corporation for breach of the covenant for quiet enjoyment in his lease. It was held that the right to discharge water was conditional upon the landlord's reserved right to repair the drain if Cairns wished to use it. It was therefore the case that the landlord could do something about the flooding but had failed to do so. Berwick was the landlord of both Sanderson and Cairns which was responsible for the damage caused by its badly constructed drain, although it was not responsible for damage which occurred solely due to excessive use by Cairns. It seems that it was crucial to that decision that Cairns was doing what his lease authorised him to do and no more. In respect of the badly designed drain, as opposed to his excessive user of the drainage facility, Cairns was therefore acting under the authority of his landlord. Furthermore there had been a substantial interference with the tenant's physical enjoyment of the demised land, in the sense of an interference with his possession of it. Therefore Sanderson did enjoy a right of action against his landlord under the covenant for quiet enjoyment.

In *Southwark LBC v Long* [2002] EWCA Civ 403 the Court of Appeal followed the *Mills* case and rejected the Judge's conclusion at first instance that the Council could be responsible for various nuisance related complaints relating to the rubbish disposal facilities in a large block of flats. The Court of Appeal reiterated that the covenant for quiet enjoyment was prospective in character and found that there was no finding of fact that the facilities provided at the time of the alleged breach were any less commodious than those at the date of the grant of the lease. However the point was also made that there is nothing to stop a tenant suing for breach of the covenant based on a commission or an omission.

It may therefore be seen that to found an action solely on the basis of an alleged breach of the covenant for quiet enjoyment is highly problematic. This result is consistent with the very limited tortious or implied contractual obligations on those who let premises for their physical state. In practice a breach of this covenant is likely to be allied with a claim for breach of the obligation not to derogate, considered earlier in this chapter and, as in the *Mills* case, under the Human Rights Act 1998, which will be considered in Ch.13.

Relying on the covenant as a defence

Sometimes the covenant will be relied on by the tenant as a defence, **6–08** for example, when the landlord wishes to gain access to carry out repairs. In that situation the obligation to carry out repairs on the part of the landlord and the right of the tenant to quiet enjoyment during the term appear to be in conflict. Resolution of this conflict requires considering both the obligation and the right together, not in isolation.

There is an implied right for the landlord to enter premises which he lets for the purposes of viewing their state and then taking a reasonable period to bring them into a state of repair (*Saner v Bilton* (1878) 7 Ch. D. 815). If the tenant then refuses access to complete the repairs within a reasonable period the landlord will not be in breach of his repairing obligation. Obviously the effect of the tenant's unreasonable refusal to allow his landlord access to perform his repairing obligation would, effectively, bring to an end that repairing obligation in any event.

However, the landlord's implied right (which will also be express in many leases or, pursuant to certain statutes) must be exercised reasonably, so that the tenant is entitled to know broadly the nature of the work the landlord is to carry out. Generally speaking, the landlord is bound to take *reasonable* precautions to minimise disturbance in carrying out repairs under the lease but they are not bound to take *every possible* precaution. The extent of those precautions may be illustrated by *Goldmile Properties Ltd v Speiro Lechouritis* [2003] 1 E.G.L.R. 60.

In that case the tenant argued that the landlord was in breach of covenant for quiet enjoyment when he carried out external repair works using scaffolding. In particular he argued that the dust from the work disrupted the tenant's restaurant business. The Court of Appeal found that the landlord had taken all reasonable steps to avoid *unnecessary* disturbance but some disturbance was inevitable and there was no breach of the covenant consequent on that disturbance.

In summary, therefore, the landlord who performed his repairing obligation in a reasonable manner would not be in breach of the repairing obligation provided he did so within a reasonable time nor would his actions amount to a breach of the covenant for quiet enjoyment provided that he performed that covenant in a reasonable way. However, a landlord would be liable for breach of the covenant for quiet enjoyment where:

1. He has interfered with the tenant's enjoyment of the demised premises during the term but not simply demised premises to the tenant which contain a defect which is likely to interfere with that tenant's enjoyment of those premises. Therefore the covenant does not provide any form of warranty as to the quality of the premises, merely an assurance that during the term the landlord will not interfere with that occupation whether actively or passively.

2. He will be liable for his own actions or for those over whom he has control. Thus he will be liable for the acts of his tenants where he has the ability to control their actions, for example by inserting appropriately worded covenants into their leases. However, the assurance that landlords give is not an assurance against interruption by third parties, for example neighbours, over whom they have no control. In a situation where the tenant's neighbours, who are not tenants or licensees of the same landlord, interfere with the tenant's enjoyment of the demised premises the tenant will need to take action directly against those responsible, however impracticable that appears.

Chapter 7

Implied obligations on tenants relevant to the repair or maintenance of the premises

The law relating to defective premises cannot be fully considered **7–01** without considering the implied obligations on tenants in relation to their defective state.

There are number implied obligations which remain relevant, particularly where there is no written lease governing the relationship between landlord and tenant. Obviously, the landlord will be able to sue for any breach of the repairing covenant if he has the benefit of an express repairing covenant. Otherwise he may need to sue for a breach of a number of implied obligations that arise.

In practice these causes of action are more likely to be raised by the landlord as defences to an action by the tenant against the landlord, e.g. as a response to a claim that the landlord has breached his repairing obligation, rather than be pleaded as the landlord's main cause of action against the tenant.

The most commonly raised of these implied obligations is the obligation on the part of the tenant to occupy the premises in a tenant-like manner. In the leading case of *Regis v Dudley* [1959] A.C. 370, considered below, Lord Denning doubted whether the tenant-like user requirement was anything more than an obligation as to the tenant's conduct and it did not in his view give rise to a repairing obligation.

In this chapter the implied obligation to occupy in a tenant like manner will be considered first followed by the less-commonly relied on obligation not to commit waste. Finally, the implied obligation which exists on tenants to permit their landlords to enter and view the state of repair of the premises during the term will be considered.

To occupy in a "tenant-like manner"

7–02   The obligation to occupy the premises in a "tenant-like manner" is thought to apply to all leases. It is unlikely to be relied on where there are adequate express provisions but where it is raised any failure to take proper care of the demised premises may breach the obligation. However although the failure to occupy premises in a tenant-like manner often overlaps with the express obligations in the lease, for example, to repair the premises, different results may flow from a breach of the tenant-like user obligation than a breach of the repairing obligation. For example, where the tenant's rent is reviewed it will take account of any onerous features of the repairing covenant in the lease whereas it will not take account of the implied obligation to occupy in a tenant-like manner. In addition, as Lord Denning has pointed out in *Regis Property Co Ltd v Dudley* [1959] A.C. 370 at 407, in deciding the level of the fair rent for the purposes of fixing that rent under the Rent Acts the rent officer is only entitled to take into account those additional requirements imposed by the lease above and beyond those implied at common law. The assumption is made that the tenant will comply with the implied obligations in the lease and his rent will be fixed in such a way that no additional value is attributed to them.

When the obligation is relevant

7–03   The obligation arises in all leases but is only likely to prove relevant where there are inadequate express terms in the lease. This will be the case in every oral lease, for example, a periodic term which arises by implication on payment of rent. However there is some debate over whether the implied obligation may be relied on where there is an (equivalent) express obligation in place. *Standen v Chrismas* (1874) 10 Q.B. 135 appears to suggest that the obligation did not arise where there was an express covenant in the lease for the tenant to repair the interior of the premises. However, in *Regis Property v Dudley* Lord Denning cast doubt on this (at [1959] A.C. 370 p.407) saying that *Standen* was not correctly decided. He held that the obligation to occupy in a tenant-like manner was a separate obligation. Lord Denning's reasoning has been described as "persuasive" by at least one commentator (Dowding and Reynolds, *Dilapidations: The Modern Law and Practice* 3rd edn at 21-06).

What is expected of the tenant

7–04   The leading case remains *Warren v Keen* [1954] 1 Q.B. 15, where Denning L.J. characterised the duty on the tenant as "doing the little jobs about the place". The jobs he had in mind-included:

- turning the water off when the tenant went away;
- cleaning chimneys when necessary;
- cleaning windows;
- mending fuses;
- unblocking the sink when it is blocked.

In a later case it has been held obiter dicta that changing a washer on a tap may be added to that list along with lagging the pipes in certain cases and keeping the house heated (*Wycombe Health Authority v Barnett* (1982) 5 H.L.R. 84). However, where the tenant left the demised premised for one night but, in fact, stayed away for two, and the unlagged pipes froze over whilst they were away, this did not on the facts constitute un-tenant-like user (*Wycombe Health Authority v Barnett* (above)). From the report it seems that the temperature had only been a little under freezing when he left. His responsibility may have been much greater if he had left the premises unoccupied for a longer period (see *Mickel v M'Coard* (1913) S.C. 896). In the latter case the tenant left the premises unoccupied for one month during the winter without turning off the water. Given that the property was situated in Scotland that did amount to un-tenant-like user. In this type of case it appears that the outcome of the case will depend on the time of year when the tenant is absent from the premises and the duration of that absence.

The extent of the obligation will also depend on the length of the lease and the character of the premises demised. Thus in relation to a short lease, an express obligation on the tenant to "maintain and keep in good and substantial condition" has been described as creating no greater obligation than the "tenant like manner" obligation (see *First Cross v Teasdale* [1983] 1 E.G.L.R. 87). But this would have been different if the repairing obligation in the lease had been to keep in "good and habitable repair". Thus "tenant-like", "husband-like" and "good and tenantable repair and condition", according to McNeill J. in that case, all mean much the same. They are all subject to the exception in respect of ordinary or reasonable use or fair wear and tear.

Consequences of breach

The effect of finding that the tenant is in breach of this obligation will usually be to absolve the landlord of responsibility for the same defect. Clearly in a case where the landlord is sued for the defective state of the premises he has demised to the tenant he cannot be responsible for any part of the defective state of the property which   **7–05** arose as a result of the tenant's failure to occupy the premises in a tenant-like manner. On the other hand there is some authority for the view (albeit expressed obiter dicta by Lord Denning in *Regis Property v Dudley* [1959] A.C. 370 referred to above) that the landlord may rely on the tenant-like user obligation even where he has the benefit of, for example, an internal repairing obligation in the lease.

Furthermore, in a case to which s.11 of the Landlord and Tenant Act 1985 applies (short leases of dwellings) by virtue of s.11(2) of that Act the landlord is not obliged to carry out works of repair for which the lessee is liable by virtue of his duty to occupy the premises in a tenant-like manner, or would be liable but for an express obligation on his part:

> "to rebuild or reinstate the premises in the case of destruction or damage by fire, or by tempest, flood or other inevitable accident, or to keep in repair or maintain anything which the lessee is entitled to remove from the dwelling-house."

Limitation

7–06   The obligation to use the premises in a tenant-like manner continues throughout the term so that a failure to remedy the defect continues up to the last day of the tenancy. Therefore where the tenant fails to yield up the premises in repair it will not be an answer to the landlord's claim that they failed to occupy the premises in a tenant-like manner to point to the fact that the default the landlord relies on arose more than six years before the commencement of the action provided the action takes place no more than six years after the end of the term (*Marsden v Edwards Heyes Ltd* [1927] 2 K.B. 1). However, that case was concerned with an alteration of the demised premises by removal of an internal partition. It was held that the actions of the tenant amounted to voluntary waste as well as un-tenant-like user. The tenant was in continuing breach of both obligations as long as he failed to reinstate the premises. It was held that although the actions had occurred more than six years before the issue of the landlord's claim they were not statute barred. Nevertheless the position may be otherwise if the tenant was in breach of his tenant-like user obligation on one occasion, for example going away on holiday and leaving the heating switched off during a cold spell resulting in the pipes bursting, as opposed to being in continuing breach. The covenants in the lease would need to be studied to see whether in fact the tenant was in continuing breach of an obligation in that lease. Where the claim is based solely on the implied obligation at common law the limitation period ought to be six-years from the date of breach of that obligation.

Not to commit waste

As the word would suggest, "waste" is the destruction of the demised   **7–07**
premises or the ground they stand on so as to damage the landlord's
reversion. It is divided into two types: voluntary waste and permissive
waste.

The obligation not to commit waste arises in tort (see *Defries
v Milne* [1913] 1 Ch.98) but it also forms part of the implied
contractual obligation to occupy in a tenant-like manner (see
Whitman v Kershaw (1886) 16 Q.B.D. 613). This has a number of
important consequences, including the fact that the directors of a
corporate tenant which commits waste may be personally liable in
tort and may not hide behind the corporate veil. Also the privity rule
will not apply and the tenant and the others responsible for the waste
may equally be sued. In practice most leases will insert a covenant
on the part of the tenant not to commit waste but where they do not
the landlord may rely on the tortious obligation not to commit waste
or an implied obligation not to commit waste where it arises. This
was explained in the case of *Marsden v Heyes* [1927] 2 K.B. 1 by
Atkin L.J. at pp.7–8).

The fact that the commission of waste gives rise to a potential
action in tort may have a number of important consequences, for
example, in relation to limitation and in relation to forfeiture. In
particular a different limitation period operates in tort than in contract
and forfeiture is not available for a tort but will normally be available
for breach of a covenant or condition in a lease. Arguably this will
include an implied covenant, such as an implied obligation not to
commit waste.

It seems to follow logically from the decision of Atkin L.J. in
Marsden v Heyes (above), that where there is an implied obligation
on the tenant not to commit waste, where the lease can be forfeited
for breach of that obligation. However, there would be no right to
forfeit a lease where the landlord pleads his case entirely on the basis
of the commission of tortious waste.

Therefore, in summary, before a lease can be forfeited for waste
the lease must contain an express prohibition on committing waste,
or it must be at least arguable that the tenant is liable under an
implied contractual obligation for any waste they commit. Also the
lease must provide that a breach of that covenant or condition gives
rise to a right to forfeit. Otherwise, no such right is thought to exist.

As will be explained, the two types of waste set out below have
different origins leading to potentially different results but it is sometimes
difficult to identify what type of waste one is concerned with. In particular
before sound advice may be given about the most advantageous remedy
for the landlord to pursue it may be important in an individual case to

know what type of waste one is concerned with. Because of the potential for different results depending on the type of waste it is necessary to understand the difference between the two types of waste.

Voluntary waste

7–08   The term "voluntary waste" (also known as "commissive waste") refers to any deliberate or negligent acts which damage the demised premises in contrast to permissive waste (considered below) which relates to damage which occurs to the property during the demise. "Damage" means damage to the landlord's reversion. Thus the tenant will be guilty of this type of waste where they pulls down or damages all or part of the premises.

As mentioned previously, the extent to which the commission of waste is a separate obligation from the tenant-like user obligation remains unclear. In *Marsden v Heyes* (above) the Court of Appeal treated them as synonymous. It is thought that the obligation to occupy in a tenant-like manner gives rise to a right to forfeit and the fact that the commission of voluntary waste is synonymous with un-tenant-like user is therefore helpful to the landlord. If the claim were purely tortious such a right would not arise (see above). However, once a breach of an express term in the lease arises, for example an express obligation not to commit waste, it will not to be necessary to rely on any implied term or liability in tort.

7–09   *Examples of voluntary waste*

- Once any fixtures and fittings are added to demised premises they become part of the realty and any removal by the tenant will normally amount to the commission of voluntary waste (see *Mancetter v Germanson* [1986] 2 W.L.R. 871). Thus in that case the tenant's actions in removing trade fixtures were tortious. However, whether or not an item becomes a landlord's fixture is a difficult area and the reader is referred to the leading textbooks on landlord and tenant for a fuller discussion.

- The carrying out of major alterations to the premises so as to alter the thing demised may also amount to voluntary waste. In order to determine this issue the court will have to give consideration to the user permitted under the lease (see *Hyman v Rose* [1912] A.C. 623). In that case the court was concerned with a chapel which had been turned into a cinema. In the process railings had been removed and there had been internal alterations. However, despite the apparently extensive nature of those alterations, the court found the tenant had not been guilty of voluntary waste.

Reasonable wear and tear

Many repairing covenants exempt reasonable wear and tear. The   **7–10**
position is thought to be similar in the law of waste so that ordinary
and reasonable use of the premises is thought not to constitute waste.
This will be so even where in consequence serious damage occurs to
the building in which the demised premises are situated (see
Manchester Bonded Warehouse Ltd v Carr (1880) 5 C.P.D. 507).
However, the tenant who is responsible for serious damage to the
premises will face a heavy onus of establishing that it was not caused
by waste but rather by his ordinary and reasonable user of the
premises.

Remedies for breach

Remedies generally are more fully considered in Pt IV.   **7–11**

In so far as voluntary waste is relied on as a breach of covenant
the remedy of forfeiture as well as an injunction apply. In so far as
the landlord pleads his case in tort then he may bring a claim for an
injunction and for damages. The normal measure of these damages,
as for disrepair claims during the term, will be the extent to which
the reversion has been damaged (see *Whitam v Kershaw* (1886)
16 Q.B.D. 613). It is thought that in a particularly outrageous case
exemplary and/or aggravated damages may be claimed. The correct
principles for the award of these are considered in more detail in
Ch.17 para.17–22, p.207.

Permissive waste

Permissive waste involves *allowing* damage to occur, rather than   **7–12**
actually *causing* that damage, i.e. it is an act of omission rather than
commission. Thus the tenant will be liable for not plastering the
walls where they decay as a result or if the house is damaged by
tempest the tenant must normally repair it to prevent further damage
as a result. However the obligation is potentially more limited than
the repairing obligation because the tenant is only bound to keep the
premises in the state they were in when demised whereas under many
repairing covenants the tenant must *put and keep* the premises in
repair. Indeed, unless the wording of the covenant expressly limits
his obligation to its pre-existing state the tenant will be liable to put
the premises in repair as well as keep them in that state.

Several commentators have thought the law on permissive waste
largely defunct. In particular, it has been noted elsewhere (see
Dowding and Reynolds 21–20 to 20–21) that Lord Denning (in
Warren v Keen) thought that "the only duty on the tenant is the duty
to use the premises in a husband like or ... a tenant like manner" and
there was no implied obligation on the tenant beyond the obligation

of tenant-like user ([1954] 1 Q.B. 15 at 20). The Law Commission, in its report "Responsibility for the Condition and State of the Premises" (1996) (referred to below), were critical of the lack of guidance as to what was or was not permissive waste (see 10–19 et seq).

However, the law of permissive waste has since been considered in the case of *Dayani v Bromley LBC* [No.1] [1999] 3 E.G.L.R. 144, where the High Court reviewed the authorities and concluded that the law on permissive waste, although it was arcane and somewhat anomalous, was nevertheless still relevant. It had been the historic position that the law on permissive waste only applied to tenancies for years or for life rather than year to year (i.e. fixed terms not periodic terms). The judge, Judge Havery Q.C. sitting as a High Court Judge, thought that the distinction between fixed terms and periodic terms still applied. He pointed out that the origins of the law of permissive waste lay in the Statute of Marlborough 1267. Thus it is an obligation under a statute and not under the lease.

Remedies for breach

7–13   The *Dayani* decision (above) may have implications for the landlord who wishes to forfeit for the causing of permissive waste. In particular, the landlord will wish to insert a covenant or condition into the lease to the effect that the tenant shall not commit waste and a right to forfeit in the event this occurs. Otherwise, it would seem based on the decision in the *Dayani* case, that they will not be able to forfeit for permissive waste to the premises.

In so far as the obligation not to permit waste, as opposed to the commission of waste, is concerned, because it is negative in character, it doubtful that the landlord may compel the tenant to comply with his contractual obligations by obtaining an order for specific performance. Indeed, there is still a general reluctance on the part of the courts to compel a tenant to comply with his repairing obligation in a lease. That topic will be considered more fully in Ch.15. However, the landlord will be able to claim damages for his damaged reversion as they can for voluntary waste.

To keep the premises wind and watertight

In relation to a tenancy from year to year, at common law there was **7–14** thought to be an obligation on the tenant to maintain the premises in such condition that they were wind and watertight throughout the term. This was based on the old authority of *Auworth v Johnson* (1832) 5 C & P 239. However, in *Warren v Keen* (above) the Court of Appeal doubted whether this represented any separate concept from the obligation of tenant-like user. Most commentators agree with the Court of Appeal in *Warren v Keen* (see *Woodfall* 13.020) so that even in a tenancy from year to year there is no additional requirement that the tenant must keep the premises wind and watertight beyond the tenant-like user obligation. On the other hand, if there is any additional obligation to keep premises wind and watertight it is probably limited to tenancies from year to year.

In any event the requirement that a tenant under a tenancy from **7–15** year to year keep the premises wind and watertight appears to add nothing to the tenant-like user obligation in practice. Indeed, it is difficult to see how the tenant could successfully argue that they have been occupying the premises in a tenant-like manner if in fact the premises let in wind and water! Furthermore the obligation to keep the premises wind and watertight may be subject to the fair wear and tear exception, referred to above in relation to voluntary waste, whereas the obligation of tenant-like user may not be.

To permit the landlord to view the state of repair and carry out repairs

As well as being an express term in most written leases there is a **7–16** statutory right on the part of the landlord to view the condition and state of the premises in s.11(6) of the Landlord and Tenant Act 1985, where the repairing obligation under that section is implied (i.e. short residential leases). This has already been referred to in Ch.5 but there is a range of other powers to enter and view the state, particularly of residential premises, at common law and under miscellaneous legislation. These powers include:

- the power under s.116 of the Rent Act 1977 to seek an order permitting the landlord to carry out works to the premises subject to a statutory tenancy without the tenant's consent; and
- the implied right under s.16 of the Housing Act 1988 to gain access to premises let on an assured tenancy to gain access and have all reasonable facilities to execute any repairs the landlord is entitled to execute.

Even without these powers there is an implied licence at common law for the landlord to enter the premises to establish the extent of the landlord's obligation to effect repairs under the lease and subsequently effect those repairs (see per Fry J. in *Saner v Bilton* (1878) 7 Ch.815). If the tenant does not allow the landlord to do so, it will normally result in a court concluding that the landlord had discharged his contractual duty to the tenant.

The scope of this right was considered in *McGreal v Wake* [1984] 1 E.G.L.R. 42, where Lord Donaldson said that although the tenant could claim the reasonable removal and other costs of moving out this did not necessarily mean that the tenant was obliged to give his landlord exclusive possession for the entire duration of the works. The landlord's right of access was limited to what was "strictly necessary in order to do the work of repair".

Proposals for reform

7–17   The Law Commission (in "Responsibility for the Condition and State of Property" Law Com. No.238 (1996)) recommended the abolition of the implied obligation to occupy rented premises in a tenant-like manner and its replacement with an obligation on the part of the tenant to take care of the property and a comprehensive obligation on the part of the landlord to keep the premises wind and watertight throughout the term. Although generally well received, the proposals have not seen the legislative light of day.

PART II

NON-CONTRACTUAL LIABILITY

Chapter 8

Negligence, nuisance and the rule in Rylands v Fletcher

Cavalier v Pope [1906] A.C. 428 establishes that, subject to certain   **8–01**
exceptions, unless the parties expressly so contract there will be no
warranty as to the fitness of the premises for habitation as between
landlord and tenant. It also establishes that, again subject to
exceptions, there is no liability for the landlord's negligent acts or
omissions relating to the state of the property *when let*. The rule is
stated in this way in *Hill and Redman* (at D47.1):

> "where the landlord is a 'bare' landlord, i.e. was not the builder of
> the premises, but simply let unfurnished, then the rule in *Cavalier
> v Pope* [1906] AC 428, HL (that such a landlord owes no duty of
> care to a tenant as to the state of the premises when let) applies."

Thus tortious liability for the defective state of buildings when let is
generally excluded at common law. That situation is very different
from that pertaining in the modern law of negligence as it affects
many areas of daily life. However, the remainder of this chapter is
largely concerned with the exceptions which exist to the general
exclusion of liability at common law on landlord to their tenant by
considering a variety of situations where liability may attach.

It will be seen that as well as the liability which may arise under
the lease there may be liability on the part of the landlord of defective
premises in respect of his negligent acts or omissions or those of his
servants or agents, after the lease. These situations will be considered
in this chapter.

In addition, there are a number of situations where landlords,
tenants and other owners of defective premises may be liable to third
parties for the defective state of their premises which will also be
considered below.

In embarking on a discussion as to tortious liability the point needs to be made that frequently allegations of tortious and contractual liability will be made in the alternative (as they were in the case of *Southwark v Long*, referred to at p.25 above) and they do not fall within watertight compartments. Furthermore the Human Rights Act is, increasingly, being used to fill any gap in the domestic law as it applies to these situations. in particular negligence, nuisance and, so far as it is relevant to defective premises, strict liability under the rule in *Rylands v Fletcher*, are frequently indistinguishable in the modern case law. However, whilst the result may be the same whether the claimant establishes liability in tort or for breach of contract, the means by which the claimant arrives at that result may differ. The case will need be pleaded accurately, which will require the claimant to identify whether his claim is in contract or tort and what form of tortious liability. In addition, the limitation period and the extent of the recoverable loss may differ as between claims in contract and tort. Hence it is appropriate to maintain the distinction here.

Negligence

8–02   The following are the more important categories of possible negligence claim that may arise in practice in the context of defective premises. These examples are concerned principally with the relationship between owners of premises and their neighbours for the defective state of those premises. Landlords, tenants and freehold owners may be sued by their neighbours for their mode of occupation and use of their premises.

Rights and liabilities between adjoining occupiers

Liability of landlords to adjoining occupiers

8–03   In the landlord and tenant situation if the landlord has retained land or part of the building in which part has been demised to a tenant, e.g. the exterior of a block of flats or other shared building, the landlord will be liable to any third party affected by that retained part as opposed to the demised part. This will commonly arise where damage is caused to adjoining premises. The landlord in that situation will be liable to his neighbour in negligence or nuisance for foreseeable damage. Similarly the landlord may have retained responsibility for repairing the structure of the premises even if it forms part of the demise, so that if the tenant is sued they may join the landlord into the action for failing to perform his obligations under the lease.

One particular case in which this sometimes arises is where the neighbour alleges the withdrawal of support. Rights of support and the subject of party walls go beyond a discussion under the "negligence" heading and are largely concerned with various species of easements between adjoining owners but it is helpful to know something of these rights before looking specifically at the topic of negligence. The reader is referred to the texts on the two principal pieces of legislation (the Party Wall Act 1996 and the Access to Neighbouring Land Act 1992) where these topics are considered in greater details (for example Bickford - Smith and Sydenham "Party Walls: Law and Practice" Jordans 2nd edn).

Rights of support between neighbours

Where the landlord remains responsible for the structure of a **8–04** subdivided building he will be liable to his neighbour for the withdrawal of any support that neighbour enjoys from that building. They may also be liable if they dig away land at or near the boundary as a result of which the neighbour's land suffers collapse or other damage.

However, easements of support are not straightforward to acquire in the absence of an express obligation in the deeds of the servient property (the property providing the support). In the absence of such provision, rights arise naturally for land but not for buildings which are built on the land. An easement of support for buildings, for example, between a part of a building separated vertically or horizontally from another part of the same building, may be created by the deeds. More commonly these rights between neighbours will be claimed under the Prescription Act 1832 through a long period of user, usually 20 years. Assuming such prescriptive rights of support are established, any removal of that support either deliberately or, as more commonly occurs, through neglect, the owner who retains control of the structure or land that has collapsed may be sued. Where the entire premises are demised to the tenant it is the tenant who is usually responsible to the neighbour as the person in control of the premises. Whether or not the tenant may also sue his landlord will depend on the provisions in his lease.

A claim for the removal of support may be brought in negligence or nuisance (as is illustrated by *Bradburn v Lindsay* [1983] 2 All E.R. 408).

Negligence of occupiers arising out of unlawful acts of third parties

The extent to which the landlord or owner of a vacant property may **8–05** be liable for the deliberate acts of a third party to a neighbour is also a problematic area. In *King v Liverpool City Council* [1986] 1 E.G.L.R. 181 the local authority failed to board up an empty property in an area prone to vandalism. As a consequence a vandal entered the premises and damaged a rising water main causing flooding to the claimant's adjoining premises. It was held that the acts of the vandals could not have been foreseen within a day or two of the property becoming vacant. Indeed as a general rule, in the absence of a special relationship, a landlord is not responsible for the act of a third party entering the premises and causing damage to a neighbour.

The same principle has been applied in relation to a burglar who, perhaps due to the neglect of the occupier, enters property A, but then enters property B (in *Perl v Camden LBC* [1984] Q.B. 342). The Court of Appeal reiterated in that case the well-known rule that a person is not liable for the acts of independent third parties, for example an independent sub-contractor. Furthermore, even if the claimant could establish one of the duty situations arising out of a special relationship, the claimant would have to prove a high degree of forseeability on the part of the defendant and that damage was the probable result. In that case whilst the entry into property A was foreseeable the entry onto property B was not.

Landlord's right to sue adjoining occupiers

8–06   A landlord may not sue a third party for trespass in respect of premises he has let out because the tort of trespass protects the person in *possession* against third party interruption not the owner of the *reversion*. Thus if a trespass occurs, for example, by an encroachment over the boundary of premises by C into land which A has demised to B, it is B that must sue C not A.

Unlike trespass, negligence and nuisance may only be established if the claimant proves special damage. It would seem to follow that where the landlord suffers damage to his reversionary interest in the premises which he has demised; he ought to be able to recover for that loss. However, in the majority of situations it will be for the tenant to sue in respect of the negligent acts or omissions of third parties affecting his occupation of the premises. In respect of nuisance by adjoining occupiers that affects his enjoyment of the demised premises this too will be tenant's right of action and not the landlord's.

Tenant's liability to adjoining occupiers

8–07   A tenant may be sued under the Occupiers Liability Acts 1957 to 1984 as the occupier of premises demised to him by his visitor or, to a more limited degree, by a trespasser onto the land which he occupies. This form of liability is considered in Ch.10.

However beyond the important duties the tenant owes to his visitors as the occupier of premises which are exclusively let to him, there is also the potential for liability to other occupiers of the building in which the demised premises are situated. This would be determined on ordinary principles of landlord and tenant law together with the modern law of negligence and nuisance.

In *Hawkins v Dhawan* (1987) 19 H.L.R. 232, [1987] 2 E.G.L.R. 157 the Court of Appeal had to consider a case in which the tenant had allowed his washbasin to overflow causing damage to his neighbour's property below.

The claim in *Hawkins v Dhawan* was brought solely in negligence. The tenant successfully argued that he had no prior knowledge of the defect (a blocked overflow) and he was not under a duty to carry out an inspection. As the judge at first instance commented, "Just as every dog is allowed his first bite, so every basin is allowed its first overflow"! The Court of Appeal agreed. It is not entirely clear whether the neighbour affected by the overflowing washbasin would have been able to succeed in nuisance since the law of negligence and nuisance have been largely subsumed in recent years (see *Cambridge Water v Eastern Counties Leather Plc* [1994] 2 A.C. 264). Both are based on reasonable foresight of damage. *Rylands v Fletcher* also poses significant problems, as will be explained later in this chapter. Therefore the result may well have been the same even if nuisance had been relied on.

The tenant's right to sue adjoining occupiers
The tenant's right to sue adjoining owners in respect of any act or **8–08** omission that causes him loss is governed by ordinary principles of negligence, nuisance and *Rylands v Fletcher*. However, these may not be placed in neat compartments and often overlap. Often a neighbour who causes damage to the adjoining premises will be able to argue that the defect that is alleged to have caused the loss or damage was not known about before that loss or damage occurred. In theory *Rylands v Fletcher* places liability on the occupier for the escape of certain substances without proving fault on his part, but as will be seen when this doctrine is considered, the modern law effectively limits this to certain unusual situations.

Builder's and builder-landlord's liability to the tenant
Quite apart from of the liability under s.1 of the Defective **8–09** Premises Act 1972, which is considered in the next chapter, the landlord-builder and indeed the non-landlord builder of a dwelling house may be liable in negligence for his work. Whilst the rule in *Cavalier v Pope* severely limits the scope of the landlord's responsibility for injury, loss and damage where he did not build the house, there was no immunity in relation to builder-owners and builder-landlords. Broadly speaking the builder has similar liability under the principle of *Donoghue v Stevenson* as a manufacturer.

8–10 *Examples*

- In *Sharpe v Sweeting* [1963] 1 W.L.R. 665 the builder-vendor had so negligently constructed the canopy above the door of the premises that it fell onto the wife of a subsequent tenant. It was held that the negligent builder was liable in the same way as a manufacturer of a faulty product could be sued by the claimant even though she was not herself the tenant.

- On the other hand in *Auto Scooters (Newcastle) v Chambers* (1966) 197 E.G. 457 the High Court had to decide a case where a chimney breast forming part of the building demised fell onto the tenant's cars parked outside that building causing him loss. It was held that the chimney had been defective when the lease had been entered into and the tenant could be expected to take the premises as he found them.

However, there is a severe limitation of the scope of duty given the law relating to the recovery of economic loss as developed by the House of Lords in *Murphy v Brentwood DC* [1990] 1 A.C. 398, 1 W.L.R. 414 H.L.. Although that case has been widely criticised and has been practically difficult to apply it remains good law at the date of publication in relation to negligence claims. Any claim to rectify defects left by the builder or landlord builder will normally be characterised as pure economic loss. Whereas the owner, be he freehold owner or tenant, will be able to claim for the damage he suffers to his person or property for the negligent acts or omissions of the builder he will not be able to claim the cost of putting those defects right.

There is an important qualification to the prohibition on recovering for economic loss. Where, for example, as a result of the way the building was built, the premises create potential hazard to an owner of adjoining premises, the owner of the defective premises may well be able to sue the builder of those premises in negligence in respect of his potential liability to the neighbour, including the cost of rectifying those defects (see *Murphy v Brentwood* [1990] 1 A.C. 398 at 475 F-G). However, their Lordships were considering a point of principle and the situation postulated did not arise on the facts before them.

Nuisance

The landlord will rarely be liable in nuisance to his tenant, who will **8–11** usually be able to claim against his landlord on one of the more obvious bases referred to above, for example a breach of the obligation to repair or maintain the premises. The tenant is generally more likely to be able to establish a breach of one of the express or implied terms of the lease or establish tortious liability under s.4 of the Defective Premises Act 1972 than pursue a common law nuisance claim. Usually such liability will fall within the concept of caveat lessee, i.e. let the lessee beware of any defects existing at the date the lease was entered into.

However, the tenant as the occupier of the premises may well be liable to third parties who are affected by his nuisance behaviour and may, as the occupier, be able to sue third parties who cause him a nuisance.

Nature of the tort of nuisance

Nuisance protects the tenant or other occupier in his occupation of **8–12** land. Thus it not only protects the right to peaceful occupation of the land but also the right to enjoy the legal rights ancillary to that occupation, for example easements granted to him. Nuisance may be established where the tenant or other occupier shows that the tortfeasor has created a nuisance in one of the ways described below. It is for the person causing and continuing the nuisance to take reasonable steps to abate that nuisance. The onus then shifts to the tortfeasor to show that he cannot by taking those reasonable steps abate the nuisance (see *Southwark LBC v Long* [2002] EWCA Civ 403 at para.65). If that onus is not discharged the appropriate order for the court to make is for the tortfeasor to take reasonable steps to abate the nuisance.

When liability arises

Liability and rights of the tenant
Just as the tenant may, in a number of circumstances, be liable to **8–13** third parties for negligent acts or omissions on land which he occupies, the tenant as the occupier of land let to him may be liable in nuisance to third parties. The tenant may also sue his neighbour where he is in occupation of land and suffers a material degree of discomfort as a result of the acts or omissions of a neighbour. The key point is that the action in nuisance must be brought by the person with rights over the land in respect of the other party's interference with those rights, be they limited rights in the form of easements or

rights in the nature of exclusive possession of the land (see *Hunter v Canary Wharf* [1997] A.C. 655 at 702). The tenant is therefore entitled to sue his landlord in respect of his interference with easements granted under the lease (see *Woodfall* 14. 031).

Where such interference is established, or there is a genuine fear that in the immediate future it will be established, the tenant is entitled to an injunction to abate the nuisance or prevent the nuisance continuing.

Liability and rights of landlord

8–14   Generally speaking, liability for injury, loss and damage to a third party caused by nuisance or negligence falls on the tenant, as the occupier, whether under the Occupiers Liability Act 1957 or at common law. However, the landlord may want to sue the tenant if as a result of his acts or omissions his reversion is damaged. Also there are a number of instances where the landlord may be liable for a nuisance causing or continuing damage to his neighbour even where subsequently the premises from which the nuisance emanated are let.

In particular, a landlord may be liable if:

- He *causes* a nuisance by creating it in the first place. He may not by granting his tenant a lease pass the blame onto that tenant, although the tenant may by his lease assume contractual responsibility for putting it right (as in *Brew Bros v Snax* [1970] 1 Q.B. 612, see below). The landlord may ultimately be liable for continuing that nuisance if he cannot establish that the tenant was bound to put it right or if the defects giving rise to liability are within a part of the premises retained by the landlord.

- He *continues* a nuisance by adopting it or authorising its continuance. Just as a freehold owner is bound to take reasonable steps to abate a nuisance that he is aware of (as in *Sedleigh-Denfield v O'Callaghan* [1940] A.C. 880 at 894) a landlord who knows of a nuisance that is present on a property that falls into his possession by reversion, who fails to take adequate steps to abate that nuisance, will be liable. He will also be taken to have authorised the nuisance where he buys the reversion from an earlier landlord who caused the nuisance with knowledge that a nuisance is being caused. In this case he may be said to have adopted that nuisance. This is illustrated by *Sampson v Hodson-Pressinger* [1981] 3 All E.R. 710.

   In that case the landlord laid tiles on a terrace which formed part of the first defendant's demise. Noise nuisance was caused to the tenant below as a consequence of the manner in which those tiles had been laid. The landlord then sold his reversion to the second defendant.

It was held that the new landlord (the second defendant) had adopted the nuisance and was in breach of the covenant for quiet enjoyment on acquiring the reversion. It was also held that by accepting rent from the first defendant, who continued to occupy the flat from which the noise emanated, the second defendant impliedly authorised the continuance of the nuisance. This was so even though nuisance would be caused by ordinary user of the terrace as opposed to excessive or unreasonable user. As a result of the original landlord's work to the terrace on the flat above, it was not capable of being used in a way that would not cause some nuisance to the flat below.

The landlord has the same right to pursue the tenant for nuisance, or his tenant's visitors where they have committed a nuisance with the consent of that tenant, as the tenant has to pursue his landlord for nuisance affecting his occupation of the demised premises. However, the landlord must first establish some damage to his reversion and these claims are relatively rare in practice.

Common categories of nuisance by landlords

In practice, liability of a landlord for nuisance is likely to fall into one of the following categories: **8–15**

Nuisance in common or retained parts affecting demised premises
One exceptional case where nuisance may be relied on in a claim by the tenant against the landlord is where the defects arose in the common parts of a building of which the demised premises form part: **8–16**

- In cases to which s.11(1A) of the Landlord and Tenant Act 1985 applies, or in cases where there is an express repairing obligation on the landlord in relation to areas within his control, it will rarely be necessary to rely on the tort of nuisance. Under that Act there is an obligation to repair the structure and exterior, including, in relation to leases granted on or after 15th January 1989, the common parts. However, cases will arise from time to time where it must be shown that the landlord has notice of the defect in question, before he may be liable to repair under this repairing covenant. The landlord may nevertheless be liable for causing, continuing or adopting a nuisance even if the requirements of valid notice of disrepair would not necessarily be made out provided the damage which occurs to that tenant was reasonably foreseeable. In *Sharpe v Manchester City Council* (1977) 5 H.L.R. 71 the common parts were infested with Cockroaches which in turn infested the demised flat. As the landlord retained the common parts he was liable for the defect giving rise to the infestation.

• In *Tennant Radiant Heat Ltd v Warrington DC* [1988] 1 E.G.L.R. 41 the claimant was the lessee of part of a warehouse building. The roof of the premises, which was outside the demise, collapsed due to an accumulation of rainwater. In particular the water did not drain away due to certain outlets being blocked. The tenant put its argument on the basis of an implied term to give business efficacy to the lease but succeeded in the Court of Appeal on the basis of common law nuisance or negligence. The court held that, save insofar as the damage to the tenant's goods arose as a result of a failure by the tenant to perform its own repairing obligation, the damage to the tenant had been caused by a defect in an area within the landlord's control. Although the landlord did not have an express repairing obligation in relation to that part of the premises the outlets that became blocked gave rise to a reasonably foreseeable risk of damage. Since they were within the landlord's control the landlord would be liable.

• However in the first instance county court case of *Jackson v JH Watson Investment Property Ltd* [2008] P. & C.R. D.G. 17 (also reported at [2008] Env. L.R. 30) the tenant tried to attach liability to the landlord in respect of a defect to a water pipe in the common parts of a converted mansion block which caused water to ingress into his nearby flat. The judge held that the case fell within the *caveat lessee* rule. The claimant had taken his lease shortly before assignment from the landlord, which had granted him the lease, to a new landlord, the defendant. The defect in question was present at that time of that assignment and at the earlier date when the lease had been granted. The defendant therefore argued successfully that if the original landlord could not have been liable for causing the nuisance because it had been present when the lease had been granted, the assignee of the reversion could not be liable for adopting that nuisance. Therefore the tenant had to be taken as having bought the flat subject to the defect in question.

In giving judgment the judge (Judge Behrens) considered

he was bound by the case of *Baxter v Camden* [2001] 1 Q.B. 1. As the editors of *Hill and Redman* have pointed out (Bulletin 68) that case illustrates the inadequate state of the present law in that the landlord is the only person who could put right the defect but he would have no incentive to do so given that most service charge provisions allow the landlord to recover the cost of repairs and not improvements. Both sides agreed the was not a repair because the premises had been let in that state and the repairing obligation would be by reference to that date.

Nuisance at the date of the lease-liability to third parties

Where the landlord grants a lease and the premises demised are a **8–17** source of a nuisance to a third party on the adjoining highway or to an adjoining owner caused by that landlord's acts or omissions, the landlord will normally be liable. The landlord may not absolve himself from liability to that third party merely by placing a repairing obligation on his tenant in the lease. However, the landlord may be able to pass the blame onto the tenant when the covenant becomes effective, e.g. because the tenant by covenanting to repair the premises was also liable to put the premises into repair. In practice this will mean that provided the defect causing injury loss or damage is within the landlord's control he may be successfully sued by the third party even if as a matter of contract law the landlord can recover the cost from the tenant, for example under the service charge provision in the lease.

If the landlord is sued he will want to bring the tenant into the action under Pt 20 of the CPR so that the appropriate apportionment of liability may be made in one set of proceedings. If the lease is one which requires the tenant to keep in repair the relevant part, which includes putting that part into repair, the landlord may pass all the blame onto the tenant provided a reasonable time had elapsed for the tenant to effect the necessary repair.

On this principle, in *Brew Bros v Snax* [1970] 1 Q.B. 612 at 639 the landlord was held liable for a wall that was defective at the start of the tenancy, which caused subsequent injury, loss or damage to a neighbour. It was held that the landlord ought to have known of its defective state at the date of the tenancy and was liable for causing a nuisance.

Nuisance arising after the commencement of the lease

Where a landlord let premises abutting a highway, but did not impose **8–18** a repairing obligation on his tenant in respect of that part, he would not be liable to the tenant's visitor for an accident which occurred within that part of the demised premises and not on the adjoining highway (*Howard and Wife v Walker and Lake* [1947] K.B. 860). Goddard C.J. made it clear that the decision may have been different if the accident had occurred on the highway. Thus if the claimant had been passing over the pavement, but had deviated from her intended course into the area where the accident occurred, which was within the curtilage of the landlord's property, there may well have been liability on the part of the landlord. But the position was otherwise on the facts as they were found to be. In particular the injured claim was there at the invitation of the tenant and within the area demised to him. The dispute would now be litigated under the Occupier's Liability Act 1957 but the wider principles have not altered.

Where premises are let on a lease that places a full repairing obligation on the tenant, once a reasonable opportunity has passed to effect the necessary repair the landlord will be able to pass the blame to the tenant. However, as has been seen, there may be cases where there is no liability under the repairing obligation but where the landlord has retained adjoining land or the common parts and is liable in nuisance.

Liability of landlords for acts of tenants towards other tenants or neighbours

8–19 Obviously, a tenant is directly liable to other tenants for the nuisance he has caused them and a landlord is directly liable to others where the manner of his occupation of his own land affects his tenants. However, a problem that has had to be grappled with in recent years has been the extent to which the landlord is required to intervene to prevent one tenant causing a nuisance to another tenant or to another occupier who is not a tenant of that landlord. In other words, to what extent is the landlord liable for the nuisance behaviour of his tenant?

8–20   The solution to that problem has generally been favourable to landlords as is illustrated by the following cases:

  - In *Hussain v Lancaster City Council* [2000] Q.B. 1 the court was concerned with nuisance caused by tenants on a council estate and their households. The council was the landlord of those tenants, who were secure tenants. It was held the council were not liable for failing to control the unruly tenants and others who were causing racial and other abuse to Mr Hussain, the owner of a shop on the council estate in question. The tenants and their households had not been using their land at the time and it was not within the scope of the law of nuisance for the landlord to control their behaviour to other owners, given that the local authority had neither authorised nor adopted their behaviour. Mr Hussain had argued unsuccessfully that the landlord had failed to use its powers to control nuisance behaviour including bringing possession proceedings against those responsible.

• In the leading case of *Tanner v Southwark LBC, Baxter v Camden LBC* [No.2] [2001] 1 A.C. 1 Southwark were held not to be liable for noise nuisance caused by their tenants to adjoining tenants in the same council block. The noise was as a result of their normal use of the flat from which the noise eminated (which had inadequate insulation). Nor can a landlord be liable for letting to a "problem tenant" unless he authorised the tenant to act in a particular manner. The position is even clearer where the tenant *becomes* a problem tenant *after* the grant. Nor would the covenant for quiet enjoyment normally be breached in this situation. Lord Millett summarised the law thus (at 22 A–B):

> "The person or persons directly responsible for the activities in question are liable; but so too is anyone who authorised them. Landlords have been held liable for nuisances committed by their tenants on this basis. It is not enough for them to be aware of the nuisance and take no steps to prevent it. They must either participate directly in the commission of the nuisance, or they must be taken to have authorised it by letting the property: see *Malzy v Eichholz* [1916] 2 KB 308. But they cannot be held liable in tort for having authorised the commission of an actionable nuisance unless what they have authorised is an actionable nuisance. The logic of the proposition is obvious. A landlord cannot be liable to an action for authorising his tenant to do something that would not be actionable if he did it himself."

But recently (in *X v Hounslow LBC* [2008] EWHC 1168) a High Court judge was able to place blame on the landlord for tormenting and harassment of its tenants by youths from the locality. This was on the basis that the landlord owed a duty of care to the tenants under the principle in the *Caparo Industries v Dickman* ([1990] 2 A.C. 605) case. However, that case seems likely to be appealed.

Entry to abate nuisance

The right of entry to abate a nuisance which exists at common law is **8–21** exercisable by and against the occupier who is responsible for that nuisance. It seems a tenant may enter the landlord's retained part of a building of which the demised premises form part for the purposes of abating a nuisance and, presumably, the landlord would enjoy the same common law right against the tenant. Both would enjoy that right against a third party causing them nuisance. Under this principle of common law abatement, in *Abbahall v Smee* [2003] 2 E.G.L.R. 66 it was held that the owner of the ground floor unit was able to enter the upper floors for the purposes of preventing damage to his part of the premises and indeed he was given an injunction for this purpose.

Rylands v Fletcher

8–22   The rule in *Rylands v Fletcher*, where it applies, creates strict liability for the occupier of land in respect of the escape of non-natural substances. This type of liability, effectively an offshoot of the law of nuisance referred to above, remains relevant despite the trend in recent years to limit its ambit. For example *Rylands v Fletcher* has been held to apply where large quantities of highly flammable plastic foam, were stored on land (owned by the defendants) together with the products manufactured with that foam a large amount of which caught fire.

It has also been held that there could be liability for the escape of fire onto adjoining land (*LMS v Styrene Packaging Ltd* [2005] EWHC 2065 (TCC). In that case the fire in question was accidentally caused by an employee of the defendant's. It caused extensive damage to the premises owned by 2nd and 3rd claimants, which were rented to the 1st claimant.

Cases where *Rylands v Fletcher* liability does not arise

8–23   *Rylands v Fletcher* does not apply to acts of God. This is illustrated by *Nichols v Marsland* [1876] 2 Ex. D. 1, where a dam failed as a result of abnormal rainfall. But for that abnormal rainfall the dam would have operated normally. Therefore there could be no liability on the part of the owner of the land to his neighbour. However, the act of God exception is rarely applied in the modern case law and its continued usefulness has been doubted.

More pertinent to liability for defective premises are those cases where, as frequently occurs between occupiers of flats and other buildings in multiple occupation, there is an escape of water seeping into an adjacent or subjacent unit. *Rylands v Fletcher* does not apply to the use of ordinary domestic appliances for accumulating water within buildings such as boilers, cisterns and tanks nor the pipes and vessels connected with them (see Clerk and Lindsell 21–42). Where one occupier suffers the ingress of water from premises above, he must prove negligence or nuisance and cannot rely on *Rylands v Fletcher*.

Examples: **8–24**

- A blocked gutter on the roof of a building overflowed damaging the claimant's premises beneath. It was held that his landlord, who was in control of the roof, could not be liable unless the tenant could prove that this was foreseeable and on the facts he could not (*Bishop v Consolidated London Properties* (1933) 102 LJKB 257).

- The tenant of the second floor of a house (A) caused damage to the business premises occupied by the tenant (B) on the ground floor below when his water closet overflowed. It was held that A was not liable under the principle of *Rylands v Fletcher*. Furthermore negligence could not be established because the defect could not have been found without close inspection and the defendant A had not been aware of the defect before damage occurred (*Ross v Fedden* (1872) L.R. 7 Q.B. 661).

Furthermore, the majority of modern authorities have restricted the ambit of *Rylands v Fletcher* to cases where the innocent party cannot for whatever reason adequately guard against the risk by obtaining insurance and there has been a tendency for the law of negligence, nuisance and *Rylands v Fletcher* to be subsumed into one. Thus in *Cambridge Water v Eastern Counties Leather Ltd* [1994] 2 A.C. 264 (pollution of borehole by release of solvent from defendant's factory) and *Transco Plc v Stockport MDC* [2004] 2 A.C. 1 (escape of water causing an embankment to collapse) the House of Lords have suggested that in all cases where such insurance was available or statutory provision was made it was unnecessary to rely on *Rylands v Fletcher*. Otherwise reasonable forseeability would need to be proved.

Chapter 9

Tortious liability of builders and landlords under the Defective Premises Act 1972 and other statutes

In this chapter, a type of tortious liability of builders and landlords is **9–01** considered. The Defective Premises Act came about as a result of the recommendations of the Law Commission in Civil Liability of Vendors and Lessors for Defective Premises (Law Com. No.40). A second report by the Commission ("Obligations of Landlords and Tenants" Law Com. No.67) was never implemented and the law remains somewhat unsatisfactory, for reasons that will be explained more fully below. These unsatisfactory features have been more recently identified by the Law Commission in LC 238 "Landlord and Tenant: Responsibility for the State and Condition of Property" (1996).

The duty created by s.1 of the Act overlaps with the duty that a builder of premises owes at common law in respect of premises which he has built as well as the liability which arises under certain other statutes, for example, potentially, under the Building Act 1984. It therefore seems appropriate to consider the position at common law before considering the Act in greater detail.

Liability under s.4 is of particular importance because it extends the class of persons to whom the landlord may be liable and provides a broader definition of notice than that under most repairing covenants. There is an area of overlap between this Act and the Occupiers Liability Acts considered in the next chapter. However, as a general rule liability under the latter is wider than under the former and liability of occupiers to their visitors is not expressly related to the repairing obligation, as is the liability of landlord's to tenants and their visitors in respect of the defective state of the premises under s.4 of the Defective Premises Act.

Before considering the Act in detail it is necessary to have some understanding of the nature of liability at common law and it is therefore that issue which will be considered first.

Liability of the builder to the purchaser in negligence at common law

9–02 In contract the starting position remains the caveat emptor principle. Generally, a seller of a property, be it a dwelling house or other accommodation, is only liable for latent rather than patent defects which he fails to reveal. Latent defects are those that would not become apparent to a buyer on reasonable inspection whereas patent defects are those which would be obvious on that prudent inspection. This is reflected in the various conditions of sale which apply to a sale of freehold property. In particular, cl.3.2.1 of the Standard Conditions of Sale, incorporated by the National Conditions of Sale, 23rd edn, provides that the purchaser is expected to be aware of physical defects and specifically:

> "… accepts the property in the physical state it is in at the date of the contract unless the seller is building or converting."

However, there are important instances where the builder/provider of the accommodation may be liable at common law (although the extent to which this is still the case in the light of *Murphy v Brentwood DC* [1998] 1 A.C. 398 will need to be considered later). For example in *Hone v Benson* [1978] 2 E.G.L.R. 164 the judge, Judge Edgar Fay Q.C., held the defendant's liable for the building work they had carried out to that accommodation, consisting of the construction of the building and the installation of the water system. This negligent building work subsequently caused the claimant loss and damage. It was held that the seller was not absolved from tortious liability by reason of an exclusion clause, in similar terms to the clause above (in that case under the Law Society's General Conditions of Sale 1970 edn).

A builder of premises, which he sells or lets, is liable in tort for the defects in those premises even though those defects were latent (*Anns v London Borough of Merton* [1978] A.C. 728) but this liability has been significantly abrogated by the decision of the House of Lords in *Murphy v Brentwood DC* [1991] 1 A.C. 398 in relation to claims for pure economic loss. To what extent the builder or other professional is liable for the losses which flow from the negligence or breach of duty is a complicated question in the light of the *Murphy* decision.

This issue will therefore be considered later in the chapter. However, it seems reasonably clear that liability under the Defective Premises Act is largely unaffected by that decision. Pursuing a remedy under that Act will be the primary means by which the purchaser of a dwelling and his successors in title within the limitation period may attach liability to the negligent builder or, in some cases, negligent construction professional.

Liability of the landlord-builder at common law

The nature of the liability on landlord-builders is illustrated by **9–03** *Targett v Torfaen BC* [1992] 3 All E.R. 27. In that case the local authority landlord had been responsible for designing and building a house which was let to the claimant. The house had no handrail and no lighting on the steps leading to the entrance to the property. The claimant had complained of the state of the steps but nothing had been done about it. The Court of Appeal followed the well-known principle (established in *Rimmer v Pearson* [1984] 1 All E.R. 930) that the landlord, designer and builder would be liable in such circumstances and rejected the submission that such liability could not survive the decision of the House of Lords in *Murphy v Brentwood DC* (where their lordships had refused a claim to the cost of rectification of defects in a dwelling, based on negligence, on the grounds that it was a claim for pure economic loss). However, liability will be limited by the principle in *Murphy* to the physical injury to the person or his possessions flowing from the negligent acts or omissions complained of. At common law there will be no liability on the part of the builder, seller or landlord for pure economic loss.

Commenting on the nature of that liability in Targett, Leggatt L.J. indicated (at pp.34–35) that it is the latency of the defect that founds liability because there is no possibility of intermediate examination either by the claimant or anyone else. Otherwise the chain of causation may be broken, although this would not necessarily be so. Indeed the chain of causation was not broken on the facts of that case. The landlord was liable for any defect to any person that they "ought reasonably have in contemplation as likely to be affected by such defect". On the facts of that case the chain of causation had not been broken by the fact that the tenant knew of the defect which subsequently caused him injury.

Therefore, in the landlord and tenant situation, the tenant who suffers injury can recover damages against the builder landlord on the principle in the *Rimmer* case. The tortfeasor would only be able to avoid liability where the claimant, having had an opportunity for examination, failed to take any steps to remedy the defect where it would have been reasonable for them to do so. In some cases this may break the chain of causation. Alternatively, there may be a finding of contributory negligence in that situation. Thus, in *Torfean* the Court of Appeal found primary liability on the part of the local authority but upheld the judge's finding of 25 per cent contributory negligence.

The statutory duty to build dwellings properly

Who does the duty apply to?

9–04   Section 1 of the DPA 1972 places an obligation on the builder of a dwelling to exercise reasonable care and skill. The duty also applies to a wider class of construction professionals carrying out work in connection with the provision of a dwelling but not merely suppliers of materials used in that dwelling. Thus the section catches architects, engineers and builders, including those builders who carry out a one-off construction or conversion project (see s.1(4)).

What type of work is covered?

9–05   The Act imposes liability in respect of those carrying out work "*in connection with the <u>provision</u> of a dwelling*" which will not cover those who carry out repair work to an existing dwelling (*Jacobs v Morton and Partners* (1994) 72 B.L.R. 92). But, as stated above, the duty will apply to those who carry out "conversions" (i.e. turning buildings into dwellings) as opposed to the restructuring of existing dwellings.

Which premises are included?

A "*dwelling*" has been defined (in *Catlin Estates Ltd v Carter Jonas (a firm)* [2005] EWHC 2315 (TCC)) as "a building used as a dwelling not being a building that was used predominantly for commercial or industrial purposes". In that case the argument that the building in question was not a dwelling, so as to avoid liability under s.1 of the 1972 Act, failed. As well as deciding this important point of construction the case also contains a discussion over the meaning of "fit for habitation" in which Judge Toulmin drew the distinction between premises which were "substantially defective", as in that case and premises which were actually "unfit".

The Act does not apply to work to premises which are to be used partly for business and partly for residential purposes, as such premises would not be dwellings, whereas work to a particular dwelling unit within a building in multiple occupation which enables it to be used as a dwelling will be within the Act.

The duty under s.1 does not apply to premises constructed under an "approved scheme" (s.2(3)) provided that it is stated in a document of an approved type that the requirements as to design or construction imposed by or under the scheme have been, or appear to have been, substantially complied with (see s.2(2)). "Approved" means approved by the Secretary of State. However, it appears that no schemes have been approved for many years. Those that are approved include the NHBC schemes of 1973, 1975, 1977 and 1979 (see the House Building Standards (Approved Scheme etc) Order 1973, SI 1973/1843; the House Building Standards (Approved Scheme etc) Order 1975, SI 1975/1402; and the House Building Standards (Approved Scheme etc) Order 1977, SI 1977/642). **9–06**

Nature and scope of the duty

This poses one of the more difficult questions in relation to the Act. Section 1 places an important duty on builders and construction professionals to exercise reasonable care and skill in carrying out work. In particular a builder or construction professional has to ensure that the "work which he takes on is done ... in a professional manner, with proper materials and so that as regards that work the dwelling will be *fit for habitation* when completed" (DPA 1972, s.1(1)). **9–07**

The duty is owed to the person who employs the builder or professional and to every person who acquires an interest whether legal or equitable. The duty of care owed to persons who might reasonably be expected to be affected by defects in the premises, created by the carrying out of that work, is not abated by the subsequent disposal of the premises by the person who owed the duty (see s.3).

Is it necessary for the claimant to show that in every case the dwelling is unfit for human habitation before they can bring a claim under s.1? HH Judge Essr Lewis Q.C. in *Thompson v Clive Alexander and Partners* (1992) 59 B.L.R. 81 thought that in every case this was something the claimant had to prove. In *Catlin Estates Ltd v Carter Jonas (a firm)* (above) Toulmin J. was invited not to follow that decision but he failed explicitly to rule on the point.

It appears from Judge Esyr Lewis's decision in the earlier case that the words "fit for habitation" qualify both the requirement to perform the work in a workmanlike manner and the requirement to use proper materials and that this remains the law (see *Halsbury's Laws* "Building Contracts, Architects, Engineers and Builders" Vol.4(2) (reissue) at para.77). However, the decision has been criticised and it is generally thought to be liable to be reconsidered by a higher court.

The duty at common law is threefold: (i) to exercise proper workmanship or professional methods; (ii) to use proper materials; and (iii) to produce a dwelling fit for habitation. However, the duty under s.1 has been held in the above case to impose a single standard on those whom it affects: that the dwelling should be on completion fit for habitation. Therefore, in important respects the duty owed under s.1 may be more limited than the duty at common law.

It has been held by the Court of Appeal in *Andrews v Schooling* [1991] 3 All E.R. 723 that liability under s.1 of the 1972 Act applied both to misfeasance and non-feasance, i.e. to acts of commission as well as acts of omission.

What is the limitation period?

9–08   This is set out in s.1(5) of the Act. That section provides that any cause of action in respect of a breach of duty imposed by the section shall be deemed to have accrued when the dwelling was completed and goes on to provide that "if after that time a person who has done work for or in connection with the provision of the dwelling does further work to rectify the work he has already done, any such cause of action in respect of that further work shall be deemed for those purposes to have accrued at the time when the further work was finished."

In *Catlin v Carter Jonas* (above) at para.299 of his judgment, Toulmin J. had to consider these words in the context of work after completion. He followed *Alexander and Anor v Mercouris* [1979] 1 W.L.R. 1270 and decided that the cause of action accrued on the date the person who is alleged to be liable took on the work. As he pointed out, this may constitute an advantage for many employers because they will not have to await completion of the further work to the dwelling before they can sue and they can do so as soon as the builder or other professional falls below the required standard.

However, in *Alderson v Beetham* [2003] EWCA Civ 408 (considered in Emden's Building Contracts at 594) the Court of Appeal held that the limitation period under s.1(5) of the Act would, on the facts of that case, run from the date that the builder *last* carried out work to the dwelling and not from the date that the property was built. There the builder had returned to the property to carry out remedial works after he had completed the property. That work had not been completed to the required standard. It was held that a new cause of action accrued from the date that the builder had carried out fresh work to the building. He had returned to the property during the original limitation period and therefore the case fell within the words of s.1(5) of the Act. Effectively the claimant could claim in respect of both the original work and the fresh work undertaken.

It has been held that the Latent Damage Act 1986 does not apply to claims under s.1 of the DPA, because that provision (inserted into the Limitation Act 1980 at s.14A) applies only to a claim for negligence at common law and not to breach of a statutory duty (see *Warner v Basildon Corporation* 7 Const. L.J. 146 and HHJ Humphrey Lloyd Q.C. in *Payne v John Setchell Ltd* at [2002] PNLR 7 at paras H7 and 57). This has the important consequence that although liability under the Act is extensive it is subject to a strict six-year limitation period.

Can the employer or purchaser recover for economic loss?

In the law of negligence, following the decision of the House of **9–09** Lords in *Murphy v Brentwood Council* [1991] 1 A.C. 398 (also considered in Ch.15), the claimant may only claim for physical damage to his person or his possessions and not for the cost of reinstating the premises themselves. A potential problem under s.1 of the Act relates to the fact that the claimant may wish to recover for economic loss, for example the cost of rectifying a building rather than damage to his person or possessions. Would such a claim fall foul of the restriction on the recovery of damages for economic loss in tort?

In *Murphy v Brentwood* [1991] 1 A.C. 398 the House of Lords held that the restriction on the recovery of damages for economic loss did not apply in the case of claims under s.1 (per Lord Bridge at 480 H-B). Nor does the restriction on the recovery of pure economic loss apply to a claim, for example against a construction professional, under the principle in *Hedley Byrne v Heller* [1964] A.C. 465 (negligent misstatement arising out of a special relationship).

In practice, however, the buyer of a new but defective house will often be better advised to pursue the developer in contract and/or claim under the relevant NHBC scheme that applies to that property rather than pursue the negligent builder in tort. This is because of the superior limitation period that would normally apply to such a scheme (normally two to ten years after completion, the builder being liable for the initial two years the remaining period being covered by the scheme). The advantages of the NHBC scheme include its informality and lack of expense on the part of the house owner. In addition there is limited insurance in the event of the builder's insolvency, which would normally be fatal to any litigation claim.

Section 3 of the 1972 Act provides that liability is not abated by the disposal of the premises by the original purchaser or employer.

The Supply of Goods and Services Act 1982

9–10 Although this Act would be properly considered in books about consumer and contract law rather than a book about defective premises, s.13 of the Act has some relevance to the subject. It applies to goods supplied and services rendered in relation to the provision of a dwelling as it applies to the provision of other goods and services. It creates a duty on those providing such services to do so with reasonable care and skill. This implied warranty would therefore apply to the builder of a dwellinghouse to achieve this minimum standard and complete the work within a reasonable time (s.14) in return for payment of a reasonable charge (s.15). However, any implied term as to the supply of a service under the Act may be excluded by express provision in the contract provided that exclusion complies with the Unfair Contract Terms Act 1977 (s.16).

The seller / builder

9–11 In addition to the above general implied warranties a builder who contracts to build and then sell a house impliedly warrants that they will do so in a good and workmanlike manner, using proper materials and so that it is fit for habitation (see Denning M.R. in *Hancock v BW Brazier (Annerly) Ltd* 1 W.L.R. 1317). This is a collateral warranty which does not merge on completion.

The implied warranty does not apply to the sale of an already built house even on new housing estate but it does apply where a house is sold whilst it is in the course of construction.

This implied warranty may be excluded by the contract. Thus in *Lynch v Thomas* [1956] 1 W.L.R. 303 it was held that where the contract referred to the house having been built in accordance with the specifications and plans, the purchaser could not rely on the implied warranty when a defect appeared. This was because there was an express term, which was by its nature more limited than the implied term. The claimant could not rely on the implied warranty as to fitness for human habitation.

Goods

9–12 As well as the above terms as to the supply of services there are implied terms as to the provision of goods, which may be relevant, where, for example, the property is a new build with some furniture included. Section 4(2) of the Supply of Goods and Services Act 1982 places a duty on all those supplying goods to ensure they are of "satisfactory quality" (formerly "merchantable quality"). This extends to minor defects.

Section 4(5) provides that where goods are supplied with the intention that they should have a certain purpose they must be fit for that purpose. The implied term as to fitness to purpose applies wherever the consumer relies on the skill and judgment of the supplier of those goods but not otherwise. This will include goods and services supplied in connection with the provision of a dwelling-house. The buyer of a new house would, ordinarily, rely on the skill and judgment of the seller where that seller is a professional house builder. Breach of the implied term gives rise to a theoretical right to reject the goods; theoretical in the case of property transactions because it most unlikely that the purchaser would wish to reject the house they have bought on the basis of some defect to the chattels within it.

Liability of landlords under the Defective Premises Act 1972

The duty to tenants and third parties

At common law a landlord who had not built or designed a dwelling, **9–13** which he lets, owed no duty of care in negligence. The extent of his contractual liability would depend on the covenants in the tenancy agreement. Contractual liability would not apply, for example, where the tenant's wife sustained injury, loss or damage due to the defective state of the premises, as it would have been restricted to those to whom the obligation to repair is owed, i.e. the tenant (see *Cavalier v Pope* [1906] A.C. 428 and *Woodfall*, "Landlord and Tenant" para.15.033). The Defective Premises Act 1972 was therefore enacted to render the landlord liable for personal injury, loss and damage to all visitors to the premises. This is considerably wider than the right to sue in negligence at common law.

However, statutory liability is closely related to the extent of the repairing obligation. Thus a tenant or a member of the tenant's family who suffers accidental injury, but who cannot establish a breach of the repairing covenant or the extended form of liability under the Act, may still be left without a remedy. Therefore, it remains relevant to know something of the common law position (considered earlier) before considering the position under the 1972 Act. It also remains relevant to know something of the terms of the lease when advising about the ambit of s.4.

The nature of the duty under section 4

In practice the duty under s.4 is the most important single basis upon **9–14** which a landlord may be made liable for injury, loss and damage to his tenant and tenant's family. Unfortunately, despite its importance, the Act is sometimes poorly understood by practitioners and the fact that many claims are of modest value has meant that relatively few cases have gone to the higher courts.

It is worth setting out the section in full before considering its more important components.

9–15   Section 4 provides:

> "(1) Where premises are let under a tenancy which puts on the landlord an obligation to the tenant for the maintenance or repair of the premises, the landlord owes to all persons who might reasonably be expected to be affected by defects in the state of the premises a duty to take such care as is reasonable in all the circumstances to see that they are reasonably safe from personal injury or from damage to their property caused by a relevant defect.
>
> (2) The said duty is owed if the landlord knows (whether as the result of being notified by the tenant or otherwise) or if he ought in all the circumstances to have known of the relevant defect.
>
> (3) In this section 'relevant defect' means a defect in the state of the premises existing at or after the material time and arising from, or continuing because of, an act or omission by the landlord which constitutes or would if he had had notice of the defect, have constituted a failure by him to carry out his obligation to the tenant for the maintenance or repair of the premises; and for the purposes of the foregoing provision "the material time" means the earliest of—
>
> > (a) where the tenancy commenced before this Act, the commencement of this Act; and
> >
> > (b) in all other cases, the earliest of the following times, that is to say—
> >
> > > (i) the time when the tenancy commences;
> > >
> > > (ii) the time when the tenancy agreement is entered into;
> > >
> > > (iii) the time when possession is taken of the premises in contemplation of the letting.

(4) Where premises are let under a tenancy which expressly or impliedly gives the landlord the right to enter the premises to carry out any description of maintenance or repair of the premises, then, as from the time when he first is, or by notice or otherwise can put himself, in a position to exercise the right and so long as he is or can put himself in that position, he shall be treated for the purposes of subsections (1) to (3) above (but for no other purpose) as if he were under an obligation to the tenant for that description of maintenance or repair of the premises; but the landlord shall not owe the tenant any duty by virtue of this subsection in respect of any defect in the state of the premises arising from, or continuing because of, a failure to carry out an obligation expressly imposed on the tenant by the tenancy.

(5) For the purposes of this section obligations imposed or rights given by any enactment in virtue of a tenancy shall be treated as imposed or given by the tenancy.

(6) This section applies to a right of occupation given by contract or any enactment and not amounting to a tenancy as if the right were a tenancy, and "tenancy" and cognate expressions shall be construed accordingly."

Key points

Under s.4 of the 1972 Act the premises must be: **9–16**

"let under a tenancy"
This will include a tenancy at will but the Act does not apply to   **9–17**
licences (see s.6(1));

"which puts on the landlord the obligation for the maintenance or repair of the premises"
This has to be read with s.4(4) so that the landlord can be liable for a   **9–18**
defect that does not fall within the repairing obligation provided they
had a "right to enter the premises to any description of maintenance
or repair of the premises". Thus it has been said that the duty under
s.4 is "linked to the repairing obligation" (see *McAuley v Bristol City
Council* [1992] Q.B. 134). Indeed, it may be more accurately said to
be linked to the other obligations in the lease since if the lease does
not give the landlord the right to enter and carry out a repair or
improvement of the type responsible for the injury loss or damage

complained of the landlord cannot be liable. If the defect is of a type which the landlord had no right to repair or maintain then the duty does not arise. Furthermore it has been held a defect in design, as opposed to a lack of repair or maintenance, cannot be within s.4. This point will be considered further below.

"a duty to take such care as is reasonable in all the circumstances"
9–19   See below for the nature of the duty.

"to see that they are reasonably safe from personal injury or from damage to their property"
9–20   This is largely self-explanatory.

"caused by a relevant defect"
9–21   "*Relevant defect*" means "*a defect in the state of the premises*" existing at one of the dates described above (subs.(3)), i.e. a defect in the state of the repair of the premises which constitutes disrepair or would constitute disrepair if the landlord had notice of it. But the duty under s.4 does not extend to rectifying matters that were not in need of repair or maintenance even though they exposed the tenant to a risk of injury (*Alker v Collingwood Housing Association* 14/2/07, *The Times*). Thus, in that case, the danger came from annealed glass, which had been installed in compliance with the building regulations that applied when the property had been built. It was held that this was a safety issue not an item of disrepair. The landlord did not covenant for the premises to be safe and therefore there could be no liability even though the tenant suffered serious injury.

"The said duty is owed if the landlord knows (whether by being notified by the tenant or otherwise) or ought in all the circumstances to have known"
9–22   As the Court of Appeal explained in *Sykes v Harry* [2001] EWCA Civ 167, [2001] E.G.L.R. 53, there is not a straightforward test for constructive notice. The Court of Appeal held that the broad duty of care under s.4 of the Defective Premises Act 1972 does not depend upon the person making the claim showing that the landlord has express notice of the defect (see para.A 6401 in *Hill and Redman*). The landlord would have the necessary notice if they had failed to take "such care as is reasonable in the circumstances to see that they (the tenant and his family) are reasonably safe from personal injury or from damage to their property" (s.4(1)).

In that case the tenant suffered from carbon monoxide poisoning from a gas fire which had not been regularly serviced for eight years. The faulty condition of that gas fire would have been revealed if the landlord had engaged contractors to carry out an annual safety check. It was held that the landlord was liable. The purpose of the 1972 Act was to break away from the historic limitations of the common law. By failing to service the fire or to make any relevant inquiries of the tenant, the landlord had failed in his duty. But the tenant was guilty of contributory negligence in not drawing defects to the landlord's attention and the court refused to disturb the judge's assessment of contributory negligence at 80 per cent.

Liability where there is a right to enter to carry out any repair or maintenance as well as duty to repair
It should be noted that the duty only arises where the landlord is either under a *duty* to repair or has a "*right* to enter the premises to carry out any description of *maintenance or repair*" (s.4(4)). The landlord is not under a duty to carry out improvements merely because they have the right to carry repairs. This may be illustrated by a number of the cases: **9–23**

- In *Wadsworth v Nagle* [2005] EWHC 26 Q.B. the lease did not provide for any right of access on the part of the landlord. A defect developed in the sealant around the bath in the flat demised to the tenant, which resulted in the tenant of the flat below suffering loss and damage. As a consequence of the damage sustained he claimed that he had to sell his flat at a lower price than he would otherwise have done. It was held that in the absence of a right on the part of the landlord in those circumstances to enter the flat where the defect arose this was fatal to the claim succeeding.

- The failure to eradicate condensation-related damp in residential accommodation is a well-known cause for complaint in poorly designed or constructed dwellings. We have seen (in Ch.2) such a complaint more often constitutes a defect in quality, the rectification of which would constitute an improvement rather than a repair. As such there would be no right of access on the part of the landlord and hence no duty under s.4(4) (see *McNerny v Lambeth LBC* [1989] 1 E.G.L.R. 81). Stephenson L.J. said in that case, obiter dicta, that the duty under s.4 "goes no wider than the repair covenant" (at p.83). In the sense that there may be a duty where there is merely a right to enter to carry out repairs, that is an over-simplification. However, it is imperative to consider how liability may be established and not simply assume it exists. The fact that, outside the landlord and tenant situation, such a claim would arise does not mean that it will arise where the relationship between claimant and defendant is that of landlord and tenant.

However:

- It has been held that the landlord would have a *right* to carry out a repair where lease gave him a right to enter the premises "for any purpose". In *McNerny* there was a defect to a step in the rear garden of a dwelling house. Although that dwelling house was one to which s.11 of the Landlord and Tenant Act 1985 applied (structural and repairing obligation in short leases), the defect in a rear step would not fall within s.11 because it did not form part of the structure or exterior of "the dwelling house". However, it was held that where there was a dangerous defect in the demised premises, as opposed to a design fault or defect in quality, including a defect in the garden, this impliedly created a right to enter those premises to remedy that defect (*McAuley v Bristol City Council* [1992] 1 All E.R. 749, (1991) 23 H.L.R. 586). Unlike *Alker v Collingwood* described above the work did not involve an improvement to the premises and was within the extended definition of the duty under s.4(4). By implying a reservation on the part of the landlord to rectify a dangerous defect the Court of Appeal were able to find that liability had been established.

Remedies

9–24   The remedy of specific performance will be available where a defect in the demised premises is such as to amount to a breach of the landlord's repairing obligation. However in the rare case where a danger is present in premises which has not yet caused any damage within the repairing covenant, technically there will be no complete cause of action. Nevertheless, the courts will restrain the landlord or compel the landlord to carry out work where serious harm is feared. This type of injunction (known as a quia timet injunction) is rare in litigation surrounding the defective state of premises. It is granted sparingly and only when the possibility of damage is high (see *Clerk and Lindsell on Torts*, 19th edn at 30–15).

There will also be a claim for damages, usually for personal injury, where accidental damage occurs. However, a claim under s.4 of the Act would normally fall within the Housing Disrepair Protocol and not the Personal Injury Protocol (see para.3.1(b) of the former). On the other hand claims under s.1 of the Act will normally fall within the Pre-action Protocol for Construction and Engineering Disputes even if they involve an allegation of negligence against a professional architect or engineer. Claims against architects and engineers are dealt with under that Protocol rather than the Professional Negligence Protocol.

These remedies will be considered in greater detail in Pt III of this book.

Secure and assured tenancies

Where the tenant is a secure or assured tenant there is an additional **9–25** complication. The history of his tenancy should be carefully considered, because it may be that in the past they were subject to a possession order. Agreements following such an order generally have the effect of giving the tenant the status of a tolerated trespasser not of reviving the tenancy, although this can subsequently be done by court order. The effect of a tolerated trespasser argument succeeding is to suspend the right to sue under s.4 of the 1972 Act until the tenancy is revived (*Lambeth LBC v O'Kane* [2006] H.L.R. 2). Unfortunately the law in this area is in a state of flux but it appears that the decision of the House of Lords in *Burrows v Brent BC* [1996] 4 All E.R. 577, the case which established the law relating to tolerated trespass, remains good law at the time of going to press.

There is nothing to prevent a judge extending the period that an order for possession has been suspended for and the courts will not allow the judge's discretion given to them by the primary legislation to be limited (see *Richmond v London Borough of Kensington* [2006] EWCA Civ 68).

Therefore at the present time it may be very difficult, if advising a landlord, to say whether a particular tenant is or is not a tolerated trespasser to whom liability under the 1972 Act is suspended.

The Court of Appeal has recently confirmed that the status of tolerated trespass may also exist where the tenancy was assured rather than secure (see *White v Knowsley Housing Association* [2007] EWCA Civ 404). In particular, the payment of arrears of rent by instalments pursuant to a court order for possession of an assured tenancy also created a tolerated trespasser situation in the view of the Court of Appeal. Section 4 will not apply to those cases either, it would appear. However, leave to petition the House of Lords has been given in that case. Furthermore the Housing and Regeneration Bill presently before Parliament will abolish the status of tolerated trespasser altogether.

Position of licensees

The duty of care under s.4 applies to "landlords" and not licensors. **9–26** Therefore a licensee or his guest who is injured must rely on the common law if they are to establish a claim arising out of the defective state of the premises as a result of its negligent construction by the defendant. For example, it may be possible to establish liability on the basis that the licensor designed and built the dwelling. This was the position in *Targett v Torfean DC* [1992] 3 All E.R. 27 discussed above, although that case involved a lease not a licence. However, the principle that the designer, builder or converter of premises owes a duty of care at common law applies equally whether the claimant is a tenant or a licensee or one of their visitors. Furthermore this principle has survived the general prohibition on a claim to pure economic loss in *Murphy v Brentwood District Council* [1991] 1 A.C. 398 (at 487 H) provided there is a defect which has caused or is likely to cause injury, loss or damage to the tenant or his visitors.

Chapter 10

The Occupiers' Liability Acts 1957–1984

The last chapter was concerned with the tortious liability of landlords **10–01** and builders under the Defective Premises Act 1972. Here the tortious liability of occupiers to visitors and trespassers is considered. Clearly, there is an overlap between the liability of occupiers and the liability of landlords, but in the landlord and tenant situation the tenant is likely to be liable as occupier whereas the landlord would be liable under the Defective Premises Act 1972 if the defect which causes loss of damage results from a want of repair or a defect for which he is responsible. In addition there is also an overlap between the liability of an occupier and the liability of other types of legal owner or those with other types of responsibility for land, for example highways authorities. The latter have statutory responsibility for the maintenance of roads and pavements. Subject to important defences, that liability is strict.

As was commented on at the start of the last chapter, an occupier may be liable to a visitor whether or not they are liable to repair the defect in question. However, the background as far as the repairs history is concerned may be relevant and where the responsibility under a lease to repair the defect in question lies on a person other than the occupier that person may be joined into the action as a third party.

The Occupiers' Liability Acts 1957 and 1984 represent some of the more straightforward legislation in this area, but they have given rise to some difficult questions of law. Nevertheless, the function of the 1957 Act in particular was to substantially simplify the law and it largely succeeded in that aim.

The duty to visitors

10–02 When considering the liability of occupiers to visitors it is necessary to leave on one side the well-established notions of negligence that apply, for example, where one is concerned with injuries suffered in the consumer field. Generally those cases of negligence based broadly on the *Donoghue v Stevenson* principle have no application to persons suffering injury whilst on another's land. This is largely because the principles on which tortious liability attached to occupiers of land arose well before the principles under which *Donoghue v Stevenson* liability arose. However, as the Court of Appeal have recently indicated, liability under the 1957 Act is no more onerous than that which attached to occupiers at common law (*Cole v Davis-Gilbert* [2007] EWCA Civ 396).

The 1957 Act

10–03 The 1957 Act abolished the distinction between an occupier's liability towards non-contractual and contractual visitors and the Court of Appeal has confirmed that this distinction is no longer relevant (in *Maguire v Sefton BC* [2006] 1 W.L.R. 2550). The question in every case where a lawful visitor is injured, be he visiting the premises under a contract or not, is whether the occupier has discharged the common duty of care to him.

The purpose of the Act is to establish the liability of occupiers to visitors, in whatever capacity they are visiting, but not to establish liability on the part of the occupier for other accidents which happen to occur on his land but which have nothing to do with his occupation of the land in question (see *Donoghue v Folkstone Properties Ltd* [2003] Q.B. 1008). That case involved a claim under the 1984 Act but nevertheless contains an important discussion (at para.36 et seq.) about the need for the accidental injury in question to be caused by the *state of the premises* rather than *happening to occur on* those premises. The Act is about relationships arising out of the occupation of the land not relationships that happen to arise from activities on that land. Thus, a shooting accident or a motor accident which happens to take place on that land does not arise from "using the premises" (s.2(2) of the 1957 Act).

However, the Act is thought to cover all types of loss and not only damages for personal injury and death, indeed s.1(3)(b) of the 1957 Act seems to make this clear. However, in practice accidental injury is the most likely loss to arise.

What premises are covered?
10–04 "Premises" are not defined in the 1957 Act but are widely interpreted

to include both buildings and external areas, such as pavements in private ownership. The Act also explicitly applies to moveable structures by including any "vessel, vehicle or aircraft" (s.1(3)(a)) within the definition of "premises", provided the occupier is in occupation of the land or vessel on which the accident occurs (see Clerk and Lindsell 19th edn at 12–07).

Who is the "occupier"?

A question of overriding practical relevance to anyone advising a **10–05** person injured whilst visiting premises is: who is the occupier? Unfortunately, the answer is not always straightforward.

The "occupier" is not defined in the Act. However, in the case law it has been defined as the person with *effective control* of the premises (*Wheat v Lacon* [1966] A.C. 552 H.L.). Clearly there can be more than one such person and more than one may be liable at the same time. Therefore liability may be apportioned between them to reflect the degree of control they exercise over the land or premises concerned. The occupation of the premises need not be lawful and need not be exclusive possession in the legal sense. As Diplock L.J. indicated in *Wheat v Lacon* (at Court of Appeal level [1966] 1 Q.B. 355 at 366) the Act is not concerned with occupation in the sense of the law of landlord and tenant or rating law. Indeed some commentators have expressed the view that there is no reason on this basis why a squatter should not be liable as occupier as the person having relatively the best title (see *Clerk and Lindsell on Torts* London: Sweet & Maxwell, 2007 19th edn pp.12–10).

Examples

- A, the owner, is having building works carried out by B at his property. As a result of a defect arising at the premises whilst the work is being done C is injured. C will have the option of suing A or B or may sue both on the basis they were both in occupation of the property at the time. If he sues only A, B may be joined into the proceedings on the basis that he substantially caused the accident and it would be just and equitable for liability to attach to B (see *Ferguson v Welsh* (1987) 1 W.L.R. 1553).

- On the other hand a landlord will rarely be liable as the occupier of part of the premises which he has let out because once he was parted with possession of that part he does not retain any physical control over that part of the premises. Therefore, classically, if C is injured on the stairway which forms part of the common parts of the building retained by B, the landlord, of which A's flat forms only one unit, it is difficult to see how A could be liable and normally B would be (*Fairman v Perpetual Investment Building Society* [1923] A.C. 74). But there are obviously much more borderline cases than this. The fact that the landlord has retained an obligation to repair the part in question will not necessarily be decisive given that it is the degree of *control* that he exercises that is important, not the nature of his contractual obligations to the tenant (per Lord Denning in *Wheat v Lacon* [1966] A.C. 552 at 579).

Even where there is only one occupier there may be shared liability for an accident. This was the case in *Lough v Intruder Alarm Systems* [2008] All E.R. (D) 364 (Jun) in which the claimant had suffered accidental injury whilst carrying out work to premises owned by a third party during the course of his employment. His employer was held to be 75 per cent to blame for the accident but the occupier of the premises was held to blame for the other 25 per cent.

Trustees and unincorporated associations

10–06 Difficult questions relating to the correct person to sue arise where the potential defendant is a trust or unincorporated association. This will frequently be the case of club and other premises used for leisure.

Where the accident occurs at a club the club itself cannot be sued as the occupier because it has no legal personality but the committee frequently may be sued on the basis that they normally hold the assets of the club on behalf of its members. It is not always clear that the committee actually owe the duty and it may be necessary to identify the member or members of the committee to whom specific responsibility for health and safety has been delegated (see *Prole v Allen* [1950] 1 All E.R. 476).

However, it seems reasonably clear that where premises are held on trust for members of a club or organisation, the trustees should collectively be sued as acting by or on behalf of that club or organisation. In practice, the rules permit the action to be begun or continued against one trustee "as representatives of … other persons who have that interest" (CPR 19.6(1)). The court has a discretion to direct that a party may not act as a representative (CPR 19.6 (2)) but where the representative action is properly constituted any judgement it order against the representative is binding on all those represented by that individual or those individuals.

Who is a "visitor"?

The Act contains a straightforward definition of "visitor", which **10–07** replaced the distinction at common law between "licensees" and "invitees". Visitors are defined in s.2(6) as:

> "...persons who enter premises for any purpose in the exercise of a right conferred by law."

That sub-section goes on to state that those persons:

> "...are to be treated as permitted by the occupier to be there for that purpose, whether they in fact have his permission or not."

"Permission" may take any number of guises, from express consent, contractual or otherwise, or more commonly any number of different species of licence to enter or remain. In fact members of the public have an implied licence to enter or remain in a number of public spaces unless their purpose in being there is wholly nefarious. But difficult questions sometimes arise when a visitor deviates from the correct or normal path and enters into private land. Such a person may become a trespasser at that point (*Mersey Docks and Harbour Board v Proctor* [1923] A.C. 253). Generally speaking, if the occupier wishes to avoid an argument that there was no implied licence to go to the area of the premises where the accident occurs they should erect suitable warning signs or fences to make this clear. Otherwise the court will be likely to find a licence to go to any area where members of the public frequently gain access.

However, whereas an adult may be considered to have deviated from the correct course, particularly where it is well marked, and thus to have become a trespasser to whom a lower duty is owed, the same may well not apply to children. They may not be expected to know the difference between a defined path and a wider area to which they can conveniently gain access. The treatment of children as a class of visitors will be more fully considered below.

Visitors exercising rights of way or other legal rights
Those exercising lawful rights under numerous pieces of legislation, **10–08** for example those in lawful pursuance of local authority powers, are not trespassers whether or not the landowner consented to their presence on his land. However, those exercising rights under the Countryside and Rights of Way Act 2000 are owed the modified duty under the 1984 Act not the duty to visitors in the 1957 Act (s.1(4) of the 1957 Act as substituted by s.13 of the 2000 Act).

Those exercising private rights of way pursuant to various forms of easement are also owed the lower duty in the 1984 Act. However such persons, where they are the owners of the dominant land entitled to the benefit of the easement of way, may have other contractual remedies, for example, to compel the servient owner to maintain the way.

Those accessing common parts of a shared building were regarded at common law as visitors (*Fairman v Perpetual Investment Society* [1923] A.C. 74) and will be regarded as visitors under the 1957 Act. However, those exercising public rights of way are not owed any duty under the Act (*McGeown v Northern Ireland Housing Executive* [1995] 1 A.C. 233) but may be able to sue at common law (as in *Thomas v BR Board* [1976] Q.B. 912) or under s.41 of the Highways Act 1980, where a failure to maintain the highway in question may be established.

The nature of the duty and standard of care to visitors

10–09 A broad definition is adopted by the legislature. The occupier owes the visitor the "common duty of care", i.e. "such care as in all the circumstances of the case is reasonable". All visitors are owed the same duty which extends to both acts and omissions.

Recent illustrations of the standard of care expected to visitors include the following:

- In *Brioland v Searson* [2005] EWCA Civ 55 the claimant was injured when she tripped and fell on a raised sill on a doorway. The Court of Appeal criticized the defendants for obtaining a report which appeared to indicate that the defect in question did not amount to a hazard. The premises had not been reasonably safe for the claimant and liability had been established, or at least that had been a conclusion which had been open to the trial judge. The expert strayed onto the judge's discretion, which involved deciding whether there was a hazard giving rise to potential liability under the Act. The court therefore declined to interfere with the trial judge's findings.

- In *Cole v Davis-Gilbert* (*The Times* 16th April 2007) the Court of Appeal decided that the organiser of a village fete had not breached its duty of care to the claimant. The claimant had broken her leg due to a hole in the village green, which had been dug to hold a maypole. She alleged that, by failing to take sufficient steps to ensure the hole was filled in adequately, the operators of the village fete, who were occupiers for the purposes of the Act, were statutorily liable.

The court found against the claimant and gave guidance on the standard of care to be applied to landowners and others involved in organising social activities. The case is likely to provide the benchmark for some time.

Nature and standard of care to particular classes of visitors

(i) *Children*
Broadly, a higher standard of care is expected to children than to **10–10** adults because the occupier should expect children to be less careful than adults (s.2(3) of the 1957 Act). Common sense dictates that a warning sign or notice, which may well discharge the common duty of care in the case of an adult, will be of no effect where one is concerned with a six-year old child. However, in deciding whether the duty of care has been discharged the occupier is entitled to expect a reasonable degree of parental control and supervision (see *Phipps v Rochester Corporation* [1955] 1 Q.B. 450).

The standard of care expected to children is best illustrated by reference to the case law:

- In *Moloney v Lambeth LBC* (1966) 198 EG 895 a 4 year old child fell through a balustrade. That balustrade was perfectly well maintained and would not have constituted a danger to adults. However, it was held foreseeable that a child would attempt to get through the gap and therefore the Council had to design the balustrade so that this hazard was removed.

- In *Boyd v Galloway* [1923] S.C. 758 children were in the habit of visiting birds that nested on a wall in premises under the control of the defendant. When one such child was visiting and stood on the wall it collapsed because it could not take the weight. It was held that although the wall was not designed for bearing such an additional load it was nevertheless foreseeable that children would visit and that such an accident would occur.

(ii) *Rescue workers*
The occupier is not generally liable to emergency workers simply **10–11** because there is a temporary hazard on his premises but, if they created that hazard deliberately they would be liable. Thus, the occupier would be liable where, for example, he deliberately started a fire at the premises and as a result a fireman was injured (see *Merrington v Ironbridge Metalworks Ltd* [1952] A.C. 1101). However, in *Ogwo v Taylor* [1988] A.C. 431 the Court of Appeal pointed out that in some cases it will be unnecessary to rely on the Act. Liability falls on the person who negligently starts a fire for all

reasonably foreseeable consequences. In that case the fireman fighting a fire, started negligently by the defendant, had been injured by scalding steam when they attempted to extinguish the blaze with water and not from any defect as such in the premises. The claimant established liability for common law negligence. As the court pointed out it will in many cases be easier to succeed at common law since the claimant will not need to prove any particular hazard in the premises merely that there was reasonable foresight that the claimant would suffer some damage.

Defences

Obvious dangers

10–12 A visitor is expected to guard against obvious dangers but obviously it is more difficult to establish that a danger would be obvious to a child than to an adult. In relation to a person carrying out his calling, s.2(3)(b) of the 1957 Act states that the occupier:

> "may expect that a person, in the exercise of his calling, will appreciate and guard against any special risks ordinarily incident to it."

Volenti non fit injuria (voluntary assumption of risk)

10–13 Section 2(5) of the 1957 Act provides that a risk willingly assumed will not be laid at the occupier's door:

> "The common duty of care does not impose on an occupier any obligation to a visitor in respect of risks willingly accepted as his by the visitor."

However the concept is rarely relied on in practice in relation to visitors, as there will be no voluntary assumption of risk where the claimant acted reasonably in all the circumstances. Nor may the defence be relied on where the risk that was voluntarily accepted was a different risk than the one which gave rise to the accident (as in *White v Blackmore* [1972] 2 Q.B. 651). Thus if A voluntarily accepted risk A, but was actually was injured by risk B, which was of a different character, there will not be any voluntary assumption of risk.

Contributory negligence

10–14 This will often be relied on in cases of occupiers' liability, although in some cases the argument that the accident was caused or contributed to by the claimant's own negligence will be sufficiently weighty to defeat the claim altogether on the grounds that it was *wholly* caused by the claimant's own negligence.

Can the occupier exclude or restrict liability?

The 1957 Act did not prevent exclusions or restrictions of liability as **10–15** long as they were "reasonable" in all the circumstances (s.2(1)). However, by the Unfair Contract Terms Act 1977 (s.2(1)), there is a total prohibition on the exclusion or restriction of liability for personal injury and death, whether by a term of the contract or by notice. Furthermore, an important limitation on that general prohibition is that it only relates to premises occupied for the purposes of a business (s.1(3)). As liability under the 1957 Act may extend to losses other than liability for personal injury and death, and may relate to residential premises, it follows that there is some limited scope for excluding or restricting liability in relation to consensual entry onto one's land by visitors. However, where that entry was contractual (entry as a visitor necessarily involves at least an implied licence) liability may only be excluded or restricted as long as it satisfies the requirement of "reasonableness" in s.3 of the 1977 Act. A notice placed at the premises must also satisfy that requirement.

The definition of a "business" is sufficiently broad to cover professional activities (see s.14) and it is thought that premises for mixed-use may be covered but it is possible to mark off an area for business or professional use from a part cordoned off for residential use. Where the visitor is injured, at least in part, because they are visiting the occupier for some business reason, liability may not be entirely excluded under the Unfair Contract Terms Act but where they are visiting for entirely domestic purposes the residential part of mixed use premises, the occupier may be able to exclude that liability as described above.

Guests

As a consequence of s.3(1) of the 1957 Act, a landlord or other **10–16** occupier could not limit liability to his tenant or exclude liability to third parties who were guests of his tenant (i.e. strangers to the contract) provided the contract permitted the tenant to admit persons who were "strangers to the contract to enter or use the premises". The above section therefore makes express provision for the occupier of premises not only to be liable to their own tenants, with whom they have a contractual relationship, but also their visitors. However, as was noted in Ch.1, a contract which confers benefits on a third party or class of persons may in any event place liability on the landlord under the Contracts (Rights of Third Parties) Act 1999.

Liability of the occupier for his independent contractors

Generally A will not be liable for B's acts or omissions where B is an **10–17** independent contractor provided he exercises reasonable care and skill in the selection of that contractor. The 1957 Act makes this clear in s.3(2) when it provides that in the absence of express wording A will not be liable for the negligent acts or omissions of B provided he acted reasonably in employing B.

The point is illustrated by *Maguire v Sefton BC* [2006] 1 W.L.R. 2550 where the claimant was injured by a malfunctioning machine in a leisure club. It was held that the defendant could rely on the defence that it had selected a reasonably competent firm of engineers to service the machine and was not liable for the defect which caused the claimant injury.

The duty to trespassers

10–18 Unlike the 1957 Act, which applies to all types of loss, the Occupiers Liability Act 1984 applies only to claims for personal injury and death. As for claims by visitors, trespassers may only claim under the 1984 Act for defects in the state of the premises and not for accidents which occur through other negligent acts or omissions on the occupier's land. Thus in *Keown v Coventry NHS Trust* [2006] 1 W.L.R. 953 a child was injured when he fell off a fire escape at a hospital for which the defendant was responsible. As the fire escape was not defective, although it might have been hazardous, he had no right of action. Furthermore, in contrast to the situation which applies in relation to visitors, the fact that a trespasser is a child would rarely make a difference to the outcome (per Longmore L.J. below at para.12). If no duty would have been owed to an adult there would probably be no duty to a child although it was a matter of "fact and degree" in every case (see also *Young v Kent CC* [2005] EWHC 1342 for a further recent illustration).

Intentions of trespasser

10–19 There are many different types of trespasser, from the innocently mistaken person who enters onto the land of another, to the person who deliberately enters the occupier's land with the intention of damaging the property. They are all in the same category for the purposes of the legal duty, although the circumstances of and reasons for entering onto the occupier's land may be highly relevant. The former rule that trespassers could only sue if they could prove that they were injured intentionally or recklessly was removed by the 1984 Act. Parliament substituted a wider duty which is flexible to the circumstances.

Nature of duty under 1984 Act and the standard of care

A lower duty applies to trespassers under the 1984 Act than to visitors **10–20** under the 1957 Act. Section 1 of the 1984 Act removed the restrictions which formerly applied and placed a duty on the occupier (see above for the definition) to a trespasser in respect "any risk of their suffering injury on the premises by reason of any *danger* due to the state of the premises or to things done or omitted to be done on them". However, the occupier must either know, or ought to have known, of the risk. In addition the risk must be one that in all the circumstances it would be "reasonable" to offer the trespasser some protection against.

Section 1(3)–(4) of the 1984 Act provides that:

"(3) An occupier of premises owes a duty to another (not being his visitor) in respect of any such risk as is referred to in subsection (1) above if—

(a) He is aware of the danger or has reasonable grounds to believe that it exists;

(b) He knows or has reasonable grounds to believe that the other is in the vicinity of the danger concerned or that he may come into the vicinity of the danger (in either case, whether he has lawful authority for being in that vicinity or not); and

(c) The risk is one against which, in all the circumstances of the case, he may reasonably be expected to offer the other some protection.

(4) Where, by virtue of this section, an occupier of premises owes a duty to another in respect of such a risk, the duty is to take such care as is reasonable in all the circumstances of the case to see that he does not suffer injury on the premises by reason of the danger concerned."

The principles, which apply in relation to the 1984 Act, are well illustrated by:

- *John Peter Tomlinson v Congleton BC and Cheshire CC* [2003] UKHL 47. In that case the House of Lords had to consider the nature of liability under the 1984 Act. There the claimant had dived into a lake occupied by the Council. There were signs warning of the danger of swimming in the lake and C was aware of that risk. He suffered serious injuries. It was held that he became a trespasser at the point where he ignored the signs. The risk was clear and obvious and not one that the Council would be expected to guard against. The Council had not therefore owed C any duty under s.1(3). Even if it had owed C a duty of care the Council would not have been in breach of it by preventing C taking a clear and obvious risk. There was no liability where, as was the case here, the risk was clear and obvious.

- A landlord was not liable as an occupier of land for injuries sustained by a tenant who had, whilst dancing on a garage roof that formed no part of her tenancy, fallen through a Perspex skylight! The danger had arisen from the tenant's activity rather than the state of the premises. The tenant had not enjoyed any licence to access the roof where she was injured and was therefore a trespasser (*Siddorn v Patel* [2007] EWHC 1248 Q.B., [2007] All E.R. (D) 453, per Sir John Blofeld on the 28/3/07).

Defences

Warnings and exclusions

10–21 Section 1(5) provides for warnings as follows:

> "(5) Any duty owed by virtue of this section in respect of a risk may, in an appropriate case, be discharged by taking such steps as are reasonable in all the circumstances of the case to give warning of the danger concerned or to discourage persons from incurring the risk."

Generally, an occupier will find it difficult to limit liability under the 1957 Act because many visitors will be at the premises under some form of licence, express or implied. Therefore the Unfair Contract Terms Act 1977 will apply so as to limit the ability of the occupier to exclude or restrict liability and prevent that exclusion altogether in the case of personal injury and death. Opinion is divided on the question of whether an occupier may exclude or restrict liability in respect of injuries suffered by a trespasser but the predominant view is that he can. As Clerk and Lindsell point out (19th edn at 12–75) the exclusion or restriction of liability for personal injury or death in s.2(1) relates to liability at common law for negligence and under the Occupiers' Liability Act 1957 but the 1977 Act has not been extended to cover claims by trespassers under the 1984 Act. Therefore the occupier has greater freedom to restrict liability to a trespasser than a visitor and the restriction on excluding or restricting liability for personal injury or death in the 1977 Act appears not to apply.

Furthermore, where a large notice is prominently displayed to the effect that no responsibility will be accepted towards trespassers a strong argument exists that the occupier should be able to rely on this notice and there should be no liability at all. Alternatively, the effect of such a notice will often be to render it reasonable for the occupier "in all the circumstances of the case", to offer the trespasser no protection against the hazard in question, given the presence of the warning sign or notice (see s.1(3)(c)).

Volenti non fit injuria
Section 1(6) of the 1984 Act provides that: **10–22**

> "(6) No duty is owed by virtue of this section to any person in respect of risks willingly accepted as his by that person (the question whether a risk was so accepted to be decided on the same principles as in other cases in which one person owes a duty of care to another)."

The defence is frequently relied on in trespass cases. Thus in *Ratcliff v McConnell* [1999] 1 W.L.R. 670 the claimant, who was a trespasser, dived into a shallow swimming pool and suffered injury. The Court of Appeal interfered with the trial judge's finding in the claimant's favour because the risk was clear and obvious which he could be taken to have voluntarily assumed under s.1(6) of the 1984 Act. The reader is also referred to the leading case of *Tomlinson* (referred to above) where the House of Lords reached the same conclusion on this point.

Chapter 11

Obligations under miscellaneous statutes and regulations

It is rarely possible to confine a discussion as to liability for defective **11–01**
premises to one area of the law. It is necessary to bear in mind
common law and statutory rules as well as EU and domestic
intervention in those rules. Many of the statutes and regulations that
follow are considered in the context of defective buildings but in fact
apply to a wider range of circumstances. They demonstrate that there
is a greater level of statutory intervention in the housing and building
field. This is stimulated by the demands of greater energy efficiency
and higher standards for all types of accommodation. Most health
and safety regulations relating to buildings are backed up by criminal
sanctions for non-compliance but some also create civil liability.

Unfortunately, the complexity of many regulations in this area and
the diverse sources of these, make it difficult to give comprehensive
guidance. The following is therefore merely a selection of the more
important statutes and regulations affecting building owners.

The Building Act 1984

Wide powers are conferred on local authorities to enforce building **11–02**
standards under this Act, which is the enabling legislation for the
current building regulations (the Building Regulations 2000 (SI
2000/2531)). The origin of those regulations lies in local authority
bye-laws, which first found their way into legislation of national
application in the Public Health Act 1936. Now the various pieces of
legislation that regulated building activity in the past, including that
Act, have been largely consolidated into the Building Act 1984.

The Act also creates the duty on local authorities to supervise building works in their areas and contains various other provisions for maintaining building standards. In addition, there are wide powers to control structurally unstable buildings. With some qualification, s.44 of the 1984 Act applies the Building Regulations to the Crown. The scope of the obligations in the 1984 Act has been considerably widened in terms of the efficiency standards to be demanded, for example, by the Sustainable and Secure Buildings Act 2004.

Other provisions in the 1984 Act and the Building Regulations themselves are more fully summarised in the next chapter where the local authority controls over defective premises are considered.

As well as domestic legislation there are also a number of regulations emanating from the EU which will be briefly considered.

The building regulations

11–03 There have been regulations controlling the safety and utility of buildings for more than 100 years. Enforcement of the regulations is under the control of local authorities.

The current regulations introduce tough new building standards. The regulations were originally concerned more with the basic safety of buildings but are now increasingly concerned with the utility and efficiency of buildings. For example, Pt E of Sch.1 of the current regulations (the Buildings Regulations 2000 (2000 SI/2531) (as amended)) is concerned with airborne and impact noise on adjoining occupiers. Part N of Sch.1 to the Building Regulations is likely to be of some importance. This part provides that glazing must be protected or toughened so that it breaks in a safe manner. This part came into force on January 1, 2001 (see reg.1) and therefore only applies to properties built on or after that date. However although the majority of landlords will own properties built before that date they should aspire to achieve these standards to avoid potential arguments arising out of their alleged failure to comply with these regulations. Also whether or not a particular property complies with the regulations may be relevant when judging whether the landlord has fallen below the standard expected of a reasonable landlord, for example, if he came to be sued under the Defective Premises Act 1972 (although this will rarely be decisive). Part P of the regulations relates to electrical installations. These will be more fully discussed below.

Liability in negligence or breach of duty following a breach of the building regulations

The regulations create criminal liability on the part of the building **11–04** owner who fails to comply with them and there are other measures available to local authorities, for example, to require the owner to pull down or remove the work which contravenes the regulations (see s.36 of the Building Act 1984). However other than the local authority and the building owner, a number of other people may be affected by a building which does not satisfy basic building standards and the important question arises: to what extent is the building owner or his agent liable in civil proceedings for non compliance?

Section 38 of the Building Act 1984 clearly would have created liability in tort for a breach of the regulations, presumably to any person affected, but it has never been implemented (See *Emden's Building Contracts and Practice*, pt IV, Ch.1, para.205). Thus the purchaser of a property who wishes to consider suing the builder will have to bring an action in contract, for common law negligence, breach of duty (see below) or, more probably, an action under s.1 of the Defective Premises Act 1972.

Establishing civil liability for a breach of the regulations and the economic loss problem

One potential problem with attaching liability for breach of statutory **11–05** duty for non-compliance with the buildings regulations on the builder is the economic loss problem. Clearly a builder or other construction professional may be liable under s.1 of the Defective Premises Act 1972 for physical damage or injury caused by his building work, as well as pure economic loss incurred by the purchaser or his successors in title. The House of Lords have characterised the duty on the negligent builder of the defective building under that Act as a "transmissible warranty of quality" (per Lord Bridge in *Murphy v Brentwood DC* at [1990] 2 All E.R. 908 at 929).

But the question that arises is whether liability attaches for a breach of the building regulations which does not itself constitute a breach of s.1. Clearly the prohibition on recovering damages for pure economic loss illustrated by *Murphy v Brentwood DC* [1990] 2 All E.R. 908 and *D and C Builders v The Church Commissioners* [1989] A.C. 177 would apply to any such action as opposed to an action under s.1 of the Defective Premises Act.

The case of *Eames London Estates v North Herts DC* (1980) 18 B.L.R. 50 suggests that an action may be brought against a builder or local authority for breach of the building regulations but the case of *Perry v Tendring* (1984) 5 Con L.R. 74 suggests otherwise. *Perry v Tendring DC* is in line with decisions of the higher courts which, particularly in relation to local authorities, have limited their liability (see, for example, *Peabody Donation Fund v Sir Lindsay Parkinson and Co* [1984] 3 W.L.R. 953). It has been pointed out that the decisions in the cases of *Eames* and *Perry* came before the prohibition on the recovery of pure economic loss in *Murphy* (see *Emden's Building Contracts and Practice*, pt IV Ch.1, para.204). However the point has also been made that the buildings regulations are concerned with *health and safety* not with the recovery of *economic losses* and therefore it could plausibly be argued that the recovery of damages for personal injury and death is adequately covered by the common law tort of negligence without placing an additional tortious liability for breach of building regulations.

As long as there remain two conflicting first instance authorities it is difficult to advise that there are clear prospects of successfully pursuing the builder who fails to comply with the building regulations in civil proceedings for a breach of those regulations, as opposed to pursuing other contractual and tortious remedies.

Liability under miscellaneous health and safety legislation

11–06   There has been a plethora of regulation in relation to every aspect of health and safety in recent years, much of it driven by EU directives. The more important regulations are summarised below. In addition to the regulations considered below there are regulations controlling various dangers and risks created by commercial activities, which may need to be referred to by those advising landlords, building owners and construction professionals, for example, the use of lead in buildings is heavily controlled as is the use of radioactive materials.

The general approach to health and safety in this country, adopted by the Heath and Safety Executive and other public bodies, may be summarised as reducing risk to as low a level as is reasonably practicable. The relevance of the many legislative controls that exist in relation to health and safety is that if landlords refuse to implement basic standards they may face not only criminal sanctions but also possible liability to the tenant. This may include the possible right to recover any sum paid over by the tenant to public enforcement authorities. However, many commercial leases will stipulate that the tenant is himself to comply with the obligations under, for example, the fire regulations, although often these stipulations are in very general terms.

Health and Safety at Work Act 1974

This Act creates a number of criminal offences, including offences **11–07** relating to the maintenance of premises at which people work, as well as numerous duties on employers and others on whom responsibility for health and safety is imposed. However, for the purposes of this work the provisions in the Act which enable the creation of a raft of statutory instruments controlling these matters are likely to be of greatest relevance. For example, the Construction Design and Management Regulations 2007 (SI 2007/320) will place extensive duties on those responsible for designing construction sites in relation to health and safety matters. In particular they impose duties on clients, designers and contractors at such sites. The regulations came into force on April 6, 2007.

The duties under, for example, s.3 of the 1974 Act, are wide in their ambit so that an employer may not only be liable to his employees but also to employees of an independent contractor (see *R. v Associated Octel Limited* [1996] 4 All E.R. 846).

The general duties under the 1974 Act do not give rise to civil liability (see s.47(1)(a)). However, specific regulations made under that Act may give rise to civil liability. The relevance of non-compliance with the Act to those suing for damages will largely be that it will provide an indication of the standard expected of the employer or other person responsible for health and safety at the workplace.

Liability for asbestos

In the past asbestos was widely used in the construction and in other **11–08** industries because of its fire retardant qualities, but throughout the twentieth century the substance came to be seen increasingly as a threat to health and safety as well as a fire preventative material. There is now a substantial amount of law controlling its use. Given the highly technical and specialist nature of much of this law the following is only a summary of some of the more important provisions.

Asbestos causes expensive problems for property owners. At common law, the presence of asbestos would be unlikely to form the subject matter of any claim in the absence of any warranty as to fitness or safety of the premises demised. Given the prospective nature of the covenant for quiet enjoyment this is unlikely to provide a tenant with a remedy either (see *Tanner v Southwark LBC (No.2)* [2001] 1 A.C. 1 (also known as *Mills v Southwark LBC*)). The precedents section of this book includes a defence to an inappropriate claim that the presence of asbestos constitutes a breach of the repairing obligation in s.11 (precedent B12).

The management and removal of asbestos is subject to a complex web of rules and regulations. The Control of Asbestos Regulations 2006 (SI 2006/2739), which replaces the Control of Asbestos at Work Regulations 2002 (SI 2002/2675), implements the EU Asbestos Worker Protection Directive 83/477/EEC. Under these regulations, those carrying out work with asbestos have a duty to minimise exposure by implementing various measures.

The Asbestos Regulations 2006 also apply to owners of certain types of non-domestic premises (commercial, industrial and public buildings but only the common parts of residential buildings). Owners of those buildings, including tenants, who are all defined as "duty holders" in reg.4, have a duty to *manage* the asbestos within that building. This will include the assessment of risk and devising a plan for dealing with it. In some cases, leaving it in situ will be the best option but in others its removal by specialist contractors will be required.

The duty to manage requires duty holders to:

- take reasonable steps to determine the location and condition of materials likely to contain asbestos;
- presume materials contain asbestos unless there is strong evidence that they do not;
- make and keep an up to date record of the location and condition of the asbestos containing materials (ACMs) or presumed ACMs in the premises;
- assess the risk of the likelihood of anyone being exposed to fibres from these materials;
- prepare a plan setting out how the risks from the materials are to be managed;
- take the necessary steps to put the plan into action; review and monitor the plan periodically; and
- provide information on the location and condition of the materials to anyone who is liable to work on or disturb them.

Regulation 4 further requires every person to co-operate with duty holders to enable them to comply with their duties. In the landlord and tenant situation that may include allowing the landlord access to hidden parts within the curtilage of the premises let to a tenant to comply with these duties.

There are also extensive duties on employers to control the presence of asbestos in the workplace.

Guidance on the management of asbestos may be found in the *Approved Code of Practice*, "The Management of Asbestos in Non-domestic Premises" L127, ISBN 978-07176-6209-8, a link to which is found on the HSE website, which also contains other helpful guidance on dealing with this material.

Fire regulations

The Regulatory Reform (Fire Safety) Order 2005, which came into **11–09** force on October 1, 2006, creates new fire safety standards. The order is made under powers conferred by s.1 of the Regulatory Reform Act 2001.

This statutory instrument, which replaces about 70 earlier pieces of legislation, places an obligation on business owners, landlords and other property owners to promote fire safety and not merely to take the lesser steps required by the old fire certification regime. There are a large number of detailed requirements. These include carrying out a risk assessment and, where the business carried on at the premises employs more than five persons, keeping a record of that assessment. The duties imposed by the regulations are, however, within the limits of reasonable practicability.

Local authorities have an important role in enforcing fire safety standards under legislation such as s.352 of the Housing Act 1985, which is now replaced by new powers in the Housing Act 2004, dealt with in the next chapter.

Liability for gas installations

In earlier chapters I have referred to the increasing web of regulations **11–10** which affect property owners in general and landlords in particular. These regulations are particularly important when one has to consider gas and electrical installations in premises which are let.

In addition to the landlord's duty, in certain types of leases, to maintain the gas installations in leasehold property under s.11 of the Landlord and Tenant Act 1985 or under the terms of the lease, the quality and maintenance of gas installations is extensively regulated by statutory instrument. In many cases a breach of the regulations will give rise to a claim in tort under s.4 of the Defective Premises Act 1974. The advantage of the latter claim in tort is that it will generally be easier to fix the landlord with notice of the relevant defect (see *Sykes v Harry* [2001] EWCA Civ 167).

Miscellaneous technical regulations about gas installations

Construction and design of gas appliances

11–11   There are numerous statutory instruments which regulate the serviceability of gas installations, for example the Gas Appliances (Safety) Regulations 1995, SI 1995/1629 (in force partly on July 18, 1995; fully on July 1, 1996), which replaces the Gas Appliances (Safety) Regulations 1992 (SI 1992/711).

These provide for such technical matters as the design of each gas appliance. Every such appliance, including a cooking appliance, must meet certain essential requirements. The regulations were introduced to implement EU Council Directive (EC) 90/396. They do not apply to second hand appliances but earlier less onerous regulations do still apply to them (see *Halsbury's Laws* Vol.41 (2005 reissue) para.613).

The 1995 Regulations referred to above, have been made under s.11 of the Consumer Protection Act 1987. That Act provides for duties on the part of "suppliers". Therefore, these regulations apply to those erecting a building or structure on land or carrying out other building work on land. However, the regulations probably do not apply to those disposing of an interest in land, e.g. creating a lease of premises which contain a gas installation which is non-compliant with the Gas Appliances (Safety) Regulations 1995 (see ibid. para.523). Those 1995 Regulations also create criminal liability.

In addition to those regulations there are numerous other regulations. A number of earlier regulations governing the construction, design and maintenance of gas installations were consolidated in the 1995 regulations but some, e.g. in relation to second hand installations, were not.

Duties on landlords and others under the 1998 Gas Safety Regulations

11–12   These are the most important regulations governing the servicing and maintenance of gas installations of which all those who rent property should be aware, whatever form of tenure they grant (and whatever the size of their operation). The 1998 Regulations (the Gas Safety (Installation and Use) Regulations 1998 (SI 1998/2451)), that are presently being considered, are of more general application but they are of importance, especially for landlords. They were introduced under s.15 of the Health and Safety at Work Act 1974 and commenced on October 31, 1998 but have since been amended by the Construction Design and Management Regulations 2007 (SI 2007/320).

Who the regulations apply to
The 1998 regulations, which replaced the Gas Safety (Installation **11–13**
and Use) Regulations 1994, place a duty on the landlord, or any
person who owns a gas appliance, to ensure that appliance is in
proper working order. The landlord's agent may also in certain
circumstances be liable for a criminal offence (see s.36 of the Health
and Safety at Work Act 1974).

What the regulations say
Any person who carries out any installation or pipework must ensure **11–14**
it is in safe condition and does not represent any risk to health and
safety (reg.36). Regulation 36 of the current regulations also requires
an annual safety check to be carried out by a Corgi registered gas
engineer and for a record to be kept, which must be available for
inspection.

The Regulations need to be read in conjunction with the *Approved
Code of Practice and Guidance*, "Safety in the installation and use
of gas systems and appliances" (available from HSE Books). These
include a requirement that all flues are maintained in good condition.
There are also provisions relating to other parts of gas installations.
Most accidents occur because of defects in the flue whereby carbon
monoxide fails to escape causing a dangerous build-up in the
property below. Despite the strict duties on landlords and others in
the regulations, claims for carbon monoxide poisoning remain fairly
common.

As well as making extensive provision for safety and record
keeping the Regulations contain criminal sanctions for non-
compliance, which the HSE is responsible for enforcing.

Liability under the regulations is strict. However reg.39 provides
a defence where the landlord took all steps which were reasonably
practicable to prevent contravention of the regulations.

As to civil liability, however, s.47(2) of the Health and Safety at
Work Act 1974 appears to create a possible breach of statutory duty
for any breach of the regulations created under that Act provided the
regulations so specify. However there is nothing in these regulations
which suggest they are intended to give rise to civil liability. Hence
in the *Sykes v Harry* case (above) the court found for the tenant under
s.4 of the Defective Premises Act 1972 although the breach of the
regulations was highly relevant to establishing that liability.

Carbon monoxide poisoning
Complaints about gas fires are most likely to arise in the context of **11–15**
claims made for carbon monoxide poisoning. Although these claims
are common, because they often involve relatively minor symptoms
in the affected person some of the more problematic areas have

tended to be ignored. In particular, even if it is established that the resident has suffered carbon monoxide poisoning, which is swiftly diagnosed following the exposure, it is not always easy to establish that this was a consequence of a defective gas installation. This will especially be the case where the person concerned was a smoker at the time of the alleged exposure. Cigarettes produce damaging amounts of Carbon Monoxide which often finds its way into the blood stream and thus makes establishing causation more difficult than it would otherwise be.

Notice

11–16 Whereas a claimant under s.11 must show actual notice to his landlord or at least to his servants or agents, liability under s.4 of the DPA will arise wherever the landlord "failed to take such care as was reasonable in all the circumstances to see that the claimant was reasonably safe from personal injury" (headnote in *Sykes v Harry* above). Once causation is established it will be difficult in practice for the landlord to avoid liability on the basis of lack of notice.

Access

11–17 A problem of practical importance that arises however relates to access in order to comply with these obligations. Tenants who are uncooperative may place their landlords at risk of prosecution. It is therefore sometimes necessary to obtain an injunction to allow access for inspection and servicing. The circumstances in which a court will grant such an injunction are considered in Ch.16.

Liability for electrical installations

11–18 Many of the regulations which apply to electrical installations are made under the Consumer Protection Act 1987, under which some of those relating to gas installations referred to above have also been made. The following may be of particular relevance to those renting out premises which contain electrical installations:

- If electrical appliances are provided for the tenant or licensee they must comply with the Electrical Equipment (Safety) Regulations 1994 (SI 1994/3260). These regulations were introduced under s.11 of the Consumer Protections Act 1987 and are designed to achieve minimum standards throughout the European Union. These include the requirement that electrical installations have adequate electrical insulation and earthing to prevent electric shock.

- Plugs and electrical sockets must be tested and marked under the Plugs and Sockets (Safety) Regulations. 1994 (SI 1994/1768). These regulations were also introduced under the Consumer Protection Act 1987 and also provide for such matters as fuses and wires.

Civil liability under the above regulations is provided for by s.41 of the Consumer Protection Act 1987. Generally speaking any person affected by a breach of regulations made under that Act, including any of those summarised above, may being an action for breach of duty.

In addition any electrical work carried out to the building must comply with the Buildings Regulations 2000. Part P is relevant to the electrical installations and the reader is referred to those regulations for the details which cannot be included here.

There is a new set of wiring regulations which apply from July 1, 2008, known as the IEE Wiring regulations. They are in their 17th edition and must comply with BS: 7671. They will set the standard of wiring and for other electrical installations. They cover such things as the design, inspection and certification of electrical wiring. Landlords are generally recommended to go with an NICEIC registered contractor but there is also a Government-sponsored scheme called "Trustmark" to assist with this. The NICEIC is the national body responsible for regulation of electrical standards and implementing the relevant standard.

Finally, any electrical equipment provided to the tenant or licensee with the premises will need to be disposed of in accordance with the Disposal of Electrical Equipment Directive (2002/96) which came into force in January 2007.

Energy efficiency standards

This is a fruitful area of EU and national government activity at present. **11–19** The EU Directive on Energy Performance in Buildings (Directive 2002/91/EC) seeks to raise standards of energy efficiency, principally in new buildings, by setting energy performance targets. The Energy Performance of Buildings (Certificates and Inspections) (England and Wales) Regulations 2007 (SI 2007/991) and the Energy Performance of Buildings (Certificates and Inspections) (England and Wales) (Amendment) Regulations 2007 (SI 2007/1669) introduce a system of certification to be used when buildings are sold or let. Those regulations apply to all buildings, both commercial and residential. In respect of commercial buildings the requirement that landlords display energy performance certificates came into force on April 1, 2008. The remaining provisions will come into force in stages, depending on the size of the premises from that day. Subject to certain exceptions, certain dwellings will come within this certification regime. The certification process is similar to the certification requirement in relation to electrical appliances. A certificate will be valid for ten years. The energy efficiency rating will need to be displayed.

These regulations need to be read with the Home Information Pack Regulations (2007/992) and the Home Information Pack (No.2) Regulations 2007, which came into force on July 2, 2007. These regulations are in the course of implementation at the time of writing. In particular they are being implemented in stages based on the size of dwelling. When fully implemented these regulations will introduce various rules about energy efficiency which readers should be aware of. Article 8 introduced the requirement that every home information pack shall contain, amongst other things, a predicted energy assessment. The regulations will apply to existing dwellings and not just to newly marketed ones.

The Energy Performance in Buildings Directive (referred to above) seems likely to have a major impact on commercial buildings as it includes the requirement that energy assessments be displayed and that air conditioning assessments be carried out. It seems likely that few buildings comply with these standards at the present time. However, this is an area where there is likely to be greater intervention by the state and voluntary sectors in the future, for example the Carbon Trust now provides grants to commercial tenants with a view to lowering their carbon emissions.

This topic will be considered more fully in the next chapter.

Legislation applying to particular types of premises

11–20 The legislation referred to in the following three paragraphs are largely repealed by a number of statutory instruments which implemented EU Directives in the 1990s. In the case of the Factories Act 1961, the entirety of that Act in so far as it may have any relevance to defective premises, has been repealed. The new regulations, which for the sake of completeness are referred to below, apply to all workplaces and workers and not just to those in specific industries. However, the statutes which follow still have some extant provisions.

Offices Shops and Railway premises Act 1963

11–21 The 1963 Act applied to offices shops and railway premises from 1964 onwards. Those premises were defined in s.1. However, some of the provisions were soon supplemented and replaced by certain sections in the Health and Safety at Work Act 1974.

As mentioned above, the 1963 Act was subject to more major amendment and repeal by various EU Directives and the regulations made under them. In particular the main regulations which now govern general health and safety standards to premises where people work or to which the people have access are as follows:

- Workplace (Health, Safety and Welfare) Regulations 1992 (SI 1992/3004);
- Provision and Use of Work Equipment Regulations 1992 (SI 1992/2932);
- Manual Handling Operation Regulations 1992 (SI 1992/2793).

But it will be obvious that those regulations go substantially beyond the scope of a publication about defective premises.

However, a small number of sections in the 1963 Act have survived, In particular:

- section 42, which places an obligation on the occupier of premises to which the Act applies to clean the furniture, fixtures and fittings therein, adequately light to those premises and ensure that the windows are kept clean to facilitate adequate illumination;
- section 43, which applies to buildings which are "plurally occupied" i.e. occupied by more than one person and extends duties as to cleanliness and maintenance of common parts including those above to such persons;
- section 44, which deals with premises with adjoining fuel storage facilities.

Disability Discrimination Act 1995 and 2005

These Acts are not really about defective premises at all; rather they **11–22** are designed to enable a disabled person to enjoy a minimum standard of access to certain buildings. Such persons may bring a claim for damages, for example, against landlords and other occupiers of premises if they have not carried out appropriate adaptation to facilitate disabled access.

In practice, an allegation of disability discrimination is often raised as a defence to possession proceedings. There have been a number of recent cases which discuss the meaning of "disability" and the ambit of the legislation. The relevance of the 1995 Act to possession proceedings has recently been considered by the House of Lords in *Lewisham LBC v Malcolm* [2008] UKHL 43. That case places sensible limits on the extent to which the Act may be used as a defence to those proceedings. A more detailed analysis is beyond the scope of this book.

Nevertheless, the new Acts create significant compliance obligations not only on employers but also in some cases on landlords, tenants and other occupiers.

The legislation should also be borne in mind by landlords because the need to comply with the Act may be more extensive than the duties under the lease and at common law. In particular, s.21 obliges the provider of "services", including a landlord who provides accommodation to a disabled person, to take steps to remove any unreasonable obstacle in the way of a disabled person.

As well as placing a duty on a landlord, in respect of any part of the premises over which he has retained control, a tenant may be permitted, indeed is required, to carry out alterations to the premises to comply with the Acts (see s.27 of the 1995 Act). As a consequence he will not, for example, be in breach of a covenant in the lease prohibiting alterations to the fabric of the building.

Chapter 12

Local authority control of defective premises

Since the mid-19th Century local authorities have had an important **12–01**
role in enforcing minimum housing and building standards (see, for
example, the Artisans and Labourers Dwellings Act 1875). This has
included the power to control dangerous and defective dwellings.
Until recently the majority of the provisions relating to housing
standards were to be found in the Housing Act 1985 but they are now
in the Housing Act 2004. This major piece of new legislation
dominates this area (see the Law Commission's consultation paper
(Law Com. 181) "Encouraging Responsible Letting" for the
legislative background in relation to the private sector).

The new regime in the 2004 Act, which was introduced from April
6, 2006 onwards, is not only aimed at defective premises but also
seeks to raise the standard and quality of the housing stock. It does
this by introducing a new system for assessing housing conditions
and ensuring the provision of basic amenities within those dwellings.
There are also important changes to the method of enforcing
standards in houses in multiple occupation (HMOs) which will need
to be considered.

The requirements of the new Act have to be enforced by local
authorities and do not give rise to civil law remedies. Nor do they
apply to local authorities themselves, which are subject to other
regulation such as the Environmental Protection Act 1990 (see
R. v Cardiff City Council ex p. Cross (1982) 6 H.L.R. 1). The
Environmental Protection Act 1990 will be considered below.

Given that the main focus of this book is on civil law remedies,
detailed coverage of the new regime under the 2004 Act is beyond
the scope of this work. However, since the excessively complex
new regime is aimed at the private sector, where it is believed the
worst housing conditions still exist, it is necessary to have some

understanding of the application of the new regulations introduced under the 2004 Act. Other provisions in the 2004 Act, such as the controversial new provisions with regard to home information packs, do not impact upon the subject matter of this publication and have therefore been only briefly referred to above.

Before the detailed provisions in the 2004 Act are considered it is helpful to have an overview of the earlier legislation, especially since case law decided under that legislation might still be relevant to the new Act.

Powers and duties under housing, building and public health legislation

Background

12–02   There is a raft of public health legislation extending back to the 19th Century controlling health-related issues that impact on building owners. The more important legislation is summarised here.

The Public Health Act 1936

12–03   Although some of the provisions in the Public Health Act 1936 have now been placed into more modern legislation, some provisions remain in force. Under that Act local authorities were given the power to take action in relation to premises which were in an unwholesome condition and were bound to take action if the premises were such as to be prejudicial to health. The Act also gave local authorities powers to control dangerous buildings and consolidated many provisions found in local byelaws in relation to numerous matters affecting public health.

Those powers and duties are now found in later legislation and in particular the Building Act 1984, which is the principal Act controlling building standards and conditions. However the following sections may still be relevant:

- section 45 which provides that defective closets are to be maintained in such a state that they are not prejudicial to health or a nuisance;
- sections 79—80 which require the removal of any noxious matter;
- section 83, as amended, which deals with dirty or verminous premises.

Under the 1936 Act local authorities had the power to make byelaws relating to the erection of buildings within their locality. Those bye-laws originally controlled building standards but those powers and duties to control building standards were eventually placed into the Building Act 1984. The present regulations (the Building Regulations 2000) apply nationally. Although the Act and the regulations have been considered more fully in the previous chapter, for the sake of completeness they are also considered here.

The Building Act 1984 and regulations made thereunder
The Building Act 1984 includes powers: **12–04**

- to ensure drainage is satisfactory and not prejudicial to health (s.59);
- to control buildings that are dangerous (s.77);
- to force owners to take action in relation to buildings that are ruinous or dilapidated (s.79).

The regulations made under the 1984 Act (the Building Regulations) have been considered in the last chapter. These regulations are now made by the Secretary of State for Communities and Local Government. The principal regulations currently in force are the Building Regulations 2000, as amended. As from July 1, 1987 the national system of building regulation has also applied to Inner London.

The Housing Act 1985
The sections of this Act contained in Part XVIII, which dealt with   **12–05** unfit dwellings, have now been repealed by s.266 of the Housing Act 2004 and replaced with the licensing system described below. In particular s.604, which set out a fitness standard which dwellings had to achieve, failing which they would be the subject to various notices, orders and charges, has gone.

There were also powers in this Act, originally found in the Housing Defects Act 1984, for the Secretary of State to designate property as defective due to its design or construction (s.528). This also enabled compensation to be paid to property owners whose properties were affected by the designation.

The Environmental Protection Act 1990
This legislation contained the important power to control statutory   **12–06** nuisance, which will be considered below.

The Housing Grants Construction and Regeneration Act 1996

12–07 This Act enables the landlord to carry out works of improvement with the benefit of a grant and introduced an adjudication procedure which helped to speed up the resolution of building disputes.

The new system for assessing housing conditions in the Housing Act 2004

12–08 The 2004 Act introduces a new system of licensing houses in multiple occupation and for dealing with various hazards in housing accommodation. It swept away many of the existing powers, some of which had been around for a long time in one guise or another. More specifically, the Act, which came into force by various statutory instruments between 2004 and 2007, replaced the old fitness standard and introduced a housing, health and safety-rating regime (HHSRR). Subject to minor exceptions the Act only applies to England and Wales (s.270(11)).

Broadly, local authorities are given increased powers of enforcement to a standard which is supposed to be more tightly defined and by reference to clearer criteria. The new regime contained in Pt 1 of the Act, is supposed to identify hazards before they cause a danger to human health and remove those hazards.

Structure of the legislation in outline

12–09 The broad scheme of Pt 1 of the Act, the majority of which came into force in 2006, is as follows:

- Chapter 1 sets out general housing standards to be achieved and defines the various hazards that are to be dealt with under the new regime.

- Chapter 2 introduces a system of notices and orders in relation to empty dwellings.

- Chapter 3 provides for emergency measures and procedures in relation to overcrowded dwellings.

- Chapter 4 re-enacts the powers of slum clearance and demolition formerly in Pt XVIII of the Housing Act 1985.

- Chapter 5 contains general and miscellaneous provisions connected with enforcement.

Part 2 of the Act introduced the new licensing system for houses in multiple occupation (HMOs) and Pt 3 introduced selective licensing for other types of residential accommodation in areas of low housing demand, known as "designated selected licensing areas". There is also a Housing and Regeneration Bill, currently before Parliament, which will create further rules to rehabilitate areas in need of such expenditure. Part 4 of the 2004 Act contains additional provisions to control residential accommodation. Part 5 of the Act introduces Home Information Packs and is therefore beyond the scope of this book. However, Pt 6, Ch.5 of the 2004 Act, is worthy of mention. It allows the introduction of public money to non-RSL landlords and developers to improve the housing stock (s.27A(1) H.A. 1996, added by s.220 of H.A. 2004).

The new housing health and safety-rating regime in outline
The duties under Pt 1 of the Act apply to "residential premises", **12–10**
which include dwelling houses, and unoccupied HMOs. The duties also apply to common parts of buildings containing one or more flats. Thus the 2004 Act:

- avoids some of the difficult questions that arose under the Housing Act 1985 as to the meaning of "house", which included a flat;
- does not distinguish between different accommodation types as long as the accommodation is used for housing. Under the 2004 Act it does not matter how the building was constructed provided it is now used as a dwelling of the type described above.

The aim of the new system (see "Housing, Health and Safety Rating System Guidance" (version 2) ODPM November 2004) is to identify faults and hazards in dwellings before they have an affect on the health and safety of occupants, whereas the old system required a local authority to serve a notice when the property fell into disrepair. Once these defects are found they are supposed to be eradicated before the premises deteriorate further. This will either be by completing the required work or, where that work cannot be effected, by closing the premises down.

The aim of eradicating defects before they render the premises uninhabitable is intended to be achieved by a complicated system of risk identification and eradication. The local authority is supposed first of all to identify whether the hazard falls within "category 1" or "category 2" of s.1. A "hazard" is:

"any risk of harm to the health or safety of an actual or potential occupier of the dwelling or HMO which arises from a deficiency in the dwelling or HMO or any building or land in the vicinity (whether the deficiency arises as a result of the construction, an absence of maintenance or repair, or otherwise." (s.2(1))

But "category 1" hazards and "category 2" hazards are only defined in very general terms in the above section and it has been left to the regulations to indicate how those hazards are to be identified.

Twenty-nine "matters and circumstances" are to be taken into account when determining the level of hazard. These are provided for in reg.3 and Sch.1 of the relevant regulations (the Housing Health and Rating System (England) Regulations 2005 (SI 2005/3208) and the Housing Health Safety and Rating System (Wales) Regulations 2006 (SI 2006/1702) . The method by which they are to be found and assessed is included in those regulations. The matters taken into account will include such things as poor energy efficiency which has not featured in housing legislation in the past. Once the seriousness of the hazard has been identified it is then allocated points according to seriousness. Those hazards with high points are required to be remedied.

Hazards covered by the legislation

12–11 As indicated above, regulations under Pt 1 of the Act were introduced by the Housing, Health and Safety Rating System (England) Regulations 2005 (SI 2005/3208), which came into force on April 6, 2006, and the Housing Health and Safety and Rating System (Wales) Regulations 2006, which came into force on June 30, 2006. These regulations distil the stated hazards down to "category 1 hazards" (those found in bands A, B or C of table 3) and "category 2 hazards" (those found in any other band in that table).

The hazards are identified by looking at four classes of harm that may arise. These are set out in Sch.2 of the 2005 and the 2006 regulations and may be summarised as follows:

- *Category 1:* psychological requirements including thermal efficiency, the removal of pollutants such as asbestos and carbon monoxide.
- *Category 2:* psychological requirements including space, security, adequate light and freedom from excessive noise.
- *Category 3:* protection from infection, poor hygiene, sanitation and inadequate water supply.
- *Category 4:* protection against accidents including falls on stairs and similar hazards.

Category 1 is the most serious but it should be noted that category 4 includes such things as "severe bruising" which would be considered very serious by most people!

Enforcement measures
The duties and powers in Pt 1 are to be enforced by housing **12–12**
authorities, which are bound to carry out annual inspections for the
purposes of the legislation. It should be noted that the enforcement
of the licensing regime is not a bar to the statutory nuisance scheme
under the EPA 1990.

In substance the local authority is required to take enforcement
action to ensure that premises which contain one or more of the
proscribed hazards are rendered safe either by carrying out work or
closing the dwelling.

Those hazards which fall within category 1 *must* be enforced
whereas those within category 2 *may* be enforced.

There are a wide variety of enforcement measures available under Ch.2
of Pt 1 to secure compliance with the new rating standard. These include:

- an improvement notice;
- a prohibition notice;
- a hazard awareness order;
- emergency remedial measures;
- an emergency prohibition order.

Where the hazard is such as to constitute an imminent threat to the
health and safety of inhabitants an emergency prohibition order will
be made. However, local authorities have a number of emergency
enforcement measures available including carrying out the work
themselves and recovering the cost from the landlord.

There is a right of appeal against a notice under the Act to the
Residential Property Tribunal but failing that a landlord who does
not comply will be guilty of a criminal offence.

Application of the new scheme
The new scheme applies to all residential premises (s.1) including **12–13**
houses in multiple occupation (HMOs) whether occupied or not,
premises occupied by students and premises occupied by religious
communities. For the purposes of achieving the minimum standard
there is a wider definition of HMO than elsewhere.

Duties and powers with respect to houses in multiple occupation

At present houses in multiple occupation are thought to provide some **12–14**
of the worst accommodation in England and Wales and it has long
been a political aim to improve the standard of this accommodation.

The law has been extensively reformed in the Housing Act 2004 by which the old provisions in the Housing Act 1985 were repealed. A new regulatory framework introduced by the 2004 Act applies to all HMOs and does not exempt all student houses, as the old regime did.

Part 7 of the new Act contains a new definition of a "house in multiple occupation" in s.254, which is not the same definition of "HMO" as is used for all purposes in the Act. "HMO" is defined in that section, inter alia, as "one or more units of living accommodation not consisting of a self-contained flat or flats" and self-contained flats where there is living accommodation occupied by persons who do not form part of a single household (s.254(3)). However, the definition is deliberately wide and will include bed and breakfast accommodation, hostels, halls of residence, and various types of supported housing such as women's refuges. The new licensing scheme applies to any yard, garden or outhouse linked to an HMO just as it applies to the house itself.

The compulsory licensing scheme described for premises in multiple occupation (s.61), is subject to an exemption in relation to temporary accommodation (s.62). The licensing scheme is administered by local authorities (s.63).

The power to control statutory nuisances

12–15   The Environmental Protection Act 1990 is a useful piece of legislation, which enables tenants and other occupiers to prevent "statutory nuisances". In particular the aggrieved person will be able to achieve a relatively swift remedy backed up by criminal sanctions for non-compliance. However, he will not be able to recover any compensation. The enforcement powers are via local authorities and, ultimately, by using the magistrates courts rather than the civil courts. A tenant of modest means will not qualify for legal aid to make such an application since legal aid is not available to fund those proceedings but those with the resources to do so may lay an information at the magistrates court for the area in which the property is situated and force action. The local environmental health officer, who identifies a statutory nuisance where it has occurred, will be able themselves to bring a claim in the magistrates' court and will therefore be responsible for the costs. However, perhaps as a consequence of the lack of public funding to individual complainants, the powers have not been as widely used as might have been expected.

The law is sufficiently detailed to have spurred more than one textbook on the subject and the reader is referred to those for more in-depth treatment of the subject (for example *Statutory Nuisance: Law and Practice*, Malcolm and Pointing, (2002) OUP). The following provides only an outline.

The statutory nuisance power in outline

Essentially the legislation is aimed at environmental nuisances and **12–16** has its origins in the public health legislation. The main provisions are found in Pt III. Section 79(1) provides that every local authority has a duty to inspect in its area for any statutory nuisance and investigate any complaint of statutory nuisance. A "statutory nuisance" is widely defined in that section so as to include any matter which is prejudicial to health and any insect emanating from trade, industrial or business premises. The section does not apply to contaminated land which has its own intricate regime of protection. It applies to Crown land but not to premises held by the Secretary of State for Defence for naval, military or air force purposes.

What constitutes a statutory nuisance?

A statutory nuisance is anything prejudicial to the health of the **12–17** claimant. Fortunately for such claimants, the legislation adopts a broad definition in s.79 by stating that any state "prejudicial to health" will constitute such a nuisance. The section then gives a number of examples where a statutory nuisance will be found, for example, any accumulation or deposit which is prejudicial to health or a nuisance and any escape of fumes or gases.

The Divisional Court in *London Borough of Hackney v Rottenberg* [2007] EWHC 166 (Admin) made it clear that this was a question upon which the magistrates' court could hear subjective evidence from environmental health officers. However that evidence was not ultimately decisive and the judge who finds the facts (or jury in a Crown Court case) had to decide whom he believed and whom he did not believe. It was preferable for local authorities bringing these prosecutions to support their cases with verifiable data. In a case involving noise nuisance this may consist of decibel readings but in a case involving damp it would involve producing damp readings.

The application of s.79 appears to have been weakened somewhat by the decision of the House of Lords in *Birmingham City Council v Oakley* [2001] 1 A.C. 617. In that case their Lordships were concerned with a council house in which the kitchen had a lavatory in a separate room on one side and a wash basin in another room on the other side. It was argued that the absence of any hand washing facility in the lavatory constituted a statutory nuisance, given its proximity to the kitchen. Their Lordships decided that the *premises themselves* must have some feature which is prejudicial to health and this did not include the layout of those premises even though that might mean that they may be used in a way that is prejudicial to health.

"Prejudice to health" is not thought to include physical injury to the complainant or his visitors, but rather refers to the indirect effects of defective accommodation, for example, loss of sleep (see *R. v Bristol City Council ex p. Everett* [1999] Env. L.R. 587 and *Lewisham v Fenner* (1995) ENDS 44). But the question whether the premises are "prejudicial to health" or not will be judged objectively and not based on the health or lack of it of individual occupiers (see *Cunningham v Birmingham City Council* [1998] Env. L.R. 1).

What powers are there to deal with statutory nuisances?

12–18   Sections 80 and 80A set out the means by which these statutory nuisances may be dealt with. In particular, those sections lay down the summary procedure referred to above which utilises the magistrates' courts and allows for the service of abatement notices. Those sections need to be read with various other sections, for example, s.160 which provides for service of these notices. This section allows a person served with a statutory notice to specify more than one address. However, in *Butland v Powys CC* [2007] All E.R. (D) 251 the Court of Appeal, overturning the Divisional Court, made it clear that they would not allow this to be used as a method of defeating the legislation. They found that the notice by the local authority requiring the abatement of noise had been correctly served on the address from which the noise emanated, given that was the address the respondent had himself given at which he should be served.

Local authority powers to enforce energy efficiency standards

12–19   This has been considered in greater detail in Ch.11 (see para.11–19). However, local authorities also have an important role in enforcing these powers. In particular, under reg.38 of the Energy Performance of Buildings (Certificates and Inspections) (England and Wales) Regulations 2007, SI 2007/991, weights and measures authorities are given the power to enforce these standards. They are county district and borough councils throughout England and county or county borough councils in Wales. Therefore, these standards are also considered here.

A significant challenge in the future is likely to be achieving higher environmental standards in all types of housing, including new and rejuvenation projects. This ought to include not only the efficiency of the unit in question but also the sustainability of the products used in its construction or restoration. On the former point there are substantial energy efficiency standards being introduced in the light of the EU Directive on Energy Performance of Buildings (Dir. 2002/91/EC). As a consequence of that Directive the energy performance certificates have been introduced in various regulations and in particular in the Energy Performance of Buildings (Certificates and Inspections) (England and Wales) Regulations 2007 (SI 2007/991) and the Energy Performance of Buildings (Certificates and Inspections) (England and Wales) (Amendment) Regulations 2008 (SI 2008/647). The 2007 regulations also introduced air conditioning assessments in relation to commercial premises. The 2007 regulations, which are the principal regulations, came into force on April 19, 2007 whereas the 2008 regulations came into force on April 6, 2008. All public buildings will have to display their energy certificates. These new regulations are set to give rise to significant compliance issues.

Section 217 of the Housing Act 2004 requires the Secretary of State to take "reasonable steps" to ensure the level of energy efficiency of new buildings and in particular provides that the new buildings should be 20 per cent more energy efficient by 2010 compared with 2000 levels. The Secretary of State will issue appropriate guidance on this but how this guidance is interpreted and the precise content of the relevant regulations are likely to be important.

These powers are in addition to the powers that exist under the Sustainable Energy Act 2003, which placed various burdens on the Government to achieve energy efficiency.

The 2004 Act (which amends the Home Energy Conservation Act 1995) also has in mind the taking of reasonable steps to ensure a general level of energy efficiency and appropriate guidance will be issued in this regard.

Energy efficiency is also increasingly becoming a requirement of the planning system, for example, the Planning and Energy Bill currently before Parliament will, if it passes through all stages of Parliament, set requirements for energy generation and energy efficiency in local plans.

The "Decent Homes Standard"

An increasing amount of housing stock formerly held by local **12–20** authorities is passing into the private sector. That part of the public sector housing stock that has not passed into the hands of a wide variety of social landlords, e.g. housing associations and charities, is being run by arms-length management organisations (ALMOs) or is being restored within the private finance initiative (PFI).

The present Government links the above developments to improving the standard of the housing stock. The "Decent Homes Standard" is an initiative by the Department of Communities and Local Government (formerly the Office of the Deputy Prime Minister) whereby the Government claims to be committed to bringing 95 per cent of homes up to a "decent standard" by 2010. However, the "decent standard" was never defined accurately and it has been left to various surveyors and other providers of energy measures in the private sector to do so (e.g. Applied Energy Products Ltd whose website has been included in Appendix 3 of this work). In practice it is likely to mean a reasonable standard of repair, modern facilities and a reasonable level of thermal comfort.

It is clear that the Government has in mind "targeting" its resources at particular deprived and vulnerable groups within the public or registered social landlord sectors. Although the official bidding for funding for these projects is now at an end, in practice it seems likely that local authorities that wish to improve their housing stock in line with the standard will be able to do so. However, they are supposed to do so via one of three accepted routes: direct transfers into the private social rented sector, the use of "arms length management organisations" (ALMOs) and the private finance initiative (PFI) but this approach has been criticised, for example, by the Local Government Association in March 2007. That Association challenged the Government to provide adequate funds for all these avenues to be explored. That is looking less and less likely in the light of the economic decline which has subsequently occurred.

However, there are a number of successful schemes in place including one in Sheffield, where the local authority in conjunction with its ALMO "Sheffield Homes" is investing about £700 million on a decent homes project (source: Sheffield Homes Website).

RSLs are encouraged to find finance from the private sector but they may well be constrained by their constitution, particularly if they are charities. The Housing Act 2004 amended earlier legislation to allow public money to be used for non-registered landlords/private developers as well for this type of project (see s.27A(1) H.A. 1996, added by s.220 H.A. 2004 supra).

There will also be further new powers to deal with urban regeneration in the Housing Regeneration Bill currently before Parliament. That Bill, if passed, will set up the Homes and Communities Agency.

Proposals for reform

The Law Commission is currently consulting on wider improvements **12–21** in the condition of housing stock and has recommended that specific provision be made for energy efficiency standards in all residential lettings (in "Encouraging Responsible Letting": Law Com. 181 (2007)). The Commission recommends that energy efficiency be a specific requirement for premises which are let out. In "Renting Homes" (Law Com. 284 (2006)—final report Law Com. 297) the Commission has also recommended important changes to terms in tenancy agreements in relation to the terms and conditions on which they are held with the aim of simplifying these and achieving greater clarity.

PART III

REMEDIES

Chapter 13

Use of the Human Rights Act 1998

The Human Rights Act 1998 has mainly been used as a defence and **13–01** mainly where, the present law being deficient in some way, the claimant seeks to rely on the Act to provide an additional remedy. Hence its consideration here.

Outside the area of litigation against the Government, where the Human Rights Act has substantially increased the scope of judicial review and related challenges, the Human Rights Act has been a less obvious generator of property-related litigation. However, as a living instrument it is by no means clear that this will remain the case.

The effect of the Act on property law may be illustrated by cases like *Price v Leeds City Council* [2006] UKHL 10 (possession order against gypsies—whether subject to art.8) and *JA Pye (Oxford) v Graham* (2006) 43 EHRR 3 (concerning the UKs limitation rules for dealing with squatter's claims against registered owners). More pertinent to this area is *Lee v Leeds City Council* [2002] EWCA Civ 06 (also considered in Ch.2 at p.19), in which tenants of a local authority tried to attack the decision in *Quick v Taff-Ely* [1986] Q.B. 809 and attach liability for design faults onto the landlord. Although the attack in that case was unsuccessful, it is by no means clear that future challenges will be.

Because of the potential long-term impact of the incorporation of Convention rights into domestic law the subject demands proper consideration in a book about defective premises. A particular difficulty in considering the subject relates to the difference between the language of rights and the language of domestic property law. This often makes it difficult to apply unfamiliar concepts from European Convention law to domestic situations.

The relevant Convention rights

13–02 The main articles that are likely to be relevant are art.8, which protects the right to a person's home, private and family life within countries that are members of the Convention, and art.1 of the First Protocol entered in 1967, which protects a person's right to their possessions. However, art.6, which protects the right to a fair and impartial hearing, may also be relevant. That article is thought to ensure due process in such things as housing allocation and in that context challenges are likely to arise from time to time (see for example, *R. (on the application of Gilboy) v Liverpool City Council* [2007] LGR 837). It is less likely to arise in the context of disputes over defective premises.

The above rights are qualified. In the case of art.8, art.8(2) provides that there shall be no interference by a state with the rights of the individual save where it is in accordance with the law and in the interests of the economic well-being of the country. Under art.1 of the First Protocol the prohibition on interference with the right to enjoy one's possessions may be impaired where it is deemed necessary by the state "in accordance with the general interest" or in the interest of securing the payment of taxes.

Article 6 is concerned with substantive legal rights and not merely with procedural matters. It is unlikely to be raised as a defence to a claim arising out of the defective state of a building, although there is a significant argument that the remedy of physical re-entry by a commercial landlord may be liable to challenge under art.6. Article 6 also carries with it the proviso that certain proceedings may be carried out without the public being admitted where this is in the interests of morals or public order.

Who is liable under the Human Rights Act?

13–03 The Act applies to "public authorities" (s.6 of the HRA 1998). This expressly includes the courts and any "person whose functions are of a public nature" (s.6(3)(a) and (b)).

In certain circumstances, hybrid authorities, which carry out public functions, such as housing associations, may be subject to the Act. Thus in *Donoghue v Poplar Housing Regeneration and Community Association Ltd* [2001] EWCA Civ 595, [2002] Q.B. 48, the housing association in question begun possession proceedings against a tenant it had inherited from the local authority. This followed an earlier attempt by that local authority to evict that tenant. The Court of Appeal said that provided the housing association was performing a public function it would be subject to the Human Rights Act. The feature that established that the housing association was discharging a public function in that case, which meant it would be subject to the Act, was "the role of the housing association in providing accommodation for the defendant and then seeking possession ... [This] was so closely assimilated to that of the local housing authority that it was performing public functions and was, to that extent, a functional public authority ..."(headnote at [2002] Q.B. 48). More recently, in *R. (on the application of Weaver) v London and Quadrant Housing Trust* [2008] EWHC (Admin) a registered social landlord was held to be a public authority for the purposes of the Human Rights Act.

How a challenge may be made

Challenges arise in one of two principal ways: **13–04**

- It is possible to apply for a declaration of incompatibility under s.7(1)(a) of the 1998 Act. Such an application may only be made to the High Court or an appellate court but such applications are not particularly common in practice. It is likely that such an application will result in the secretary of state for the relevant department applying to be joined as a party to the proceedings.

- The court when considering existing case law and legislation may look at European jurisprudence and interpret the common law and statute law, both primary and secondary, in such a way as to render it compatible with the Convention. This is the means by which most human rights challenges come before the courts, i.e. on an argument that existing law should be re-interpreted to make it compatible.

The challenges so far

The Convention gives no general right to housing or housing of a **13–05** particular quality (see *O'Rourke v UK* (App. No.390 22/97)). However, European jurisprudence suggests that the former right may arise in certain exceptional circumstances (see *Marzari v Italy* App. No.36488/97, where the applicant had a serious disease) but even where that is established a large "margin of appreciation" would be allowed to the domestic authorities as the actions of that state tend to be treated as necessary in a democratic society. The "margin of appreciation" referred to is the respect of international courts for decisions made locally by national parliaments of signatory countries.

It is thought appropriate to accord those local decisions a proper degree of respect. In *Marzari* the claimant had effectively brought his eviction for non-payment of rent on himself by failing to take steps to protect his own position properly. Therefore his eviction was justified when the system in place in Italy for dealing with that default was considered. It was right for the court to consider the remedy in its context and, even though a breach of art.8 had been established, it was nevertheless justified.

The wide margin of appreciation to domestic law is also illustrated by *Hatton v UK* 036022/97 [2003] ECHR 338 (July 8, 2003). In that case eight members of the Heathrow action committee were unsuccessful before the Grand Chamber in their challenge against the UK Government's policy on night flights. The Grand Chamber is a panel of five judges composed of the President of the Court, the Section Presidents, with the exception of the Section President who presides over the Section to which the Chamber that gave the preliminary judgment belongs. The Grand Chamber is the highest level that the litigant disgruntled by a human rights decision can go. More recently in *Pye v Graham* (App. No.44302/02), somewhat surprisingly, the Grand Chamber of the ECtHR declined to find that the law on adverse possession as it pertained to registered proprietors before the advent of the Land Registration Act 2002, contravened art.1 of the First Protocol.

The cases summarised above are in line with a generally conservative approach by both domestic courts and the ECtHR itself in the property field.

One recent case that appears to be out of line with that approach has been *McCann v UK* (App. No.19009) where the ECtHR determined that the law which allowed one joint tenant to terminate the agreement on behalf of both joint tenants, but without the other's consent or even knowledge, was not compliant with art.8. The Court were particularly concerned with the lack of procedural safeguards for the joint tenant who faces a loss of a valuable right to a joint secure tenancy without his knowledge or consent where the co-tenant had given notice to quit in somewhat dubious circumstances.

The whole question of the extent of art.8 seems set to be reconsidered by domestic courts therefore and it seems only a matter of time before the application of the Convention to building standards and the standard of accommodation generally also receives attention.

A recent attempt to apply the obligations under art.8 to local authorities in the context of nuisance behaviour by residents to its tenants did not succeed on the basis of the Human Rights Act (in *X v London Borough of Hounslow* [2008] EWHC Q.B.). However that case was decided on the basis that negligence had been established and the judge, Maddison J., therefore did not consider it necessary to decide on the application of the Convention. However it is by no means clear that the judge could not have decided the case on the basis that the tenant's art.8 rights had been breached.

Decisions relevant to defective premises litigation

In *Lee v Leeds City Council* [2002] LGR 305 it was argued that art.8 **13–06** of the European Convention on Human Rights was engaged by the local authority's failure to ensure that the premises were in a state that was fit for human habitation. The Court of Appeal found that both the argument in that case and the way that it had been raised (at the appeal stage) were flawed. But although they did not rule out such a challenge in the future, it ran into a number of hurdles. Not least of these was that the rule that lettings of unfurnished premises do not carry with them any warranty as to the quality of the accommodation was well-known and would probably fall within the wide margin of appreciation which is allowed to national parliaments. Secondly, it was pointed out by the Court of Appeal in *Lee* that there were other remedies available to the tenant affected by poor housing conditions under, for example, the Environmental Protection Act 1990.

In *Leeds City Council v Price* (above) the House of Lords were not concerned with a defective premises type claim nor did they consider that type of case. Nevertheless the case was thought at the time to put clear limits on the application of the Convention in general and art.8 in particular to well-established domestic practices. They held that where possession proceedings were brought against those without any licence or consent on the land in question, the local authority's claim could not be defeated by art.8. In theory a disgruntled squatter could argue in the High Court that the primary legislation was contrary to the Convention but in practice this was very unlikely to be successful.

However, recent European jurisprudence suggests the ECtHR may be developing a more active degree of involvement in domestic affairs. In particular, in *McCann v UK* (App. No.19009/04) 13/5/08 the ECtHR suggested that the principle of English property law, whereby one joint tenant could serve notice on behalf of both, could cause serious injustice. In particular it thereby deprived the other joint tenant of his home, where he had not served nor known of the notice. Thus it will be liable to challenge. The circumstances of that case did point to a contravention art.8. More recently still the House of Lords have cast doubt on its own decision in *Price* (above) by stating (in *Doherty v Birmingham City Council* [2008] UKHL 57

(30/7/08)) that in relation to cases to which art.8 applies (in that case involving a traveller) the facts must be examined on a case by case basis to see whether the article is engaged. The court would then go on to consider whether the second part of the article (which allowed for the interference with that right in certain circumstances) was established. The law at the moment is therefore very far from being finally settled.

Possible future challenges

13–07 It has long been thought that forfeiture is an area rife for challenge. In particular a number of commentators have speculated that the forfeiture by physical re-entry would be one of the first challenges after the new Act was introduced. At the time of writing this has still not occurred, but forfeiture by physical re-entry is still liable to be overturned (see most recently Janet Bignell, "L and T Review 2007", Vol.11 No.5). From the point of view of the tenant facing the loss of a valuable asset it is surprising that it has not yet been argued that forfeiture by physical re-entry represents an unlawful deprivation by the landlord of the tenant's possessions. Alternatively, it may be argued that the exercise of the ancient right of forfeiture without court proceedings represents a breach of art.6, which gives the right to a fair hearing.

However, any attack on English legislation on the basis that it is not compliant with the Human Rights Act runs into the problem that, in relation to most English legislation, a large margin of appreciation will be given to our national Parliament. It seems inevitable in a mature legal system that procedures will be well developed and will balance the needs of a tenant for a roof over his head, or to carry on his business, as the case may be, with the needs of the landlord for a reasonable return on his investment. It is only likely to be in those cases where the respondent is a local authority or housing association and thus owes the duties of a public authority to the tenant or in cases where there is a genuine challenge to the validity of the legislation itself that any successful challenge is likely to be launched under the Human Rights Act. These are likely to be rare cases especially in the case of defective premises type complaints.

Chapter 14

Self help

The right of self-help continues to have a role in eradicating defects **14–01** in buildings and enforcing maintenance obligations. The principal method of self-help that continues to be relevant is the commercial landlord's right, where certain conditions are met, to forfeit a lease by physical re-entry. In many cases the landlord will decide to do this by bringing proceedings. Nevertheless the exercise of the ancient right of physical re-entry is still used and is often an effective way of ensuring either compliance with the leasehold covenants or bringing an early end to the lease. Because of the continuing importance of forfeiture and because nowadays it is commonly effected by proceedings rather than by self-help, this is dealt with separately in the next chapter.

The present chapter is concerned with the methods of self-help available to freehold owners, tenants and certain types of licensees who suffer from defects to their properties. This involves considering the extent to which an adjoining owner has a right to access his neighbour's land at common law and by statute as well as the means by which maintenance and repair obligations may be enforced by a tenant against his landlord. In addition, where the premises demised to the tenant are in disrepair the tenant often faces the difficult question tactically of whether to do the repairs himself or to continue to press the landlord to do them. Finally there is the related question of whether he should deduct the actual or estimated repair costs against the rent. The extent to which the tenant can do the work himself and recover the cost from the landlord will therefore be considered below.

Freehold owners' access to adjoining land

14–02 Much of the commentary that follows applies equally to all types of owner but it is more common for freehold owners to become involved in disputes with neighbours than for tenants to do so. However, in some cases similar principles will apply as between adjoining occupiers of flats as between owners of land or buildings separated vertically from adjoining land or buildings.

The starting position for resolving any dispute between adjoining freehold owners is a consideration of the deeds but these are often silent as to important matters such as access rights. However, they may help at least to identify where the boundary lies. If so, at least it will be possible to determine where responsibility lies to reinstate a physical feature that is in disrepair. If the dispute essentially involves a defective or dangerous party wall then this ought properly to be determined under the Party Wall Act 1996. As this does not entail self-help but rather embarking on a process of notice and counter-notice with a view ultimately to resolving any dispute by reference to a surveyor, and is a specialist area requiring detailed consideration, the Act is not considered further in this work. The rights of access and related points do, however, warrant further consideration here.

Common law rights between neighbours

14–03 It was a major deficiency of the common law that in the absence of an express or implied right of access to neighbouring land in the deeds, the owner who needed to enter his neighbour's land or buildings normally had to establish a prescriptive or other easement to do so. Alternatively he would need the agreement of his neighbour. There was no right of access for the purposes of, for example, maintaining his property. This problem theoretically existed however parlous the state of the property in question. An alternative solution was the common law right to abate a nuisance if such nuisance could be shown to have been caused or continued by the neighbour. These rights are considered in greater depth in the following paragraphs.

Establishing an easement
14–04 The problem of access to adjoining land to effect repairs was the addressed in *Ward v Kirkland* [1967] Ch.194. There the judge, Ungoed-Thomas J., was able to find an easement to allow access over a neighbour's land for repair purposes. A farmyard, a cottage and the land had been in common ownership. On the sale-off of the cottage and some land a problem arose over maintenance of a wall dividing the two parcels of land. The purchaser claimed the benefit of an easement to maintain the wall in question. It was held that the

sale had converted a quasi-easement into an easement under s.62 of the Law of Property Act 1925. A quasi-easement is the user of some part of one's own land that would constitute an easement if the land over which that advantage were exercised, was owned or occupied by another person. Section 62 provides that a variety of easements and advantages, including quasi-easements, are converted into legal easements on a conveyance. It was held that this had occurred on the sale off of the cottage and therefore the cottage had the benefit of an easement to maintain the wall in question. It had crystallised into an easement under that section when the cottage and the land that went with it had been sold off.

Common law right to abate a nuisance

This was also considered in Ch.8. Where the source of damage **14–05** amounts to a nuisance caused by a neighbouring property or land it may well be necessary to consider the rights of the occupier to abate affected by the defective neighbouring property nuisance at c affected by the defective neighbouring property to abate the nuisance. In *Abbahall v Smee* [2002] 1 W.L.R. 1472 the claimant's flat suffered damage when the owner of a flat above failed to maintain it. It was held that the tenant below, the claimant, did have the right to enter the flat above to exercise his common law right to abate a nuisance.

Statutory intervention in relation to access rights

Fortunately the difficulty of access rights has now been largely **14–06** addressed by the legislature in the Access to Neighbouring Land Act 1992. The combination of that Act and the Party Wall Act 1996, which deals with repairs and new work to various structures on or near to the boundary but not, generally, existing features wholly owned by one neighbour, has been largely to remove the need to rely on express or implied easements or the common law right to abate a nuisance. In particular, the Access to Neighbouring Land Act 1992 gives access rights on obtaining a court order where work to the dominant land is reasonably necessary. There is no reason why an access order should not be obtained by the owner of one flat against the owner of an adjoining flat, as the definition of "land" would appear to include buildings, although "land" is not defined in the Act. Therefore it should not matter whether the division is horizontal or vertical, nor would the right be limited to adjoining freehold owners provided the land over which the access is required is physically contiguous.

The law as it exists since the Access to Neighbouring Land Act appears to be much more favourable to property owners facing the need to repair damage or to maintain their own properties. The Party Wall Act 1996 addresses the linked problem of maintaining party walls and carrying out certain building work in the vicinity of the boundary. However, invoking the procedures in the 1992 Act may be protracted and costly given that a claim in the county court will need to be brought and the claimant will need to establish that the order is reasonably necessary. Also it is by no means clear that the 1992 Act allows access to land forming part of a highway (see s.8(3)) and it cannot be assumed that highway authorities will always co-operate.

To date there has been little litigation under the Act and it may well be that it takes some time for the problem of access to an adjoining highway and other problems to be addressed. In addition the Access to Neighbouring Land Act does not address the need to establish fault for any damage caused by a defective structure. To do that the owner of land or buildings affected by defective premises must bear in mind his common law rights in nuisance as well as investigating thoroughly those rights which there are under the deeds and under the Party Wall Act 1996.

The tenant's right to self-help

Carrying out the works

14–07   This is sometimes the cheapest and easiest way for the tenant to gain redress. Frequently it will also be the quickest way to achieve a satisfactory solution. The nature of this right will be considered and, later, the extent to which the tenant may deduct the costs he incurs in carrying out this work against rent and other charges.

Defects to the common parts

14–08   Where the defect arises within the demised premises the tenant will obviously be able to do the work or employ another person to do the work. However, the position may be more complex when the defect in question arises in the common parts of the building in which the demised premises are situated, rather than the demised premises themselves. There the tenant will need to rely on an express or implied right to enter those common parts to view the state and carry out the repairs. The right is similar to the landlord's equivalent right to enter and view the state of the demised premises and, if necessary, carry out the required repairs (considered more fully at para.7–16, p.74).

The lease will sometimes provide for this and in the absence of an express provision it may be possible to argue for an implied term. Further, where the landlord ought to have carried out repairs to that area as part of his repairing obligation, the case law suggests that the tenant has an implied licence to enter the landlord's property just as the landlord could enter the tenant's property in equivalent circumstances (see *Loria v Hammer* [1989] 2 E.G.L.R. 249). In that case the judge, John Lindsay Q.C. sitting as a deputy High Court Judge, saw no reason to distinguish between the landlord's implied licence, which undoubtedly exists, and the tenant's. Both were necessary to give proper effect to the covenants which were contained in the lease. The case illustrates that there are often several ways of approaching this type of problem requiring consideration of the law of easements, implied contractual terms and tort.

Withholding repair costs against rent

Invariably the cheapest and quickest way for the solvent tenant to **14–09** have his property repaired will be to have the repairs done at his expense and set-off that cost against future rent demands. Alternatively, he may wish to obtain an estimate and retain sufficient monies from the periodic rent to pay for those necessary repairs in the future. Choosing this method of self-help has pitfalls and it will generally be advisable to give the landlord proper notice that this is what the tenant is doing (see *Asco Developments v Gordon* [1978] 2 E.G.L.R. 41, LAG Bulletin, p.293). The problem will often arise in modern residential leases that the tenant will not enjoy much by way of long-term protection from removal and the landlord can relatively easily serve the necessary notice to terminate the lease and start possession proceedings. As will be seen, whilst a damages claim may operate as a set off to any rent arrears claim by the landlord, it will not usually prevent the court granting outright possession where the necessary conditions are met.

The dangers of not keeping the landlord informed of the reasons for withholding rent are illustrated by *Bluestorm v Portvale* [2004] EWCA Civ 289. In that case the Court of Appeal had to consider the tenant's right of set-off in the context of a transfer of the landlord's freehold reversion. The landlord claimed unpaid service charges against the defendant and the defendant counterclaimed for alleged disrepair. It was held that the defendant's failure to pay service charges on the 11 flats that it owned was the substantial cause of the failure of the claimant to repair the building of which those premises formed part. In addition the defendant had liquidated its subsidiary in circumstances that the trial judge had found unacceptable. On the facts the claimant had been justified in failing to do the repairs and the tenant's counterclaim failed. It would have been inequitable for the counterclaim to succeed in those circumstances. The Court of Appeal did not feel that they had to follow the earlier case of *Yorkbrook v Batten* (1985) 18 H.L.R. 25. In that case the landlord had unsuccessfully argued that the payment of a maintenance contribution by the tenant was a condition precedent for the discharge by the landlord of an obligation on the part of the landlord to provide hot water and central heating. Consequently the landlord was bound to renew and replace antiquated and unserviceable equipment in order to fulfil an obligation to provide adequate hot water and heating.

Setting off the repair costs in subsequent proceedings

14–10 Although not strictly a right of self-help but rather a set-off to a claim, it seems logical to deal with it here, as it is often a consequence of the withholding of rent discussed above that proceedings will be issued.

Frequently either the landlord begins proceedings to recover the outstanding rent or the tenant brings a claim for specific performance of the landlord's repairing obligation. Where the former occurs the extent to which the tenant may deduct the outstanding repair costs against that outstanding rent must be determined.

The tenant's equitable right of set-off against a rent arrears claim is of great practical importance. The tenant's claim is one for an unliquidated sum in damages, unlike the landlord's claim which is for a liquidated amount of rent fixed in the lease. It used to be thought that the equitable set-off of repair costs did not arise in these circumstances. However, it has for some time been recognised that such a claim can succeed and old authorities that said the tenant's counterclaim had to be for a liquidated sum, as opposed to an unliquidated sum, have not survived (see *British Anzani (Felixstowe) v International Management Ltd* [1980] Q.B. 137). Provided a counterclaim is closely related to the claim it may be set off against that claim. This will include a claim for disrepair arising under the covenants in the lease.

Subject to the tenant's claim being connected with the landlord's claim there are no limits on which items the tenant may set-off against a rent claim. Therefore an unquantified claim may be set-off against a liquidated claim. It is desirable tactically from the tenant's point of view to protect himself against the full force of the landlord's claims by raising any set-off available to him.

Set-off following assignment

14–11 The limits of the right have been set by such cases as *Muscat v Smith* [2003] 1 W.L.R. 2853 where Sedley L.J. drew attention to the need for a close relationship between claims and counterclaims. He found that upon taking the assignment of the landlord's reversion the assignee could only pursue those rent arrears which post-dated the assignment unless he was expressly assigned the benefit of the accrued rent claim. Nor would the assignee be liable for breaches of the repairing covenant which occurred prior to the assignment. Where the assignee of the reversion took an assignment of the outstanding rent arrears claim then the tenant was entitled to set off his own claim for despair against that claim.

However, there are dangers in attempting to set-off claims given that the right of set-off arises in equity (these are illustrated by the case of *Bluestorm v Portvale* [2004] EWCA Civ 289, more fully considered at p.163).

More recently in *Edlington Properties Ltd v JH Fenner and Co Ltd* [2006] EWCA Civ 403 the Court of Appeal had to consider the important question of the ability of a tenant to counterclaim against the assignee of his landlord's freehold reversion and the right of set off in the following circumstances. The Welsh Development Agency ("the WDA") entered an agreement ("the agreement") with Fenner (F) whereby WDA would build a factory on its land and then enter into a lease with F. After this occurred, however, the freehold reversion was assigned to Edlington (E).

E sued F for rent and insurance premiums due *after* assignment but F counterclaimed damages against E in respect of alleged breaches of the agreement by the WDA, i.e., which had arisen *before* the assignment.

Neuberger L.J. began by setting out the following propositions for the tenant:

1. that the transferee of the reversion took the benefit of the lease subject to any equities which could be invoked against the transferee;
2. that F's right of set off against the original landlord (the WDA) was a right which ran with the reversion.

Both those propositions were wrong in his view. In particular, neither s.141 of the LPA (rent and benefit of lessee's covenants runs with the reversion), which applies where the transfer had taken place before January 1, 1996, nor s.3 of the Landlord and Tenant (Covenants) Act 1995 (benefit and burden of covenant shall pass on an assignment), which applies to transfers after that date, provided for any right of the debtor to set-off a claim for damages in respect of claims before the tenant had been given notice of the assignment. The right of the assignee of the reversion to claim the rent due after assignment was not a chose in action but simply an incident of the reversion. The right of set-off, on the other hand, was a right personal to the tenant, whether or not it arose under the lease.

Attempts to limit the right of set-off

14–12 Leases, particularly commercial leases, frequently try to limit the ambit of the right of set-off or try and exclude it altogether. However, very clear words must be used to achieve this. A clause to the effect that rent was to be paid "without deduction" was held to be ineffective (see *Connaught Restaurants Ltd v Indoor Leisure Ltd* [1993] 2 E.G.L.R. 108). But a covenant to pay rent by direct debit has been held to effectively exclude the right of set-off (*Esso Petroleum v Milton* [1997] 1 W.L.R. 938).

There are also instances where a right of set-off in relation to compensation payments due to the tenant arises by statute (e.g. under the Agricultural Holdings Act 1986, s.17). That section is due to be repealed by the Tribunals, Courts and Enforcement Act 2007 but at the time of writing it remains in force.

The position of licensees

14–13 The majority of licensees will occupy land or buildings on short term arrangements and are unlikely to become involved in disrepair claims but where their premises do fall into disrepair they often have much lesser rights than tenants. However, there is no reason why contractual licensees, in the absence of express terms, should not be able to argue for similar terms to be implied into their contracts as tenants. Thus the discussion above in relation to implied access rights to effect repair to common parts and in relation to mutuality of remedy should in theory apply to them. Licensees also have the same rights as other occupiers to pursue neighbours for nuisance but cannot acquire easements or their equivalent unless they are expressly given the contractual equivalent rights. Obviously, any action in trespass vests in the owner of a legal estate and not in a mere licensee.

The rights of tenants of local authorities to compel the landlord to carry out repairs

14–14 Section 96 of the Housing Act 1985 (as amended by s.121 of the Leasehold Reform, Housing and Urban Development Act 1993) enabled secure tenants and introductory tenants to serve a notice requiring certain qualifying repairs to be carried out by their landlords, which must be local authorities. The scheme was extended to introductory tenants by the Secure Tenants (Rights to Repair) Regulations 1997 (SI 1997/73) which amended the 1994 regulations referred to below.

Regulations were made under that provision by the Secure Tenants of Local Authorities (Right to Repair Scheme) Regulations 1994 (SI 1994/133) setting out the prescribed information to be included in the notice and the description of the repairs to be included. Notices may then be issued by the landlord specifying the work required and stating the period within which they are to be done. If the contractor specified in the notice fails to do the work within the prescribed period the landlord shall specify a new contractor failing which they will pay compensation to the tenant.

However, as a result of the regulations the scheme is limited to small claims not exceeding £250 in value (see reg.4). This very much reduces the utility of the duty enshrined in the legislation. In addition the scheme does not apply to small landlords who have less than 100 houses or flats. Nor can the tenant claim compensation where he neglected or refused to allow his landlord access.

The right to carry out improvements

Many leases, including all local authority leases, provide that the **14–15** tenant may not carry out improvements without the landlord's consent, such consent not to be unreasonably withheld. In relation to secure tenants, the qualified right to carry out improvements is enshrined in the legislation (see s.97 Housing Act 1985). That section provides that "any alteration in, or addition to, a dwelling house will require consent but that such consent is not to be unreasonably withheld"). Similar rights exist for protected tenants under the Rent Act 1977 However, tenants of other premises who wish to carry out improvements will be able to obtain the consent of the landlord unless there is an absolute prohibition in the lease.

In addition secure tenants who carry out certain types of improvements are entitled by statute to be compensated for these. A formula is contained in the regulations for calculating this (see the Secure Tenants of Local Authorities (Compensation for Improvements) Regulations 1994 (SI 1994/613)).

In relation to commercial premises the lease should make clear whether the tenant is allowed to carry out improvements. Those improvements may or may not become part of the realty depending on their nature and will often give rise to arguments at the end of the term as to compensation.

The rights of long leaseholders

14–16 Tenants of long leases of flats (i.e. those of 21 years or more) have the additional right under s.21 of the Landlord and Tenant Act 1987 which provides for the appointment of a manager by obtaining an order from the Leasehold Valuation Tribunal under s.24 of that Act. Alternatively, the LVT has the right to appoint a receiver.

However, these powers may only be exercised where the LVT is satisfied that the premises are not being properly managed and that state of affairs is likely to continue if those powers are not exercised.

Chapter 15

Forfeiture

Where a landlord has to deal with disrepair to premises, forfeiture is **15–01**
often an effective way of either compelling the tenant to remedy the
breach of covenant or obtaining an early end to the lease whereby the
landlord may perform the required repairs himself. Where commercial
premises are involved, by forfeiting the lease the landlord can bring
a premature end to the term without the expense and delay of court
proceedings. This is because physical re-entry is still allowed in
relation to such premises and is often the cheapest and most effective
way to enforce compliance with the conditions and covenants in the
lease. Where residential accommodation is involved, court action
will be needed and will in many cases not achieve the desired
outcome.

Forfeiture for non-payment of rent is beyond the scope of this book
but other types of forfeiture are related to the subject matter of this
book and the relevant principles are therefore considered here. The
reader is referred to specialist text books and in particular *Woodfall*
and *Hill and Redman*, for more specialist guidance.

When the right to forfeit arises

The ancient right to forfeit arises when there is a breach of a covenant **15–02**
or condition in a lease or, it follows, in an agreement for lease. The
landlord must exercise that right within twelve years of the cause for
forfeiture arising (s.15(1) Limitation Act 1980, also considered in
Ch.18 at para.18–03, p.224).

The following essential conditions must be met before forfeiture,
whether by physical re-entry or court action, may be contemplated:

- the lease must contain a forfeiture clause;
- there must be a breach which justifies invoking that clause;

- the landlord must have gone through certain preliminary steps;
- the landlord must not have waived the cause for forfeiture.

The first and second requirements are largely self-explanatory but it is not always clear that a particular repairing obligation, for example, falls on the tenant. The landlord should be confident that the breach alleged will be made out before contemplating forfeiture. As to the third hurdle, before the landlord may forfeit for a breach other than non-payment of rent he must serve an s.146 notice (see below). This third requirement may give rise to difficult questions of law and fact. As to the fourth requirement, whether any waiver has occurred is also sometimes difficult to identify and a great deal of care is needed when advising landlords how they should proceed after a cause for forfeiture has arisen.

What method of forfeiture should be chosen?

15–03 Despite substantial statutory protection for business and residential tenants and the incorporation into English law of international obligations to respect for one's possessions, forfeiture by physical re-entry is still permitted in relation to commercial premises and is relatively common. However, this form of self-help has long been frowned on (see *WG Clark (Properties) Ltd v Dupre Properties Ltd* [1992] 1 All E.R. 596 at 606) and the Law Commission has recommended wholesale reform of this area of the law (Law Com. 303 "Termination of tenancies for tenant default" December 2006). The right to physically re-enter has been removed from residential premises by the introduction of the requirement (in s.2 of the Protection from Eviction Act 1977) that a court order is required before possession may be demanded. The requirement that forfeiture may not take place when a person is lawfully residing at the premises has also largely removed forfeiture as a method of lease determination from mixed business and residential premises (see *Patel v Pirabakaran* [2006] 1 W.L.R. 3112).

In any event where the landlord is considering the quickest way to gain possession of residential premises forfeiture is unlikely to assist because the tenant is likely to have the protection of one of the schemes of protection which apply. For example, an assured tenant whose tenancy is brought to an end by forfeiture, may remain in possession because a statutory periodic tenancy arises under s.5 of the Housing Act 1988 and he does not assume the status of a trespasser (see s.5(1)–(2)). The landlord must bring possession proceedings having served notice in correct form and established a ground under Sch.2 of the Act.

Commercial landlords frequently choose to physically re-enter and it remains a powerful weapon available to them. However, adopting such a course has some potential pitfalls. If the cause for forfeiture transpires not to have been established the landlord runs the risk of an action for trespass and a claim for substantial business losses on the part of the tenant. Also it is a criminal offence to use excessive force in carrying out re-entry contrary to s.6 of the Criminal Law Act 1977.

When will the landlord be taken to have waived the cause for forfeiture?

The argument that the landlord has waived the right to forfeit the **15–04** lease often arises in practice. The effect of a successful waiver argument is to vest the remainder of the term in the tenant for all purposes and the landlord may only avail himself of a new cause for forfeiture, the old one being lost.

What constitutes waiver?

This is rarely straightforward. As Professor Goode has pointed out (in **15–05** "Commercial Law" 3rd edn p.105) waiver has different meanings in different contexts. However, waiver in this context is a form of election. Essentially, where a breach of the covenants or conditions in the lease occurs, the landlord has two options: he can treat the lease as being on foot or he can treat the lease as forfeit. Once he has chosen the latter course any conduct on his part which is inconsistent with that position will be taken to waive the breach (see *Doe d. Morecraft v Meux* (1825) 4 B & C 606). Thus, typically, after a cause for forfeiture has arisen, an acceptance of rent by the landlord will be seen as waiving that right and treating the lease as being on foot. But disrepair by the tenant is a continuing breach of the repairing covenant so that waiver affects breaches which have arisen in the past not breaches that arise in the future. As long as the premises remain in disrepair a new cause for forfeiture will arise the day after the waiver and each day thereafter that the premises remain in disrepair.

It has been held that the landlord may accept rent up to the date fixed for a s.146 notice to be complied with (*Doe'd Rankin v Brindley* (1832) 4 B & Ad. 84). However, the acceptance of rent *after* the date for complying with the s.146 notice has passed will have the effect of waiving the breaches referred to in that notice. As long as the breaches which gave rise to the notice continued without any waiver the landlord could forfeit for those breaches without serving a new notice (*Penton v Barnett* [1898] 1 Q.B. 276).

However, more recently in *Greenwood v WEF* [2008] EWCA Civ 47 the tenant had come to agreement with his landlord as to the payment of arrears of rent and service charges that had built up but the landlord did not then demand rent fearing a waiver. Subsequently, the landlord demanded payment of the sum agreed. The tenant argued that this amounted to a waiver of any cause for forfeiture. In the circumstances it was argued that subsequent forfeiture proceedings should not succeed. Alternatively the tenant claimed to be entitled to relief.

Thomas L.J. noted that an unequivocal demand for rent may be regarded in the same manner as the payment and acceptance of rent but went on to say that he need not decide that point because the solicitor's letter was not a demand for rent. The landlord was simply trying to enforce payment of the amount agreed.

In summary, therefore, any unequivocal demand for or acceptance of rent may amount to waiver and will have the potentially far reaching consequence that the landlord will have to either await the recurrence of a further cause for forfeiture or will have to claim possession on a different basis.

What procedural steps must the landlord take before forfeiting?

Restrictions on the landlord's right to forfeit

15–06 Whatever method is chosen the landlord cannot avoid the important regulation of the landlord's right to forfeit contained in s.146 of the Law of Property Act 1925 and the Leasehold Property (Repairs) Act 1938. These restrictions only apply in cases other than for non-payment of rent. The effect of those Acts will now be considered.

The section 146 notice

15–07 In all cases of forfeiture other than for non-payment of rent it is an essential requirement that the landlord should, first of all, serve a notice under s.146 of the Law of Property Act 1925. The notice serves two functions; first of all it informs the tenant of the breach complained of. Secondly, where the breach is capable of remedy, the notice gives the tenant an opportunity to remedy the breach. It should allow him a reasonable opportunity to do this. What will be a "reasonable period" will depend on the nature of the covenant and its breach.

The notice need not be in any prescribed form but where the breach is capable of remedy should inform the tenant of the steps he is to take and in any event the notice should inform the tenant of the need to pay compensation to the landlord.

Which breaches are capable of remedy?
This is a complex area. Historically the position has been that the **15–08**
tenant may remedy breaches of positive covenants and this will make
it difficult for the landlord to proceed with the forfeiture, because
relief would be likely to be given, but a negative covenant may not
be remedied. The modern law looks at the substance of the covenant
and the mischief it is aimed at. If in substance it can be put right then
it will be regarded as capable of remedy and relief against forfeiture
may be given on that basis. Thus a breach of a user covenant by
using the premises for illegal or immoral purposes may be
irremediable because that use is thought to taint the premises.
However, a breach of the covenant not to commit alterations may be
remedied by reinstating the premises to their former state. Each case
must be looked at on its own facts therefore.

The effect of the Leasehold Property Repairs Act 1938
This Act came about to protect tenants of small properties held under **15–09**
long leases from having to pay heavy bills for dilapidations under the
threat of forfeiture for breach of the repairing covenant. The Act was
originally intended to apply to low value houses only. However, it
was extended by s.51 of the Landlord and Tenant Act 1954 to apply
to all leases which fulfil the relevant conditions. The Act applies to:

- tenancies *for terms of 7 years or more*;
- of which there are *at least 3 years unexpired.*

But

- The tenancy must not be an agricultural holding to which
  the Agricultural Holdings Act 1986 applies or a new farm
  tenancy.
- The Act does not apply to covenants to "put" the premises in
  repair, e.g. where, for example, the tenant covenants to put
  the premises into repair within a reasonable time of taking
  possession (see s.3).

Lord Denning explained the reason for the Act in *Sidnell v Wilson*
[1966] 1 All E.R. 681 at 683:

"The Act of 1938 was passed shortly before the war because
of a great mischief prevalent at that time. Unscrupulous people
used to buy up the reversion of leases and then bring pressure
to bear on tenants by an exaggerated list of dilapidations. The
Act of 1938 applied to leases for seven years or more which
had three years or more to run. In such cases Parliament enacted
that a landlord, when he gave a notice under s 146 of the Law

of Property Act, 1925, to make good dilapidations, must state on the notice that the tenant was entitled to give a counter-notice. The effect of a notice (was) that the tenant was entitled to give a counter-notice. The effect of a counter-notice is that the landlord cannot proceed to forfeit the premises or to claim damages *unless he has the leave of the court*."

The Leasehold Properties Repairs Act 1938 was enacted to impose a bar on forfeiture in certain cases and claims for damages for breach of the repairing covenant until certain conditions (summarised by Lord Denning above) have been fulfilled. In particular, it is aimed at claims for damages during the term as well as claims for forfeiture.

In a case to which the Act applies, the sanction of the court is required to pursue a claim for forfeiture or damages. But the Act does not prevent the landlord claiming an injunction or pursuing a debt under the terms of the lease (*Middlegate Properties v Goldlow Jackson* (1977) 34 P. & C.R. 4). Indeed , in *Jervis v Harris* [1996] 1 E.G.L.R. 78 the Court of Appeal held that the Act did not afford protection to a tenant whose lease enabled the landlord to enter the premises, view their state and thereafter recover the costs off the tenant.

The requirements of the Act in overview
15–10 Where the Act applies, its scheme is as follows:

- where the 1938 Act applies where the landlord (L) serves an s.146 notice on the tenant (T) it should contain the information prescribed by the 1938 Act (s.1(4));
- T then has 28 days to serve a counter notice (s.1(1));
- if he does not do so the Act ceases to apply;
- if T does serve a counter notice L cannot proceed with the forfeiture without the leave of the court (s.1(3));
- the court will only grant leave where it is satisfied that leave ought to be granted and it may do so subject to conditions (s.1(5));
- L is not entitled to his solicitor and surveyor's costs (under s.146(3)) unless the court so directs.

The requirement of the court's leave
15–11 Under s.1(5) of the 1938 Act there are five grounds on which the court will give leave to the landlord to continue with the forfeiture or dilapidations claim. The landlord needs to prove only one of the following:

"(a) that the immediate remedying of the breach in question is requisite for preventing substantial diminution in the value of his reversion, or that the value thereof has been substantially diminished by the breach;

(b) that the immediate remedying of the breach is required for giving effect in relation to the [premises] to the purposes of any enactment, or of any bye-law or other provision having effect under an enactment, [or for giving effect to any order of a court or requirement of any authority under any enactment or any such byelaw or other provision as aforesaid];

(c) in a case in which the lessee is not in occupation of the whole of the [premises as respects which the covenant or agreement is proposed to be enforced,] that the immediate remedying of the breach is required in the interests of the occupier of [those premises] or of part thereof;

(d) that the breach can be immediately remedied at an expense that is relatively small in comparison with the much greater expense that would probably be occasioned by postponement of the necessary work; or

(e) special circumstances which in the opinion of the court render it just and equitable that leave should be given."

The court will not grant leave unless and until it is satisfied that the landlord needs a remedy immediately to protect the value of his interest.

How the 1938 Act works in practice
The way the Act works is illustrated by *Landmaster Properties Ltd v* **15–12** *Thackeray Property Services* [2003] 2 E.G.L.R. 30, which indicates that in a commercial context the Act overrides the repairing obligation. In that case C was the tenant of a public house in a shopping precinct. The demised property was left empty. It became dilapidated and a target for vandals and squatters. The landlord served an s.146 notice. The tenant claimed the protection of the 1938 Act in response. The landlord sought leave to proceed with the forfeiture but before it did so the property was destroyed in an arson attack. It was held that the relevant date for judging the position was the date of the hearing. At that date there was no substantial damage to the value of the reversion, for the fire had removed the disrepair;

indeed, it could be argued that the potential purchaser may be interested in the bare site. Nevertheless the judge's decision to grant leave to proceed with the forfeiture was upheld in the special circumstances that applied.

Claims under the 1938 Act, for example by a landlord of leave to commence a claim where the tenant has the protection of the Act, are "landlord and tenant claims" for the purposes of Pt 56.1 of the CPR (see Civil Procedure 2008 "White Book" at 56PD.2). These claims are started by Pt 8 claim form, as modified by that Part and its Practice Direction. An example of such a claim is to be found at Appendix B2.

Can the 1938 Act be avoided?

15–13 In *Jervis v Harris* [1996] 1 All E.R. 303 the Court of Appeal had to consider whether a clause in a commercial lease which stated that gave the landlord a right to enter and effect repairs himself and recover cost from tenant was subject to the leave of the court under s.1(3) of the 1938 Act. It was decided that this type of clause, often found in commercial leases, succeeded in avoiding the requirements of the 1938 Act. Those responsible for drafting leases should therefore consider inserting such a clause.

Relief against forfeiture

15–14 The court has a wide discretion to grant relief against forfeiture. Although that jurisdiction was originally equitable, it now arises under statute, the power to give relief being given by s.146(2) LPA (see below). However, this will often be subject to conditions. These will usually include a requirement that the tenant remedy the breach. But the court will not order the tenant to remedy a breach consisting of decorative disrepair if it considers this unreasonable (s.147 LPA 1925, see *Woodfall*: 17.177, but this will be considered in more detail below). Those breaches that are normally considered capable of remedy are those which do not damage the premises in the long term, the classic example being an unlawful assignment which by its nature cannot be remedied (see para.15–08, p.173).

The statutory jurisdiction

15–15 The statutory discretion to grant relief under s.146(2) of the LPA 1925 applies to all breaches other than non-payment of rent. In practice, relief is widely granted.

The court is exercising an equitable jurisdiction which allows a considerable discretion. However, the courts have emphasised that relief is not automatic. Important factors to consider (see *Shiloh Spinners v Harding* [1973] A.C. 691 and *Woodfall* 17.166) will include:

- the conduct of the parties;
- whether the breach is wilful or merely inadvertent;
- whether the effect of the breach will stigmatise the premises so as to make them difficult to re-let. This will be the case of immoral and illegal user which are uses beyond the scope of this book;
- whether the breach has had some lasting effect on the value of the premises (*Scala House and District Property Co v Forbes* [1974] 3 W.L.R. 14);
- whether the damage sustained by the landlord is proportionate to the damage sustained by the tenant if no relief is given (*Billson v Residential Apartments Limited* [1992] 1 A.C. 494);
- where the tenant is in breach of a qualified covenant, whether the landlord would have consented to whatever the covenant prohibits;
- the interests of those who are not parties to the lease;
- the degree of hardship to the tenant if relief is refused.

Thus in *Greenwood v WEF* [2008] EWCA Civ 47 (referred to above) the Court of Appeal refused to intervene with the trial judge's decision not to grant relief. They would only do so on the basis that the trial judge had misdirected himself. The discretion was sufficiently wide to allow the granting of relief on the basis that the property demised would be sold and the proceeds of sale used to defray the outstanding amount due to the landlord (as had occurred in *Khar v Delmounty* (1996) 75 P. & C.R. 232). In *Greenwood*, contrary to the tenant's submission, the court found that amount claimed by the landlord was not disproportionate to the value of the demised premises, particularly since the tenant had attempted to evade the landlord's claim by assigning the tenancy to a company which was a party to the action. The judge's refusal to grant relief was well within his discretion.

Terms on which relief will be granted

Obviously, this will depend on the type of case the court is concerned **15–16** with. Ordinarily, however, and where the breach is capable of remedy the tenant will be required to remedy the breach complained of as a condition of relief. But the unfettered discretion in the legislation will not be weakened by any rule that relief must be subject to remedying the defect complained of (see *Rose v Hyman* [1912] A.C. 623 and Lord Templeman in *ABP v C H Bailey* [1990] 2 A.C. 703).

Thus where the work required to remedy the breach will be of no benefit to anyone, the court may decide to grant relief without the need for remedy. However in cases to which the Leasehold Property (Repairs) Act 1938 applies (i.e. cases where there is a lease of seven years or more of which three remain), the landlord will have to obtain leave under that Act before he can proceed with the forfeiture.

Payment of compensation is stated by s.146(2) to be a condition of relief but in practice compensation is only ordered where the landlord has suffered some damage and in many cases the landlord will not seek compensation.

Effect of the grant of relief

15–17 The effect of the grant of relief is to vest the remainder of the term in the tenant as if the forfeiture had not taken place. Furthermore the relief relates-back to the commencement of proceedings. The status of the tenant between the two events (the commencement of forfeiture proceedings or physical re-entry and the granting of relief) has caused a certain amount of judicial concern (see *Liverpool Properties v Oldbridge Investments* [1985] 1 E.G.L.R. 111). In that case Parker L.J. (at p.112) characterised the position of the tenant between forfeiture and relief as one of "limbo". During that period it could not be said for certain what would happen, for it was only when the tenant applied for relief, which he could do at any time, and complied with all the terms of the relief, that the original lease may be said to continue. Where the physical re-entry was effected there is a new lease on the same terms as the old.

Sub-tenant's position

15–18 This is dealt with by s.146(4). Where the landlord is "proceeding by action or otherwise" against the tenant and whether for non-payment of rent or other breach of covenant, proviso or stipulation in the lease, any person claiming as under-lessee may claim relief under this sub-section. He may bring that claim in the tenant's action or in an action of his own. If he is successful the remainder of the term may be vested in that under-lessee but subject to the same conditions that might have applied if the tenant were granted relief. Indeed the statute specifies that it is to be on such terms "as the court shall think fit". In no circumstances may the under-lessee require a lease to be granted to them for a longer term than the original term.

Costs

Payment of the landlord's costs is frequently a term for the grant of **15–19** relief. Indeed s.146 (3) provides that these are payable where the breach has been waived "at the request of the tenant" or the tenant is granted relief against forfeiture.

The provision does not mean that in other circumstances there may be no claim for costs or that the tenant has no opportunity to challenge either the reasonableness of the claim for costs or the amount of that claim. However, it does mean that the costs claim will be a form of statutory debt which entitles the landlord to pursue that debt by all means other than forfeiture itself.

Generally speaking the landlord will be able to recover their costs, whether or not this is made a condition of the granting of relief.

Where the parties agree to follow the Property Litigation Association's Protocol in respect of terminal dilapidations claims a failure to follow that Protocol may be looked at when the question of costs is determined. Even where the Protocol does not apply the failure to follow the appropriate pre-action behaviour, as encouraged by the CPR and in accordance with the overriding objective, may result in adverse costs consequences. In particular the Practice Direction on Pre-action Protocols at para.4.1 (at p.2136 in the current *White Book 2008*) states that pre-action behaviour is to be in accordance with the overriding objective even in cases which are not subject to any particular protocol. This will almost invariably require the claimant to set out his position pre-action in correspondence (see ibid. at p.2128).

The particular case of decorative repairs

This is dealt with by s.147 of the Law of Property Act 1925 which **15–20** provides that the court has the power to order that the tenant is relieved from liability under such a covenant altogether. Effectively the tenant may in certain circumstances be able to prevent the forfeiture taking place at all.

The section only applies where the claimed forfeiture is for internal disrepairs to a house or other building. The court may relieve the tenant from the obligation to do the repairs as well as from the adverse effects of the notice. But the section does not apply where the tenant agreed to *put* the premises into decorative repair but has not done so. Nor does it apply where the tenant agreed to keep the property in a sanitary condition or where the repairs stipulated in the landlord's 146 notice amount to structural items which are necessary for the maintenance of that structure. The section does not apply to any statutory duty to keep the premises fit for human habitation or where the lease merely requires the tenant to *yield up* the premises in a specified condition at the end of the term.

Despite the limited ambit of s.147, where it applies it may be a vital tool available to the tenant to avoid forfeiture. In practice however, it is relatively unusual for a landlord to rely only on decorative disrepair.

How and when to apply for relief

15–21 The landlord should bring their forfeiture claim under Pt 55 whether the claim is to commercial or residential premises, even where the claim relates to land rather than buildings.

Where the landlord brings forfeiture proceedings the tenant has the option of seeking relief by way of counterclaim in that action or bringing his own separate claim. If he brings a separate claim it should also brought under Pt 55 CPR. CPR 55.7 applies CPR 15.2 to the action so that although no acknowledgement of service is needed, a defence will still need to be served within 14 days of service of the claim form. A counterclaim may be brought as of right in response to a Pt 7 claim and by virtue of CPR 15.7 which applies Pt 20.4(2), a counterclaim may be brought as of right to a Pt 55 claim provided it is filed with the defence. Where a claim is brought under Pt 8, the court's permission is required to bring a counterclaim.

In cases where the landlord proceeds by physically re-entering the tenant will have little choice but to bring his own separate action for relief. Where he brings his own action it is also governed by Pt 55. Specifically, Pt 55.2(1)(c) provides that the tenant should use form N5A. Some helpful notes are provided at form N7B in relation to residential premises.

In terms of *when* the tenant should apply, the tenant can apply at any stage after the service of the s.146 notice up to the time when possession is finally yielded up. After that it is usually too late (*Rogers v Rice* [1892] 2 Ch.170).

Whether the landlord should forfeit?

Tactical considerations

In practice forfeiture is sometimes used as a negotiating tool but **15–22** once a landlord has elected to proceed by forfeiture it is difficult if not impossible to reverse that decision without the consent of the tenant. This is illustrated by the following cases:

- In *GS Fashions v B and Q Limited* [1995] 4 All E.R. 899 the landlord terminated the lease by service of a writ on the basis that the tenant had unlawfully assigned or sublet but he then tried to change his mind and wished to retain the benefit of his covenants with the tenant. He argued that the writ had been served on the wrong, i.e., mistaken, basis. However, there had been a mutual confirmation that the lease was forfeit in the pleadings because the tenant admitted the cause for forfeiture arose in his defence. The judge (Lightman J.) thought that the landlord's decision to proceed with the forfeiture was unequivocal and thus irreversible. The fact that he had undoubtedly made the wrong decision did not mean he could reverse his decision to forfeit the lease. By electing to forfeit the lease came to an end and the only means the tenant could remain the tenant was by entering a new tenancy agreement.

- In *London Borough of Kingston v Marlow* [1996] 1 E.G.L.R. 101 the landlord demanded the payment of service charges that were due and issued a writ when they were not paid. The tenant did not apply for relief and subsequently vacated the premises. The consequence of the landlord's early termination was that he became liable for business rates, the Court of Appeal held. This is because the effect of forfeiture is to bring to an end the tenant's right to possession of the premises and there could not be two persons in possession of the premises for the purposes of rating law.

Therefore the landlord will only wish to contemplate forfeiture if they are confident of reletting the premises or because the state of the premises is such that it would be unwise to allow them to continue to deteriorate.

On the other hand the tenant may have good economic reasons for allowing his lease to be forfeited and he may not wish to seek relief. Nevertheless in a case where the landlord has adopted the forfeiture route, he may have no option but to proceed to re-enter even if he subsequently change his mind.

Proposals for reform

15–23 There have been a number of proposals to reform the law of forfeiture over the years. The most recent has been by the Law Commission in 2006 (in "Termination of Tenancies for Tenant Default", October 31 2006 (Law Com. 303, 2006)). This report proposed the abolition of forfeiture and its replacement with a statutory scheme that will regulate if, and how, a tenancy can be terminated during its term and was accompanied by a draft bill. However, whilst Parliament has now intervened in relation to distress for rent and certain other types of physical seizure for tenant default during the term (in the Courts, Tribunals and Enforcement Act 2007 which received Royal assent on July 19, 2007 and came into force on December 31, 2007 (Commencement Order No.2 SI 3613)), the Government has not so far shown any inclination to act in relation to forfeiture. This is despite having considerable support from property professionals (see for example the lecture given by Stuart Bridge, a Law Commissioner, to the Property Bar Association on November 9, 2006—available on the Law Commission's website). The bill has not featured in the 2007 Queen's speech so it seems that it is unlikely to be introduced in the foreseeable future.

Chapter 16

Specific performance and mandatory injunctions

In most cases where leasehold premises are in disrepair the landlord **16–01** and tenant will come to an agreement as to the work to be carried out. In some cases the agreement will be in the form of an undertaking which, in the correct form, may be enforceable like an order of the court. It will be a relatively rare case where it will be necessary to obtain an order for specific performance. However, that remedy and the associated remedy of a mandatory injunction, represent powerful remedies which can be an effective way of ensuring that repairing obligations are complied with.

The term "specific performance" is used effectively synonymously with the term "mandatory injunction" for these purposes, although strictly speaking a mandatory injunction may issue for a tortious remedy as well as a contractual one. Specific performance, on the other hand, only issues to enforce a contractual obligation. In most cases in this area the claim will be under a lease, although specific performance would also be available to a contractual licensee who can identify a clear breach of a contractual obligation on the part of his licensor.

Historically, equity demonstrated considerable reluctance to grant the remedy of specific performance in favour of the landlord to compel his tenant to comply with an obligation (see *Jeaune v Queen's Cross* [1974] Ch.97 for the reasons for this reluctance). It was argued before that case that because the tenant could not be compelled by specific performance to comply with the covenants in the lease so the landlord should not be compelled to perform his obligations under the lease. This lack of mutuality enabled landlords sometimes to argue that the court should not award specific performance against them. The modern case law suggests that this remedy may be used to compel both the landlord *and* the tenant to carry out their repairing obligations.

Under the modern law it seems that specific performance is just one of the remedies in the landlord's armoury just as the tenant may pursue such a remedy against his defaulting landlord (see *Rainbow Estates v Tokenhold* [1999] Ch.64, although in that case the leases considered by the Judge (Lawrence Collins Q.C. sitting as a deputy) were unusual in that they did not contain forfeiture clauses). In theory, at least, the same remedy is available to both landlord and tenant and the lack of mutuality will only be one factor to consider in deciding how to do justice in the case. However, in practice the landlord is more likely to avail himself of more powerful weapons such as, in the commercial field, forfeiture or, in the residential field, to bring a possession claim on the grounds that the lease has not been complied with than pursue a claim for specific performance.

General principles

16–02   The old equitable rule that the remedies of an injunction and specific performance would only be awarded where damages represented an inadequate remedy still applies. However, where the claim is by a residential tenant under a short lease of less than seven years, there is a statutory basis for the award which avoids this difficulty. This will be considered below (in para.16–06).

A breach of the repairing obligation represents a continuing breach in that, technically, a new cause of action arises each day that the property is in disrepair. This means that a claim needs to be brought for each and every breach that occurs if full compensation is to be achieved. Obviously, this is impractical and may cause the court to lean towards granting specific performance instead. The court will in practice consider the extent of the continuing breach as well as the practicality of supervising the execution of repairs in deciding whether specific performance is the appropriate remedy.

It has been held that specific performance may be claimed where the landlord has forfeited the lease but the tenant has applied for relief. In such a case it is thought that the covenants in the lease have the potential to become live again and the tenant could by this means be made to perform his repairing obligations again. However, the landlord will not be able to enforce the covenants in the lease during the intervening period, i.e. before the application for relief is heard (see *Peninsula Maritime v Padseal* [1981] 2 E.G.L.R. 43).

It is the modern law illustrated by the *Tokenhold* case referred to above that specific performance is available to either landlord or tenant but not as a matter of routine. Outside the statutory basis for the award available to tenants of short leases, considered below, the discretion will be exercised cautiously but on the other hand it will not be interfered with on appeal lightly.

When specific performance or mandatory injunctional will be refused

In short, as equitable remedies specific performance or a mandatory **16–03** injunction will be refused wherever an equitable defence arises or wherever the court considers that damages are a more "appropriate" remedy. It must be just and equitable to award specific performance so that the benefit to the applicant must be real and tangible, not merely tactical. Thus the remedy may not be successfully sought merely to give the landlord a tactical advantage over the tenant nor will it be granted near the end of the term where the landlord can sensibly present his terminal dilapidations claim against a solvent tenant.

Delay

Equitable defences include delay amounting to acquiescence but this **16–04** will only arise where the delay is such as to make it unconscionable to allow the claimant to enforce his rights. This will particularly be a problem where the landlord has lulled the tenant into a false sense of security and in consequence the tenant has altered his position. Strictly, the related equitable defence of laches is only available where there has been *negligent* delay and not merely inadvertence. This must be coupled with knowledge of the facts and only where there is no limitation period for the commencement of the claim in question.

Lack of particularity

The most common reason for refusing the award of specific **16–05** performance or a mandatory injunction is because the tenant has failed to present a clear enough schedule of the work that needs doing and the time scale within which it needs to be done. The court will expect a high degree of particularity before it will award specific performance of works which may take many weeks and this will be of particular importance where an application is made for an interim order for specific performance or an injunction (as in *Parker v Camden LBC* [1986] Ch.162, where Lord Donaldson pointed out that in many cases building work is not simply a case of "throwing a switch").

The statutory basis for the award

16–06 Section 17 of the Landlord and Tennant Act 1985 creates a specific power to apply for specific performance of the landlord's obligation to repair the structure and exterior of the premises under s.11 of that Act. Under this section the equitable requirements that damages must be inadequate and that the remedy is mutually available, in so far as that restriction still applies, do not apply in relation to premises to which the section applies (s.17(1)).

Furthermore the section does not just apply to work to the demised premises but also to "any part of the premises in which the dwelling is comprised" (s.17(1)) and although the power to award specific performance is couched in discretionary terms, in practice the order is readily made in the housing cases to which the section applies.

Interim relief

16–07 Jurisdiction to give this form of interim relief exists under s.37 of the Supreme Court Act 1981, s.38 of the County Courts Act 1984 and Pt 25.1 CPR. This gives the court the power to award a range of interim remedies, including an interim injunction, interim declaration and interim order for inspection of the property subject to the claim. Normally these applications should be made on three clear days notice but in an urgent claim a without-notice application is permitted. In a really urgent case the applicant will not have had the opportunity to issue his claim. In every case where the applicant seeks an injunction, usually pending trial, he will have to give an undertaking in respect of any loss the other side suffers in the event that he is unsuccessful at that trial.

A claim to interim relief by way of a *mandatory* injunction, as opposed to *prohibitory* injunction, will only rarely be successful and only in an urgent case. The breach of the agreement should be particularly clear. Such an award will only be made in "exceptional cases" and not in the run of the mill type of dispute. In practice the order would have to be reasonably straightforward and uncontroversial (see *Parker v Camden LBC* [1986] Ch.162). The applicant would need to show a strong case and not merely a prima facie case.

By contrast an interim prohibitory injunction would issue much more easily. Such an application would be based on the need to maintain the balance of convenience until trial. That test, introduced by *American Cyanamid v Ethicon* [1975] A.C. 396, is now regarded as well-established and will be applied to all interim prohibitory injunction applications. In practice an applicant for an injunction will need a good arguable case before an injunction will be granted, although the court will tend to give the applicant the benefit of any doubt which exists as to whether the case is good and arguable provided that the purpose of the exercise is to maintain the status quo.

An example of a case where interim relief should not have been given is *Hi Fi Elevator Services v Temple* (1996) 28 H.L.R. 1). There the Court of Appeal said the lower court had been wrong to grant an interim injunction to prevent the landlord carrying out repairs which he could ultimately recover under the service charge provision in the lease. The landlord had the right to enter and carry out repairs to the structure and exterior including the roof, the area in disrepair.

One argument that was often raised in response to a landlord's application for an injunction to perform his repairing covenant was that it would involve a trespass into the premises demised to the tenant but in fact the *Hi Fi Elevator* and other cases illustrate that the landlord has the right to carry out repair work within his repairing covenant. Where the work was to the common parts of a building, that did not pose a problem, but arguably he may be entitled to enforce his rights to repair within any part of the building in which the demised premises are situated also, provided the lease allowed this. Essentially, the landlord could not be prevented from entering any part of the premises, whether or not they were demised to the tenant, for the purposes of maintaining the structure and exterior of those premises. That right existed at common law and under a number of statutes with the aim of maintaining the value of the landlord's interest.

Claims under section 4 of the Defective Premises Act 1972

Where the claim is under s.4 of the Defective Premises Act 1972, as well **16–08** as claiming damages a tenant whose home is defective may bring a claim for specific performance or an injunction (see *Barrett v Lounova (1982) Ltd* [1990] Q.B. 348). Although the decision on that point was strictly obiter dicta, it was nevertheless in accordance with principle. If the tenant can prove that there is an imminent risk to the health and safety of the occupants of a property to which the Act applies, there is no reason why he should not claim such an injunction.

Which court?

By virtue of s.38 of the County Courts Act 1984 the county court has **16–09** the power to order free-standing injunctive relief and there need not be any other claim, e g. for damages. Indeed the county court may award all the remedies that the High Court can award. As will be seen, essentially that duplicates the powers of the High Court under s.37 of the Supreme Court Act 1981. There are some restrictions on the ability of the county court to award injunctions (for example freezing injunctions) but they are largely beyond the scope of this book.

It will be appropriate to issue the injunction claim in the High Court because that is the likely trial forum or because the claim is sufficiently urgent or serious to justify issuing there. Jurisdiction will be more fully considered in Ch.18.

How is the order or undertaking enforced?

16–10   A landlord who fails to carry out repairs that are ordered as part of a specific performance or injunction order or who fails to comply with an undertaking enforceable as an order of the court, will be in contempt and in some cases may be imprisoned for up to six months and/or fined (as in *Hackney v Mullen* (1996) 29 H.L.R. 592). Not every undertaking is "an undertaking enforceable as an order of the court". It needs to be worded appropriately to ensure that result. Obviously the power to impose penalties for contempt is only used where a clear breach has been proved in circumstances where the guilty party clearly understood what they were to do, when they were to do it, and the consequences of their failure to do so. Specifically the undertaking should be served on the party giving it and preferably a penal notice should be attached to undertakings as they must be attached to orders if they are to be enforced (see sc45.5 in *White Book* Vol.I 2008 at p.1897).

The liability of individual directors of a corporate tenant or landlord is sometimes more difficult to establish, but where it is possible to make a director personally responsible on behalf of the company, on the basis that he had the appropriate level of knowledge of the breach of the order or undertaking in question, he may be held in contempt. There is also a rarely used power to sequestrate the company's assets if a corporate party is found to be in contempt.

Damages in lieu of an injunction/specific performance

16–11   Jurisdiction to award damages in lieu of these equitable remedies has existed since Lord Cairns' Act of 1858, which is still referred to. However, the power is now contained in s.50 of the Supreme Court Act 1981. The same power exists in county courts. These damages compensate for future losses and not past damage and are therefore partly restitutionary as well as compensatory. They are unlikely to be appropriate in a claim for damages for disrepair but are commonly awarded where there is a permanent infringement of a right to light or trespass over the boundary of an adjoining property. As such the reader is referred to other texts, for example, Snell's Principles of Equity 31st edn at Ch.16, for a fuller summary of the principles.

The leading case remains *Shelfer v City of London Electric Light Ltd* where Lindley L.J. thought it a good working rule to award damages in lieu of an injunction where:

> "(1) The injury to the plaintiff's legal right is small, (2) ... and is one which is capable of being estimated in money, (3) and is one which can be compensated by a small money payment, (4) and the case is one which it would be oppressive to the defendant to grant an injunction."

In *Jaggard v Sawyer* [1995] 1 W.L.R. 269 the Court of Appeal indicated that the court would consider awarding damages in lieu where the claimant had established his right to an injunction but nevertheless damages appeared to the court to be the more appropriate remedy. The claimant had to first overcome any equitable defence that was relied on. Where the defendant successfully defended the claim to relief, for example, on the basis that there has been excessive delay, the claimant would be denied any relief. But where the right to an injunction had prima facie been established it was still open to the court to exercise its discretion against awarding an injunction or specific performance and in favour of damages.

In practice, damages in lieu tend to be awarded in certain categories of case. For example they are often awarded in cases of actual and threatened trespass (see p.284 in *Jaggard*) as well as infringements of restrictive covenants and rights to light. In *Jaggard* the court explained that the principles on which they would refuse an injunction or specific performance included any case where the damage to the defendant from having to comply with such an order was out of all proportion to the loss to the claimant.

As has been indicated, these damages are less likely to be awarded where, for example, a landlord is attempting to compel the tenant or the tenant is attempting to force his landlord to comply with his repairing obligations. An example of a case involving defective premises in which they were awarded was *Hammersmith and Fulham LBC v Creska (No.2)* [2000] L. & T.R. 288. In that case the landlord claimed the right to carry out work under a *Jervis v Harris* type clause (giving landlord right to enter and effect repairs in default and recover the cost from the tenant, see above at p.176, para.15–13). Jacob J. refused this on the basis that the award of the remedy sought (an injunction) would cause unnecessary and excessive disruption to the tenant whereas the landlord could be adequately compensated in money for its loss.

The actual quantum of these damages varies according to the nature of the right that the claimant has lost. However, the following broad principles may be stated as follows:

1. the court will compensate the claimant for what he has lost not what the guilty party has gained (per Millett L.J. in *Jaggard v Sawyer* at p.276–277 and 291–292);

2. the claimant will generally to be awarded such a sum as might reasonably have been agreed by him in return for allowing that which would otherwise be prohibited (see *Wrotham Park Estate Co v Parkside Homes* [1974] 1 W.L.R. 798);

3. no ransom price could be demanded but the parties were entitled to make use of their respective bargaining positions (*Jaggard v Sawyer* at p.283);

4. the relevant date for the valuation exercise to be undertaken is generally immediately before the wrongful act complained of but circumstances may dictate a different date (see *Lunn Poly v Liverpool and Lancashire Properties Ltd* at paragraphs 17-19 and 27-29);

5. the whole exercise was a matter of judgement and not of precision; the award must "feel right" (see Wynn *Jones v Bickley* [2006] EWHC 1991).

Chapter 17

Damages

Most claims arising out of defective premises will include a claim **17–01** for damages. In some cases, such as dilapidations claims, this will be the only claim. In others it will be added on to the main claim for specific performance. Although contractual and tortious claims frequently overlap, they involve different considerations and the distinction between the two will therefore be maintained in this chapter.

The compensatory principle has long governed the award of damages in tort (see *Livingstone v Rawyards Coal* (1880) App. Cas. 25) whereas contractual damages are supposed to be about allocating and rewarding risk. Generally, where damages are awarded for breach of contract, they will compensate the claimant for all their expectations whether they are commercial, personal or even eccentric provided they are not too remote (see *Radford v De Froberville* [1977] 1 W.L.R. 1262 per Oliver J.).

Damages for disrepair, which form the core of the discussion on damages in this book, compensate a number of different things. It is therefore difficult to lay down guidelines of universal application. The award may be very different in a commercial context than in a residential one. However, as a general rule, in a residential case, the court is mainly concerned with the upset and inconvenience caused by living in a defective dwelling. In a commercial case the court is more concerned with damage to the business. In addition the court will compensate the innocent party for any direct physical injury, damage to his property and for his out of pocket expenses (special damages).

In this chapter the heads of damage which commonly arise in residential leases are considered, including long-leases. These claims are primarily contractual claims by the tenant which aim to compensate them for the inconvenience and other losses that flow from the landlord's breach. The most common types of damages' claims by landlords in commercial leases will then be looked at. These are subject to important limitations on the amount the landlord can recover and often give rise to difficult practical questions of quantification in practice. The types of tortious claims which frequently arise, including those cases where the tenant or a member of his family suffers personal injury as a result of the physical condition of the premises, will also be looked at. Although these claims most commonly arise in a domestic context, there is no reason why a commercial tenant or his employee should not claim against the landlord under the lease or under s.4 of the Defective Premises Act 1972, as the case may be, provided that defect flows directly from a breach of the landlord's repairing obligation (the 1972 Act will be relied on by those who are not owed contractual duties under the lease).

However, both damages for breach of contract and in tort are subject to important limitations on the right to recover compensation common to all damages claims. The principal limitations relate to the need to establish causation, the fact that even though the claimant has suffered a loss it may be, for largely policy reasons, that it is treated as too remote and the fact that there is in every case, what has been called, a "duty to mitigate". These arguments most commonly arise in the context of claims for damage to the tenant's possessions. They are considered in the context of defective premises at p.211 Some of the more important limits on liability for damages will be summarised there. Finally, the question of interest will be briefly considered.

Damages for disrepair in residential leases

17–02   Generally these claims will be by tenants against their landlords. Those claims form the focus of the discussion here. The more important principles which apply to these claims were stated in *Calabar v Stitcher* [1984] 1 W.L.R. 287. The fundamental object of the award was to put the claimant, in so far as money could do this, in the position he would have been in had the wrong complained of not occurred. The court considered various heads of claim by the tenant, who was a long leasehold owner of a flat which suffered from disrepair over a long period. He was awarded a lump sum for the period he had lived in defective accommodation due to the landlord's breach of covenant and his consequential losses.

The starting point is to construe the covenant. Obviously, the extent of the landlord's liability for damages will depend on the scope of that covenant. But there are several heads of claim which commonly arise in practice, including:

- inconvenience and discomfort;
- actual repair costs where the tenant does not claim specific performance;
- losses consequential on the landlord's failure to comply with his repairing obligation.

Later in this chapter other general damages will be considered, such as claims to any personal injury sustained by the tenant or his family. Some examples of the types of claim that commonly arise in residential housing litigation under, for example, the Defective Premises Act 1972, will also be looked at. In particular common complaints such as those for carbon monoxide poisoning and for respiratory conditions associated with damp will be considered.

Inconvenience and discomfort

When these damages are recoverable
In the normal case of disrepair involving residential premises, where, **17–03** for example, the landlord has failed to repair the structure and exterior of the premises, the tenant falls to be compensated for his *inconvenience* in having to endure defective housing conditions. These damages will be awarded from the date from which the landlord has had both reasonable notice of the disrepair and an opportunity to effect the necessary repair, to the date that he actually discharges his obligation; be it by offering to do the work, providing alternative accommodation or actually rectifying the defects. However, where the tenant actually vacates to alternative premises they will be entitled to special damages for that alternative accommodation and related expenses but not to damages for inconvenience and discomfort for the period he is away, whereas if he remains in possession these damages will be awarded.

The correct method of assessment
Damages for inconvenience and discomfort are linked to the level of **17–04** rent payable in respect of the premises and indeed are often referred to as damages for the "diminution in value". The proper approach in most cases is to arrive at a weekly or monthly loss of rental value and multiply that by the duration of the defects. Although a judge is at liberty to award a lump sum the guidance suggests that he would be "well advised to cross check his prospective award by reference to the rent payable for the period equivalent to the duration of the landlord's breach of covenant" (*Wallace v Manchester City Council* [1998] 3 E.G.L.R. 38). This has been reiterated in *Shine v English Churches Housing Association* [2004] EWCA Civ 434. The amount

awarded should relate to what the tenant has lost and this necessarily involves considering the amount of rent that he pays.

Four propositions were set out by Morritt L.J. in *Wallace v Manchester City Council*, which remain good law: (at p.42):

> "*First*, the question in all cases of damages for breach of an obligation to repair is what sum will, so far as money can, place the tenant in the position he would have been in if the obligation to repair had been duly performed by the landlord. *Second*, the answer to that question inevitably involves a comparison of the property as it was for the period when the landlord was in breach of his obligation with what it would have been if the obligation had been performed. *Third*, for periods when the tenant remained in occupation of the property notwithstanding the breach of the obligation to repair the loss to him requiring compensation is the loss of comfort and convenience which results from living in a property which was not in the state of repair it ought to have been if the landlord had performed his obligation (*McCoy v Clark*; *Calabar Properties Ltd v Stitcher* and *Chiodi v De Marney*). *Fourth*, if the tenant does not remain in occupation but, being entitled to do so, is forced by the landlord's failure to repair to sell or sublet the property he may recover for the diminution of the price or recoverable rent occasioned by the landlord's failure to perform his covenant to repair (*Calibre Properties Ltd v Stitcher*)."

Residential leases at a ground rent

17–05   The majority of residential leases where damages have been claimed against the landlord for disrepair have involved short leases for which a periodic rent, be it monthly or weekly, is paid either by the tenant or commonly by housing benefit. However, there are cases where no weekly or monthly rent is payable but merely a ground rent. In such cases different principles might apply than in cases where the tenant rents on a monthly or other periodic term on a shorthold lease.

Calabar v Stitcher (referred to above) was such a case. In that case the Court of Appeal had upheld the judge's award to the tenant at first instance of £3,000 for her inconvenience and discomfort based on a lump sum and not on any assessment of the notional rack rent of the flat in question. The tenant was a tenant of a flat under a 99 year lease. The premises suffered from serious disrepair and but for a failure to plead the cost of alternative accommodation the tenant would have been able to claim that item because the tenant had moved out for a period, but since it was not pleaded the tenant was limited to the inconvenience and discomfort and some re-decoration costs. Stephenson L.J., giving the leading judgment, saw no reason not to regard the redecoration costs as reflecting any diminution in the capital value of the flat. This is a slightly confusing way of looking at the problem because any diminution in value is more properly characterised as an item of general, not special, damage and should reflect any inconvenience and discomfort. The Court declined to award an additional sum under that head because it was adequately reflected in the award by the Judge of the special damages for redecoration costs.

In *Earle v Charalambous* [2006] EWCA Civ 1090, [2007] H.L.R. 8 the Court of Appeal had to re-visit the question: to what extent is the tenant who pays a ground rent entitled to claim a notional loss of the rental value against the landlord who has allowed part of the premises, for which he is responsible, to fall into disrepair?

The facts in *Charalambous* were that the tenant, like the tenant in *Calabar*, held a flat on a 99-year lease for which he had paid a premium. The premises comprised a shop on the ground floor and living accommodation above. The claimant occupied one flat of eight flats on the upper floors. Water came into C's flat from the roof above in 20 different places. For 35 months of the period during which the property remained in disrepair C remained in occupation but for the next 21 months he moved in to live with his parents. The court had to consider how he should be compensated. The judge at first instance awarded him a notional monthly rent for the duration of the defects. The landlord appealed.

The Court of Appeal observed that it had long been recognised that the starting position was the difference in value (*Hewitson v Reynolds* [1924] 93 LJKB 1080) but in *Wallace v Manchester City Council* [1998] 1 E.G.L.R. 38 Morritt L.J. rejected the notion that this was any different from a claim for inconvenience; the two were effectively two sides of the same coin or as he put it, "they are alternative ways of expressing the same concept".

It was argued that since the claimant was only liable for a ground rent it was inappropriate to award him a notional rack rent for the premises. It was contended that the correct approach to the inconvenience claim (or diminution in value as it is more properly called) was that it should depend on the awards in comparable cases. These suggested an annual figure of £3,300. There was in any event no satisfactory evidence of the comparable market rent.

The court rejected the defendant's argument that the award of a lump sum by the judge at first instance was too high or wrong in principle. The Court held that where, as here, the premises provided a home to the claimant, the notional reduction in rental value was likely to be the appropriate starting position. The award would

not be a modest sum as for a protected periodic tenant. Nor was
the position precisely analogous to the situation where one buys a
property entirely as an investment, although both would take as their
starting position the loss of rental value. The award was not capable
of precise analysis being an award of general damages by the court. It
was not susceptible to expert evidence. In that case the judge appears
to have carried out his own research into the level of the rent and to
have taken account of the tenant's own evidence. His award of half
the cost of the notional loss of rental value of part of the premises
for the period for which damages for disrepair were claimed was
upheld. A further award by the judge of a lump sum of £20,000 was
characterised as excessive and ill-reasoned. Although the Court of
Appeal was critical of some of the judge's methodology they did not
interfere with his overall approach. However, some of the figures
were reduced, specifically the £20,000 was removed altogether from
the award.

Repair costs

17–06   In an appropriate case these may be claimed by the tenant as an
alternative to specific performance. However, it is relatively rare for
these to be awarded in practice because the landlord will frequently
undertake to carry out the works rather than risk an order for specific
performance. The availability of the remedy for specific performance
may, for reasons that will be explained in Ch.18 (at para.18–31,
p.239) lead to a different track allocation if a claim is issued.
Tactically, therefore, it is often advantageous for the landlord to
undertake to do works for which he is liable at the earliest opportunity.
Where the court is satisfied that the landlord genuinely intends to do
the works which are required it may well refuse damages for the
repair costs.

Where the court is concerned, for example, with a long lease of a
flat, it often occurs that the landlord has the right to recover the cost
of any repairs carried out from the tenant under the service charge
provision. This will need to be reflected in any award the court makes
for these damages.

Consequential losses

The landlord is liable for losses consequential on his failure to repair
the premises and, it was established in *McGreal v Wake* (1984)
13 H.L.R. 107, that this will include damages to furnishings and
decorations that do not themselves fall within the repairing obligation.
Indeed, all the costs of clearing up after the landlord's works will fall
at the latter's door as part of the tenant's special damages.

Other consequential losses will include:

* removal costs;
* costs associated with the storage of furniture;
* additional heating costs;
* any additional travel or insurance costs.

The limits on these claims will be considered later but the categories of claim are not closed provided they fall within the over-arching compensatory principle.

Damages for disrepair in commercial leases

The landlord's claim

Damages are awarded in commercial cases to preserve the value of the landlord's investment in the premises as a capital asset. The function of the landlord's damages is to put him in the position he would have been in had there been no breach of the repairing covenant (see *Costain Properties v Finlay* (1989) 57 P. & C.R. 345).   **17–07**

At common law a different measure of damages applied where the landlord's claim was during the term as opposed to at the end of the term. During the term the common law measure was the *diminution in value* measure (*Doe'd Worcester School Trustees v Rowland* (1841) 9 C & P 734). Indeed in respect of other common law claims, such as trespass, the landlord's claim is limited to the extent of their damaged reversion. In relation to the claim to damages for disrepair, the longer the lease had to run the less the damages would be. This had to be qualified in a case where the *cost of repairs* was a more accurate guide to the diminution figure (*Ebbetts v Conquest* [1896] A.C. 490).

At the end of the term the common law measure was the *cost of repairs* (*Woodfall* 13.081.1). However, the potential to claim the full repair costs at the end of the term is materially reduced by statute.

The Landlord and Tenant Act 1927

Section 18 (1) of the Landlord and Tenant Act 1927 provides that: **17–08**

> "Damages for breach of the covenant or agreement to keep in repair during the currency of the lease or put the premises in repair at the termination of a lease ... shall in no case exceed the amount (if any) by which the value of the reversion in the

premises (whether immediate or not) is diminished owing to the breach of such covenant or agreement as aforesaid; and in particular no damage shall be recovered for a breach of any covenant or agreement to leave or put the premises in repair at the termination of a lease, if it is shown that the premises in whatever state of repair they might be, would at or shortly after the termination of the tenancy have been or be pulled down, or such structural alterations made therein as would render valueless the repairs covered by the covenant or agreement."

Section 18 places a cap on the landlord's damages for dilapidations, regardless of the terms of the lease. The Act was introduced because it was thought to be unfair of the landlord to claim damages for the repair costs which exceeded the value of the reversion.

In *Culworth Estates v Licensed Victuallers* [1991 2 E.G.L.R. 54 Dillon L.J. explained that there were two limbs to s.18(1):

1.   whether the damages "exceed the amount, if any, by which the reversion is diminished";

2.   if it is shown that the premises, "in whatever state they might be" would shortly after the tenancy expired have been pulled down or such structural alterations made therein as to render the repairs valueless then no damages shall be recoverable.

However, the two limbs are not obvious from a first reading of the sub-section, the second half appearing to qualify the first.

In summary, s.18 of the Landlord and Tenant Act 1927 provides the important limitation that the landlord's damages for disrepair must not exceed the value of their damaged reversion. By the second limb to s.18, in relation to premises which are to be demolished or structurally altered, no damages at all are recoverable. The statute does not merely provide a cap but puts in place a total bar to recovery. The two limbs operate in a different way and will be considered separately below.

When does section 18 apply?

17–09   Section 18 applies to breaches of *repairing* obligation whether during the term or at the end of the term. Any claim to damages other than damages for *disrepair* will fall to be determined without the need for the cross-check in s.18(1). For the purposes of s.18, the fact that the covenant relates to *decorative* repair as opposed to structural repair does not mean that it is outside the limitation on damages provided for by s.18. The important point is that the covenant must involve *repair* and not merely decoration.

It follows that section will *not* apply inter alia to the following covenants:

- to reinstate at the end of the term as a result of alterations;
- to decorate at the end of the term;
- to expend a specified sum each year on repairs.

However the view has been expressed (in N. Dowding and K. Reynolds, *Dilapidations: The Modern Law and Practice*, 3rd edn (London: Sweet and Maxwell, 2007) at para.29–19) that the first limb of s.18(1) will apply to a covenant to reinstate after fire. Where the covenant to repair carries with it an incidental obligation to decorate or paint the premises as part of this process then s.18 is thought also to apply.

The first limb

The effect of the first limb of s.18 of the 1927 Act is not to change the **17–10** *basis* of assessment of damages but to place an upper *ceiling* on the quantum that is recoverable for the tenant to pay. By this means a cap is placed on liability for his damages to the landlord.

The burden of proof to establish that the damages do not exceed the diminution in the value of the reversion is on the landlord who is seeking damages. However, where the landlord has actually repaired the premises, or intends to do those repairs, the burden of proof is thought to rest on the tenant to establish that the cost of repairs is not the same as the diminution in value of the reversion, i.e. they exceed that value (see Woodfall at 13.081–13.082 and *Mather v Barclays Bank Plc* [1987] 2 E.G.L.R. 254). Where the landlord has to go to the cost of proving the cost of repairs do not exceed the value of the diminished reversion, they may recover that cost from the tenant.

When repair costs will be awarded and when the diminution in value
As has been indicated, at common law the general rule was that **17–11** during the term the landlord's damages were the extent of the depreciation in the *reversion*. Where the term had come to an end the normal measure would be the sum to put the premises into the state of *repair* in which the tenant ought to have left them in at the end of the lease. This was likely to match closely the degree of damage to the reversion. These principles of assessment still operate since s.18 was enacted subject to the cap imposed by that section. The latter rule would apply even where the claimed cost of repairs did not equate with the landlord's true level of loss (see *Joyner v Weeks*

[1891] 2 Q.B. 31).

However, which of these measures more closely related to the landlord's loss depended on the facts of each case. In particular the landlord's loss varied depending on how long the lease had left to run. If the lease had a long time left to run, the diminution in the value of the reversion was unlikely to be great. If, on the other hand, there was a short time left to run, the landlord's loss may be substantial. At the end of the term there may often have been good reasons why the landlord would wish to pursue a claim for damage to the reversion rather than the cost of repairs, i.e. sometimes this would be a higher figure. For example, the existence of a claim under s.4 of the Defective Premises Act against the landlord would significantly damage the value of the reversion which would not necessarily be reflected in the repair costs. Can the landlord in such circumstances claim that enhanced diminution in value measure?

In some cases, subject to the cap, it is possible to claim for the repair costs during the term and the reversion damage at the end of the term. Where, for example, the term only has a short time to run it may be that the real loss to the landlord is better represented by the repair costs and not by the diminution in value (See *Culworth Estates v Licensed Victuallers* [1990] 2 E.G.L.R. 36), although the limitation on the diminution in value will put a check on the amount they can recover. As the principles under which damages for disrepair at common law are now well-established, the landlord would have to provide a cogent reason for departing from those principles and this would only be likely to be in an unusual case.

How the diminution in value figure is identified in practice

17–12 Generally speaking, when valuing the diminution in value, what the court is valuing is the extent to which the premises have deteriorated during the term (see, by comparison, the shipping case of *Voaden v Champion* [2002] EWCA Civ 89). This will be a matter for expert evidence. However, in practice this exercise will involve considering the value of the premises had the tenant performed his repairing obligation according to the lease and then discounting the value of the premises in their present state. The difference between those two represents the diminution in value.

The following are examples of the correct valuation method to apply in certain recognised situations:

When the landlord is likely to carry out or has carried out the repairs
17–13 The fact that the landlord in any case has actually expended the money on the repair of the premises is normally a good reason for awarding them these damages.

Where there is little likelihood of the landlord doing the repairs
In a terminal dilapidations claim, where there was evidence that the **17–14**
landlord was not going to undertake the repairs this was a good
reason for not allowing the undiscounted costs of repair (*Crewe
Services & Investment Corp v Silk* [1998] 2 E.G.L.R. 1). Evidence of
the actual diminution will normally be needed.

Where there is only a nominal time for the term to run, the value
of the reversion may be commensurately nominal unless the landlord
can justify more extensive repairs. This was the situation in *Espir v
Basil Street* [1936] 3 All E.R. 91.

In that case the tenant (E) sublet part of the premises to B for 99
years but subsequently B acquired a new lease of the whole premises
for a much longer term (i.e. 999 years) from the head landlord. B did
major alterations to the premises in breach of their lease with E. It
was held that E could not claim the full reinstatement cost but was
limited to the diminution in value of the premises, which the Court of
Appeal assessed to be nominal only. This was because the reversion
only fell into possession for a period of 15 days before the end of
the term.

However in *Culworth Estates v Society of Licensed Victuallers*
(supra) the diminution in value was substantial. There the landlord had
never intended to carry out remedial works. Following expiry of the
lease he decided to sell the property to a third party. The third party
intended to convert the premises into workshops. The premises were
worth £320,000 in disrepair but if restored the landlord would, the
judge found, have been able to sell the building on. Alternatively he
would have been able to realise the value of the premises by renting
them out but for the fact that they needed work. Either way he would
have been able to realise their commercial value.

The judge found that the diminution in value exceeded the repair
costs by a substantial margin and therefore the landlord was entitled
to realise the value of the premises notwithstanding that he did not
intend to do the work but to sell them. The judge awarded the full
repair costs and the loss of rent during the period of those works.

Where it may be assumed the premises will be redeveloped
In *Ravengate Estates Ltd v Horizon Housing Group Ltd and another* **17–15**
[2007] EWCA Civ 1368 the court had to consider inter alia a claim
for diminution in the value of the reversion. The tenant successfully
relied on s.18.

The premises consisted of a large building on Streatham High Street.
The part of the premises demised to the tenant consisted of six-flats
within that building. At the end of the lease the landlord prepared a
substantial schedule of dilapidations following an inspection by his
surveyor. The trial judge found the premises ripe for redevelopment. The

question before the Court of Appeal was whether in respect of the claim for breach of the repairing covenant the judge should have taken into account the prospects for redevelopment. It was argued by the tenant, successfully both at first instance and before the Court of Appeal, that any purchaser of those premises would be looking to redevelop them.

It was held that the Judge was right to state that any potential purchaser of the property would have regard to the level of disrepair in giving effect to redevelopment of the property. On the facts the amount of the diminution in value was less than the cost of repairs and the trial judge was right to apply this measure of damages because of the cap in s.18. The diminution in value would reflect the fact that the purchase price would be substantially reduced to reflect the cost of those works of redevelopment that would be likely to be carried out. Any repairs carried out by the landlord would be rendered otiose by the substantial refurbishment works that would be carried out. Furthermore, the trial judge found as a fact that the landlord did not intend to carry out the repairs that he claimed he would carry out.

Where there is a sub-tenancy

17–16 Generally speaking, the landlord will suffer no diminution in value where he allows, or is required by legislation to allow, a sub-tenant to remain in possession at the end of the lease. This is illustrated by the recent case of *Lyndendown v Vitamol* [2007] 29 E.G. 142.

In that case Court of Appeal held that an undertaking by the tenant's parent company to the effect that the sub-lessee's repairing obligations would be limited to keeping the premises wind and watertight was ineffective for the purposes of satisfying the requirement in s.18 that the damages for disrepair should not exceed the value of the damaged reversion. In that case the sub-lessee held over under the Landlord and Tenant Act 1954. By s.65 of that Act, the sub-tenant therefore became directly liable to the landlord on expiry of his lease and commencement of the continuation tenancy. Effectively the sub-tenancy became the tenancy immediately expectant on the expiry of the superior tenancy. Furthermore the rent under a new tenancy (under s.34 of the 1954 Act) will be assessed without reference to any breaches of covenant which have occurred in the sub-tenant's tenancy with the tenant, so that the sub-tenant could not take advantage of their own wrong.

The question was whether the undertaking given by Lyndendown's parent had the effect of limiting the value of the landlord's dilapidation claim. It was held that the value of the reversion was nil and the undertaking was of no value. Thus it did not affect the value of the reversion for the purposes of s.18. However, this was based on the evidence given before the trial judge. He held on a preliminary issue that the head landlord could not recover substantial damages from the tenant. The Court of Appeal did not interfere with that decision.

Furthermore the Court of Appeal clarified that, in a terminal dilapidations claim, the correct date for assessing the diminution in value of the reversion is normally the termination date but in some cases it may be appropriate to look at later events if they shed light on the extent of the diminution in value at that date.

Where an arrangement as to the completion of repairs is reached with the new tenant

This was the situation in *Haviland v Long* [1952] 2 Q.B. 80. In that **17–17** case the court considered that, in deciding the correct value of the reversion, it should not look at subsequent transactions.

However, as many commentators have pointed out, this is a little simplistic. What parties subsequently paid for the premises concerned, in a genuine transaction, might be good evidence of their true value and in practice valuers always often consider comparable properties in arriving at a valuation.

What is meant by diminution in the value of the reversion?

This is a formula that experts find difficult to apply in many cases in **17–18** practice. The evidence of the experts will be supplemented to a significant degree by the evidence from the parties. In a case where the landlord gives evidence that they actually intend to expend £x on the property this will, obviously, be a crucial piece of evidence. The fact that the landlord wishes to carry out major works of refurbishment will not of itself prevent them recovering substantial damages under the first limb, although it might be highly relevant to limb two. This is illustrated by *Latimer v Carney* [2006] EWCA Civ 1417.

In *Latimer v Carney* the landlord granted a six-year lease of a carpenter's shop with upstairs living accommodation. Just before the end of the lease the landlord served a surveyor's report suggesting that the premises were in disrepair and claimed the cost of rectification. The tenant paid towards the cost of the repairs. The landlord set about finding a new tenant but that involved waiting several months and substantially refurbishing the premises. The landlord claimed the total remedial costs in fitting the premises out for the new tenant; alternatively the total costs of rectifying the defects on the schedule of dilapidations.

The court considered that the starting position was to ascertain the diminution in value. It was only if the sum claimed by the landlord exceeded that figure that the court would need to consider whether the claim offended s.18. In obvious cases, the court could infer damage to the reversion but generally there needed to be some evidence of the value of the reversion. In this regard inferences could be drawn from circumstantial evidence. In that case the court drew the inference that the damage to the reversion equated with the estimated repair costs. However, as a general rule, it is always preferable to bring any expert evidence to court to show a diminution in value.

The second limb

17–19 The second limb is different from the first because it involves the court concluding, based on the subjective intentions of the landlord, that he intends to pull-down, or substantially alter, the premises in question. This is judged at the date when the lease or continuation lease comes to an end by whatever means. Where only parts of the premises are to be rendered valueless by the alterations that the landlord intends to carry out it is believed that the landlord may recover damages in respect of the balance of the premises. Because of the high test to be surmounted in relation to the second limb it is rarely relied on successfully in practice.

A recent example of an attempt to rely on the second limb in s.18 arose in *Strachan v Henshaw* [2007] EWHC (TCC) 1289. There the judge first of all had to consider fact that the landlord required major overcladding works at the end of the term in circumstances where only patch repairs had been agreed to as being appropriate under the terms of the covenant. A secondary argument was that since the landlord was to perform those cladding works which fell outside the repairing covenant the landlord could not claim the cost back off the tenant as they fell within the second limb of s.18 (structural alterations rendering the claimed reinstatement valueless). The tenant succeeded on the first argument but not the second before Judge Peter Coulson Q.C., who held that the overcladding had not superseded the patch repairs and it was doubtful whether it amounted to a structural alteration.

The tenant's damages claim

17–20 Tenant's claims for disrepair to commercial premises are less common than they are in residential premises, due in part to the more onerous repairing obligations typically placed on commercial tenants. Section 18 does not apply to a tenant's claim for disrepair against his landlord.

The object of the award is to put the tenant in the position he would have been in had the landlord complied with his obligation. The principles as set out above in relation to claims for disrepair to residential premises apply to a degree in relation to claims by commercial tenants, save that commercial tenants are less concerned with the aesthetic quality of the premises and more concerned with the effect on their businesses.

However, where the tenant does not move out for the work to be done, inconvenience and discomfort are a factor in commercial as well as residential claims. The tenant will be entitled to compensation for the full duration of the disrepair, from the date the landlord has failed to perform his obligation, to the date the premises are finally put into their pre-breach of covenant state. Thus in *Beegas Nominees v British Gas Plc* (1994) 11 E.G. 151 the judge (Lindsay J.) awarded a lump sum of £40,000 for what he called "inconvenience". But this explicitly did not "simply (reflect) … the diminution in prospective letting value". The judge rejected an award of 20 per cent loss in rental value contended for by the tenant's counsel.

Subsequently, the Court of Appeal have recognised that inconvenience may be a factor in commercial cases as well as residential (in *Larksworth Investments v Temple House* [1996] EGCS 86), but obviously it will be necessary to justify an award which exceeds the diminution in rental value of the premises.

Where a tenant complained of a loss of or inadequate services provided by the landlord the diminution in value method applied but inconvenience was a factor in the judge's calculation. Expert evidence was admissible to determine the diminution in value in one commercial case (*Electricity Supply Nominees Ltd v National Magazine Co Ltd* [1999] 1 E.G.L.R. 130). This contrasts with the position in relation to long residential leases, where such evidence is not normally permitted (see *Earle v Charalambous* [2006] EWCA Civ 1090). In a commercial case the judge may, as in *Beegas*, order a lump sum or they may, as in *Electricity Nominees*, adopt a more scientific approach. It is suggested that there was a lack of scientific analysis in the *Beegas* case which makes the task of advising commercial tenants what sum they should accept in compensation very difficult. In addition the identification of corporate inconvenience is problematic. If it includes those of the customers of the corporate entity it runs into the difficulty that they are not parties to the contract and are not necessarily within the class expected to suffer loss. The approach adopted by Judge Hicks Q.C. in *Electricity Nominees* does at least have the attraction of some degree of certainty and resulted from proper analysis, but, as the judge in that case pointed out, the award in the *Beegas* case did equate roughly to 10 per cent of the rent. Therefore the result may have been more scientific than at first sight appears to be the case.

In addition to the damages for inconvenience the tenant is entitled to the consequential losses and special damages that he is able to prove. The reader is referred to the discussion in relation to residential premises for more detailed consideration of these.

Damages in tort

Liability for those responsible for the safety of premises

17–21 In tortious claims under the Defective Premises Act 1972 or under the Occupiers Liability Act 1957 by the tenant or a member of his family or their visitors, the major head of claim will invariably be the personal injury element which will be considered next. In addition there will often be claims for damage to possessions. In theory a claim under the Occupiers Liability Act 1957 may extend to other "damage" but claims to heads of loss other than personal injury, damage to clothing and other special damages flowing from that injury are rare in practice. The duty in respect of trespassers under the Occupiers Liability Act 1984 only applies to any injury that trespasser suffers.

Where damages are claimed under s.1 of the Defective Premises Act for physical injury to the tenant or licensee or their possessions for the landlord's failure to design and build premises correctly, those damages do not fall within the prohibition on damages for economic loss in *Murphy v Brentwood DC* [1990] 2 All E.R. 908 and *Dept of the Environment v Thomas Bates & Son Ltd* [1990] 2 All E.R. 943. However, the position may be otherwise where the tenant claims at common law for the cost of rectifying defects before any actual injury or damage of the type described occurs (see *Clerk and Lindsell on Torts* at 8–112). A claim at common law, as opposed to under s.4 of the Defective Premises Act 1972, may well fall foul of the prohibition on the recovery of damages for economic loss. The expenditure in rectifying the premises may constitute pure economic loss which, absent a contractual claim, would be irrecoverable (see *Targett v Torfaen BC* [1992] 3 All E.R. 27). That case, and *Rimmer v Liverpool City Council* [1985] Q.B. 1 before it, were concerned with defects which were latent not patent. The claim was for personal injuries not for the type of loss that appears to be ruled out by the *Murphy* decision. Therefore the position cannot be said to have been finally decided and *Murphy* is an unsatisfactory decision for a number of reasons. However, until it is overruled any claim to indirect losses in tort for one of these claims should be avoided.

There may be exceptional cases where liability may attach for negligent misstatement in the absence of contract and in the absence of physical injury or damage to property (see e.g. *Offer-Hoar v Larkstore Ltd* [2006] 1 W.L.R. 2926). However, such cases seem unlikely to arise outside the context of professional negligence claims against architects and construction professionals.

Exceptional cases—aggravated or exemplary damages

Aggravated damages and exemplary damages are awarded in tort not **17–22** in contract. They are not compensatory in character but rather, in the case of aggravated damages aim to punish the tortfeasor and, in the case of exemplary damages, aim to indicate the opprobrium of the court for the tortfeasor's conduct.

Aggravated damages are awarded where the conduct of the tortfeasor has caused such upset or injury as to aggravate the injury to the victim so as to justify going beyond the compensatory measure. There must be

> "exceptional and contumelious conduct or motives on the part of the defendant in committing the wrong or subsequently to the wrong and, secondly, mental distress, injury to feelings, indignity, insult, humiliation and a heightened sense of injury or grievance." (para.74 of the unreported case of *Owers v Bailey* per Nicholas Strauss Q.C. quoting *Appleton v Garrett* [1997] 8 Med. L.R. 75 at 77 per Dyson J.)

The only cases where such damages would be considered would be cases involving deliberate assaults, particularly unlawful eviction claims where, for example, the landlord has requested heavy assistance in encouraging the tenant to vacate.

Exemplary damage on the other hand are only awarded in the landlord and tenant context where there has been a calculation of profit by the landlord and the court wishes to sound its disapproval of the conduct under scrutiny. In practice these too are often awarded in unlawful eviction cases but are rarely awarded in disrepair cases. However, exceptional cases may arise where the housing conditions are so bad or the landlord's behaviour so lamentable that exemplary damages will be awarded for poor housing conditions, particularly where they are associated with an attempt to evict the tenant (see, for example, *Brown v Mansouri* CLY 97/3287 Uxbridge County Court).

Liability for personal injury and death

Personal injury damages may be claimed for a breach of ss.1 and 4 **17–23** of the Defective Premises Act and in the rare cases where liability in negligence may be established. The tenant himself may claim under the lease in respect of such injuries as are caused by a breach of the landlord's repairing obligation. Such claims are also often made under the Occupiers Liability Act 1957 by visitors against tenants who occupy defective premises. However, it has been doubted whether they may be claimed in a case based purely on nuisance (see Atkins Court forms Vol.28, para.11, *Read v Lyons* [1947] A.C. 156 and *Hunter v Canary Wharf* [1991] A.C. 655).

The reader is referred to works on the assessment of damages for the principles by which the correct level of damages is arrived at, such as *McGregor on Damages* 17th edn and *Kemp and Kemp: Personal Injury Law and Practice*. The Judicial Studies Board Guidelines (currently in their 8th edition) also provide helpful guidance on the assessment of damages in respect of all types of condition. However, of particular relevance to this area are damages awarded for asthma, which frequently arise as a result of damp premises, and for the consequences of carbon-monoxide poisoning, usually in the context of defective heating installations. Personal injury claims are also made for respiratory and related conditions falling short of asthma. These also normally arise out of damp housing conditions often affecting young children. These will now be considered in greater detail.

Carbon-monoxide poisoning

17–24 This often occurs where the claimant is exposed to fumes from a defective gas fire. The symptoms are usually those of nausea, headaches and lethargy. Provided the causal link may be shown, the tenant or other occupier will usually be able to claim damages on one of the bases described above. The level of damages will vary between those where the symptoms are transitory and those where permanent brain damage is sustained.

At the less serious end of the scale, awards for shorter periods of headaches, nausea and other adverse reactions to gas and other carbon-monoxide ingestion are frequently reported in Current Law. The following is a typical example:

- In *Harvey v Fairscope* CLY 97/2022 the claimant suffered from 10 months of headaches, lethargy and other symptoms. These symptoms cleared up within three months of the defective boiler that had caused them being rectified. The claimant was awarded £5000 for her injuries.

However, some claims are of the utmost seriousness as the following examples help to illustrate:

- In *Chandler v Goodman & others* (October 16, 2000, unreported) Q.B.D. a 28-year-old woman was awarded £475,000 for brain damage and severe post-traumatic stress disorder sustained as a result of CO poisoning. The claimant was rendered comatose for nine days. Her short-term memory was impaired and she suffered attention deficit and inability to concentrate. The claimant required extensive psychological treatment and was not able to pursue a career in textile design.

- In *Bateman and others v British Gas Plc* (March 23, 1998, unreported) Q.B.D. the claimant, aged 51, received £315,102 total damages for brain damage caused by CO poisoning from a defective boiler. The claimant inhaled carbon-monoxide fumes causing significant brain damage, and visual disturbance, a change in personality and marked cognitive impairment. Short-term memory was seriously damaged.

Asthma

These cases often give rise to difficult causation arguments. It is **17–25** necessary in every case to establish identifiable damage before any claim may be brought. As the House of Lords have recently confirmed (in *Johnston v NEI International Combustion Ltd* [2007] UKHL 39), without some damage there is no cause of action in negligence at all. Frequently the medical evidence does not support the proposition that the housing conditions were *the* cause of asthma. In many cases, they will have been merely a cause. Provided there is a causal link between the symptoms and those conditions. Courts, particularly at county-court level, seem content to gloss over the possible causation argument and award damages in such circumstances. These cases appear from time to time in Current Law. The following help to illustrate both the level of the awards in individual cases and the approach to establishing causation in practice:

- In *L (a child) v Empire Estates* (2002) 6 Q.R. 13 the court had to consider two children's claims for housing-related asthma. In the first claim the claimant was four years old. The child contracted and suffered an exacerbation of previous coughing, wheezing and so forth. He became so bad that he had to take steroids daily as well as using inhalers frequently. However, the medical evidence indicated that he would probably have suffered this at some stage anyway but that he was more prone to future episodes. He was awarded general damages of £8,500.

- In the same case (2002) 6 Q.R. 20 the second claimant was a six-year-old. It was claimed that although he already had asthma this became worse after living for 8 months in damp and mouldy accommodation. It was held that the causal link had been established. There had been a clear improvement in the child's state of health when they had moved to drier premises in 2002. He was awarded £1,750 in 2002.

- In *Conroy v Hire Token Ltd* 29/5/01 CLY Digest 02/3540 a boy aged two and a girl aged four at the date of the hearing both suffered coughs and colds over a six month period as a result of severe mould growth at a their home. Neither child sought medical attention nor was there a diagnosis of asthma. Each child was awarded £650 under s.4 of the Defective Premises Act 1972.

The issue of causation is more fully considered later in this chapter at para. 17–30, p.213.

Other conditions relating to damp housing conditions

17–26 In many cases, particularly of first-instance cases at county court level, no distinction is made between the damages for inconvenience and the personal-injury element and no evidence of cause and effect is given so that it is not possible to know whether the claimant has a recognised condition, such as asthma, or merely an exacerbation of some vaguer condition such as the recurrence of colds. The following are examples of the types of awards made in cases of damp where other conditions are contracted falling short of a full diagnosis of asthma:

- *Mc Coy v Clark* (1982) 13 H.L.R. 87 where the claimant suffered pneumonia caused by damp housing conditions. He was awarded £100 in 1982 in respect of this injury, as well as 10 per cent loss of rental value for the first two years followed by 20 per cent for the next year. The tenant was also awarded £5 for nuisance in the form of threats from the landlord or the landlord's agent. However, the Court of Appeal increased the award to reflect the period of the inconvenience damages, saying that the appropriate periods would be: 20 per cent in respect of the first 113 weeks and 40 per cent in respect of the last 68 weeks. However the figures appear to have reflected a degree of fault on the part of the tenant.

- *Chiodi v Marney* [1988] 2 E.G.L.R. 64 in which the claimant suffered arthritis / exacerbation of arthritis and colds. She was awarded £1500 for a period of three and a half years of these symptoms. On appeal to the Court of Appeal that award was not challenged but there was an unsuccessful appeal on the grounds that the award of more than £5,000 lump sum for her inconvenience was contrary to principle. The latter award would probably not be sustainable today in the light of the case of *Shine v English Churches Housing Association* (see above at para.17–04, p.193).

- *Ogefere v Islington LBC* (CLY 99/1391) in which the tenant's premises suffered from pronounced damp which produced a strong smell. The tenant suffered from depression as a result as well as other injuries. £1250 was awarded for the first year and £700 for the next six months. £1,500 was awarded for the last year. £750 in total was awarded specifically for "ill health".

Future employment prospects

Where it is difficult to quantify the loss of employment and apply the **17–27** conventional multiplier/multiplicand approach owing to too many imponderables about the claimant's future earning capacity, the court may be invited to look at the matter globally and assess the present value of the risk of the future financial loss (*Blamire v South Cumbria Health Authority* C.A. [1993] PIQR Q1). These loss-of-earning capacity awards will be rare in a housing case but they may arise if the symptoms are particularly serious or protracted.

Limitations on the damages award

Contributory negligence

Claims based on negligence or breach-of-statutory-duty awards are **17–28** frequently reduced to reflect an element of contributory negligence. Such a reduction is particularly a feature of personal injury litigation.

It is worth noting however that contributory negligence cannot be used to reduce an award of damages for breach of contract, even one based essentially on allegations of negligent breach of duty (see *Tennant Radiant Heat Ltd v Warrington DC* (1988) 11 E.G. 71). In that case the claim was brought in tort but the counterclaim was brought in contract. The apportionment of liability was therefore determined on the principles of causation discussed below and not based on contributory negligence as such. Only an award of damages in negligence, whether breach of statutory duty or liability at common law, may found such a reduction (*Forsikringsaktieselskapet Vesta v Butcher* [1989] A.C. 852 (October 30 1987, *The Times)*).

The extent of the court's finding of contributory negligence will depend on its assessment of the claimant's "share in responsibility for the loss or damage" that he claims for (s.1(1) of the Law Reform (Contributory Negligence) Act 1945). Essentially this is based on the "causative potency" of the claimant's own acts or omissions when weighed against those of the defendant's. Often the defendant will be primarily liable, whether or not he actually knew of the defect which is proved to have caused some injury to the claimant, before the accident occurred. This was the position in *Harry v Sykes* (2001) 17 EWCA 221, although there the landlord had failed to service the gas fire, which caused the tenant injury, as he should have done under the relevant regulations. However, the tenant was aware of the defect but failed to notify the landlord of the need to have the gas fire serviced. The final award was reduced by as much as 80 per cent.

Although such a reduction is at first sight surprising, there is no theoretical limit on the extent of contributory negligence that may be found; such awards can be reduced by as much as 100 per cent, although such a reduction would only be in a wholly exceptional case.

17–29 *Examples*

- In the Scottish case of *Craig v Strathclyde RC* reported in 1998 Hous. L.R. 104 (a Scottish series of reports, not to be confused with the Housing Law Reports) the claimant was a nine-year-old child who was injured whilst ascending an unlit staircase. His damages were reduced by 10 per cent to reflect the fact that he was attempting to carry a bicycle down the unlit stairs in total darkness at the time of his accident. It was completely dark at the time. The result is a little surprising given the age of the child but not unheard of.

- On the other hand in the Northern Ireland case of *Devine v Northern Ireland Housing Executive* [1992] N.I. 74 the Court of Appeal of Northern Ireland upheld a decision of a trial judge that a ten-year-old child had not been guilty of contributory negligence. The child in question had got onto a roof of a garage roof 4 feet off the ground level and suffered serious injury when he fell off that roof. However, the court stressed that such damages could be reduced even for young children as the above case illustrates.

Causation, remoteness and the failure to mitigate

17–30 Claims for damages in tort and contract often include claims for damage to the tenant's property or property belonging to his family or visitors. In commercial cases loss-of-profit claims sometimes feature. These claims may be consequent on a breach of the repairing obligation or at common law. Where the claim is in tort by a member of the tenant's family or by one of his visitors it will usually be under the Defective Premises Act 1972 or Occupiers Liability Act 1957.

In these cases and indeed in all claims, in order to limit the exposure of the defendant or their insurers to compensation, arguments as to causation, remoteness and failure to mitigate will often be raised. Although different considerations apply in different types of case, some general guidance may be set out.

Causation

In every claim, be it contract or tort, the claimant must establish **17–31** causation. Where the claim is in contract often the contract will determine the losses that may be said to flow from breach but where the claim is in tort the court sometimes has the difficult task of deciding the extent to which there is a causal link between the tort and the loss. In principle the test for causation is the same but the test for remoteness of damage, considered next, is not. Often causation and remoteness are considered together, the principles of remoteness placing policy limits on the extent of recoverable loss.

There have been significant developments in recent years and this is an area that has generated much litigation, particularly where the court is concerned with awarding damages for personal injury which may be due to multiple causes. A leading recent case in tort is *Fairchild v Glenhaven* [2002] UKHL 22. Although that case involved a number of employers' liability claims arising out of asbestos exposure, rather than claims in the housing or defective-premises field, the principle that it laid down was important. Their lordships held that where an employee had worked for a number of different employers but could not say which one had caused him to contract asbestosis, he could succeed if he could show against that employer that he had *materially* increased the *risk* of contracting that disease. He did not need to show that the employer had in fact caused the disease or increased the severity of that disease whilst working for that employer.

Although causation arguments are most likely to arise in construction and professional negligence litigation they do sometimes arise in all types of claims arising out of defective premises. It seems that a person defending a contractual claim may, in practice, use causation in much the same say as a person defending a negligence claim may use contributory negligence (see *Tenant Radiant Heat v Warrington DC* (above)). However, the material-contribution test is likely to lead to a limit on the ability of defendants to run causation arguments in practice.

A recent case which discusses some of the principles, as they apply to this area, is *Hilda Drake v Harbour* 21/8/07 TCC, [2008] EWCA Civ 25. There the Court of Appeal found that the judge at first instance had been correct to find that the defendant, who had been employed as an electrician by the claimant to carry out electrical work, was negligent. The claim arose out of the manner in which he carried out electrical work at the defendant's premises. A fire broke out and damaged the claimant's premises. All the claimant had to show was that the fire that broke out at the claimant's premises was more likely than not to have been caused by the defendant's negligence. The claimant did not have to prove the precise mechanism by which the fire had started. It was for the defendant faced with the claimant proving that the fire had probably been caused by his acts or omissions to attribute a different non-negligent cause. Thus the doctrine of res ipsa loquitur (i.e. the facts speak for themselves) was applied.

By and large therefore, as in that case, where a claimant is pursuing a remedy in tort, it was sufficient to show the causal link between the negligence and the loss and it would not normally be necessary to go on to show the precise mechanism by which the damage had occurred. In that case it was therefore unnecessary to show how the fire had started.

Remoteness

17–32 The ordinary rules of remoteness apply to disrepair and related claims. However different rules apply in contract and tort. In the classic formulation in *Hadley v Baxendale* (1854) 9 Exch.341 there are two limbs to the rules on remoteness in contract; under the first the defendant is liable for such loss as may fairly and reasonably be considered to arise *naturally* from the breach of contract. Under the second limb the defendant may be liable for all losses which may be said to have been in the *reasonable contemplation* of him and the claimant at the date of the contract. This limitation is imposed for policy reasons. Although the application has varied according to the contractual context, these ancient principles have survived despite the hugely varying circumstances to which they apply.

To establish the tort of negligence pre-supposes some foreseeable damage but it frequently arises that consequences flow which are both unintended and unforeseen. These unforeseen consequences will fall at the door of the tortfeasor where they are within the type or class of harm that was foreseen. This is illustrated by *Hilda Drake v Harbour* (above) Similar rules apply to claims in nuisance.

There remains considerable debate as to the extent of the losses that may be said to flow from the negligent acts or omissions in question and to what extent this goes to the issue of forseeability. This is well-described in Clerk and Lindsell 19th edn in Ch.2, but that discussion goes beyond the scope of this book.

Issues of remoteness do not often arise in defective premises claims but one example where the argument that the loss claimed was too remote was ventilated was the case of *Marshall v Rubypoint* [1997] EGCS 12 C.A. That case involved a flat within a building controlled by the landlord. Section 11 of the Landlord and Tenant Act 1985 applied to the lease. In any event, the lease contained a covenant that R should maintain, repair, redecorate and renew the common parts of the building which included the front door. The tenant's premises were burgled whilst he was out, due to the defective state of the front door. There was no fault on the part of the tenant, as the door to his own flat was properly secured. It was held that the landlord was liable for the loss of the tenant's possessions that ensued. The tenant's losses were not too remote.

Another example arose in *Coleman v British Gas* (17/2/02 unreported) where the court reached the opposite conclusion. There the judge, Toulmin J., held that the exacerbation of the claimant's psychological symptoms was too remote from the cause (the presence of carbon monoxide emanating from a defective gas fire). In addition, he held this did not satisfy the test in *Page v Smith* [1996] A.C. 310 (Hillsborough disaster case) in that the clamant was not the primary victim.

Loss of profit

The claimant may seek to establish a loss of profit arising from the **17–33** tortious acts or omissions or breaches of contract on the part of his landlord. Arriving at a reasonable assessment of future losses is in practice difficult as it often involves considerable speculation. However, some assistance is derived from the cases now considered.

In one recent case *Watermoor Meat Supply Ltd v Walker and another* [2007] All E.R. (D) 292 (Oct) Q.B.D. the judge had this in mind when he refused a loss of profit claim based on the retail prices index and the claimant's generous estimates of profits growth. The claimant had rented a butchers shop from the defendant, which had burnt down. The defendant was responsible for its reinstatement. The claim solely concerned quantum. The court had to project forward the profit that would have been made but for the fire. It was able to do this with the assistance of expert evidence and the parties own evidence including its assessment of their business acumen, the trading location of the premises and the prospects of the retail market generally.

Loss of profit claims are hard to prove in practice (for a recent example see *Hawkins v Woodhall* [2008] All E.R. (D) 375). That was a claim for loss of profits flowing from disrepair.

Mitigation of loss

There has been a trend in recent years of treating tenancy agreements **17–34** like other contracts and applying the analysis that applies, particularly, to commercial contracts. One area where this has recently been argued is in the area of tenant abandonment during a fixed term tenancy.

What happens if the tenant abandons the premises? Can the landlord claim the lost rent off the tenant or does his duty to mitigate extend to finding a replacement tenant?

This question was considered and answered fairly conclusively in *Reichman v Gauntlett* [2006] EWCA Civ 1659. The Court of Appeal considered that there is no duty to mitigate following abandonment save in cases where the innocent party has acted wholly unreasonably in not treating the lease as repudiated.

The decision in *Reichman* may have been different if for example, the case had involved residential premises for which it would be relatively straightforward to find a new tenant, but the onus of proving a failure to mitigate would be on the tenant. Essentially it would be for such a tenant not only to plead a failure to mitigate but, if possible, to bring forward evidence (including market evidence?) to back up the assertion that the landlord's conduct had been wholly unreasonable.

The betterment problem

17–35 The tenant may wish to carry out repairs themselves and claim this cost back off the landlord. Alternatively, the tenant may wish to claim specific performance or secure an undertaking from the landlord to effect the repairs. In either case he may well suffer consequential damage to his furnishings and personal effects. In such a case the tenant will often be faced with the argument that he is in a better position than he was before the landlord's breach of contract (see *McGregor on Damages* 17th edn at 1–1027, where this debate is fully discussed). This is a debate of practical importance therefore. The problem is that if, for example, special damages are awarded which result in the claimant obtaining new goods for old, because the old goods damaged are irreplaceable, the tenant may be in a better position than he was before the disrepair arose. Do they, in these circumstances, have to give credit for that element of betterment?

The predominant view is that provided the benefit is merely incidental the innocent party need not give credit for it. The key case is *Harbutts Pasticine v Wayne Tank and Pump* [1970] Q.B. 447 in which the Court of Appeal decided that where it was not possible to restore the claimant to the position he had been in before the tort or breach of contract had occurred, any benefit to the claimant was merely incidental and should, effectively, be discounted.

Furthermore, it was held in *McGreal v Wake* (1984) 13 H.L.R. 107 that no deductions would be made in respect of redecoration consequent on the landlord's breach of repairing covenant.

Most cases in this area have adopted a similar reasoning in refusing to deduct for betterment. It does not necessarily follow that *Harbutts Plasticine* would be followed in every circumstance and many leases require the court to discount "fair wear and tear" in arriving at, for example, any claim for damages relating to fixtures at the property (see for e.g. *Burkeman v GE Capital*, [2002] EWHC 2863 (Q.B.), Stuart Brown Q.C. sitting as a High Court judge). However, it remains the predominant view that a claim by a tenant, for example, for redecoration costs, will not be discounted. Indeed a betterment argument is unlikely to succeed in this type of litigation (see *McGregor*, supra).

Interest

This seemingly straightforward area generates a good deal of **17–36** confusion.

Contractual claims

Claims for debt or damages, such as claims for claims for damages **17–37** for disrepair, will normally give rise to a claim for simple interest at the discretion of the court. Logically such an award would appear justified. Where, for example, the tenant claims for the diminution in value of the demised premises consequent on the landlord's disrepair the award of interest would reflect the fact that the damages include the tenant's notional loss of interest on the rent he has paid over to the landlord from the date it was paid over until judgement or earlier settlement. Obviously, if the tenant has not paid any rent for the duration of the disrepair but has withheld it and seeks to set off his outstanding disrepair claim against the landlord's outstanding rent claim, it is difficult to see any justification for an interest claim.

Commercial dilapidations claims are normally brought at the end of the lease; the claim being based on the tenant's failure to yield up the premises in repair. In such a case the correct date for calculating damages and hence interest is the termination date. However the court retains the right to deprive the landlord of some or all of his interest claim where he has, for tactical or other reasons, delayed in issuing the claim (see *Craven (Builders) Ltd v Secretary of State for Health* [2001] 1 E.G.L.R. 128).

Where interest is awarded both the rate and the period for which it is awarded are at the discretion of the court. However in non-personal injury claims, the practice has developed of awarding 8 per cent, which is above the current base rate, from the date the cause of action arose until the judgment is given or earlier payment made. It has remained at this high rate for many years. However, it should be properly pleaded by including a proper calculation (CPR 16.4(2) (b)).

Theoretically the court has the right to award compound interest (interest upon interest). This may arise, for example for a claim for unjust enrichment or a claim based on fraud. In practice this is unlikely to arise in this area of litigation and simple interest is more likely to be awarded. Section 35A(4) of the Supreme Court Act 1981 and s.69(4) of the County Court Act 1984, provide that the court may not award interest on a debt in respect of a period during which interest on the debt already runs, e.g. under a provision in the lease.

Personal injury claims

17–38   In a personal injury case the successful claimant is entitled to interest on his general damages for pain, suffering and loss of amenity at 2 per cent from the date he serves his claim until the date he obtains a judgment in his favour.

As to the claimant's special damages, where he claims a loss of earnings as a result of the accident interest will normally be awarded at half the full rate on the past earnings losses if that loss is continuing at the date of the trial. A once and for all loss such as the loss of or damage to possessions, rather than a continuing loss, would normally would be awarded at the full rate awardable on the court's special account (see *Jefford v Gee* [1970] 1 All E.R. 1202). Since February 1, 2002 the rate has been 6 per cent. However the rate and the period for which interest is awarded are within the discretion of the court. Thus, if there has been an inexcusable period of delay this may justify reducing the period or rate for which interest is awarded.

Where the interest claim is under a statute, as it is in all personal injury cases, the award is, in reality, as of right and the defendant has the burden of showing that interest would not be awarded.

The judgment rate

17–39   The judgment rate is specified in the Judgments Act 1838 and is varied occasionally, but is currently set at the high rate of 8 per cent.

PART IV

PRACTICE AND PROCEDURE

Chapter 18

Bringing a court claim

In this chapter the practicalities of pursuing a claim for disrepair and **18–01** other forms of property damage and injury will need to be considered. First and foremost amongst the considerations facing the potential litigant is: how long have I got to pursue my claim? However, there are also a greater range of dispute resolution methods available which will need to be considered, either as part of or as an adjunct to court proceedings. Because of the present day importance of these other methods, particularly mediation, they warrant consideration in a separate chapter at the conclusion of this book. For those going down the litigation route there are a great number of matters to consider: how the case is pleaded, who to join as a party and, in a commercial case, the all-important schedule of dilapidations. If the matter proceeds to a hearing, the Scott schedule, which serves a similar function, will also need to be considered so there will also be some guidance on this type of pleading below.

Secondly, experts assume an important role in proving disrepair and all types of property damage. In a commercial dilapidations claim it may be impossible to contemplate proceedings of any type without knowing the extent of the disrepair and the extent to which this will feed through to the final damages claim given the important statutory cap already considered. Because experts will need to be considered at an early stage as well as later stages in the litigation process, they will also be considered in this chapter. The type of expert that might be instructed in the context of a typical residential case involving an allegation of carbon monoxide poisoning arising from, say, a gas fire, will be considered including those experts likely to assist a successful outcome in the case.

Thirdly, there are a number of pre-action protocols in litigation relating to defective premises of varying degrees, some of which are binding on the litigants one of which is voluntary in character. Even if there is no protocol applies to the particular form of action being contemplated pre-action behaviour is expected to be in the post-Woolf spirit of co-operation. Negotiation and exploring settlement are encouraged and the tactic of "keeping the powder dry" until the battle or the eve of the battle is discouraged. It is important to adopt the right approach because dilapidations claims in particular, indeed, all claims involving experts, are more costly than other proceedings.

A crucial aim of the Woolf reforms was to make summary disposal of issues quicker and cheaper. Unfortunately this has not transpired to be the case to the regret of Lord Woolf and others. Part of the problem lies in the wording of the principal summary judgment power in Pt 24 of the CPR (further considered at para.18–39, p.242). Whereas the old power in the Rules of the Supreme Court 1965 and County Court Rules 1981 referred to "no defence" the new power, which refers to a "real prospect of success", has been interpreted in a way that is more generous to those with only "shadowy" claims or defences. In addition there has been a marked judicial reluctance to dispose of issues summarily where the trial itself is supposed to take place quicker and at less cost than used to be the case. Other litigation topics, such as which parties to join, need only be touched on in a specialist publication and the reader is referred to more general publications on civil procedure such as the current *White Book*.

The final topic will be the important issue of costs. Judges, particularly appellate judges, often refer to the wide discretion that judges have on costs. This makes giving decisive and sound advice difficult but such advice is at a premium, particularly to those who do not have the day-to-day experience of how courts award costs including surveyors and other non-legally qualified property professionals. Some pointers in the context of this publication are therefore included.

Limitation

18–02   In most cases the correct limitation period will depend on the type of claim. When the cause of action accrues depends on whether the action is brought in contract (in which case generally the action must be brought within six years of the date of breach under s.5 of the Limitation Act 1980) or in tort (where generally the action must be brought within six years of the date of damage under s.2 of that Act). In some cases it will also depend on the nature of the damage sustained. For example, if the claim is for damages arising out of personal injury the claim must be brought within three years of the date the injury occurred or within three years of the date of knowledge, whichever is the later. It has recently been decided by the House of

Lords (in *A v Hoare* [2008] UKHL 6) that this three-year limitation period applies even if the claimant's personal injuries were deliberately inflicted, as opposed to being occasioned by "negligence, nuisance or breach of duty". In *Stubbings v Webb* [1993] A.C. 498 the House of Lords had thought that such a claim had to be brought within six years and that there was no discretion to override the limitation period.

However, if the claim is for tortiously-caused property damage the claim must be brought within six years of that damage. Where that damage was caused negligently, as opposed to being as a result of a breach of contract, the claimant may rely on a later date of knowledge (see s.14A Limitation Act 1980). That later date of knowledge is subject to the 15 year long-stop in s.14B of the Act. The 15 year period commences on the date of the act or omission said to constitute the negligence on which the cause of action is founded.

Unsurprisingly, the Law Commission has described the present law on limitation as being "uneven, illogical and unnecessarily complex" and has recommended wholesale reform (in Law Com. No.270: "Making the law on civil limitation periods simpler and fairer"). Other than the reform of the law of limitation in relation to registered land (i.e. adverse possession claims), which was reformed as a consequence of a different Law Commission report, the Government has not shown any tendency to adopt the proposed reforms, sensible as they appear to be.

The more important limitation topics will now be considered in greater detail.

When the cause of action accrues

Contractual claims

As has already been stated, in contract all that is needed is some **18–03** breach of contract to sue for damages and there are no "long stops" or discretionary extensions available, although any fraud or concealment will have the effect of delaying the running of time (see below).

Here are the main rules relevant to the conduct of defective premises claims of a contractual nature including those arising out of a landlord and tenant relationship:

- Where the obligation being sued upon is contained in a deed under seal (an action on a "specialty") then the twelve year limitation period in s.8 of the Limitation Act applies. This will include an action on a formal written lease but not under an informal oral periodic tenancy, although some commentators have assumed that a claim for disrepair has a six year limitation period (see, for example, Knaffler and Luba "Repairs Tenant's Rights" 3rd edn para.4.34). However, this is almost certainly incorrect and it is regrettable that neither *Woodfall* nor *Hill and Redman* comment on the point). The test for a deed is whether the necessary formality requirements are met (see s.1 of the Law of Property (Miscellaneous Provisions) Act 1989). A deed no longer be "signed, sealed and delivered" but must be executed as a deed. Other claims under oral or written leases not under seal are subject to the contractual limitation period of six years from the date of breach.

- A claim to forfeit a lease must be brought within 12 years of the date the cause for forfeiture arose (s.15(1) Limitation Act 1980) but an application for relief from ejectment for non-payment of rent may be made up to six months after the order under s.210 of the Common Law Procedure Act 1852.

- On the other hand an action to recover rent is subject to the six year rule from the date that the rent became due (s.19 Limitation Act 1980).

- Where damages for disrepair are claimed a new cause of action arises on each day that the property is in disrepair. This gives rise to a number of practical problems relating to the wording of the repairing covenant. In particular, if the landlord's real complaint is that the tenant failed to deliver up the premises in repair at the end of the term (i.e. a terminal dilapidations claim) limitation will not begin to run until the termination date. As has already been noted, liability to effect repairs normally arises when the landlord has both notice of the disrepair in question and the reasonable opportunity to put that disrepair right. Therefore the landlord or tenant could not sue earlier than the date of that notice.

Tortious claims

18–04 In tort, as stated above there is a basic six year limitation period from the date the cause of action "accrued". The cause of action accrues when the claimant suffers "more than minimal damage" (see *Cartledge v Jopling* [1963] A.C. 758). This is subject to the important exception in the case of claims for damages for personal injury or death for which the claim must be brought within three years of the accrual of the cause of action (date of injury) or date of knowledge, if later (ss.11 and 14 Limitation Act 1980). There is also an important discretion to override the primary limitation period in personal injury claims in s.33 of the 1980 Act , considered briefly below (at para.18–05, p.225).

Nuisance may be a one-off act, for example, producing excessive noise and smoke on one occasion, or it may be, and more commonly is, a continuing tort, for example allowing moisture to penetrate from one flat into the flat below with reasonable foresight of the damage to that lower property. In the latter type of case, rather like the contractual equivalent type of claim, e.g. to disrepair, the claim cannot become statute barred as long as the situation continues, i.e. the tortfeasor is under a continuing legal duty to put matters right. However, a particular day of loss can become statute barred if it can be shown that it arose more than six years, or whatever the limitation period may be, prior to the day the action commenced. In short only the damage that the claimant can prove occurred within the six years prior to issue may be claimed for (see *Cartwright v GKN Sankey Ltd* [1972] 2 Lloyd's Rep 242).

Some particular cases

The normal limitation rules do not apply where the claimant dies **18–05** before bringing his claim. In those circumstances the right of action survives for his estate under the Law Reform (Miscellaneous Provisions) Act 1934. A personal injury claimant's estate has a further three years to sue (s.11(3)) provided the deceased knew of the claim. In other cases, the executors or administrators would have whatever limitation period applied to the original cause of action to bring the claim as that claim survives to the estate and can be pursued as soon as probate or letters of administration have been taken out.

The normal limitation period whether in contract or tort does not apply where there is fraud, deliberate concealment or mistake on the part of the defendant in relation to any facts relevant to the claimant's right of action (see s.32 of the 1980 Act).

More relevant to a publication about defective premises is the additional limitation period for claims to latent damage originally introduced by the Latent Damage Act 1986 already referred to. Under s.14A of the Limitation Act 1980 the claimant has an additional three years from the date of knowledge to sue, if that is later than the date of the accrual of the cause of action (date of damage) but this is subject to the 15 year long-stop after that cause of action accrued (in s.14B). Before s.14A came into force it was held, in relation to a defective building claim, that the claimant suffered some damage when cracking occurred (latent damage that was hidden from public view—*Pirelli v Oscar Faber* [1983] 2 A.C. 1 (HL)).

The date of knowledge for personal injury claims is defined in s.14 in slightly different terms to the date of knowledge for non-personal injury claims in s.14A. It is not subject to any statutory long-stop but it is subject to an overriding power to extend time where it is just and equitable to do so under s.33 of the Limitation Act already referred to. This power is widely used and sometimes results in old cases coming before the court where the court considers the prejudice to the defendant is outweighed by the potential prejudice to the claimant if the doors of the court are closed in front of him.

An action for a contribution may be made at any time up to two years following the judgment or settlement of the claim that the claimant seeks a contribution towards (s.10 of the 1980 Act).

Finally, an action to enforce a judgment must be brought within six years of the date the judgment becomes enforceable, presumably the date that the order giving effect to that judgment was sealed (s.24 Limitation Act).

Parties

18–06 It is important that any representative party should be identified as such. When claims by visitors against occupiers were considered above in the context of the Defective Premises Act 1957 it was pointed out that difficult questions arise as to the correct person or persons to sue where there is a committee who run, for example, a club. In occupiers liability claims the question often arises: who is in effective control? Sometimes a Land Registry search will not help because there may be any number of leases and sub-leases which do not appear on the proprietorship register (leases of only 7 years or more being compulsorily registerable and only then when a registerable disposition in relation to the property takes place (see s.27 Land Registration Act 2002)).

Claims to a contribution or indemnity, called "additional claims" are governed by Pt 20 CPR but where it is necessary to apply to add or substitute a party the application would need to be made under Pt 19 CPR, save where the application involved adding or substituting a party after limitation has expired (governed by Pt 17).

Instructing an expert

18–07 Before an expert can be appointed as part of the court process the party applying for such evidence must show that there is an issue which requires expert opinion evidence and that cannot be dealt with without such assistance. It must be "reasonably required" to resolve the proceedings (CPR Pt 35.1). Secondly, it must be proportionate to or the issues to be resolved in those proceedings. Thus if the value of the claim is low, for example, the case is likely to be allocated to the Small Claims' Track (claims worth not more than £5,000 or, where there is a claim for specific performance of the repairing obligation, not more than £1,000). By implication, expert evidence will normally not be justified in cases on the Small Claims Track, although the court retains complete control over this (see CPR 27.5). However, given the complexity of some disrepair claims for example, the difficulty in identifying which items of disrepair are structural and which amount merely to decorative disrepair, it is difficult to see how evidence given by the tenant himself as to the extent of the alleged disrepair would be sufficient to discharge the burden of proof.

An expert may be employed by one of the parties (*Field v Leeds City Council* [2000] 1 E.G.L.R. 54). However, he must sign a declaration under Pt 35 of the CPR to indicate that he understands and accepts the obligation to give an honest and open opinion uninfluenced by the party who is to discharge his fee / pay his wage. He must also recognise his overriding duty to the court and sign a declaration to that effect.

The proliferation of experts is discouraged under the CPR (see Pts 35.1 and 35.7) and in straightforward claims the instruction of a single joint expert will be the usual course the court will adopt. As will be seen, a number of protocols, for example the Housing Disrepair Protocol, strongly encourage this. Where a single expert has been appointed it would most unusual for the court to ignore the expert conclusions, particularly where that evidence had been read as unchallenged evidence, as normally occurs where there is only one expert. In *Montoya v Hackney* July 15 2004 (unreported SD 204705) the single expert had identified defects but concluded that they fell within the exception in s.11(3) of the Landlord and Tenant Act 1985, i.e. they were consistent with the age, character and prospective life and the locality in which the dwelling was situated. Given those facts it was perverse for the judge to reject the expert's evidence and effectively prefer the non–expert evidence of the tenant. A High Court Judge, Astill J., overturned that decision on appeal therefore.

Where the court does allow the parties to instruct their own experts it will take a good deal of persuasion to allow a third expert in the same discipline. However, where, as occurred in *Stallwood v David* [2006] EWHC 2600, the claimant's first expert effectively "caved in" on a key point during a meeting with the other side's expert, the claimant was allowed to instruct a further expert. This will usually be at the expense of the person seeking to rely on a third expert.

Any instructions to experts should comply with the Protocol on the Instruction of Experts. All material information should be supplied to the expert preferably in an agreed set of instructions. In default of agreement as to the expert's instructions the court has the power to direct the issue or issues that the expertise to deal with.

Joint statements

18–08 Where there are two or more experts in the same discipline they are generally required to meet to narrow the issues and produce a joint statement. The statement is not binding on the parties even where they reach agreement on an issue (CPR 35.12(5)) but the statement will be admissible and may well be persuasive. However the actual discussion is privileged unless the parties agree otherwise (CPR 35.12(4)).

It should be noted that if an expert is instructed for mediation the content of his disclosed evidence, including a joint statement prepared by him in conjunction with the opponent's expert, will be in the public domain and will not be protected by privilege, whether "without prejudice" privilege or otherwise (see *Aird v Prime Meridian Limited* [2006] EWCA Civ 1866 (21/12/06)). This is an exception to the normal rule that discussions which take place in mediation are without prejudice and may not be referred to if they fail. But it is always open to the parties to place whatever qualification they see fit on their discussions.

It is possible for a party to rely on another party's disclosed expert's report, even where that party is no longer a party and will not be attending the trial. However, it has been held that the weight to be attached to that report may not be very great given that he would not be attending to give oral evidence (see *Gurney Consulting Engineers v Gleeds Health and Safety* TCC 25/1/06).

What type of expert should be instructed?

18–09 Obviously the type of expert instructed will depend to a large degree on the type of dispute. For example, where the claim is that the claimant has suffered carbon monoxide poisoning as a result of a defective gas fire for which the landlord is responsible, one may have to consider each of the following:

- Heating consultant—this needs to be somebody with experience of gas heating appliances, boilers, flues and knowledge of CO poisoning. The expert should be able to measure the level of CO exposure from the faulty appliance.

- Toxicologist—this expert will need to establish the causal link between CO poisoning and effects on health.

- Consultant psychiatrist and consultant neuro-psychologist—in any case where there is an allegation of brain damage (including memory impairment and loss of concentration) it will usually be necessary to instruct both of these experts. The neuro-psychologist will establish by formal testing the extent of brain damage and its effect on cognitive functioning and memory abilities. The neuro-psychiatrist will consider the effects of CO exposure on psychiatric functioning in particular.

- Employment consultant—may be needed where there is a loss of wages claim to provide data about loss of earnings and possibly pension losses. Such an expert may also be of use where somebody cannot go back to the sort of job he was doing previously and may only be capable of working at a lower level of ability. The expert will need to quantify future deficits in income.

- Care consultant—if the injuries are severe then there may be a social care element claim for the future, the cost of which needs to be quantified as part of the special damages claim.

If on the other hand the claim is for terminal dilapidations to commercial premises, it is likely that the claimant will wish to consider one or more of the following:

- The landlord's surveyor will need to inspect. He will not necessarily be able to give opinion evidence at a trial but will almost certainly be a witness because he will need to prepare the schedule of dilapidations.

- If the matter is contentious, an independent surveyor and valuer who is capable of giving evidence in court may need to be appointed. Obviously such a person should not be connected to either party and it would be preferable if he did not work for the same firm as the landlord's surveyor.

- In many cases mechanical and electrical engineers will need to be instructed to deal with matters within their own area of specialism.

- In a complex case, for example, one involving specialist plant and equipment, experts and even contractors familiar with the latest costs and other practical difficulties may be needed. This will obviously go to the issue of repair costs albeit that these are subject to the cap in s.18 of the Landlord and Tenant Act 1927.

There is more information below about experts where the two main protocols in this field are considered.

There are dangers in relying on a single joint expert, although sometimes questions may be asked which help to elucidate the replies helpful to the client one represents. The problem of allowing the evidence to stand without further challenge or supplementary oral evidence is illustrated by *Montoya v Hackney* [2004] referred to above, where the single joint expert had reached some unfavourable conclusions as to the extent of the disrepair having regard to the age of the property and its location.

Complying with pre-action protocols

18–10 There are now a large number of these including those which apply to housing disrepair claims, professional negligence and construction disputes but none under the CPR in relation to dilapidations claims. Fortunately the Property Litigation Association's Protocol, considered below, fills the gap that would otherwise exist for terminal-dilapidations claims. These are a type of claim where the need for guidance is at its most obvious. Unfortunately in the area of enforcing liability for defective buildings several of the CPR Protocols overlap, for example, there is an obvious overlap between the Pre-action Protocol for Construction and Engineering Disputes and the Professional Negligence Protocol. There is also an obvious overlap between the Housing Disrepair Protocol and the Pre-action Protocol for Personal Injury Claims. How this apparent overlap should be resolved is set out in the introductory notes of the former Protocol, which provide that where the claimant is suing a construction professional the Pre-action Protocol for Construction and Engineering Disputes should be used. In the case of a housing disrepair claim with a personal injury element the Pre-action Protocol for Personal Injury claims should be followed for that personal injury element unless that element of the claim is minor, e.g. it will not require expert evidence other than a doctor's letter.

There is also an overlap with the guidance given in the Court Guides and the CPR protocols (found in Vol.2 of the White Book and not Vol.1 where the Protocols are found). Those of particular relevance this field of practice are the Chancery Guide and the Technology and Construction Court Guide.

These protocols will now be considered in their practical context.

Dilapidations claims

The Pre-Action Protocol—Terminal Dilapidations Claims for Damages

18–11 This Protocol was agreed by the Property Litigation Association in conjunction with the surveying profession and in particular the Royal

Institute of Chartered Surveyors (RICS). The Protocol, which was introduced in June 2002, does not have official CPR status. Indeed it is not mentioned in the current edition of the White Book. However, it is now in its second edition, having been extensively revised with effect from September 14, 2006. Some practitioners regard the Protocol as being a helpful tool.

The aims of the Protocol are similar to the CPR protocols—to encourage early settlement; enable the parties to avoid litigation and to support the efficient management of proceedings. It is aimed at actions by landlords to claim compensation for disrepair at the end of the term (i.e. terminal dilapidations claims) and not other actions between landlord and tenant, for example, claims which arise during the term. All terminal dilapidation claims relating to the physical state of the premises on the termination of a lease and not to cases involving a breach of the repairing covenant may be litigated under the Protocol.

The revised Protocol recommends the use of plain English in dilapidations claims.

Some key points are:

The landlord's claim   **18–12**

- The landlord should serve a schedule in the form annexed to the Protocol setting out the breaches alleged and specifying the steps taken to enforce compliance with the obligation or obligations in question. However, where the landlord serves his schedule before the end of the lease it should be updated at the end of the term.

- Where there are other claims, e.g. for reinstatement or to compel compliance with other obligations in the lease, these should be served separately.

- The claim should be quantified in a separate document. The schedule should enable the tenant to know what work needs to be carried out and at what cost. If the claim is for the cost of works these should be quantified. Other costs such as professional fees should be included in the landlord's claim. If the work has been done the landlord need not provide a valuation under s.18(1) of the LTA 1927. If however, the landlord has not carried out the work or if he does not intend to do so he must provide a valuation under s.18(1).

- The landlord (L) is not required to calculate his diminution in value claim until a later stage, i.e. when he finally pleads his claim.

- The RICS guidance is adopted in relation to the endorsement of the schedule. This guidance has recently been revised to reflect the new May 2008 edition of the protocol (see below). The surveyor is required to certify that the repairs claimed are a fair assessment of the likely loss to the landlord.
- L's VAT status should be identified.
- Projected surveyors and other fees and expenses should be quantified.
- The facts of the case should be summarised.

Certification of the dilapidations schedule by the landlord's surveyor

18–13 The new RICS guidance in terms of the schedule of dilapidations is as follows. In the new edition (which was published in May 2008) the Association have varied the Protocol's requirement that the landlord's surveyor should certify that "the landlord's claims are a fair assessment of the landlord's loss" because it was felt this needed to be more specific to prevent landlords advancing exaggerated claims. It provides that the surveyor who prepares the schedule confirms that the works in that schedule are reasonably required, any costs quoted are reasonable and that full account has been taken of the landlord's intentions for the property at, or shortly after, the termination of the tenancy. The RICS guidance reflects the new wording.

Timing of the dilapidations schedule

18–14 There is nothing to stop a landlord who has served a schedule of dilapidations negotiating at the same time for a new lease provided those negotiations are made "subject to contract". However, those negotiations need to be handled carefully as is illustrated by *Business Environment Bow Lane Ltd v Deanwater Estates Ltd* [2007] EWCA Civ 622.

There the landlord began to negotiate a surrender of the lease and the grant of a new five-year term. As part of the negotiations he did not serve a schedule of dilapidations on the tenant at the end of the new term. The proposed new lease allowed the landlord to enter to carry out repairs without being able / required to serve such a schedule under the old lease. The new lease was entered into. It was held that the assurance given to the tenant, that he would not be liable to repair at the end of the old lease, did not override the express terms of the new lease so as to prevent the landlord enforcing the strict terms of the new lease, whether on the basis of a collateral contract or estoppel.

The tenant's response

18–15 The tenant must be given reasonable time in which to respond, usually thought to be two months. Within that two-month period the tenant should indicate whether he is to allege that the diminution in value is less than the claim but he may simply request proportionate disclosure by the landlord of his intention to carry out the repair works with a view to deciding whether he wishes to rely on s.18. A meeting between the two sides or their experts before the response is encouraged. Any number of without prejudice meetings may be held with a view to settlement. Where the claim is not resolved and proceedings are to follow a "stock take" before issue is encouraged. Finally, the parties are encouraged to explore ADR.

The courts may take a dim view of those who fail to comply with the Protocol, even though it does not form part of the CPR, if the parties have agreed to follow it.

Other procedural steps before issue

In claims unpaid service charges, which often arise out of disrepair, **18–16** there are certain restrictions which the landlord should be aware of. In particular, as well as the legislative restrictions which exist under the Landlord and Tenant Act 1985 and 1987 in relation to certain types of tenant, there is a code on the collection of service charges prepared by the RICS. This tends to view the tenant like any other consumer and provides him with a degree of protection against over zealous enforcement.

There is also an accreditation scheme aimed at enforcing minimal standards amongst commercial landlords (the Code for Leasing Business Premises in England and Wales 2007). However, this is voluntary and in certain cases landlords will opt out of the scheme.

Housing claims

The Pre-action Protocol on Housing Disrepair follows the same **18–17** pattern as other protocols but some of the time periods are fairly onerous and the guidance is not always easy to apply in practice.

The Housing Disrepair Protocol Working Group published the draft protocol in January 2001. Earlier attempts to produce a protocol were frustrated but the protocol has now been in operation since December 2003.

Scope

The protocol is intended to apply to all civil claims arising from the **18–18** condition of residential premises by tenants, long-leaseholders, members of their families, and presumably also other household members, including those with a claim for personal injury has already been mentioned, the Protocol for Personal Injury claims needs to be followed where that element of the claim is sufficiently serious to be dealt with separately". The Housing Protocol also applies to contractual licensees. But those proceedings brought by way of set-off or counterclaim (where directions will be sought or agreed, substantially to the same effect) are excluded from the Protocol's application. The deadlines in the protocol are quite tight as the following discussion makes clear.

Aims

18–19 The Protocol recites the objectives set out in the CPR's existing Practice Direction on Protocols:

- to encourage early and full exchange of information about the claim;
- to enable litigation to be avoided by pre-action settlement;
- where litigation is unavoidable, to help the efficiency of proceedings.

Also, the Housing Disrepair Protocol has its own specific aims:

- to promote speedy and appropriate repairs;
- to ensure that any compensation due is paid speedily;
- to promote good pre-action practice, especially disclosure and experts' instructions;
- to avoid unnecessary litigation;
- to keep the costs of resolving disputes down.

Steps under the Protocol

18–20 • Step 1—the early notification letter (ENL)

This is to provide the landlord (L) with notice of the claim as early as possible, even before the letter of claim (below) but it will not be necessary in every case, e.g. where urgent repairs are sought. There is a specimen at the end of the Protocol. An ENL should contain the tenant's (T's) name and address, details of past and outstanding defects and details of notice already given to L. It should also make any request for disclosure and contain any proposals for instructing an expert.

In urgent cases, for example, where the limitation period is about to expire, an ENL may be skipped. The tenant may issue promptly. But this can be avoided if L can confirm it will not take a limitation point if T issues late.

- Step 2—the letter of claim (LOC)

This too should be sent as soon as possible. It should contain the same details as the ENL, plus:

- a history of the defects;
- details of any emergency work done;
- how the defects have affected T and his household;
- details of any special damages;
- details of the proposed expert, if not already supplied;
- the poposed letter of instruction to that expert

- Step 3—the landlord's response

L should reply within 20 working days of the date of posting of the ENL or LOC if an ENC was sent. Hence the comment above about the short deadlines.

The tenancy file should be sent, where one exists, and details of notice, any inspection of the property and works/servicing records as far as they are relevant. A response will also be needed to proposals as to choice of expert/ expert evidence generally.

If replying to a LOC:

As above, but the following matters should also be covered:

- extent (if any) to which liability is admitted;
- reasons for disputing liability;
- details of any "no access/no notice" defence;
- full schedule and timescale for works;
- any offers of compensation and costs.

It may also be necessary to make a point about the workability of the time limits and the disclosure of obscure records by large corporate or public sector landlords may well be an issue. A smaller private landlord may legitimately object to disclosure of independent contractors' records or expensive disclosure obligations.

Expert Evidence under the Housing Disrepairs Protocol

"Before and after" photographs are encouraged in order to help the **18–21** expert or experts, and ultimately the court, with their task of determining whether it falls within the relevant obligation. The principle is to instruct one joint expert on one agreed set of instructions, where possible.

Specimen letters of instruction are included in the Protocol. Where joint instructions cannot be agreed, each party can instruct the same expert separately. Alternatively, L can send its expert to the premises (preferably simultaneously with T's). The court can subsequently decide who has acted reasonably.

Inspection by the experts or single joint expert should be within 20 days of L's response to T's first letter (3.6(g)).

A single expert should report back to the parties within 10 days of the inspection, or where two experts are appointed they should report in schedule form, with details of the proposed works, on what is agreed and what is not, with reasons for the latter within the same period.

The parties can ask written questions of a single expert—the format and timetable is best agreed in advance. Otherwise the court can order it.

In really urgent cases, e.g. where there is a significant health & safety risk, or an interim injunction is needed, T can instruct an expert earlier than the Protocol suggests. Both parties are expected to honour their obligations and act reasonably over experts' access requirements.

Experts' costs and other terms should be agreed at the outset. Jointly instructed experts' fees will be shared equally.

Costs

18–22   Where works are to be carried out, and/or compensation paid, then costs incurred as a result of the claim should be paid by L "unless this would cause an injustice". This is of questionable fairness where, for example, the landlord carries out repairs but they did not constitute actionable disrepair because he had no prior notice of the defects.

Consequences of non-compliance with the protocol

18–23   This may be taken into account by the court in deciding what directions to make and whether a party should be required to pay a sum into court (CPR 3.1). It could also be taken into account in exercising the discretion on costs under CPR 44.3(5)(b).

Pleadings

18–24   Since the CPR pleadings, or "statements of case" as they are now called in Pt 16 of the CPR, may refer to evidence and law whereas they used to be solely concerned with setting out the facts and the cause of action relied on.

The intention should be to put a party's case at its highest. By so doing the initiative will start and finish with that party and the opponent will be forced to scrutinise his own case and perhaps think twice before defending the claim. The CPR assists in this undertaking, but it is suggested that the following points are borne in mind.

Rules on statements of case—the basics

The rules regarding the preparation of claims and defences are in **18–25** CPR Pt 16. Evidence can be, and is encouraged to be, included. In some cases it may be appropriate to attach copies of this evidence to the pleading itself. CPR Pt 16.5 provides that where the allegation is denied the reason for that denial must be stated. Generally time spent detailing each and every element of the case will be well rewarded in the long term. The amount of and rate of interest, as well as the statute or other provision under which it is claimed, should be specified in the particulars of claim (CPR 16.4.(2)).

Invariably claims for disrepair are brought under Pt 7 of the CPR, involving as they do disputes of fact.

If the defendant wishes to advance a limitation defence he must plead when he says the limitation period expired and particularise the basis for that defence (PD 16, para.13.1).

Amendments

CPR Pt 17 contains the rules governing the means by which **18–26** amendments to statements of case can be made. The rules are not complex to understand or apply. The threshold is not particularly high. But the costs involved in amendments should be considered.

Unfortunately CPR Pt 17 does not identify the guidelines which will be applied on an application for permission to amend, save when the limitation period has expired. However, the starting point is to seek to give effect to the overriding objective (*Thurrock BC v Secretary of State for the Environment, Transport and the Regions* (2000) *The Times*, December 20, affirmed in the Court of Appeal, [2002] EWCA Civ 226).

In *Harris v Shah* (February 22, 2002, unreported) a trial date was set in a personal injury claim. Through an oversight the court gave permission to instruct a joint expert very late. His report was seen by the claimant only three weeks before trial which led to an application by the claimant to vacate the trial date in order to amend the particulars of claim to put an alternative claim and other consequential matters. Permission was given together with permission to the defendant to appeal. The trial judge, when considering the application for permission to appeal, ventured that there was a tension between maintaining trial dates and ensuring a fair trial occurred. The Court of Appeal was asked to review the position. In due course, the court stated that there was no such dichotomy. Due weight should be given to all the criteria contained in CPR 1.1 rather than seeking to give one more weight than another.

Scott schedules

18–27 A Scott schedule, named after an Official Referee (a specialist judge in the days before the Technology and Construction Court) who lived before the Second World War, is a simple method of setting out a complex technical dispute in tabular form. It should set out the issues in columns, for example, one column will set out the approximate nature of the clause, two further columns will set out the rival contentions of the parties. There will usually be a fourth column for a judge to complete. A Scott schedule is normally ordered to be prepared at one of the case management hearings but is not automatic. The court will consider whether such a schedule will genuinely save costs and time (see the Technology and Construction Court Guide at para.5.6). In practice however these are frequently ordered in cases before the Technology and Construction Court T&CC which replaced the old Official Referees' Business). Claims before the T&CC are considered more fully below.

Guidance is given above with specific reference to dilapidations claims under the Property Litigation Association Protocol, but a Scott schedule will also be common in building-related litigation and will sometimes be used in residential disrepair claims. It is part of the standard procedure in claims before the T & CC. Practitioners will be familiar with the format of a schedule described above. It is helpful in any case involving multiple allegations of breach of covenant for the covenant, which is alleged to have been broken, to be referred to in one of the columns in addition to the content of the breach being summarised.

Claims for contribution and indemnity

18–28 Theses claims frequently arise in respect of claims by visitors. Where, for example the defect in the state of the premises in which the visitor is injured is within the area demised to the tenant the repairing covenant may place responsibility on the landlord for rectifying that defect. In those circumstances the tenant will wish to join his landlord into the claim.

Part 19 CPR governs the addition of new parties to the action and Pt 20 CPR governs adding any additional claim against a party whether he is an existing party or not. For example, where B is sued by A, his visitor, but contends he is entitled to a contribution from C, his landlord responsible for repair, he will make an application under Pt 20 to add the landlord into the claim.

Further information

Requests for further information may now elicit evidence and, **18–29** indeed, are usually intended to do so (CPR 18.1), unlike old requests for further and better particulars. If the information is not supplied the party seeking it may apply to the court who can compel that party to supply it where it will "clarify any matter in dispute" (CPR 18.1(1) (a)). In an appropriate case "teeth" will need to be added to the order by way of an "unless" order. These will be referred to below (see para.18–33, p.240).

Statements of truth

In every document which is intended to contain evidence or otherwise **18–30** be admissible, there must be a statement of truth (CPR Pt 22). Failure to include such a statement in a statement of case could lead to the court striking it out. This rarely occurs but where the court considers that there is no honest belief in the contents of the statement or that the statement was merely made in the hope that something would turn up at disclosure or trial this drastic step will be taken (*Clarke v Marlborough Fine Art (London) Ltd* (2001) *The Times*, 4 December per Patten J. [2002] EWHC 11 (Ch.)).

Case Management

Track allocation

Part 26 CPR contains important provisions for track allocation. These **18–31** have an important influence on the level of costs that can be recovered. Basically in order for a residential case to be kept on the Fast Track the tenant will wish to pursue any claim for specific performance that is available. This is due to the wording of Pt 26.6 CPR, which provides that in allocating a claim to a track the Small Claims Track will be the "normal track" where the claimant is seeking an order for the landlord to do the work and that work is estimated to cost "not more than £1000". Otherwise the Fast Track will be the normal track, as it will also be if the case includes a claim for damages for personal injury of more than £1,000. In any case where specific performance is not sought the normal track on which to allocate the case will be the Small Claims Track if the financial value of the claim is not more than £5,000. In cases where there is a counterclaim that is ignored in deciding which track to allocate the case to.

The consequence of these allocation rules will be that the represented claimant will not be able to recover his legal costs other than the fixed costs of issue, compelling witnesses to attend the hearing and related expenses.

One of the matters that the judge or master will need to address on allocation is the prospects of settlement. The rules specifically allow for a stay in order for ADR to take place (CPR 26.4(1)).

Unless orders

18–32 Wide powers to manage cases are given to the courts by Pt 3 CPR. However, in practice the more peremptory orders that used to be made under the old rules are rarer than formerly.

18–33   One of the orders the court can make is for some sanction to automatically follow from a failure to comply with the terms imposed by an order. That sanction must be appropriate.

In *Marcan Shipping v G. Kefelas and Candida Corporation* (17/5/07) [2007] 3 All E.R. 365 the Court of Appeal held that these orders were to be salutary in their effect the sanction had been imposed by the court the only way the sanction could be avoided was by applying for relief from sanctions under CPR 3.9 and the party having the benefit of the sanction did not have to justify the original order imposing the sanction. The sanction would automatically take effect unless the application under CPR 3.9 was successful. There was no need to invoke the power the court has under Pt 3.4 to strike out the other side's case where there had been a breach of an order or practice direction.

However, the old-style draconian orders that used to be made under the former rules of procedure have been replaced by an approach which is supposed to have justice at its heart. That approach is intended to promote compliance with deadlines from the point of view of all litigants and not just those in the litigation before the court (see *Biguzi v Rank Leisure Plc* [1999] 1 W.L.R. 1926 (26/7/99).

T&CC practice

18–34 The majority of dilapidations claims that are dealt with through the courts will be tried and managed by the Technology and Construction Court (T&CC) and Pt 60 CPR together with the Practice Direction which accompanies it (PD 60) provide that claims of this type are examples of cases that may be suitably brought in that court. It therefore appears appropriate to identify some key features of its practice.

Background

In 1998 the Official Referees' Buisness became the Technology and Construction Court ("the T&CC"), one of the specialist courts of the Queen's Bench Division of the High Court. However, certain county courts have T&CC jurisdiction and claims may be issued in either court in those centres. The procedure would be governed by the same rules subject to any rule particular to the court in question. A number of other important changes were introduced at the same time (e.g. the appointment of a High Court Judge to be in charge of the T&CC). However, the transition from Official Referees to T&CC was essentially seamless.

The T&CC has its own guide ("The T&CC Guide") but although there are a number of protocols which appertain to this area there is no specific protocol which applies to these claims. However, help is available in the Guide itself and a number of the other protocols may apply to proceedings before the court, for example, the Construction and Engineering Protocol will apply to claims by or against builders.

There are some special forms used in T&CC claims, found in the T&CC Guide.

Features of litigation in the T&CC

Like the Official Referees' Business before it, the T&CC deals with **18–36** claims that are technically complex. Where the claim is principally concerned with a point of law (e.g. to construe a repairing covenant) the Chancery Division might be more appropriate. However, a case involving difficult factual and expert evidence, particularly arising out of building litigation in the broadest sense, will be issued in the T&CC.

The length of the trials which are sometimes heard by the court and the cost and delay in getting them in order for a trial to be conducted has led to a more "hands-on" approach to litigation, both by way of practice and procedure. This approach normally results in one judge of trial judge status overseeing the interlocutory proceedings as well as the trial stages themselves. "Trial stages" is referred to because where the issues of liability and quantum are substantial the judge allocated will often consider paring off issues to be determined separately, principally to save costs.

Basic procedure

This is governed by Pt 60 in Vol.2 of the *White Book*. The court will **18–37** direct an early case management hearing at which directions will be given.

All claims before the T&CC are treated as having been allocated to the Multi-track (Pt 60.6) and Pt 29, which governs that track, therefore applies.

Transfer to the county court

18–38 The High Court has power under s.40(2) of the County Courts Act 1984 to order the transfer of proceedings to a county court, notwithstanding that the proceedings would otherwise fall outside the jurisdiction of the county court (see *National Westminster Bank Plc v King* [2008] EWHC 280 (Ch.)).

Costs tend to be higher on the T&CC and the court is therefore encouraged to transfer claims to the county court where there is no complex question of law or fact involved (see *Collins v Drumgold* (2/4/08 for the circumstances in which transfer will be ordered). The power to transfer is exercised under CPR 30.3(2) but this needs to be read with Pt 60 and the Practice Direction that accompanies that part. In particular 60 PD para.5.1 (found in Vol.2 of the *White Book*) should be reffered to.

Summary judgment

18–39 The defendant who fails to file a defence in time or at all will entitle the claimant to judgment. Failing that, the opportunity to strike out a claim or obtain summary judgment against one's opponent remains a key power in the court and one of the few ways to avoid an expensive trial. Although far less often used since the CPR (a development which the original architect of the CPR Lord Woolf has regarded with some concern (see *The Lawyer*, 13/3/06)), it remains an important power.

Frequently a claim for summary judgment, on the basis that the claimant or defendant does not have a real prospect of success, will be brought in tandem with a claim under Pt 3.4, which allows a court to strike out a claim or counterclaim which discloses no "reasonable grounds for bringing or defending the claim". Logically the two bases for summary disposal are distinct, one being based on the assertion that the claim or defence *cannot* succeed (Pt 3.4) and the other being based on the assertion after looking at the evidence that there is *no real prospect* of succeeding (Pt 24).

The following points should be noted:

- A court will consider giving summary of its own volition provided it gives the affected party the opportunity to set-aside that order.

- Summary judgment may be proper in a case involving the construction of documents and not only in a case involving the determination of issues after hearing oral evidence.

As to the second point, the court must ask itself in the former type of case whether evidence given at trial is likely to shed any further light on the points in issue (see *ICI Polymers v TTE Training* [2007] EWCA Civ 725) or whether in fact the court has the information it needs to summarily dispose of the case. In that case the Court of Appeal emphasised the fact that the court must have all the information necessary before it if it is to give summary judgment on a construction point. It needs to ask whether there is likely to be any oral evidence on the point which is likely to cast matters in a different light. Frequently if the case turns on the construction of a document the answer to that question will be "no" but, in practice, obtaining a summary disposal of the matter remains difficult for the applicant.

Costs

Part 36 offers

For many years the primary means by which a defendant has been **18–40** able to protect himself from the point of view of costs has been by offering to rectify any defect in the premises for which he is liable (by Pt 36 offer) and by paying into court an appropriate amount by way of compensation (by Pt 36 payment). However, since April 7, 2007 Pt 36 payments have been abolished, although there will be cases going through the court process where payments-in have been made. The Pt 36 offer is, of course, retained.

To make a Pt 36 offer the offering party (known as "the offeror") must offer in writing to settle the claim or an aspect of the claim. The receiving party (the "offeree") has 21 days to consider the terms of that offer but if he accepts the offer he has the right to his costs up to the date of the notice of acceptance (Pt 36.10). Therefore any offer which seeks to qualify or reduce the costs payable, other than by making it clear that only costs on a standard basis are payable, would not constitute a valid Pt 36 offer. Such an offer could, however, be considered under Pt 44.3 CPR (see below).

When calculating the amount to offer, the offeror (who may be the claimant or the defendant) should have regard to the incidence of interest and must state whether it takes account of any counterclaim (CPR 36.2).

Other offers to settle and conduct

In exercising its wide discretion on costs, the court will consider **18–41** those factors set out in CPR 44.3 including:

- Whether despite being the successful party the claimant has exaggerated his claim (see *Jackson v MOD* [2006] All E.R. (D) 14 in which the Court of Appeal upheld a reduction of 25 per cent in respect of the costs where the claimant had "significantly exaggerated his claim".

- Whether the parties properly considered mediation. In this context the reader is referred to *Dunnett v Railtrack* [2002] 2 All E.R. 850 and *Halsey v Milton Keynes NHS Trust* [2004] EWCA Civ 576. In the later case the court identified six factors to be taken into account when deciding whether a party had acted unreasonably in refusing mediation. The reader is also referred to *Birchell v Bullard* [2005] EWCA Civ 358 and *Hickman v Blake Lapthorne and Fisher* [2006] EWHC 12 (Q.B.) (Considered in the notes to 44.3 in the *White Book*, 2008 at 44.3.13).

- Whether a party has succeeded on an issue or not. Increasingly the courts will look at the substance of what was argued about at a trial and the old "winner takes all" principle will only apply cases where a party has decisively won on all issues (see *McGlinn v Waltham Construction* [2007] EWHC 698).

But Pt 44.3 provides comprehensive guidance on the factors to take into account when deciding the incidence of costs. There are a wide range of orders the court can make to reflect its findings. Costs will normally be ordered on the standard basis but exceptionally may be on a indemnity basis.

Chapter 19

Other methods of dispute resolution

There are now more methods of dispute resolution at the disposal of **19–01** the potential claimant than at any time in the past. There is considerable weight behind the movement towards ADR in general and mediation in particular. This movement has been largely cost-driven, encouraged by the Government, the judiciary and specialist organisations working within the professions.

The voluntary use of ADR by disputants has been accompanied with greater statutory use of alternative schemes of dispute resolution, which do not primarily rely on the courts. Thus, under s.106 the Housing Grants, Construction and Regeneration Act 1998 the legislature introduced a system of adjudication in relation to certain types of construction contract. The scheme has undoubtedly saved money and increased the pitifully slow pace of dispute resolution which used to pertain in some building litigation. There are various other schemes of various levels of formality which are relevant in the field of defective premises.

In addition to post-dispute references to ADR there is a trend towards greater use of clauses in leases and contracts which pre-determine this method of dispute resolution. Mediation clauses are now becoming more common in commercial leases, for example, the Commercial Leases Working Group, responsible for the Code of Practice for Commercial Leases (now in its second edition), recommends the inclusion of an ADR clause.

Arbitration clauses are also commonly found in commercial leases. In this chapter it will be necessary to consider mediation and its more expensive relation arbitration as well as some other methods of non-court based dispute resolution that are available.

Finally, the cheapest method of resolving a dispute is usually by negotiation. This might involve referring that dispute to an expert, whose opinion the parties agree to be bound by. Assuming that does not achieve the desired settlement some consideration will need to be given to Pt 36 of the CPR, which has been dealt with in the previous chapter, and the best means of protecting a client's position on costs.

First of all, the various methods of alternative dispute resolution will be considered, including those with varying degrees of Government backing. Then the less formal schemes will be considered. Arbitration will then be looked at because it is sometimes the dispute-resolution method pre-determined in the lease or voluntarily agreed to by the parties. Finally, expert determination as a method of dispute resolution will be considered.

ADR schemes

Mediation generally

19–02   Increasingly the potential litigant will wish to consider whether the dispute can be resolved by mediation as opposed to litigation. The advantages are that costs will probably be saved thereby; the relationship between the parties may well be less damaged than it would be by protracted court proceedings. Many of those who have their disputes resolved in this way find this particularly valuable. There is a high success rate and the mediation process is not held in public. The less formal (and frightening!) nature of the proceedings also appeals to many potential litigants.

Sometimes mediation is an adjunct to court-based proceedings but in many cases it will be the first point of reference for a dispute. Indeed it is increasingly seen as the first port of call by many potential litigants. In 2001, Sir Andrew Leggatt's Review of the Tribunal System considered that oral hearings before tribunals should be the last resort for disgruntled complainants, not the first. The trend that report encouraged is supported by a number of government-sponsored schemes of which only a few may be mentioned here.

Government sponsored and court based schemes

19–03   In relation to housing litigation the Law Commission have leant support to the use of "informal dispute resolution" wherever possible in its report "Housing: Proportionate Dispute Resolution", May 2008 (Law Com. 309). This would include using the new Housing Ombudsman to bring about a solution to housing-related problems. The service can deal with all disputes over housing management including the quality and frequency of repairs as well as any delay in completing those repairs.

The Housing Ombudsman Service applies to all registered social landlords (RSLs) other than local authorities, which have their own Local Government Ombudsman scheme in place. RSLs are required by the Housing Act 1996 to take part in the scheme. A number of private landlords and housing managers also subscribe to it.

There are also numerous court-based schemes in place. Central London County Court was the first in England to establish such a scheme in 1996 and there are now a number of such schemes in the major court hearing centres throughout England and Wales. However, a pilot in the Technology and Construction Court (T&CC), which enabled T&CC judges to mediate in cases that had not been allocated to them, was not a success. The pilot finished in July 2007 and it seems unlikely to be repeated. But the process of court-based mediation is being encouraged by the squeeze on public finance for civil justice, the higher judiciary and the Legal Services Commission. It seems likely that judges at the interlocutory stage and even later in some litigation will continue to press for the use of mediation. Usually this will result in the imposition of a stay and one of the consequences may be increased cost and delay but if successful the opposite will normally result.

Non-government or non-court-based schemes

There has been a trend towards better trained and more specialist **19–04** mediators in recent years. There are now a large number of organisations, which provide mediators with appropriate skills. Many of these organisations provide guidelines for the conduct of this method of dispute resolution and standard mediation agreements. They include:

- the Association of Northern Mediators provides a range of civil and commercial mediators in the North of England;
- many of the Bar Associations, for example the Technology and Construction Bar Association (TECBAR) provide lists of members who are qualified mediators together with an indication of their experience;
- the Centre for Effective Dispute Resolution (CEDR) provides training and guidance for potential mediators as well as accreditation for those individuals who qualify;
- the Royal Institution of Chartered Surveyors provides has a number of approved mediators who are accredited with the Civil Mediation Council and who may be particularly suited to dispute involving defective premises;
- the Chartered Institute of Arbitrators, which is setting up a mediation scheme of its own.

Choice of mediator

19–05 As well as the above organisations there are also numerous professional bodies that will assist in the identification of a suitable mediator and the drawing up of the correct agreement. The reader is also referred to Appendix 3 which lists some other organisations which may help. However, there remain more mediators than there are mediations. Those holding themselves out as mediators are of varying levels of qualification and experience and it is most likely to be by word of mouth that a suitable mediator for a particular dispute is found.

Conduct of mediation

19–06 Once a mediator has been appointed there are a large number of things that will need to be considered with the client. For example:

- What written case is to be submitted?
- What would be an appropriate venue?
- What kind of advocate possesses the appropriate skills to advance the mediation?
- What will happen to the costs if a settlement is not achieved?

The last point deserves particular emphasis. Mediation is expensive, particularly as an adjunct to litigation where there is often a duplication of costs. However, the 47th issue of the CPR update requires solicitors completing allocation questionnaires on behalf of their clients to show that they have explained the mediation option to them. There is disquiet in some quarters as to the quasi-compulsory character of these references, given that the litigant is effectively being told that if he refuses for their dispute to be referred he may be penalised on costs (see for e.g. Stephen Cantle *N.L.J.* (2008) Vol.158 No.7330 p.1042). Nevertheless at the present time mediation remains something of a perceived panacea and if mediation is not properly considered there may be adverse costs consequences. Obviously if the reference is successful there may be a considerable saving in costs in the long run.

Without prejudice nature of mediation

19–07 The process of mediation, including any evidence filed but particularly any negotiating position adopted in the mediation, will be without prejudice unless the parties expressly stipulate otherwise (but see para.18–08 at p.228 in relation to a joint experts' statement prepared for a mediation). However, the party who adopted a wholly unreasonable position in mediation but who subsequently failed to succeed to the extent claimed at trial could, no doubt, have that earlier position exposed when the question of costs was dealt with after that trial (see *Malmesbury, Earl of v Maltby* [2008] EWHC 424 (Q.B.)). Just as it is possible to go behind "without prejudice" correspondence when dealing with costs questions in relation to court claims it ought to be possible to go behind "without prejudice" statements at the earlier unsuccessful mediation when costs are determined at the subsequent trial.

Costs of mediation

The award of costs in favour of the party who is "successful" at the **19–08** mediation is less common than an award in favour of successful litigants in court proceedings. The reason for this is that generally mediation is often seen as a means of preserving a relationship between the parties. The settlement achieved in that mediation is consensual rather than imposed. Therefore it is unusual for a party to recognise that their case is so weak at the mediation stage that he will agree to pay the other side's costs. Indeed, the goodwill that often prevails following a successful mediation may well enable the party to see the costs he has incurred in that context.

Early neutral evaluation-ENE

Early neutral evaluation (ENE) is a non-binding form of alternative **19–09** dispute resolution, involving a neutral third party.

There is currently a voluntary scheme in the T&CC whereby the court goes through an early neutral evaluation of the prospects of the claim or issue in dispute succeeding (see para.7.5 of the T&CC Guide). The scheme is not much used at the time of writing but is thought to be potentially useful as a further means of ADR in some cases.

The interested parties do not necessarily need to meet together as part of the process of ENE. However, generally it is conducted by each party presenting a concise summary of his case or the issue in dispute and then the court indicating its view (see s.7 of the T&CC Guide). The judge conducting the ENE should not be the judge who ultimately tries the case.

Costs can be substantially reduced if it is successful and has received some encouragement in the legal press (see, for example, Friel at 158 *N.L.J.* 613).

Arbitration

19–10 Arbitration is used as a method of resolving commercial landlord and tenant disputes, particularly in relation to rent review but less commonly is used to resolve dilapidations type claims. It has substantial advantages over litigation but some disadvantages. The advantages are: confidentiality; having the dispute determined by a specialist forum and a greater degree of freedom to decide on the correct procedure to be adopted; and the timing of that procedure. However, arbitrators have substantial freedom to decide what directions to make and when. If this freedom is not given to them by the agreement it is given in s.34 of the Arbitration Act 1996, which provides that the arbitrator may make directions for the speedy and cost-effective resolution of the dispute. Normally the strict rules of evidence do not apply but it is open to the arbitrator to provide that they do.

A disadvantage of arbitration is that the award will prove difficult to challenge save in certain rare cases and the costs will be as high as litigation if not higher. This remains the case after the substantial increase in issue fees of £500 for Fast Track and £1000 for Multi-track cases in court with effect from October 1, 2007. Certainly arbitration does not enjoy the costs advantage that ADR enjoys at the present time.

Like mediation arbitration may only take place with the agreement of the parties. Frequently this is because there is an arbitration clause in the lease but it may be because the parties wish their dispute to be decided by a specialist forum where they can choose their arbitrator.

It is less common for residential leases to have an arbitration clause but such clauses are sometimes found in long leases and it is quite common for disputes over service charges to be determined in this way.

Model clauses for a referral to arbitration to be inserted into leases and contracts are abundant, for example, the Technology and Construction Bar Association (TECBAR) includes such a clause on its website as well as a list of members qualified to act as arbitrators. However there is nothing to stop the parties voluntarily agreeing to refer a dispute to arbitration. The Institute of Arbitrators provides more comprehensive guidance on how to put arbitration in motion and selection of a suitable arbitrator.

Statutory rules governing arbitration

19–11 Arbitration has been regulated by legislation dating back to 1889 and there have been a number of modern Acts governing all aspects of a reference. Now it is mainly governed by the Arbitration Act 1996.

One of the aims of that Act was to strengthen this method of dispute resolution. Section 9 of that Act therefore allows the party who relies on an arbitration agreement to seek a stay of any court proceedings until the reference is made.

Scope of the reference

Generally the court will broadly construe its jurisdiction, since the **19–12** assumption will be that the parties wish to determine all matters in dispute (see *Fiona Trust v Privalov* [2007] UKHL 40). This will include determination of all matters of construction; since the assumption is made that the objective businessman observer would wish all matters in dispute to be referred with a view to having those matters resolved.

Who is to arbitrate?

There is a statutory power to appoint a judge of the T&CC under s.93 **19–13** of the Arbitration Act 1996, provided the Lord Chief Justice approves of them being made available. This power may be useful, particularly where the arbitration turns on a legal issue of interpretation but is very rarely used in practice. However, more commonly the arbitrator is chose from a pool of potentially qualified persons by the parties and will often be experienced in the technical field that the dispute is about. The relevant specialist bodies will be able to assist in the task of finding an arbitrator.

Challenge

Challenging arbitrator's awards is fraught with difficulty. The courts **19–14** afford considerable respect to the expertise of arbitration and the binding quality of the reference. There must be a lack of jurisdiction, a serious procedural irregularity or bias before the arbitrator can be effectively challenged (see ss.67—68 of the 1996 Act).

Appeal

Unless otherwise agreed between the parties, there is a right of appeal **19–15** on a point of law only (s.69 of the 1996 Act). However this right is relatively rarely exercised in practice.

The award

Once the award has been made and there is no effective appeal it **19–16** becomes enforceable as an order of the court (s.66 of the 1996 Act).

Expert determination

19–17 By instructing a noted practitioner in an area that person possesses expertise in, the parties may quickly and relatively cheaply obtain a solution to his dispute. In particular, minimal time will need to be devoted by the protagonists. However, this method of dispute resolution is probably unsuited to complex matters, especially factually complex cases, and the precise basis upon which the determination is to be binding will need to be considered. Difficult questions may arise if one person wishes to challenge the determination or simply issue a claim. For example, how does privilege operate in relation to the information given to the expert and in what circumstances may a party allege the determination was flawed, for example, because some essential fact was ignored? This last point warrants further attention.

Challenging the determination

19–18 Some guidance may be gained from the authorities. The reference is essentially a matter of contract and the parties may by their contract provide for the determination to be as binding as they wish (see for example *Morgan Sindall Plc v Sawston Farms (Cambs) Ltd* (1998) C.A. (Civ Div transcript)). The decisions in this area suggest that challenging the expert on the grounds that, for example, a surveyor carrying out a valuation exercise had erred in his approach, would be very difficult. There is a strong emphasis on the lawyers acting for the referring parties providing complete and agreed instructions (see *Doughty Hanson & Co Ltd v Bruce Patrick Roe* [2007] EWHC 2212 (Ch.)).

The Court of Appeal has given further consideration to expert determination in *Homespace v Sita South East Ltd* [2008] EWCA Civ 1. That case followed the principles set out in *Norwich Union v P & O Properties* [1993] 1 E.G.L.R. 164. The court said that the following three basic questions had to be answered where an expert determination was challenged:

1. What does the lease or other agreement actually entrust to the expert for his determination?
2. Whether the expert has in fact determined that question?
3. Whether it can be shown that the expert has made a mistake, which vitiates his decision?

However, despite the emergence of case law dealing with some of the problems that the reference might throw up, this method of dispute resolution is set to grow in popularity.

PART V

APPENDICES

APPENDIX A – STATUTES AND STATUTORY INSTRUMENTS

APPENDIX A1

Landlord and Tenant Act 1927 c.36

PART II

GENERAL AMENDMENTS OF THE LAW OF LANDLORD AND TENANT

18.— Provisions as to covenants to repair.

(1) Damages for a breach of a covenant or agreement to keep or put **A1–01** premises in repair during the currency of a lease, or to leave or put premises in repair at the termination of a lease, whether such covenant or agreement is expressed or implied, and whether general or specific, shall in no case exceed the amount (if any) by which the value of the reversion (whether immediate or not) in the premises is diminished owing to the breach of such covenant or agreement as aforesaid; and in particular no damage shall be recovered for a breach of any such covenant or agreement to leave or put premises in repair at the termination of a lease, if it is shown that the premises, in whatever state of repair they might be, would at or shortly after the termination of the tenancy have been or be pulled down, or such structural alterations made therein as would render valueless the repairs covered by the covenant or agreement.

(2) A right of re-entry or forfeiture for a breach of any such covenant or agreement as aforesaid shall not be enforceable, by action or otherwise, unless the lessor proves that the fact that such a notice as is required by section one hundred and forty-six of the Law of Property Act, 1925, had been served on the lessee was known either—

    (a)   to the lessee; or

    (b)   to an under-lessee holding under an under-lease which reserved a nominal reversion only to the lessee; or

    (c)   to the person who last paid the rent due under the lease either on his own behalf or as agent for the lessee or under-lessee;

and that a time reasonably sufficient to enable the repairs to be executed had elapsed since the time when the fact of the service of the notice came to the knowledge of any such person.

Where a notice has been sent by registered post addressed to a person at his last known place of abode in the United Kingdom, then, for the purposes of this subsection, that person shall be deemed, unless the contrary is proved, to have had knowledge of the fact that the notice had been served as from the time at which the letter would have been delivered in the ordinary course of post.

This subsection shall be construed as one with section one hundred and forty-six of the Law of Property Act, 1925.

(3) This section applies whether the lease was created before or after the commencement of this Act.

Leasehold Property (Repairs) Act 1938 c.34

1.— Restriction on enforcement of repairing covenants in long leases of small houses.

(1) Where a lessor serves on a lessee under subsection (1) of section **A2–01** one hundred and forty-six of the Law of Property Act, 1925, a notice that relates to a breach of a covenant or agreement to keep or put in repair during the currency of the lease [all or any of the property comprised in the lease], and at the date of the service of the notice [three] years or more of the term of the lease remain unexpired, the lessee may within twenty-eight days from that date serve on the lessor a counter-notice to the effect that he claims the benefit of this Act.

(2) A right to damages for a breach of such a covenant as aforesaid shall not be enforceable by action commenced at any time at which [three] years or more of the term of the lease remain unexpired unless the lessor has served on the lessee not less than one month before the commencement of the action such a notice as is specified in subs.(1) of s.146 of the Law of Property Act 1925, and where a notice is served under this subsection, the lessee may, within twenty-eight days from the date of the service thereof, serve on the lessor a counter-notice to the effect that he claims the benefit of this Act.

(3) Where a counter-notice is served by a lessee under this section, then, notwithstanding anything in any enactment or rule of law, no proceedings, by action or otherwise, shall be taken by the lessor for the enforcement of any right of re-entry or forfeiture under any proviso or stipulation in the lease for breach of the covenant or agreement in question, or for damages for breach thereof, otherwise than with the leave of the court.

(4) A notice served under subsection (1) of section one hundred and forty-six of the Law of Property Act, 1925, in the circumstances specified in subsection (1) of this section, and a notice served under subs.(2) of this section shall not be valid unless it contains a statement, in characters not less conspicuous than those used in any other part of the notice, to the effect that the lessee is entitled under this Act to serve on the lessor a counter-notice claiming the benefit of this Act, and a statement in the like characters specifying the time within which, and the manner in which, under this Act a counter-notice may be served and specifying the name and address for service of the lessor.

(5) Leave for the purposes of this section shall not be given unless

the lessor proves—

(a)   that the immediate remedying of the breach in question is requisite for preventing substantial diminution in the value of his reversion, or that the value thereof has been substantially diminished by the breach;

(b)   that the immediate remedying of the breach is required for giving effect in relation to the [premises] to the purposes of any enactment, or of any byelaw or other provision having effect under an enactment, [or for giving effect to any order of a court or requirement of any authority under any enactment or any such byelaw or other provision as aforesaid];

(c)   in a case in which the lessee is not in occupation of the whole of the [premises as respects which the covenant or agreement is proposed to be enforced], that the immediate remedying of the breach is required in the interests of the occupier of [those premises] or of part thereof; (d) that the breach can be immediately remedied at an expense that is relatively small in comparison with the much greater expense that would probably be occasioned by postponement of the necessary work; or

(e)   special circumstances which in the opinion of the court, render it just and equitable that leave should be given.

(6) The court may, in granting or in refusing leave for the purposes of this section, impose such terms and conditions on the lessor or on the lessee as it may think fit.

APPENDIX A3

Occupiers' Liability Act 1957 c.31

Liability In Tort

2.— Extent of occupier's ordinary duty

(1) An occupier of premises owes the same duty, the "common duty **A3–01** of care" , to all his visitors, except in so far as he is free to and does extend, restrict, modify or exclude his duty to any visitor or visitors by agreement or otherwise.

(2) The common duty of care is a duty to take such care as in all the circumstances of the case is reasonable to see that the visitor will be reasonably safe in using the premises for the purposes for which he is invited or permitted by the occupier to be there.

(3) The circumstances relevant for the present purpose include the degree of care, and of want of care, which would ordinarily be looked for in such a visitor, so that (for example) in proper cases—

- (a) an occupier must be prepared for children to be less careful than adults; and
- (b) an occupier may expect that a person, in the exercise of his calling, will appreciate and guard against any special risks ordinarily incident to it, so far as the occupier leaves him free to do so.

(4) In determining whether the occupier of premises has discharged the common duty of care to a visitor, regard is to be had to all the circumstances, so that (for example)—

- (a) where damage is caused to a visitor by a danger of which he had been warned by the occupier, the warning is not to be treated without more as absolving the occupier from liability, unless in all the circumstances it was enough to enable the visitor to be reasonably safe; and
- (b) where damage is caused to a visitor by a danger due to the faulty execution of any work of construction, maintenance or repair by an independent contractor employed by the occupier, the occupier is not to be treated without more as answerable for the danger if in all the circumstances he had acted reasonably in entrusting the work to an independent contractor and had taken such steps (if any) as he reasonably ought in order to satisfy himself that the contractor was competent and that the work had been properly done.

(5) The common duty of care does not impose on an occupier any

obligation to a visitor in respect of risks willingly accepted as his by the visitor (the question whether a risk was so accepted to be decided on the same principles as in other cases in which one person owes a duty of care to another).

(6) For the purposes of this section, persons who enter premises for any purpose in the exercise of a right conferred by law are to be treated as permitted by the occupier to be there for that purpose, whether they in fact have his permission or not.

APPENDIX A4

Defective Premises Act 1972 c.35

1.— Duty to build dwellings properly.

(1) A person taking on work for or in connection with the provision **A4–01** of a dwelling (whether the dwelling is provided by the erection or by the conversion or enlargement of a building) owes a duty—

- (a) if the dwelling is provided to the order of any person, to that person; and
- (b) without prejudice to paragraph (a) above, to every person who acquires an interest (whether legal or equitable) in the dwelling;

to see that the work which he takes on is done in a workmanlike or, as the case may be, professional manner, with proper materials and so that as regards that work the dwelling will be fit for habitation when completed.

(2) A person who takes on any such work for another on terms that he is to do it in accordance with instructions given by or on behalf of that other shall, to the extent to which he does it properly in accordance with those instructions, be treated for the purposes of this section as discharging the duty imposed on him by subsection (1) above except where he owes a duty to that other to warn him of any defects in the instructions and fails to discharge that duty.

(3) A person shall not be treated for the purposes of subsection (2) above as having given instructions for the doing of work merely because he has agreed to the work being done in a specified manner, with specified materials or to a specified design.

(4) A person who—

- (a) in the course of a business which consists of or includes providing or arranging for the provision of dwellings or installations in dwellings; or
- (b) in the exercise of a power of making such provision or arrangements conferred by or by virtue of any enactment;

arranges for another to take on work for or in connection with the provision of a dwelling shall be treated for the purposes of this section as included among the persons who have taken on the work.

(5) Any cause of action in respect of a breach of the duty imposed by this section shall be deemed, for the purposes of the Limitation Act 1939, the Law Reform (Limitation of Actions, &c.) Act 1954 and the Limitation Act 1963, to have accrued at the time when the dwelling was completed, but if after that time a person who has done work for or in connection with the provision of the dwelling does further work to rectify the work he has already done, any such cause of action in

respect of that further work shall be deemed for those purposes to have accrued at the time when the further work was finished.

2.— Cases excluded from the remedy under section 1.

A4–02 (1) Where—

(a) in connection with the provision of a dwelling or its first sale or letting for habitation any rights in respect of defects in the state of the dwelling are conferred by an approved scheme to which this section applies on a person having or acquiring an interest in the dwelling; and

(b) it is stated in a document of a type approved for the purposes of this section that the requirements as to design or construction imposed by or under the scheme have, or appear to have, been substantially complied with in relation to the dwelling;

no action shall be brought by any person having or acquiring an interest in the dwelling for breach of the duty imposed by section 1 above in relation to the dwelling.

(2) A scheme to which this section applies—

(a) may consist of any number of documents and any number of agreements or other transactions between any number of persons; but

(b) must confer, by virtue of agreements entered into with persons having or acquiring an interest in the dwellings to which the scheme applies, rights on such persons in respect of defects in the state of the dwellings.

(3) In this section "approved" means approved by the Secretary of State, and the power of the Secretary of State to approve a scheme or document for the purposes of this section shall be exercisable by order, except that any requirements as to construction or design imposed under a scheme to which this section applies may be approved by him without making any order or, if he thinks fit, by order.

(4) The Secretary of State—

(a) may approve a scheme or document for the purposes of this section with or without limiting the duration of his approval; and

(b) may by order revoke or vary a previous order under this section or, without such an order, revoke or vary a previous approval under this section given otherwise than by order.

(5) The production of a document purporting to be a copy of an approval given by the Secretary of State otherwise than by order and certified by an officer of the Secretary of State to be a true copy of the approval shall be conclusive evidence of the approval, and without proof of the handwriting or official position of the person purporting to sign the certificate.

(6) The power to make an order under this section shall be exercisable

by statutory instrument which shall be subject to annulment in pursuance of a resolution by either House of Parliament. (7) Where an interest in a dwelling is compulsorily acquired—

    (a)   no action shall be brought by the acquiring authority for breach of the duty imposed by s.1 above in respect of the dwelling; and

    (b)   if any work for or in connection with the provision of the dwelling was done otherwise than in the course of a business by the person in occupation of the dwelling at the time of the compulsory acquisition, the acquiring authority and not that person shall be treated as the person who took on the work and accordingly as owing that duty.

3.— Duty of care with respect to work done on premises not abated by disposal of premises.

(1) Where work of construction, repair, maintenance or demolition **A4–03** or any other work is done on or in relation to premises, any duty of care owed, because of the doing of the work, to persons who might reasonably be expected to be affected by defects in the state of the premises created by the doing of the work shall not be abated by the subsequent disposal of the premises by the person who owed the duty.

(2) This section does not apply—

    (a)   in the case of premises which are let, where the relevant tenancy of the premises commenced, or the relevant tenancy agreement of the premises was entered into, before the commencement of this Act;

    (b)   in the case of premises disposed of in any other way, when the disposal of the premises was completed, or a contract for their disposal was entered into, before the commencement of this Act; or

    (c) in either case, where the relevant transaction disposing of the premises is entered into in pursuance of an enforceable option by which the consideration for the disposal was fixed before the commencement of this Act.

4.— Landlord's duty of care in virtue of obligation or right to repair premises demised.

(1) Where premises are let under a tenancy which puts on the landlord **A4–04** an obligation to the tenant for the maintenance or repair of the premises, the landlord owes to all persons who might reasonably be expected to be affected by defects in the state of the premises a duty to take such care as is reasonable in all the circumstances to see that they are reasonably safe from personal injury or from damage to

their property caused by a relevant defect.

(2) The said duty is owed if the landlord knows (whether as the result of being notified by the tenant or otherwise) or if he ought in all the circumstances to have known of the relevant defect.

(3) In this section "relevant defect" means a defect in the state of the premises existing at or after the material time and arising from, or continuing because of, an act or omission by the landlord which constitutes or would if he had had notice of the defect, have constituted a failure by him to carry out his obligation to the tenant for the maintenance or repair of the premises; and for the purposes of the foregoing provision "the material time" means—

    (a) where the tenancy commenced before this Act, the commencement of this Act; and

    (b) in all other cases, the earliest of the following times, that is to say—

        (i) the time when the tenancy commences;

        (ii) the time when the tenancy agreement is entered into;

        (iii) the time when possession is taken of the premises in contemplation of the letting.

(4) Where premises are let under a tenancy which expressly or impliedly gives the landlord the right to enter the premises to carry out any description of maintenance or repair of the premises, then, as from the time when he first is, or by notice or otherwise can put himself, in a position to exercise the right and so long as he is or can put himself in that position, he shall be treated for the purposes of subsection (1) to (3) above (but for no other purpose) as if he were under an obligation to the tenant for that description of maintenance or repair of the premises; but the landlord shall not owe the tenant any duty by virtue of this subsection in respect of any defect in the state of the premises arising from, or continuing because of, a failure to carry out an obligation expressly imposed on the tenant by the tenancy.

(5) For the purposes of this section obligations imposed or rights given by any enactment in virtue of a tenancy shall be treated as imposed or given by the tenancy.

(6) This section applies to a right of occupation given by contract or any enactment and not amounting to a tenancy as if the right were a tenancy, and "tenancy" and cognate expressions shall be construed accordingly.

[. . .]

6.— Supplemental.

A4–05 (1) In this Act—

    "disposal" , in relation to premises, includes a letting, and an assignment or surrender of a tenancy, of the premises and the creation by contract of any other right to occupy the premises, and "dispose" shall be construed accordingly;

"personal injury" includes any disease and any impairment of a person's physical or mental condition;

"tenancy" means—

(a) a tenancy created either immediately or derivatively out of the freehold, whether by a lease or underlease, by an agreement for a lease or underlease or by a tenancy agreement, but not including a mortgage term or any interest arising in favour of a mortgagor by his attorning tenant to his mortgagee; or
(b) a tenancy at will or a tenancy on sufferance; or
(c) a tenancy, whether or not constituting a tenancy at common law, created by or in pursuance of any enactment;
and cognate expressions shall be construed accordingly.

(2) Any duty imposed by or enforceable by virtue of any provision of this Act is in addition to any duty a person may owe apart from that provision.

(3) Any term of an agreement which purports to exclude or restrict, or has the effect of excluding or restricting, the operation of any of the provisions of this Act, or any liability arising by virtue of any such provision, shall be void.

[...]

Occupiers' Liability Act 1984 c.3

1.— Duty of occupier to persons other than his visitors.

A5–01   (1) [...]The rules enacted by this section shall have effect, in place of the rules of the common law, to determine—

 (a) whether any duty is owed by a person as occupier of premises to persons other than his visitors in respect of any risk of their suffering injury on the premises by reason of any danger due to the state of the premises or to things done or omitted to be done on them; and

 (b) if so, what that duty is.

(2) For the purposes of this section, the persons who are to be treated respectively as an occupier of any premises (which, for those purposes, include any fixed or movable structure) and as his visitors are—

 (a) any person who owes in relation to the premises the duty referred to in section 2 of the Occupiers' Liability Act 1957 (the common duty of care), and

 (b) those who are his visitors for the purposes of that duty.

(3) An occupier of premises owes a duty to another (not being his visitor) in respect of any such risk as is referred to in subsection (1) above if—

 (a) he is aware of the danger or has reasonable grounds to believe that it exists;

 (b) he knows or has reasonable grounds to believe that the other is in the vicinity of the danger concerned or that he may come into the vicinity of the danger (in either case, whether the other has lawful authority for being in that vicinity or not); and

 (c) the risk is one against which, in all the circumstances of the case, he may reasonably be expected to offer the other some protection.

(4) Where, by virtue of this section, an occupier of premises owes a duty to another in respect of such a risk, the duty is to take such care as is reasonable in all the circumstances of the case to see that he does not suffer injury on the premises by reason of the danger concerned.

(5) Any duty owed by virtue of this section in respect of a risk may, in an appropriate case, be discharged by taking such steps as are reasonable in all the circumstances of the case to give warning of the danger concerned or to discourage persons from incurring the risk.

(6) No duty is owed by virtue of this section to any person in respect of risks willingly accepted as his by that person (the question whether a risk was so accepted to be decided on the same principles as in other cases in which one person owes a duty of care to another).

[(6A) At any time when the right conferred by section 2(1) of the Countryside and Rights of Way Act 2000 is exercisable in relation to land which is access land for the purposes of Part I of that Act, an occupier of the land owes (subject to subsection (6C) below) no duty by virtue of this section to any person in respect of—

    (a) a risk resulting from the existence of any natural feature of the landscape, or any river, stream, ditch or pond whether or not a natural feature, or

    (b) a risk of that person suffering injury when passing over, under or through any wall, fence or gate, except by proper use of the gate or of a stile.

(6B) For the purposes of subsection (6A) above, any plant, shrub or tree, of whatever origin, is to be regarded as a natural feature of the landscape.

(6C) Subsection (6A) does not prevent an occupier from owing a duty by virtue of this section in respect of any risk where the danger concerned is due to anything done by the occupier—

    (a) with the intention of creating that risk, or

    (b) being reckless as to whether that risk is created.]

(7) No duty is owed by virtue of this section to persons using the highway, and this section does not affect any duty owed to such persons.

(8) Where a person owes a duty by virtue of this section, he does not, by reason of any breach of the duty, incur any liability in respect of any loss of or damage to property.

(9) In this section—

"highway" means any part of a highway other than a ferry or waterway;

"injury" means anything resulting in death or personal injury, including any disease and any impairment of physical or mental condition; and

"movable structure" includes any vessel, vehicle or aircraft.

APPENDIX A6

Building Act 1984 c.55

PART III

OTHER PROVISIONS ABOUT BUILDINGS

Defective premises, demolition etc.

76.— Defective premises.

A6–01 (1) If it appears to a local authority that—

    (a) any premises are in such a state (in this section referred to as a " defective state") as to be prejudicial to health or a nuisance, and

    (b) unreasonable delay in remedying the defective state would be occasioned by following the procedure prescribed by [section 80 of the Environmental Protection Act 1990],

the local authority may serve on the person on whom it would have been appropriate to serve an abatement notice under the said section 93 (if the local authority had proceeded under that section) a notice stating that the local authority intend to remedy the defective state and specifying the defects that they intend to remedy.

(2) Subject to subsection (3) below, the local authority may, after the expiration of nine days after service of a notice under subsection (1) above, execute such works as may be necessary to remedy the defective state, and recover the expenses reasonably incurred in so doing from the person on whom the notice was served.

(3) If, within seven days after service of a notice under subsection (1) above, the person on whom the notice was served serves a counter-notice that he intends to remedy the defects specified in the first-mentioned notice, the local authority shall take no action in pursuance of the first-mentioned notice unless the person who served the counter-notice—

    (a) fails within what seems to the local authority a reasonable time to begin to execute works to remedy the said defects, or

    (b) having begun to execute such works fails to make such progress towards their completion as seems to the local authority reasonable.

(4) In proceedings to recover expenses under subsection (2) above, the court—

(a) shall inquire whether the local authority were justified in concluding that the premises were in a defective state, or that unreasonable delay in remedying the defective state would have been occasioned by following the procedure prescribed by [section 80 of the Environmental Protection Act 1990], and

(b) if the defendant proves that he served a counter-notice under subsection (3) above, shall inquire whether the defendant failed to begin the works to remedy the defects within a reasonable time, or failed to make reasonable progress towards their completion,

and if the court determines that—

(i) the local authority were not justified in either of the conclusions mentioned in paragraph (a) of this subsection, or (ii) there was no failure under paragraph (b) of this subsection,

the local authority shall not recover the expenses or any part of them.

(5) Subject to subsection (4) above, in proceedings to recover expenses under subsection (2) above, the court may—

(a) inquire whether the said expenses ought to be borne wholly or in part by some person other than the defendant in the proceedings, and

(b) make such order concerning the expenses or their apportionment as appears to the court to be just,

but the court shall not order the expenses or any part of them to be borne by a person other than the defendant in the proceedings unless the court is satisfied that that other person has had due notice of the proceedings and an opportunity of being heard.

(6) A local authority shall not serve a notice under subsection (1) above, or proceed with the execution of works in accordance with a notice so served, if the execution of the works would, to their knowledge, be in contravention of a building preservation order under section 29 of the Town and Country Planning Act 1947.

(7) The power conferred on a local authority by subsection (1) above may be exercised notwithstanding that the local authority might instead have proceeded under [Part VI of the Housing Act 1985 (repair notices)].

77.— Dangerous building.

(1) If it appears to a local authority that a building or structure, or **A6–02** part of a building or structure, is in such a condition, or is used to carry such loads, as to be dangerous, the authority may apply to a magistrates' court, and the court may—

(a) where danger arises from the condition of the building or structure, make an order requiring the owner thereof—

    (i)   to execute such work as may be necessary to obviate the danger or,

    (ii)   if he so elects, to demolish the building or structure, or any dangerous part of it, and remove any rubbish resulting from the demolition, or

  (b) where danger arises from overloading of the building or structure, make an order restricting its use until a magistrates' court, being satisfied that any necessary works have been executed, withdraws or modifies the restriction.

(2) If the person on whom an order is made under subsection (1)(a) above fails to comply with the order within the time specified, the local authority may—

  (a) execute the order in such manner as they think fit, and

  (b) recover the expenses reasonably incurred by them in doing so from the person in default,

and, without prejudice to the right of the authority to exercise those powers, the person is liable on summary conviction to a fine not exceeding level 1 on the standard scale.

[(3) This section has effect subject to the provisions [the Planning (Listed Buildings and Conservation Areas) Act 1990] relating to listed buildings, buildings subject to building preservation [notices,] and buildings in conservation areas.]

78.— Dangerous building— emergency measures.

A6–03 (1) If it appears to a local authority that—

  (a) a building or structure, or part of a building or structure, is in such a state, or is used to carry such loads, as to be dangerous, and

  (b) immediate action should be taken to remove the danger,

they may take such steps as may be necessary for that purpose.

(2) Before exercising their powers under this section, the local authority shall, if it is reasonably practicable to do so, give notice of their intention to the owner and occupier of the building, or of the premises on which the structure is situated.

(3) Subject to this section, the local authority may recover from the owner the expenses reasonably incurred by them under this section.

(4) So far as expenses incurred by the local authority under this section consist of expenses of fencing off the building or structure, or arranging for it to be watched, the expenses shall not be recoverable in respect of any period—

  (a) after the danger has been removed by other steps under this section, or

  (b) after an order made under section 77(1) above for the purpose of its removal has been complied with or has been executed as mentioned in subsection (2) of that section.

(5) In proceedings to recover expenses under this section, the court shall inquire whether the local authority might reasonably have proceeded instead under section 77(1) above, and, if the court determines that the local authority might reasonably have proceeded instead under that subsection, the local authority shall not recover the expenses or any part of them.

(6) Subject to subsection (5) above, in proceedings to recover expenses under this section, the court may—

 (a) inquire whether the expenses ought to be borne wholly or in part by some person other than the defendant in the proceedings, and

 (b) make such order concerning the expenses or their apportionment as appears to the court to be just,

but the court shall not order the expenses or any part of them to be borne by any person other than the defendant in the proceedings unless it is satisfied that that other person has had due notice of the proceedings and an opportunity of being heard.

(7) Where in consequence of the exercise of the powers conferred by this section the owner or occupier of any premises sustains damage, but section 106(1) below does not apply because the owner or occupier has been in default—

 (a) the owner or occupier may apply to a magistrates' court to determine whether the local authority were justified in exercising their powers under this section so as to occasion the damage sustained, and

 (b) if the court determines that the local authority were not so justified, the owner or occupier is entitled to compensation, and section 106(2) and (3) below applies in relation to any dispute as regards compensation arising under this subsection.

(8) The proper officer of a local authority may, as an officer of the local authority, exercise the powers conferred on the local authority by subsection (1) above.

(9) This section does not apply to premises forming part of a mine or quarry within the meaning of the Mines and Quarries Act 1954.

79.— Ruinous and dilapidated buildings and neglected sites.
(1) If it appears to a local authority that a building or structure is by **A6–04** reason of its ruinous or dilapidated condition seriously detrimental to the amenities of the neighbourhood, the local authority may by notice require the owner thereof—

 (a) to execute such works of repair or restoration, or

 (b) if he so elects, to take such steps for demolishing the building or structure, or any part thereof, and removing any rubbish or other material resulting from or exposed by the demolition, as may be necessary in the interests of amenity.

(2) If it appears to a local authority that—

    (a)   rubbish or other material resulting from, or exposed by, the demolition or collapse of a building or structure is lying on the site or on any adjoining land, and

    (b)   by reason thereof the site or land is in such a condition as to be seriously detrimental to the amenities of the neighbourhood,

the local authority may by notice require the owner of the site or land to take such steps for removing the rubbish or material as may be necessary in the interests of amenity.

(3) Sections 99 and 102 below apply in relation to a notice given under subsection (1) or (2) above, subject to the following modifications—

    (a)   section 99(1) requires the notice to indicate the nature of the works of repair or restoration and that of the works of demolition and removal of rubbish or material, and

    (b)   section 99(2) authorises the local authority to execute, subject to that subsection, at their election either the works of repair or restoration or the works of demolition and removal of rubbish or material.

(4) This section does not apply to an advertisement as defined in [section 336(1) of the Town and Country Planning Act 1990].

[(5) This section has effect subject to the provisions [the Planning (Listed Buildings and Conservation Areas) Act 1990] relating to listed buildings, buildings subject to building preservation [notices] and buildings in conservation areas.]

80.— Notice to local authority of intended demolition.

A6–05 (1) This section applies to any demolition of the whole or part of a building except—

    (a)   a demolition in pursuance of a demolition order [or obstructive building order] made under [Part IX of the Housing Act 1985], and

    (b)   a demolition—

        (i)   of an internal part of a building, where the building is occupied and it is intended that it should continue to be occupied,

        (ii)   of a building that has a cubic content (as ascertained by external measurement) of not more than 1750 cubic feet, or, where a greenhouse, conservatory, shed or prefabricated garage forms part of a larger building, of that greenhouse, conservatory, shed or prefabricated garage, or

        (iii)   without prejudice to sub-paragraph (ii) above, of an agricultural building ([within the meaning of any of

paragraphs 3 to 7 of Schedule 5 to the Local Government
Finance Act 1988]), unless it is contiguous to another
building that is not itself an agricultural building or a
building of a kind mentioned in that sub-paragraph.

(2) No person shall begin a demolition to which this section applies
unless—

    (a) he has given the local authority notice of his intention to do
so, and

    (b) either—

        (i)   the local authority have given a notice to him under
section 81 below, or

        (ii) the relevant period (as defined in that section) has
expired.

(3) A notice under subsection (2) above shall specify the building to
which it relates and the works of demolition intended to be carried
out, and it is the duty of a person giving such a notice to a local
authority to send or give a copy of it to—

    (a) the occupier of any building adjacent to the building,

   [(b) any public gas supplier (as defined in Part I of the Gas Act
1986) in whose authorised area (as so defined) the building
is situated,]

   [(c) the public electricity supplier (as defined in Part I of the
Electricity Act 1989) in whose authorised area (as so defined)
the building is situated and any other person authorised by a
licence under that Part to supply electricity to the building;]

(4) A person who contravenes subsection (2) above is liable on summary
conviction to a fine not exceeding level 4 on the standard scale.

81.— Local authority's power to serve notice about demolition.

(1) A local authority may give a notice under this section to—   **A6–06**

    (a) a person on whom a demolition order or obstructive building
order has been served under Part IX of the Housing Act
1985,

    (b) a person who appears to them not to be intending to comply
with an order made under section 77 above or a notice given
under section 79 above, and

    (c) a person who appears to them to have begun or to be intending
to begin a demolition to which section 80 above otherwise
applies.

(2) Nothing contained in a notice under this section prejudices or
affects the operation of any of the relevant statutory provisions,
as defined in section 53(1) of the Health and Safety at Work etc.
Act 1974; and accordingly, if a requirement of such a notice is
inconsistent with a requirement imposed by or under the said Act of
1974, the latter requirement prevails.

(3) Where—

    (a)   a person has given a notice under section 80 above, or

    (b)   the local authority have served a demolition orderor obstructive building order on a person under Part IX of the Housing Act 1985

a notice under this section may only be given to the person in question within the relevant period.

(4) In this section and section 80 above, " the relevant period" means—

    (a)   in a case such as is mentioned in subsection (3)(a) above, six weeks from the giving of the notice under section 80 above, or such longer period as the person who gave that notice may in writing allow, and

    (b)   in a case such as is mentioned in subsection (3)(b) above, seven days after the local authority served a copy of the demolition orderor obstructive building order in accordance with Part IX of the Housing Act 1985, or such longer period as the person on whom the copy was served may in writing allow.

(5) It is the duty of the local authority to send or give a copy of a notice under this section to the owner and occupier of any building adjacent to the building to which the notice relates.

(6) It is also the duty of the local authority to send or give a copy of a notice under this section—

    (a)   if it contains such a requirement as is specified in section 82(1)(h) below, to the statutory undertakers concerned, and

    (b)   if it contains such a requirement as is specified in section 82(1)(i) below, to the fire and rescue authority, if they are not themselves the fire and rescue authority.

    [...]

82.— Notices under section 81.

A6–07 (1) A notice under section 81(1) above may require the person to whom it is given—

    (a)   to shore up any building adjacent to the building to which the notice relates,

    (b)   to weatherproof any surfaces of an adjacent building that are exposed by the demolition,

    (c)   to repair and make good any damage to an adjacent building caused by the demolition or by the negligent act or omission of any person engaged in it,

    (d)   to remove material or rubbish resulting from the demolition and clearance of the site, (e)　to disconnect and seal, at such points as the local authority may reasonably require, any sewer or drain in or under the building,

(f)　to remove any such sewer or drain, and seal any sewer or drain with which the sewer or drain to be removed is connected,

(g)　to make good to the satisfaction of the local authority the surface of the ground disturbed by anything done under paragraph (e) or (f) above,

(h)　to make arrangements with the relevant statutory undertakers for the disconnection of the supply of gas, electricity and water to the building,

[(i)　to make such arrangements with regard to the burning of structures or materials on the site as may be reasonably required by the fire and rescue authority;]

(j)　to take such steps relating to the conditions subject to which the demolition is to be undertaken, and the condition in which the site is to be left on completion of the demolition, as the local authority may consider reasonably necessary for the protection of the public and the preservation of public amenity.

(2) No one shall be required under paragraph (c), (e) or (f) of subsection (1) above to carry out any work in land outside the premises on which the works of demolition are being carried out if he has no right to carry out that work, but, subject to section 101 below, the person undertaking the demolition, or the local authority acting in his default, may break open any street for the purpose of complying with any such requirement.

(3) Before a person complies with a requirement under paragraph (e), (f) or (g) of subsection (1) above, he shall give to the local authority—

(a)　at least 48 hours' notice, in the case of a requirement under paragraph (e) or (f), or

(b)　at least 24 hours' notice, in the case of a requirement under paragraph (g),

and a person who fails to comply with this subsection is liable on summary conviction to a fine not exceeding level 2 on the standard scale.

(4) This section does not authorise interference with apparatus or works of statutory undertakers authorised by an enactment to carry on an undertaking for the supply of electricity, or gas or with apparatus or works of a water undertaker or sewerage undertaker.

(5) Without prejudice to the generality of subsection (4) above, this section does not exempt a person from—

(a) the obligation to obtain any consent required under section 174 of the Water Industry Act 1991 or section 176 of the Water Resources Act 1991 (interference with water supplies or with waterworks)

(b) criminal liability under any enactment relating to the supply of gas or electricity, or

(c) the requirements of regulations under section 31 of the Gas Act 1972 (public safety).

(6) Section 99 below applies in relation to a notice given under section 81(1) above.

83.— Appeal against notice under s. 81.

A6–08 (1) Section 102 below applies in relation to a notice given under section 81 above.

(2) Among the grounds on which an appeal may be brought under section 102 below against such a notice are—

(a) in the case of a notice requiring an adjacent building to be shored up, that the owner of the building is not entitled to the support of that building by the building that is being demolished, and ought to pay, or contribute towards, the expenses of shoring it up,

(b) in the case of a notice requiring any surfaces of an adjacent building to be weatherproofed, that the owner of the adjacent building ought to pay, or contribute towards, the expenses of weatherproofing those surfaces.

(3) Where the grounds on which an appeal under section 102 below is brought include a ground specified in subsection (2) above—

(a) the appellant shall serve a copy of his notice of appeal on the person or persons referred to in that ground of appeal, and

(b) on the hearing of the appeal the court may make such order as it thinks fit—

(i) in respect of the payment of, or contribution towards, the cost of the works by any such person, or

(ii) as to how any expenses that may be recoverable by the local authority are to be borne between the appellant and any such person.

Landlord and Tenant Act 1985 c.70

Repairing obligations

11.— Repairing obligations in short leases.
(1) In a lease to which this section applies (as to which, see sections **A7–01**
13 and 14) there is implied a covenant by the lessor—
- (a) to keep in repair the structure and exterior of the dwelling-
house (including drains, gutters and external pipes),
- (b) to keep in repair and proper working order the installations in
the dwelling-house for the supply of water, gas and electricity
and for sanitation (including basins, sinks, baths and sanitary
conveniences, but not other fixtures, fittings and appliances
for making use of the supply of water, gas or electricity),
and
- (c) to keep in repair and proper working order the installations
in the dwelling-house for space heating and heating water.

[(1A) If a lease to which this section applies is a lease of a dwelling-
house which forms part only of a building, then, subject to subsection
(1B), the covenant implied by subsection (1) shall have effect as if—
- (a) the reference in paragraph (a) of that subsection to the
dwelling-house included a reference to any part of the
building in which the lessor has an estate or interest; and
- (b) any reference in paragraphs (b) and (c) of that subsection
to an installation in the dwelling-house included a reference
to an installation which, directly or indirectly, serves the
dwelling-house and which either—
    - (i) forms part of any part of a building in which the lessor
has an estate or interest; or
    - (ii) is owned by the lessor or under his control.

(1B) Nothing in subsection (1A) shall be construed as requiring
the lessor to carry out any works or repairs unless the disrepair (or
failure to maintain in working order) is such as to affect the lessee's
enjoyment of the dwelling-house or of any common parts, as defined
in section 60(1) of the Landlord and Tenant Act 1987, which the
lessee, as such, is entitled to use.]

(2) The covenant implied by subsection (1) (" the lessor's repairing
covenant") shall not be construed as requiring the lessor—

(a) to carry out works or repairs for which the lessee is liable by
     virtue of his duty to use the premises in a tenant-like manner,
     or would be so liable but for an express covenant on his
     part,

(b) to rebuild or reinstate the premises in the case of destruction
     or damage by fire, or by tempest, flood or other inevitable
     accident, or

(c) to keep in repair or maintain anything which the lessee is
     entitled to remove from the dwelling-house.

(3) In determining the standard of repair required by the lessor's
repairing covenant, regard shall be had to the age, character and
prospective life of the dwelling-house and the locality in which it
is situated.

[(3A) In any case where—

(a) the lessor's repairing covenant has effect as mentioned in
     sub-section (1A), and

(b) in order to comply with the covenant the lessor needs to carry
     out works or repairs otherwise than in, or to an installation
     in, the dwelling-house, and

(c) the lessor does not have a sufficient right in the part of the
     building or the installation concerned to enable him to carry
     out the required works or repairs,

then, in any proceedings relating to a failure to comply with the
lessor's repairing covenant, so far as it requires the lessor to carry
out the works or repairs in question, it shall be a defence for the
lessor to prove that he used all reasonable endeavours to obtain, but
was unable to obtain, such rights as would be adequate to enable him
to carry out the works or repairs.]

(4) A covenant by the lessee for the repair of the premises is of no
effect so far as it relates to the matters mentioned in subsection (1)(a)
to (c), except so far as it imposes on the lessee any of the requirements
mentioned is subsection (2)(a) or (c).

(5) The reference in subsection (4) to a covenant by the lessee for the
repair of the premises includes a covenant—

(a) to put in repair or deliver up in repair,

(b) to paint, point or render,

(c) to pay money in lieu of repairs by the lessee, or

(d) to pay money on account of repairs by the lessor.

(6) In a lease in which the s repairing covenant is implied there is
also implied a covenant by the lessee that the lessor, or any person
authorised by him in writing, may at reasonable times of the day
and on giving 24 hours' notice in writing to the occupier, enter the
premises comprised in the lease for the purpose of viewing their
condition and state of repair.

12.— Restriction on contracting out of s.11.

(1) A covenant or agreement, whether contained in a lease to which **A7–02** section 11 applies or in an agreement collateral to such a lease, is void in so far as it purports—

(a) to exclude or limit the obligations of the lessor or the immunities of the lessee under that section, or

(b) to authorise any forfeiture or impose on the lessee any penalty, disability or obligation in the event of his enforcing or relying upon those obligations or immunities,

unless the inclusion of the provision was authorised by the county court.

(2) The county court may, by order made with the consent of the parties, authorise the inclusion in a lease, or in an agreement collateral to a lease, of provisions excluding or modifying in relation to the lease, the provisions of section 11 with respect to the repairing obligations of the parties if it appears to the court that it is reasonable to do so, having regard to all the circumstances of the case, including the other terms and conditions of the lease.

13.— Leases to which s.11 applies: general rule.

(1) Section 11 (repairing obligations) applies to a lease of a dwelling- **A7–03** house granted on or after 24th October 1961 for a term of less than seven years.

(2) In determining whether a lease is one to which section 11 applies—

(a) any part of the term which falls before the grant shall be left out of account and the lease shall be treated as a lease for a term commencing with the grant,

(b) a lease which is determinable at the option of the lessor before the expiration of seven years from the commencement of the term shall be treated as a lease for a term of less than seven years, and

(c) a lease (other than a lease to which paragraph (b) applies) shall not be treated as a lease for a term of less than seven years if it confers on the lessee an option for renewal for a term which, together with the original term, amounts to seven years or more.

(3) This section has effect subject to—

section 14 (leases to which section 11 applies: exceptions), and

section 32(2) (provisions not applying to tenancies within Part II of the Landlord and Tenant Act 1954).

14.— Leases to which s.11 applies: exceptions.

A7–04 (1) Section 11 (repairing obligations) does not apply to a new lease granted to an existing tenant, or to a former tenant still in possession, if the previous lease was not a lease to which section 11 applied (and, in the case of a lease granted before 24th October 1961, would not have been if it had been granted on or after that date).

(2) In subsection (1)—

" existing tenant" means a person who is when, or immediately before, the new lease is granted, the lessee under another lease of the dwelling-house;

" former tenant still in possession" means a person who—
- (a) was the lessee under another lease of the dwelling-house which terminated at some time before the new lease was granted, and
- (b) between the termination of that other lease and the grant of the new lease was continuously in possession of the dwelling-house or of the rents and profits of the dwelling-house; and

" the previous lease" means the other lease referred to in the above definitions.

(3) Section 11 does not apply to a lease of a dwelling-house which is a tenancy of an agricultural holding within the meaning of the Agricultural Holdings Act 1986and in relation to which that Act applies or to a farm business tenancy within the meaning of the Agricultural Tenancies Act 1995..

(4) Section 11 does not apply to a lease granted on or after 3rd October 1980 to—

a local authority,

a National Park authority,

a new town corporation,

an urban development corporation,

the Development Board for Rural Wales,

a [registered social landlord],

a co-operative housing association, or

an educational institution or other body specified, or of a class specified, by regulations under section 8 of the Rent Act 1977 or paragraph 8 of Schedule 1 to the Housing Act 1988 (bodies making student lettings).

a housing action trust established under Part III of the Housing Act 1988

(5) Section 11 does not apply to a lease granted on or after 3rd October 1980 to—
- (a) Her Majesty in right of the Crown (unless the lease is under the management of the Crown Estate Commissioners), or

(b)   a government department or a person holding in trust for Her Majesty for the purposes of a government department.

15. .— Jurisdiction of county court.

The county court has jurisdiction to make a declaration that section **A7–05** 11 (repairing obligations) applies, or does not apply, to a lease—

    (a)   whatever the net annual value of the property in question, and

    (b)   notwithstanding that no other relief is sought than a declaration.

16.— Meaning of " lease" and related expressions.

In sections 11 to 15 (repairing obligations in short leases)—   **A7–06**

    (a)   "lease" does not include a mortgage term;

    (b)   "lease of a dwelling-house" means a lease by which a building or part of a building is let wholly or mainly as a private residence, and " dwelling-house" means that building or part of a building;

    (c)   "lessee" and "lessor" mean, respectively, the person for the time being entitled to the term of a lease and to the reversion expectant on it.

17.— Specific performance of landlord's repairing obligations.

(1) In proceedings in which a tenant of a dwelling alleges a breach **A7–07** on the part of his landlord of a repairing covenant relating to any part of the premises in which the dwelling is comprised, the court may order specific performance of the covenant whether or not the breach relates to a part of the premises let to the tenant and notwithstanding any equitable rule restricting the scope of the remedy, whether on the basis of a lack of mutuality or otherwise.

(2) In this section—

    (a)   "tenant" includes a statutory tenant,

    (b)   in relation to a statutory tenant the reference to the premises let to him is to the premises of which he is a statutory tenant,

    (c)   "landlord" in relation to a tenant, includes any person against whom the tenant has a right to enforce a repairing covenant, and

    (d)   "repairing covenant" means a covenant to repair, maintain, renew, construct or replace any property.

Landlord and Tenant Act 1987 c.31

Applications relating to flats

35.— Application by party to lease for variation of lease.

A8–01 (1) Any party to a long lease of a flat may make an application to [a leasehold valuation tribunal] for an order varying the lease in such manner as is specified in the application.

(2) The grounds on which any such application may be made are that the lease fails to make satisfactory provision with respect to one or more of the following matters, namely—

   (a)   the repair or maintenance of—

      (i)   the flat in question, or

      (ii)   the building containing the flat, or

      (iii)   any land or building which is let to the tenant under the lease or in respect of which rights are conferred on him under it;

   (b)   the insurance of the building containing the flat or of any such land or building as is mentioned in paragraph (a)(iii);

   (c)   the repair or maintenance of any installations (whether they are in the same building as the flat or not) which are reasonably necessary to ensure that occupiers of the flat enjoy a reasonable standard of accommodation;

   (d)   the provision or maintenance of any services which are reasonably necessary to ensure that occupiers of the flat enjoy a reasonable standard of accommodation (whether they are services connected with any such installations or not, and whether they are services provided for the benefit of those occupiers or services provided for the benefit of the occupiers of a number of flats including that flat);

   (e)   the recovery by one party to the lease from another party to it of expenditure incurred or to be incurred by him, or on his behalf, for the benefit of that other party or of a number of persons who include that other party;

   (f)   the computation of a service charge payable under the lease[;]

[(g) such other matters as may be prescribed by regulations made by the Secretary of State].

(3) For the purposes of subsection (2)(c) and (d) the factors for determining, in relation to the occupiers of a flat, what is a reasonable standard of accommodation may include—

(a) factors relating to the safety and security of the flat and its occupiers and of any common parts of the building containing the flat; and

(b) other factors relating to the condition of any such common parts.

[(3A) For the purposes of subsection (2)(e) the factors for determining, in relation to a service charge payable under a lease, whether the lease makes satisfactory provision include whether it makes provision for an amount to be payable (by way of interest or otherwise) in respect of a failure to pay the service charge by the due date.]

(4) For the purposes of subsection (2)(f) a lease fails to make satisfactory provision with respect to the computation of a service charge payable under it if—

(a) it provides for any such charge to be a proportion of expenditure incurred, or to be incurred, by or on behalf of the landlord or a superior landlord; and

(b) other tenants of the landlord are also liable under their leases to pay by way of service charges proportions of any such expenditure; and

(c) the aggregate of the amounts that would, in any particular case, be payable by reference to the proportions referred to in paragraphs (a) and (b) would [either exceed or be less than] the whole of any such expenditure.

(5) [Procedure regulations under Schedule 12 to the Commonhold and Leasehold Reform Act 2002][1] shall make provision—

(a) for requiring notice of any application under this Part to be served by the person making the application, and by any respondent to the application, on any person who the applicant, or (as the case may be) the respondent, knows or has reason to believe is likely to be affected by any variation specified in the application, and

(b) for enabling persons served with any such notice to be joined as parties to the proceedings.

[(6) For the purposes of this Part a long lease shall not be regarded as a long lease of a flat if—

(a) the demised premises consist of or include three or more flats contained in the same building; or

(b) the lease constitutes a tenancy to which Part II of the Landlord and Tenant Act 1954 applies.]

(8) In this section " service charge" has the meaning given by section 18(1) of the 1985 Act.[...]

APPENDIX A9

Environmental Protection Act 1990 c.43

PART III

STATUTORY NUISANCES AND CLEAN AIR

Statutory nuisances

79.— Statutory nuisances and inspections therefor.

A9–01 (1) Subject to subsections (1A) to (6A) below, the following matters constitute " statutory nuisances" for the purposes of this Part, that is to say—

(a) any premises in such a state as to be prejudicial to health or a nuisance;

(b) smoke emitted from premises so as to be prejudicial to health or a nuisance;

(c) fumes or gases emitted from premises so as to be prejudicial to health or a nuisance;

(d) any dust, steam, smell or other effluvia arising on industrial, trade or business premises and being prejudicial to health or a nuisance;

(e) any accumulation or deposit which is prejudicial to health or a nuisance;

(f) any animal kept in such a place or manner as to be prejudicial to health or a nuisance;

(fa) any insects emanating from relevant industrial, trade or business premises and being prejudicial to health or a nuisance;

(fb) artificial light emitted from premises so as to be prejudicial to health or a nuisance;

(g) noise emitted from premises so as to be prejudicial to health or a nuisance;

(ga) noise that is prejudicial to health or a nuisance and is emitted from or caused by a vehicle, machinery or equipment in a street or in Scotland, road; and

(gb) smoke, fumes or gases emitted from any vehicle, machinery or equipment on a street so as to be prejudicial to health or a nuisance other than from any vehicle, machinery or equipment being used for fire brigade purposes;

(h) any other matter declared by any enactment to be a statutory nuisance;

and it shall be the duty of every local authority to cause its area to be inspected from time to time to detect any statutory nuisances which ought to be dealt with under section 80 below or sections 80 and 80A below and, where a complaint of a statutory nuisance is made to it by a person living within its area, to take such steps as are reasonably practicable to investigate the complaint.

(1A) No matter shall constitute a statutory nuisance to the extent that it consists of, or is caused by, any land being in a contaminated state.

(1B) Land is in a " contaminated state" for the purposes of subsection (1A) above if, and only if, it is in such a condition, by reason of substances in, on or under the land, that—

    (a)   harm is being caused or there is a possibility of harm being caused; or

    (b)   pollution of controlled waters is being, or is likely to be, caused;

and in this subsection " harm", " pollution of controlled waters" and " substance" have the same meaning as in Part IIA of this Act.

(2) Subsection (1)(b), (fb) and (g) above do not apply in relation to premises—

    (a)   occupied on behalf of the Crown for naval, military or air force purposes or for the purposes of the department of the Secretary of State having responsibility for defence, or

    (b)   occupied by or for the purposes of a visiting force;

and " visiting force" means any such body, contingent or detachment of the forces of any country as is a visiting force for the purposes of any of the provisions of the Visiting Forces Act 1952.

(3) Subsection (1)(b) above does not apply to—

    (i)   smoke emitted from a chimney of a private dwelling within a smoke control area,

    (ii)   dark smoke emitted from a chimney of a building or a chimney serving the furnace of a boiler or industrial plant attached to a building or for the time being fixed to or installed on any land,

    (iii)   smoke emitted from a railway locomotive steam engine, or (iv) dark smoke emitted otherwise than as mentioned above from industrial or trade premises.

(4) Subsection (1)(c) above does not apply in relation to premises other than private dwellings.

(5) Subsection (1)(d) above does not apply to steam emitted from a railway locomotive engine.

(5A) Subsection (1)(fa) does not apply to insects that are wild animals included in Schedule 5 to the Wildlife and Countryside Act 1981 (animals which are protected), unless they are included in respect of section 9(5) of that Act only.

(5B) Subsection (1)(fb) does not apply to artificial light emitted from—

    (a)   an airport;

    (b)   harbour premises;

    (c)   railway premises, not being relevant separate railway premises;

    (d)   tramway premises;

    (e)   a bus station and any associated facilities;

    (f)   a public service vehicle operating centre;

    (g)   a goods vehicle operating centre;

    (h)   a lighthouse;

    (i)   a prison.

(6) Subsection (1)(g) above does not apply to noise caused by aircraft other than model aircraft.

(6A) Subsection (1)(ga) above does not apply to noise made—

    (a)   by traffic,

    (b)   by any naval, military or air force of the Crown or by a visiting force (as defined in subsection (2) above), or

    (c)   by a political demonstration or a demonstration supporting or opposing a cause or campaign.

(6B) Subsection (1)(gb) above does not apply in relation to smoke, fumes or gases emitted from the exhaust system of a vehicle.

(7) In this Part—

"airport" has the meaning given by section 95 of the Transport Act 2000;

"associated facilities", in relation to a bus station, has the meaning given by section 83 of the Transport Act 1985;

"bus station" has the meaning given by section 83 of the Transport Act 1985;

"chimney" includes structures and openings of any kind from or through which smoke may be emitted;

"dust" does not include dust emitted from a chimney as an ingredient of smoke;

"equipment" includes a musical instrument;

"fumes" means any airborne solid matter smaller than dust;

"gas" includes vapour and moisture precipitated from vapour;

"goods vehicle operating centre" , in relation to vehicles used under an operator's licence, means a place which is specified in the licence as an operating centre for those vehicles, and for the purposes of this definition " operating centre" and " operator's licence" have the same meaning as in the Goods Vehicles (Licensing of Operators) Act 1995;

"harbour premises" means premises which form part of a harbour area and which are occupied wholly or mainly for the purposes of harbour operations, and for the purposes of this definition " harbour area" and " harbour operations" have the same meaning as in Part 3 of the Aviation and Maritime Security Act 1990;

"industrial, trade or business premises" means premises used for any industrial, trade or business purposes or premises not so used on which matter is burnt in connection with any industrial, trade or business process, and premises are used for industrial purposes where they are used for the purposes of any treatment or process as well as where they are used for the purposes of manufacturing;

"lighthouse" has the same meaning as in Part 8 of the Merchant Shipping Act 1995;

"local authority" means, subject to subsection (8) below,—

(a) in Greater London, a London borough council, the Common Council of the City of London and, as respects the Temples, the Sub-Treasurer of the Inner Temple and the Under-Treasurer of the Middle Temple respectively;
(b) in England outside Greater London, a district council;
(bb) in Wales, a county council or county borough council;
(c) the Council of the Isles of Scilly; and
(d) in Scotland, a district or islands council or a council constituted under section 2 of the Local Government etc (Scotland) Act 1994;

"noise" includes vibration;

"person responsible" —

(a) in relation to a statutory nuisance, means the person to whose act, default or sufferance the nuisance is attributable;
(b) in relation to a vehicle, includes the person in whose name the vehicle is for the time being registered under the Vehicle Excise and Registration Act 1994 and any other person who is for the time being the driver of the vehicle;
(c) n relation to machinery or equipment, includes any person

who is for the time being the operator of the machinery or equipment;

, and

"prejudicial to health" means injurious, or likely to cause injury, to health;

"premises" includes land and, subject to subsection (12) and, in relation to England and Wales, section 81A(9) below, any vessel;

"prison" includes a young offender institution;

"private dwelling" means any building, or part of a building, used or intended to be used, as a dwelling;

"public service vehicle operating centre" , in relation to public service vehicles used under a PSV operator's licence, means a place which is an operating centre of those vehicles, and for the purposes of this definition " operating centre" , " PSV operator's licence" and " public service vehicle" have the same meaning as in the Public Passenger Vehicles Act 1981;

" railway premises" means any premises which fall within the definition of " light maintenance depot" , " network" , " station" or " track" in section 83 of the Railways Act 1993;

"relevant separate railway premises" has the meaning given by subsection (7A);

"road" has the same meaning as in Part IV of the New Roads and Street Works Act 1991;

"smoke" includes soot, ash, grit and gritty particles emitted in smoke;

"street" means a highway and any other road, footway, square or court that is for the time being open to the public;;

"tramway premises" means any premises which, in relation to a tramway, are the equivalent of the premises which, in relation to a railway, fall within the definition of " light maintenance depot" , " network" , " station" or " track" in section 83 of the Railways Act 1993;

"vehicle" means a mechanically propelled vehicle intended or adapted for use on roads, whether or not it is in a fit state for such use, and includes any trailer intended or adapted for use as an attachment to such a vehicle, any chassis or body, with or without wheels, appearing to have formed part of such a vehicle or trailer and anything attached to such a vehicle or trailer.

and any expressions used in this section and in the Clean Air Act 1993 have the same meaning in this section as in that Act and section 3 of the Clean Air Act 1993 shall apply for the interpretation of the expression "dark smoke" and the operation of this Part in relation to it.

(7A) Railway premises are relevant separate railway premises if–
   (a) they are situated within–
        (i)   premises used as a museum or other place of cultural, scientific or historical interest, or (ii) premises used for the purposes of a funfair or other entertainment, recreation or amusement, and
   (b) they are not associated with any other railway premises.

(7B) For the purposes of subsection (7A)–
   (a) a network situated as described in subsection (7A)(a) is associated with other railway premises if it is connected to another network (not being a network situated as described in subsection (7A)(a));
   (b) track that is situated as described in subsection (7A)(a) but is not part of a network is associated with other railway premises if it is connected to track that forms part of a network (not being a network situated as described in subsection (7A) (a));
   (c) a station or light maintenance depot situated as described in subsection (7A)(a) is associated with other railway premises if it is used in connection with the provision of railway services other than services provided wholly within the premises where it is situated.

In this subsection "light maintenance depot", "network", "railway services", "station" and "track" have the same meaning as in Part 1 of the Railways Act 1993.

(8) Where, by an order under section 2 of the Public Health (Control of Disease) Act 1984, a port health authority has been constituted for any port health district or in Scotland where by an order under section 172 of the Public Health (Scotland) Act 1897 a port local authority or a joint port local authority has been constituted for the whole or part of a port, the port health authority, port local authority or joint port local authority, as the case may be shall have by virtue of this subsection, as respects its district, the functions conferred or imposed by this Part in relation to statutory nuisances other than a nuisance falling within paragraph (fb), (g) or (ga) of subsection (1) above and no such order shall be made assigning those functions; and " local authority" and " area" shall be construed accordingly.

(9) In this Part " best practicable means" is to be interpreted by reference to the following provisions—

(a) "practicable" means reasonably practicable having regard among other things to local conditions and circumstances, to the current state of technical knowledge and to the financial implications;

(b) the means to be employed include the design, installation, maintenance and manner and periods of operation of plant and machinery, and the design, construction and maintenance of buildings and structures;

(c) the test is to apply only so far as compatible with any duty imposed by law;

(d) the test is to apply only so far as compatible with safety and safe working conditions, and with the exigencies of any emergency or unforeseeable circumstances;

and, in circumstances where a code of practice under section 71 of the Control of Pollution Act 1974 (noise minimisation) is applicable, regard shall also be had to guidance given in it.

(10) A local authority shall not without the consent of the Secretary of State institute summary proceedings under this Part in respect of a nuisance falling within paragraph (b), (d) or (e), (fb) and in relation to Scotland, paragraph (g) or (ga), of subsection (1) above if proceedings in respect thereof might be instituted under Part I or under regulations under section 2 of the Pollution Prevention and Control Act 1999.

(11) The area of a local authority which includes part of the seashore shall also include for the purposes of this Part the territorial sea lying seawards from that part of the shore; and subject to subsection (12) and , in relation to England and Wales,section 81A(9) below, this Part shall have effect, in relation to any area included in the area of a local authority by virtue of this subsection—

(a) as if references to premises and the occupier of premises included respectively a vessel and the master of a vessel; and

(b) with such other modifications, if any, as are prescribed in regulations made by the Secretary of State.

(12) A vessel powered by steam reciprocating machinery is not a vessel to which this Part of this Act applies.

80.— Summary proceedings for statutory nuisances.

(1) Subject to subsection (2A) where a local authority is satisfied that **A9–02** a statutory nuisance exists, or is likely to occur or recur, in the area of the authority, the local authority shall serve a notice (" an abatement notice") imposing all or any of the following requirements—

(a) requiring the abatement of the nuisance or prohibiting or restricting its occurrence or recurrence;

(b) requiring the execution of such works, and the taking of such other steps, as may be necessary for any of those purposes,

and the notice shall specify the time or times within which the requirements of the notice are to be complied with.

(2) Subject to section 80A(1) below, the abatement notice shall be served—

(a) except in a case falling within paragraph (b) or (c) below, on the person responsible for the nuisance;

(b) where the nuisance arises from any defect of a structural character, on the owner of the premises;

(c) where the person responsible for the nuisance cannot be found or the nuisance has not yet occurred, on the owner or occupier of the premises.

(2A) Where a local authority is satisfied that a statutory nuisance falling within paragraph (g) of section 79(1) above exists, or is likely to occur or recur, in the area of the authority, the authority shall–

(a) serve an abatement notice in respect of the nuisance in accordance with subsections (1) and (2) above; or

(b) take such other steps as it thinks appropriate for the purpose of persuading the appropriate person to abate the nuisance or prohibit or restrict its occurrence or recurrence.

(2B) If a local authority has taken steps under subsection (2A) (b) above and either of the conditions in subsection (2C) below is satisfied, the authority shall serve an abatement notice in respect of the nuisance.

(2C) The conditions are–

(a) that the authority is satisfied at any time before the end of the relevant period that the steps taken will not be successful in persuading the appropriate person to abate the nuisance or prohibit or restrict its occurrence or recurrence;

(b) that the authority is satisfied at the end of the relevant period that the nuisance continues to exist, or continues to be likely to occur or recur, in the area of the authority.

(2D) The relevant period is the period of seven days starting with the day on which the authority was first satisfied that the nuisance existed, or was likely to occur or recur.

(2E) The appropriate person is the person on whom the authority would otherwise be required under subsection (2A)(a) above to serve an abatement notice in respect of the nuisance.

(3) A person served with an abatement notice may appeal against the notice to a magistrates' court or in Scotland, the sheriff within the period of twenty-one days beginning with the date on which he was served with the notice.

(4) If a person on whom an abatement notice is served, without reasonable excuse, contravenes or fails to comply with any requirement or prohibition imposed by the notice, he shall be guilty of an offence.

(5) Except in a case falling within subsection (6) below, a person who commits an offence under subsection (4) above shall be liable on summary conviction to a fine not exceeding level 5 on the standard scale together with a further fine of an amount equal to one-tenth of that level for each day on which the offence continues after the conviction.

(6) A person who commits an offence under subsection (4) above on industrial, trade or business premises shall be liable on summary conviction to a fine not exceeding £20,000.

(7) Subject to subsection (8) below, in any proceedings for an offence under subsection (4) above in respect of a statutory nuisance it shall be a defence to prove that the best practicable means were used to prevent, or to counteract the effects of, the nuisance.

(8) The defence under subsection (7) above is not available—

    (a)   in the case of a nuisance falling within paragraph (a), (d), (e), (f), (fa) or (g) of section 79(1) above except where the nuisance arises on industrial, trade or business premises;

    (aza) in the case of a nuisance falling within paragraph (fb) of section 79(1) above except where–

        (i)   the artificial light is emitted from industrial, trade or business premises, or

        (ii)   the artificial light (not being light to which sub-paragraph (i) applies) is emitted by lights used for the purpose only of illuminating an outdoor relevant sports facility;

        (aa) in the case of a nuisance falling within paragraph (ga) of section 79(1) above except where the noise is emitted from or caused by a vehicle, machinery or equipment being used for industrial, trade or business purposes;

    (b)   in the case of a nuisance falling within paragraph (b) of section 79(1) above except where the smoke is emitted from a chimney; and

    (c)   in the case of a nuisance falling within paragraph (c) or (h) of section 79(1) above. (8A) For the purposes of subsection (8)(aza) a relevant sports facility is an area, with or without structures, that is used when participating in a relevant sport, but does not include such an area comprised in domestic premises.

(8B) For the purposes of subsection (8A) " relevant sport" means a sport that is designated for those purposes by order made by the Secretary of State, in relation to England, or the National Assembly for Wales, in relation to Wales.

A sport may be so designated by reference to its appearing in a list maintained by a body specified in the order.

(8C) In subsection (8A) " domestic premises" means–

    (a)   premises used wholly or mainly as a private dwelling, or

    (b)   land or other premises belonging to, or enjoyed with, premises so used.

(9) In proceedings for an offence under subsection (4) above in respect of a statutory nuisance falling within paragraph (g) or (ga) of section 79(1) above where the offence consists in contravening requirements imposed by virtue of subsection (1)(a) above it shall be a defence to prove—

    (a)   that the alleged offence was covered by a notice served under section 60 or a consent given under section 61 or 65 of the Control of Pollution Act 1974 (construction sites, etc); or

    (b)   where the alleged offence was committed at a time when the premises were subject to a notice under section 66 of that Act (noise reduction notice), that the level of noise emitted from the premises at that time was not such as to a constitute a contravention of the notice under that section; or

    (c)   where the alleged offence was committed at a time when the premises were not subject to a notice under section 66 of that Act, and when a level fixed under section 67 of that Act (new buildings liable to abatement order) applied to the premises, that the level of noise emitted from the premises at that time did not exceed that level.

(10) Paragraphs (b) and (c) of subsection (9) above apply whether or not the relevant notice was subject to appeal at the time when the offence was alleged to have been committed.

80A.— Abatement notice in respect of noise in street.

A9–03 (1) In the case of a statutory nuisance within section 79(1)(ga) above that—

(a)   has not yet occurred, or

(b)   arises from noise emitted from or caused by an unattended vehicle or unattended machinery or equipment,

the abatement notice shall be served in accordance with subsection (2) below.[]

(2) The notice shall be served—

(a)   where the person responsible for the vehicle, machinery or equipment can be found, on that person;

(b)   where that person cannot be found or where the local authority determines that this paragraph should apply, by fixing the notice to the vehicle, machinery or equipment.

(3) Where—

(a)   an abatement notice is served in accordance with subsection (2)(b) above by virtue of a determination of the local authority, and

(b)   the person responsible for the vehicle, machinery or equipment can be found and served with a copy of the notice within an hour of the notice being fixed to the vehicle, machinery or equipment,

a copy of the notice shall be served on that person accordingly.

(4) Where an abatement notice is served in accordance with subsection (2)(b) above by virtue of a determination of the local authority, the notice shall state that, if a copy of the notice is subsequently served under subsection (3) above, the time specified in the notice as the time within which its requirements are to be complied with is extended by such further period as is specified in the notice.

(5) Where an abatement notice is served in accordance with subsection (2)(b) above, the person responsible for the vehicle, machinery or equipment may appeal against the notice under section 80(3) above as if he had been served with the notice on the date on which it was fixed to the vehicle, machinery or equipment.

(6) Section 80(4) above shall apply in relation to a person on whom a copy of an abatement notice is served under subsection (3) above as if the copy were the notice itself.

(7) A person who removes or interferes with a notice fixed to a vehicle, machinery or equipment in accordance with subsection (2)(b) above shall be guilty of an offence, unless he is the person responsible for the vehicle, machinery or equipment or he does so with the authority of that person.

(8) A person who commits an offence under subsection (7) above shall be liable on summary conviction to a fine not exceeding level 3 on the standard scale.

81.— Supplementary provisions.

(1) Subject to subsection (1A) below, where more than one person is **A9–04**
responsible for a statutory nuisance section 80 above shall apply to
each of those persons whether or not what any one of them is
responsible for would by itself amount to a nuisance.

(1A) In relation to a statutory nuisance within section 79(1)(ga)
above for which more than one person is responsible (whether or
not what any one of those persons is responsible for would by itself
amount to such a nuisance), section 80(2)(a) above shall apply with
the substitution of " any one of the persons" for " the person" .

(1B) In relation to a statutory nuisance within section 79(1)(ga)
above caused by noise emitted from or caused by an unattended
vehicle or unattended machinery or equipment for which more than
one person is responsible, section 80A above shall apply with the
substitution—

    (a)   in subsection (2)(a), of "any of the persons" for "the person"
               and of "one such person" for "that person" ,

    (b)   in subsection (2)(b), of "such a person" for "that person",

    (c)   in subsection (3), of "any of the persons" for "the person"
               and of "one such person" for "that person" ,

    (d)   in subsection (5), of "any person" for "the person", and

    (e)   in subsection (7), of "a person" for "the person" and of "such
               a person" for "that person".

(2) Where a statutory nuisance which exists or has occurred within
the area of a local authority, or which has affected any part of that
area, appears to the local authority to be wholly or partly caused by
some act or default committed or taking place outside the area, the
local authority may act under section 80 above as if the act or default
were wholly within that area, except that any appeal shall be heard
by a magistrates' court or in Scotland, the sheriff having jurisdiction
where the act or default is alleged to have taken place.

(3) Where an abatement notice has not been complied with the local
authority may, whether or not they take proceedings for an offence
or, in Scotland, whether or not proceedings have been taken for
an offence, under section 80(4) above, abate the nuisance and do
whatever may be necessary in execution of the notice.

(4) Any expenses reasonably incurred by a local authority in abating,
or preventing the recurrence of, a statutory nuisance under subsection
(3) above may be recovered by them from the person by whose act or
default the nuisance was caused and, if that person is the owner of the
premises, from any person who is for the time being the owner thereof;
and the court or sheriff may apportion the expenses between persons
by whose acts or defaults the nuisance is caused in such manner as the
court consider or sheriff considers fair and reasonable.

(5) If a local authority is of opinion that proceedings for an offence under section 80(4) above would afford an inadequate remedy in the case of any statutory nuisance, they may, subject to subsection (6) below, take proceedings in the High Court or, in Scotland, in any court of competent jurisdiction, for the purpose of securing the abatement, prohibition or restriction of the nuisance, and the proceedings shall be maintainable notwithstanding the local authority have suffered no damage from the nuisance.

(6) In any proceedings under subsection (5) above in respect of a nuisance falling within paragraph (g) or (ga) of section 79(1) above, it shall be a defence to prove that the noise was authorised by a notice under section 60 or a consent under section 61 (construction sites) of the Control of Pollution Act 1974.

(7) The further supplementary provisions in Schedule 3 to this Act shall have effect.

81A.— Expenses recoverable from owner to be a charge on premises.

A9–05 (1) Where any expenses are recoverable under section 81(4) above from a person who is the owner of the premises there mentioned and the local authority serves a notice on him under this section—

    (a) the expenses shall carry interest, at such reasonable rate as the local authority may determine, from the date of service of the notice until the whole amount is paid, and

    (b) subject to the following provisions of this section, the expenses and accrued interest shall be a charge on the premises.

(2) A notice served under this section shall—

    (a) specify the amount of the expenses that the local authority claims is recoverable,

    (b) state the effect of subsection (1) above and the rate of interest determined by the local authority under that subsection, and

    (c) state the effect of subsections (4) to (6) below.

(3) On the date on which a local authority serves a notice on a person under this section the authority shall also serve a copy of the notice on every other person who, to the knowledge of the authority, has an interest in the premises capable of being affected by the charge.

(4) Subject to any order under subsection (7)(b) or (c) below, the amount of any expenses specified in a notice under this section and the accrued interest shall be a charge on the premises—

    (a) as from the end of the period of twenty-one days beginning with the date of service of the notice, or

    (b) where an appeal is brought under subsection (6) below, as from the final determination of the appeal,

until the expenses and interest are recovered.

(5) For the purposes of subsection (4) above, the withdrawal of an appeal has the same effect as a final determination of the appeal.

(6) A person served with a notice or copy of a notice under this section may appeal against the notice to the county court within the period of twenty-one days beginning with the date of service.

(7) On such an appeal the court may—

    (a)   confirm the notice without modification,

    (b)   order that the notice is to have effect with the substitution of a different amount for the amount originally specified in it, or

    (c)   order that the notice is to be of no effect.

(8) A local authority shall, for the purpose of enforcing a charge under this section, have all the same powers and remedies under the Law of Property Act 1925, and otherwise, as if it were a mortgagee by deed having powers of sale and lease, of accepting surrenders of leases and of appointing a receiver.

(9) In this section—

    "owner", in relation to any premises, means a person (other than a mortgagee not in possession) who, whether in his own right or as trustee for any other person, is entitled to receive the rack rent of the premises or, where the premises are not let at a rack rent, would be so entitled if they were so let, and

    " premises" does not include a vessel.

[(10) This section does not apply to Scotland.]

81B.— Payment of expenses by instalments.

(1) Where any expenses are a charge on premises under section 81A **A9–06** above, the local authority may by order declare the expenses to be payable with interest by instalments within the specified period, until the whole amount is paid.

(2) In subsection (1) above—

    " interest" means interest at the rate determined by the authority under section 81A(1) above, and

    " the specified period" means such period of thirty years or less from the date of service of the notice under section 81A above as is specified in the order.

(3) Subject to subsection (5) below, the instalments and interest, or any part of them, may be recovered from the owner or occupier for the time being of the premises.

(4) Any sums recovered from an occupier may be deducted by him from the rent of the premises.

(5) An occupier shall not be required to pay at any one time any sum greater than the aggregate of—

(a)   the amount that was due from him on account of rent at the date on which he was served with a demand from the local authority together with a notice requiring him not to pay rent to his landlord without deducting the sum demanded, and

(b)   the amount that has become due from him on account of rent since that date.

[(6) This section does not apply to Scotland.]

82.— Summary proceedings by persons aggrieved by statutory nuisances.

A9–07   (1) A magistrates' court may act under this section on a complaint or, in Scotland, the sheriff may act under this section on a summary application, made by any person on the ground that he is aggrieved by the existence of a statutory nuisance.

(2) If the magistrates' court or, in Scotland, the sheriff is satisfied that the alleged nuisance exists, or that although abated it is likely to recur on the same premises or, in the case of a nuisance within section 79(1)(ga) above, in the same street or, in Scotland, road, the court or the sheriff shall make an order for either or both of the following purposes—

(a)   requiring the defendant or, in Scotland, defender to abate the nuisance, within a time specified in the order, and to execute any works necessary for that purpose;

(b)   prohibiting a recurrence of the nuisance, and requiring the defendant or defender, within a time specified in the order, to execute any works necessary to prevent the recurrence;

and , in England and Wales, may also impose on the defendant a fine not exceeding level 5 on the standard scale.

(3) If the magistrates' court or the sheriff is satisfied that the alleged nuisance exists and is such as, in the opinion of the court or of the sheriff, to render premises unfit for human habitation, an order under subsection (2) above may prohibit the use of the premises for human habitation until the premises are, to the satisfaction of the court or of the sheriff, rendered fit for that purpose.

(4) Proceedings for an order under subsection (2) above shall be brought—

(a)   except in a case falling within paragraph (b), (c) or (d) below, against the person responsible for the nuisance;

(b)   where the nuisance arises from any defect of a structural character, against the owner of the premises;

(c)   where the person responsible for the nuisance cannot be found, against the owner or occupier of the premises.

(d)   in the case of a statutory nuisance within section 79(1)(ga) above caused by noise emitted from or caused by an unattended vehicle or unattended machinery or equipment, against the person responsible for the vehicle, machinery or equipment.

(5) Subject to subsection (5A) below, where more than one person is responsible for a statutory nuisance, subsections (1) to (4) above shall apply to each of those persons whether or not what any one of them is responsible for would by itself amount to a nuisance.

(5A) In relation to a statutory nuisance within section 79(1)(ga) above for which more than one person is responsible (whether or not what any one of those persons is responsible for would by itself amount to a nuisance), subsection (4)(a) above shall apply with the substitution of "each person responsible for the nuisance who can be found" for "the person responsible for the nuisance".

(5B) In relation to a statutory nuisance within section 79(1)(ga) above caused by noise emitted from or caused by an unattended vehicle or unattended machinery or equipment for which more than one person is responsible, subsection (4)(d) above shall apply with the substitution of "any person" for "the person" .

(6) Before instituting proceedings for an order under subsection (2) above against any person, the person aggrieved by the nuisance shall give to that person such notice in writing of his intention to bring the proceedings as is applicable to proceedings in respect of a nuisance of that description and the notice shall specify the matter complained of.

(7) The notice of the bringing of proceedings in respect of a statutory nuisance required by subsection (6) above which is applicable is—

(a) in the case of a nuisance falling within paragraph (g) or (ga) of section 79(1) above, not less than three days' notice; and

(b) in the case of a nuisance of any other description, not less than twenty-one days' notice;

but the Secretary of State may, by order, provide that this subsection shall have effect as if such period as is specified in the order were the minimum period of notice applicable to any description of statutory nuisance specified in the order.

(8) A person who, without reasonable excuse, contravenes any requirement or prohibition imposed by an order under subsection (2) above shall be guilty of an offence and liable on summary conviction to a fine not exceeding level 5 on the standard scale together with a further fine of an amount equal to one-tenth of that level for each day on which the offence continues after the conviction.

(9) Subject to subsection (10) below, in any proceedings for an offence under subsection (8) above in respect of a statutory nuisance it shall be a defence to prove that the best practicable means were used to prevent, or to counteract the effects of, the nuisance.

(10) The defence under subsection (9) above is not available—

(a)   in the case of a nuisance falling within paragraph (a), (d), (e), (f), (fa) or (g) of section 79(1) above except where the nuisance arises on industrial, trade or business premises; (aza) in the case of a nuisance falling within paragraph (fb) of section 79(1) above except where–
  (i)   the artificial light is emitted from industrial, trade or business premises, or
  (ii)   the artificial light (not being light to which sub-paragraph (i) applies) is emitted by lights used for the purpose only of illuminating an outdoor relevant sports facility;
(aa) in the case of a nuisance falling within paragraph (ga) of section 79(1) above except where the noise is emitted from or caused by a vehicle, machinery or equipment being used for industrial, trade or business purposes;
(b)   in the case of a nuisance falling within paragraph (b) of section 79(1) above except where the smoke is emitted from a chimney;
(c)   in the case of a nuisance falling within paragraph (c) or (h) of section 79(1) above; and
(d)   in the case of a nuisance which is such as to render the premises unfit for human habitation.

(10A) For the purposes of subsection (10)(aza) "relevant sports facility" has the same meaning as it has for the purposes of section 80(8)(aza).

(11) If a person is convicted of an offence under subsection (8) above, a magistrates' court or the sheriff may, after giving the local authority in whose area the nuisance has occurred an opportunity of being heard, direct the authority to do anything which the person convicted was required to do by the order to which the conviction relates.

(12) Where on the hearing of proceedings for an order under subsection (2) above it is proved that the alleged nuisance existed at the date of the making of the complaint or summary application, then, whether or not at the date of the hearing it still exists or is likely to recur, the court or the sheriff shall order the defendant or defender (or defendants or defenders in such proportions as appears fair and reasonable) to pay to the person bringing the proceedings such amount as the court or the sheriff considers reasonably sufficient to compensate him for any expenses properly incurred by him in the proceedings.

(13) If it appears to the magistrates' court or to the sheriff that neither the person responsible for the nuisance nor the owner or occupier of the premises or (as the case may be) the person responsible for the vehicle, machinery or equipment can be found the court or the sheriff may, after giving the local authority in whose area the nuisance has

occurred an opportunity of being heard, direct the authority to do anything which the court or the sheriff would have ordered that person to do.

Gas Safety (Installation and Use) Regulations

(SI 1998/2451)

Part F

Maintenance

36.— Duties of Landlords

A10–01 (1) In this regulation—

"landlord" means—

(a) in England and Wales—

    (i) where the relevant premises are occupied under a lease, the person for the time being entitled to the reversion expectant on that lease or who, apart from any statutory tenancy, would be entitled to possession of the premises; and

    (ii) where the relevant premises are occupied under a licence, the licensor, save that where the licensor is himself a tenant in respect of those premises, it means the person referred to in paragraph (i) above;

(b) in Scotland, the person for the time being entitled to the landlord's interest under a lease;

"lease" means—

(a) a lease for a term of less than 7 years; and

(b) a tenancy for a periodic term; and

(c) any statutory tenancy arising out of a lease or tenancy referred to in sub-paragraphs (a) or (b) above,

and in determining whether a lease is one which falls within sub-paragraph (a) above—

    (i) in England and Wales, any part of the term which falls before the grant shall be left out of account and the lease shall be treated as a lease for a term commencing with the grant;

    (ii) a lease which is determinable at the option of the lessor before the expiration of 7 years from the commencement of the term shall be treated as a lease for a term of less than 7 years;

  (iii) a lease (other than a lease to which sub-paragraph
    (b) above applies) shall not be treated as a lease for a
    term of less than 7 years if it confers on the lessee an
    option for renewal for a term which, together with the
    original term, amounts to 7 years or more; and
  (iv) a "lease" does not include a mortgage term;
 "relevant gas fitting" means—

(a) any gas appliance (other than an appliance which the tenant
is entitled to remove from the relevant premises) or any
installation pipework installed in any relevant premises;
and (b) any gas appliance or installation pipework which,
directly or indirectly, serves the relevant premises and which
either—

  (i) is installed in any part of premises in which the
    landlord has an estate or interest; or
  (ii) is owned by the landlord or is under his control,

except that it shall not include any gas appliance or installation
pipework exclusively used in a part of premises occupied for non-
residential purposes.

 "relevant premises" means premises or any part of premises
occupied, whether exclusively or not, for residential purposes
(such occupation being in consideration of money or money's
worth) under—
(a) a lease; or
(b) a licence;
 "statutory tenancy" means—
(a) in England and Wales, a statutory tenancy within the meaning
of the Rent Act 1997 and the Rent (Agriculture) Act 1976; and
(b) in Scotland, a statutory tenancy within the meaning of the Rent
(Scotland) Act 1984, a statutory assured tenancy within the
meaning of the Housing (Scotland) Act 1988 or a secure tenancy
within the meaning of the Housing (Scotland) Act 1987;
 "tenant" means a person who occupies relevant premises
being—
(a) in England and Wales—
  (i) where the relevant premises are so occupied under a
    lease, the person for the time being entitled to the term
    of that lease; and
  (ii) where the relevant premises are so occupied under a
    licence, the licensee;
(b) in Scotland, the person for the time being entitled to the
tenant's interest under a lease.
(2) Every landlord shall ensure that there is maintained in a safe
condition—

(a)   any relevant gas fitting; and

(b)   any flue which serves any relevant gas fitting,

so as to prevent the risk of injury to any person in lawful occupation or relevant premises.

(3) Without prejudice to the generality of paragraph (2) above, a landlord shall—

(a)   ensure that each appliance and flue to which that duty extends is checked for safety within 12 months of being installed and at intervals of not more than 12 months since it was last checked for safety (whether such check was made pursuant to these Regulations or not);

(b)   in the case of a lease commencing after the coming into force of these Regulations, ensure that each appliance and flue to which the duty extends has been checked for safety within a period of 12 months before the lease commences or has been or is so checked within 12 months after the appliance or flue has been installed, whichever is later; and

(c)   ensure that a record in respect of any appliance or flue so checked is made and retained for a period of 2 years from the date of that check, which record shall include the following information—

(i)   the date on which the appliance or flue was checked;

(ii)   the address of the premises at which the appliance or flue is installed;

(iii)   the name and address of the landlord of the premises (or, where appropriate, his agent) at which the appliance or flue is installed;

(iv)   a description of and the location of each appliance or flue checked;

(v)   any defect identified;

(vi)   any remedial action taken;

(vii)   confirmation that the check undertaken complies with the requirements of paragraph (9) below;

(viii) the name and signature of the individual carrying out the check; and

(ix)   the registration number with which that individual, or his employer, is registered with a body approved by the Executive for the purposes of regulation 3(3) of these Regulations.

(4) Every landlord shall ensure that any work in relation to a relevant gas fitting or any check of a gas appliance or flue carried out pursuant to paragraphs (2) or (3) above is carried out by, or by an employee of, a member of a class of person approved for the time being by the Health and Safety Executive for the purposes of regulation 3(3) of these Regulations.

(5) The record referred to in paragraph (3)(c) above, or a copy thereof, shall be made available upon request and upon reasonable notice for the inspection of any person in lawful occupation of relevant premises who may be affected by the use or operation of any appliance to which the record relates.

(6) Notwithstanding paragraph (5) above, every landlord shall ensure that—

(a) a copy of the record made pursuant to the requirements of paragraph (3)(c) above is given to each existing tenant of premises to which the record relates within 28 days of the date of the check; and

(b) a copy of the last record made in respect of each appliance or flue is given to any new tenant of premises to which the record relates before that tenant occupies those premises save that, in respect of a tenant whose right to occupy those premises is for a period not exceeding 28 days, a copy of the record may instead be prominently displayed within those premises. (7) Where there is no relevant gas appliance in any room occupied or to be occupied by the tenant in relevant premises, the landlord may, instead of ensuring that a copy of the record referred to in paragraph (6) above is given to the tenant, ensure that there is displayed in a prominent position in the premises (from such time as a copy would have been required to have been given to the tenant under that paragraph), a copy of the record with a statement endorsed on it that the tenant is entitled to have his own copy of the record on request to the landlord at an address specified in the statement; and on any such request being made, the landlord shall give to the tenant a copy of the record as soon as is practicable.

(8) A copy of the record given to a tenant pursuant to paragraph (6)(b) above need not contain a copy of the signature of the individual carrying out the check if the copy of the record contains a statement that another copy containing a copy of such signature is available for inspection by the tenant on request to the landlord at an address specified in the statement; and on any such request being made the landlord shall make such a copy available for inspection as soon as is practicable.

(9) A safety check carried out pursuant to paragraph (3) above shall include, but shall not be limited to, an examination of the matters referred to in sub-paragraphs (a) to (d) of regulation 26(9) of these Regulations.

(10) Nothing done or agreed to be done by a tenant of relevant premises or by any other person in lawful occupation of them in

relation to the maintenance or checking of a relevant gas fitting or flue in the premises (other than one in part of premises occupied for non-residential purposes) shall be taken into account in determining whether a landlord has discharged his obligations under this regulation (except in so far as it relates to access to that gas fitting or flue for the purposes of such maintenance or checking).

(11) Every landlord shall ensure that in any room occupied or to be occupied as sleeping accommodation by a tenant in relevant premises there is not fitted a relevant gas fitting of a type the installation of which would contravene regulation 30(2) or (3) of these Regulations.

(12) Paragraph (11) above shall not apply in relation to a room which since before the coming into force of these Regulation has been occupied or intended to be occupied as sleeping accommodation.

Housing Act 2004 c.34

CHAPTER 1 ENFORCEMENT OF HOUSING STANDARDS: GENERAL

New system for assessing housing conditions

1.— New system for assessing housing conditions and enforcing housing standards

(1) This Part provides–   **A11–01**

   (a) for a new system of assessing the condition of residential premises, and

   (b) for that system to be used in the enforcement of housing standards in relation to such premises.

(2) The new system–

   (a) operates by reference to the existence of category 1 or category 2 hazards on residential premises (see section 2), and

   (b) replaces the existing system based on the test of fitness for human habitation contained in section 604 of the Housing Act 1985 (c. 68).

(3) The kinds of enforcement action which are to involve the use of the new system are–

   (a) the new kinds of enforcement action contained in Chapter 2 (improvement notices, prohibition orders and hazard awareness notices),

   (b) the new emergency measures contained in Chapter 3 (emergency remedial action and emergency prohibition orders), and

   (c) the existing kinds of enforcement action dealt with in Chapter 4 (demolition orders and slum clearance declarations).

(4) In this Part " residential premises" means–

   (a) a dwelling;

   (b) an HMO;

   (c) unoccupied HMO accommodation;

   (d) any common parts of a building containing one or more flats.

(5) In this Part– "building containing one or more flats" does not include an HMO;

"common parts" , in relation to a building containing one or more flats, includes–

(a) the structure and exterior of the building, and

(b) common facilities provided (whether or not in the building) for persons who include the occupiers of one or more of the flats;

"dwelling" means a building or part of a building occupied or intended to be occupied as a separate dwelling;

"external common parts", in relation to a building containing one or more flats, means common parts of the building which are outside it;

"flat" means a separate set of premises (whether or not on the same floor)–

(a) which forms part of a building,

(b) which is constructed or adapted for use for the purposes of a dwelling, and

(c) either the whole or a material part of which lies above or below some other part of the building;

"HMO" means a house in multiple occupation as defined by sections 254 to 259, as they have effect for the purposes of this Part (that is, without the exclusions contained in Schedule 14);

"unoccupied HMO accommodation" means a building or part of a building constructed or adapted for use as a house in multiple occupation but for the time being either unoccupied or only occupied by persons who form a single household.

(6) In this Part any reference to a dwelling, an HMO or a building containing one or more flats includes (where the context permits) any yard, garden, outhouses and appurtenances belonging to, or usually enjoyed with, the dwelling, HMO or building (or any part of it).

(7) The following indicates how this Part applies to flats–

(a) references to a dwelling or an HMO include a dwelling or HMO which is a flat (as defined by subsection (5)); and

(b) subsection (6) applies in relation to such a dwelling or HMO as it applies in relation to other dwellings or HMOs (but it is not to be taken as referring to any common parts of the building containing the flat).

(8) This Part applies to unoccupied HMO accommodation as it applies to an HMO, and references to an HMO in subsections (6) and (7) and in the following provisions of this Part are to be read accordingly.

2.— Meaning of " category 1 hazard" and " category 2 hazard"
(1) In this Act–   **A11–02**

"category 1 hazard" means a hazard of a prescribed description which falls within a prescribed band as a result of achieving, under a prescribed method for calculating the seriousness of hazards of that description, a numerical score of or above a prescribed amount;

"category 2 hazard" means a hazard of a prescribed description which falls within a prescribed band as a result of achieving, under a prescribed method for calculating the seriousness of hazards of that description, a numerical score below the minimum amount prescribed for a category 1 hazard of that description; and

"hazard" means any risk of harm to the health or safety of an actual or potential occupier of a dwelling or HMO which arises from a deficiency in the dwelling or HMO or in any building or land in the vicinity (whether the deficiency arises as a result of the construction of any building, an absence of maintenance or repair, or otherwise).

(2) In subsection (1)–

"prescribed" means prescribed by regulations made by the appropriate national authority (see section 261(1)); and

"prescribed band" means a band so prescribed for a category 1 hazard or a category 2 hazard, as the case may be.

(3) Regulations under this section may, in particular, prescribe a method for calculating the seriousness of hazards which takes into account both the likelihood of the harm occurring and the severity of the harm if it were to occur.

(4) In this section–

"building" includes part of a building;

"harm" includes temporary harm.

(5) In this Act "health" includes mental health.

Procedure for assessing housing conditions

3.— Local housing authorities to review housing conditions in their districts

A11–03 (1) A local housing authority must keep the housing conditions in their area under review with a view to identifying any action that may need to be taken by them under any of the provisions mentioned in subsection (2).

(2) The provisions are–
(a)   the following provisions of this Act–
(i)   this Part,
(ii)   Part 2 (licensing of HMOs),
(iii)   Part 3 (selective licensing of other houses), and
(iv)   Chapters 1 and 2 of Part 4 (management orders);
(b)   Part 9 of the Housing Act 1985 (c. 68) (demolition orders and slum clearance);
(c)   Part 7 of the Local Government and Housing Act 1989 (c. 42) (renewal areas); and
(d)   article 3 of the Regulatory Reform (Housing Assistance) (England and Wales) Order 2002 (S.I. 2002/1860).

(3) For the purpose of carrying out their duty under subsection (1) a local housing authority and their officers must–
(a)   comply with any directions that may be given by the appropriate national authority, and
(b)   keep such records, and supply the appropriate national authority with such information, as that authority may specify.

[…]

PART 7

SUPPLEMENTARY AND FINAL PROVISIONS

Meaning of "house in multiple occupation"

254.— Meaning of "house in multiple occupation"

A11–04 (1) For the purposes of this Act a building or a part of a building is a " house in multiple occupation" if–
(a)   it meets the conditions in subsection (2) ("the standard test");
(b)   it meets the conditions in subsection (3) ("the self-contained flat test");

(c) it meets the conditions in subsection (4) ("the converted building test");

(d) an HMO declaration is in force in respect of it under section 255; or

(e) it is a converted block of flats to which section 257 applies.

(2) A building or a part of a building meets the standard test if–

(a) it consists of one or more units of living accommodation not consisting of a self-contained flat or flats;

(b) the living accommodation is occupied by persons who do not form a single household (see section 258);

(c) the living accommodation is occupied by those persons as their only or main residence or they are to be treated as so occupying it (see section 259);

(d) their occupation of the living accommodation constitutes the only use of that accommodation;

(e) rents are payable or other consideration is to be provided in respect of at least one of those persons' occupation of the living accommodation; and

(f) two or more of the households who occupy the living accommodation share one or more basic amenities or the living accommodation is lacking in one or more basic amenities.

(3) A part of a building meets the self-contained flat test if–

(a) it consists of a self-contained flat; and

(b) paragraphs (b) to (f) of subsection (2) apply (reading references to the living accommodation concerned as references to the flat). (4) A building or a part of a building meets the converted building test if–

(a) it is a converted building;

(b) it contains one or more units of living accommodation that do not consist of a self-contained flat or flats (whether or not it also contains any such flat or flats);

(c) the living accommodation is occupied by persons who do not form a single household (see section 258);

(d) the living accommodation is occupied by those persons as their only or main residence or they are to be treated as so occupying it (see section 259);

(e) their occupation of the living accommodation constitutes the only use of that accommodation; and

(f) rents are payable or other consideration is to be provided in respect of at least one of those persons' occupation of the living accommodation.

(5) But for any purposes of this Act (other than those of Part 1) a building or part of a building within subsection (1) is not a house in multiple occupation if it is listed in Schedule 14.

(6) The appropriate national authority may by regulations–

    (a)   make such amendments of this section and sections 255 to 259 as the authority considers appropriate with a view to securing that any building or part of a building of a description specified in the regulations is or is not to be a house in multiple occupation for any specified purposes of this Act;

    (b)   provide for such amendments to have effect also for the purposes of definitions in other enactments that operate by reference to this Act;

    (c)   make such consequential amendments of any provision of this Act, or any other enactment, as the authority considers appropriate.

(7) Regulations under subsection (6) may frame any description by reference to any matters or circumstances whatever.

(8) In this section–

    "basic amenities" means–

    (a)   a toilet,

    (b)   personal washing facilities, or

    (c)   cooking facilities;

    "converted building" means a building or part of a building consisting of living accommodation in which one or more units of such accommodation have been created since the building or part was constructed;

    "enactment" includes an enactment comprised in subordinate legislation (within the meaning of the Interpretation Act 1978 (c.30); "self-contained flat" means a separate set of premises (whether or not on the same floor)–

    (a)   which forms part of a building;

    (b)   either the whole or a material part of which lies above or below some other part of the building; and

    (c)   in which all three basic amenities are available for the exclusive use of its occupants.

APPENDIX B – PRECEDENTS

Appendix B1

SCHEDULE 2

Precedents

Section 146 notice B1–01

To: *(name of tenant)*

[of *(address)* *(or as appropriate)* whose registered office is at *(address)*]

By a Lease made on *(date)* between (1) *(name of (original) landlord)* and (2) *(name of (original) tenant)* ('the Lease') of *(describe premises)* ('the Premises') were let to the tenant for a term of ....

I, *(name of landlord)*, [of *(address)* *(or as appropriate)* whose registered office is at *(address)*], the [current] landlord of the Premises under the Lease **GIVE YOU NOTICE** as follows:—

1   The Lease contains [a covenant *(or as appropriate)* covenants] by the tenant [not] to *(insert details of relevant covenants)*.

2   There [has been a breach *(or as appropriate)* have been breaches] of the covenant[s] in that *(insert details)*.

3   [All the *(or as appropriate)* The] matter[s] complained of in paragraph 2 above constitute[s] [a breach *(or as appropriate)* breaches] of covenant that [is *(or as appropriate)* are] incapable of remedy.

4   You are required to pay compensation in money for the breach[es] and also to pay [pursuant to clause *(number of clause requiring payment of landlord's costs of notices etc)* of the Lease] all costs, fees, charges, disbursements and expenses incurred by me, and any VAT payable on them, in relation or incidental to the preparation and service of this notice.

5   At the end of *(state period, e.g. 14 days)* from the date of this notice I intend to enforce the right of re-entry or forfeiture that has arisen by reason of the facts set out in this notice by action or otherwise and also claim damages.

Dated: *(date)*

Signed: *(signature of, or on behalf of, the landlord)*

(on duplicate)

Received a notice of which the above is a true copy.

Dated: *(date)*

Signed: *(signature of, or on behalf of, the tenant)*

APPENDIX B2

Part 8 claim under Leasehold Property Repairs Act 1938, to be **B2–01**
accompanied by a detailed witness statement in support.

<u>**IN THE LAMBTON COUNTY COURT**</u>   <u>**Claim no:**</u>

<u>**BETWEEN:-**</u>

ABC LIMITED

<u>**Claimant**</u>

and

SUMMERS RETAIL LIMITED

<u>**Defendant**</u>

DETAILS OF CLAIM

1.   This claim is brought under Part 8 of the CPR.   **B2–02**
2.   The Claimant claims relief under the Leasehold Property
      (Repairs) Act 1938.
3.   The Claimant seeks the following relief:
a.   An order that the claimant should have permission to issue a
      claim under section 1 (3) of the said Act;
b.   An order that the Claimant should be entitled to its reasonable
      costs of forfeiture pursuant to section 2 of the said Act
      together with the costs of this claim.
4.   The legal basis of the claim is as follows:
a.   The Claimant is the freehold owner of 1 Parkside Road,
      Wormwood Road, Lambton ("the Property")
b.   The Property was demised to the Claimant by a lease dated
      1st January 2000 for a term of 23 years from 20th April 1999
      ("the Lease");
c.   The rent was £7,200 per annum payable quarterly in advance
      on the usual quarter days;
d.   By clause 2 (d) the Defendant covenanted to keep the
      Property in repair throughout the term;
e.   There was a proviso for re-entry in the event that the
      Defendant failed to comply with the covenants and conditions
      in the lease;
f.   On 1st December 2007 the Claimant served a notice under

section 146 of the Law of Property Act 1925 ("146 notice");

g. On 23rd January 2007 the Defendant served a notice pursuant to section 1 of the 1938 Act to the effect that he claimed the benefit of the 1938 Act;

h. A substantial diminution in value will occur to the Property if the Defendant's breaches of covenant as specified in the 146 notice are not remedied;

i. Accordingly the Claimant seeks an order that the Claimant be allowed to proceed with the forfeiture of the lease in accordance with the covenants and conditions therein;

j. Further it is just and equitable to permit the Claimant to proceed with the forfeiture for the reasons stated in the statement of Peter Rarebit which accompanies this claim;

And the Claimant claims leave to proceed to forfeit the Lease pursuant to section 1 of the 1938 Act and in particular a declaration that one or more of the grounds specified in section 1 (5) of the 1938 are satisfied and for the further and other relief.

STATEMENT OF TRUTH

B2–03 Forfeiture claim

IN THE LAMBTON COUNTY COURT   Claim no:

BETWEEN:-

HOPE LIMITED

Claimant

and

SERVILE LIMITED

Defendant

Appendix B3

PARTICULARS OF CLAIM

1. The Claimant, a registered company (Company Registration **B3–01** 1234567) whose address is at Hope Parade, Hope Road, London N5, is the leasehold owner of 176a-178b Biggin Hill, London SW1.

2. The Claimant's leasehold title was created by an underlease dated 11th February 1997 between Saver Stores Limited and Mr Timothy Fairdeal ("the First Underlease") by which the Premises were demised to Timothy Fairdeal for a term of 125 years from 11th February 1997. The Claimant is the assignee of the lease to Timothy Fairdeal. The Claimant's leasehold title is registered at HM Land Registry under title number LAM 987654.

3. By an underlease ("the Second Underlease") dated 2nd June 1999 Timothy Fairdeal granted Battersea Dogs and Cats Housing Trust Limited a 21-year term plus 1 day of 178a Biggin Hill, London SW1 ("the Premises"). The Claimant is now the owner of the leasehold reversion immediately expectant upon the term in the Second Underlease following an assignment dated 23rd February 2000.

4. The Defendant's leasehold title to the Premises is registered at HM Land Registry under Title No: ABC 123456. The Defendant is the assignee of the remainder of the term granted by the Second Underlease to Battersea Dogs and Cats Housing Trust Limited by the said Timothy Fairdeal pursuant to an assignment details of which are not within the Claimant's knowledge.

5. The Second Underlease, a true copy of which is attached, provided as follows:

    (i) Under Clause 1 of the Second Underlease that the premises were demised in consideration of the rent and covenants reserved and contained therein excepting and reserving unto the lessor the rights reserved in the third Schedule. The Second Underlessee agreed to yield and pay an initial rent of £3,087 by instalments after completion of a specification of works dated 11th February 1997 by monthly instalments, initially, of £307.29. The current passing rent in the Second Underlease is £60.

(ii)   Under clause 2(1) of the Second Underlease the tenant agreed to pay the service charge by way of further or additional rent as a proper part of the expenses and outgoings incurred by lessor or on behalf of the lessor in repairing, maintaining or renewing the building of which the premises formed part as well as the other heads of expenditure set out in the Second Underlease.

(iii)   Under clause 4 the Second Underlease provided that if the said rents or any part thereof were unpaid for 21 days after any of the days they became due for payment, whether those payments were lawfully demanded or not, if the tenant neglected or refused to pay or any of the covenants, conditions or agreements contained in the Second Underlease where not complied with, it was to be lawful for the lessor or any of the lessor's duly authorised agents to re-enter the premises and peacefully re-possess the same.

6.   On 20th May 2008 an invoice was sent by the Claimant to the Defendant demanding payment of unpaid rent and service charge including insurance rent. The said invoice was in respect of the Premises and other premises demised to the Defendant.

7.   A further demand for payment of rent and service charges was made on 1st July 2008 and in addition a request for payment of legal costs was made.

8.   The Defendant has neglected or refused to pay any of the arrears of rent or service charges due and accordingly, the Claimant desires to forfeit the Second Underlease. By reason of the failure to pay rent and service charges and by issue of this claim the Claimant hereby forfeits the lease and claims possession of the premises.

9.   As at the date of the issue of this claim the state of the arrears of rent and service charges on the Defendant's account were as follows:

PARTICULARS

B3–02

(i)	Rent due for the period to	£ .
(ii)	Services charges due for the period to	£ .
(iii)	Interest thereon	£ .
	Total	£..........

8.   To the best of the Claimant's knowledge only the Defendant is in occupation of the Premises.

9.   The Claimant claims interest upon all arrears of rent and service charges at the rate of 8% from (Instructing Solicitors

to insert date that each payments originally became due) to the date of issue of this claim in the sum of £   a n d thereafter to continue at a daily rate of £   until judgment or earlier payment pursuant to Section 69 of the County Courts Act 1984.

AND the Claimant claims:

1.   Possession of the premises;
2.   Unpaid rent including services charges of £;
3.   Mesne profits of £ per day from the date of service of this claim until possession is yielded up;
4.   Interest thereon;
5.   Costs.

Brair Lapin

STATEMENT OF TRUTH

The Claimant believes that the facts stated in these Particulars of **B3–03** Claim are true.

Signed..

Dated this   day of   2008

<u>IN THE LAMBTON COUNTY COURT</u>   **<u>Claim no:</u>**

<u>BETWEEN:-</u>

HOPE LIMITED

<u>Claimant</u>

and

SERVILE LIMITED

<u>Defendant</u>

PARTICULARS OF CLAIM

COUNSEL:

Brair Lapin

Defence to forfeiture claim by landlord based on unlawful alterations **B4–01**
and other breaches seeking relief from forfeiture

IN THE SOUTH MIMMS COUNTY COURT   **Claim no:**

BETWEEN:-

ISAAC HATEMAN

Claimant

and

FB (SOUTHERN) LIMITED

Defendant

DEFENCE AND COUNTERCLAIM

DEFENCE

1. The Defendant admits that the Claimant is the freehold
    owner of the Land.
2. The Defendant admits the Lease and the covenants recited in
    paragraphs 2-4 of the Particulars of Claim.
3. So far as paragraph 5 of the Particulars of Claim is concerned,
    insofar as the covenants are still relevant and have not been
    waived it is admitted they would still be enforceable by the
    landlord.
4. So far as paragraph 6 of the Particulars of Claim is concerned,
    the Defendant acquired its leasehold title following a large-
    scale voluntary transfer from the Council of the City of
    Bognor on 27th July 1999 to South Mimms Housing Trust
    Ltd. On 31st July 2007 the Lease was transferred to FB
    (Southern) Ltd.
5. It is admitted that by a letter dated 1st August 2007 the
    Claimant purported to serve a notice under Section 146 of
    the Law of Property Act 1925. No admissions are made as to
    the validity of the same. It is further admitted that by a letter
    from Fobb and Co Solicitors dated 25th February 2008 to the
    Solicitors acting on the Claimant's behalf purported to serve
    a further notice under that section. No admissions are made
    as to the validity of that notice either.

6. Save that it is admitted and averred that the Defendant was the registered as the leasehold proprietor of the Land edged red on the plan annexed hereto under title number AB123456 on the date specified and that the Defendant acquired the remainder of the term of the Lease by assignment from South Mimms Housing Trust, paragraph 9 of the Particulars of Claim is not admitted.

7. Without prejudice to the foregoing, paragraph 11 is admitted.

8. As to the substance of the alleged breaches of covenant giving rise to a cause for forfeiture the Defendant says as follows in relation to the covenants in the Lease:

    (i) It is not admitted that the covenant recited at paragraph 3(i) of the Particulars of Claim can be construed as placing an obligation on the tenant to substantially repair any of the demised premises.

    (ii) As to the covenant at paragraph 3 (ii) of the Particulars of Claim it would have been unreasonable for the Claimant to refuse consent to such alterations as were proposed.

    (iii) As to paragraph 3 (iii) of the Particulars of Claim no change of user is proposed, the Land is to continue to be used for the purpose of private dwelling houses.

    (iv) The Defendant denies any breach of the covenant recited at paragraph 3 (iv) of the Particulars of Claim.

9. If, which is denied, the Claimant is entitled to avail himself of a cause for forfeiture against the Defendant the Defendant relies on its Counterclaim to relief therefrom.

COUNTERCLAIM

B4–02 10. The Defendant repeats paragraphs 1-9.

11. If, which is denied, the Claimant is entitled to forfeit the Defendant claims to be relieved therefrom under section 146(2) of the Law of Property Act 1925 or otherwise upon such terms as the Court thinks fit and to retain possession of the Land having regard, inter alia, to the following:

    (i) The fact that if the Defendant is not given relief it will cause hardship to itself and its tenants;

    (ii) Reinstatement of the altered buildings to their former state would be expensive and wasteful;

    (iii) The fact that in relation to the qualified covenants recited at paragraph 3(ii)-(iv) the Claimant would have consented to the proposed works if they fell within those covenants;

(iv)   The absence of any long-term damage to the value of the Claimant's reversion;

(v)   The fact that the Defendant's breach would not have been wilful;

(vi)   The fact that the damage sustained by the Defendant if relief is refused is disproportionate to the damage sustained to the Claimant.

12.   In addition to the Defendant the following sub-tenants may be entitled to apply for relief against forfeiture [insert a list or Schedule to the Defence]

AND the Defendant Counterclaims for:

(i)   Relief against forfeiture;

(ii)   A declaration that the Lease continues;

(iii)   An order for costs.

W E Gladstone

STATEMENT OF TRUTH

I believe/the Defendant believes that the contents of this Defence are **B4–03** true.

I am duly authorised by the Defendant to sign this agreement on its behalf

Signed...

Dated this   day of   2008

IN THE SOUTH MIMMS COUNTY COURT   **Claim no:**

BETWEEN:-

ISAAC HATEMAN

Claimant

and

FB (SOUTHERN) LIMITED

Defendant

DEFENCE AND COUNTERCLAIM

COUNSEL:

W E Gladstone

B5–01 Particulars of dilapidations claim by landlord

IN THE HIGH COURT OF JUSTICE
QUEEN'S BENCH DIVISION
TECHNOLOGY AND CONSTRUCTION COURT

Claim No.
[HC/HQ] ...
Claimant

FRANK TOPPING

Claimant

and

ABC DILAPIDATION CLAIMS LIMITED

Defendant

PARTICULARS OF CLAIM

B5–02

1. By a lease dated .... 20... and made between the Claimant and the Defendant the premises known as (address) were demised to the Defendant for a term of ... years from .... 20... at the rent of £...... a year and such further sums as were therein mentioned.

2. By the lease the Defendant covenanted with the Claimant (inter alia) as follows:

   (1) to repair the demised premises throughout the term including the drains and sanitary and water apparatus and electrical equipment boiler and central heating.

   (2) to yield up those premises in the state of repair referred to at the termination of the Lease.

3. In breach of the said covenants contained in the Lease the Defendant has failed to keep the premises in repair in the manner thereby provided or at all. Full particulars of the said breaches were set out in a schedule of dilapidations annexed to the notice referred to in the next paragraph hereof.

4. On .... 20... the Claimant caused a notice in accordance with the provisions of Section 146 of the Law of Property Act 1925 to be served on the Defendant specifying the said breaches and requiring the Defendant to remedy them, yet the Defendant has failed to remedy them or any of them within [the time specified in the said notice or a reasonable time]

or at all. [Or insert details of the dilapidations present at the termination date and allege a failure to yield up in repair].

5. By reason of the matters aforesaid the Claimant has suffered damage and the value of the reversion expectant on the termination of the lease has been greatly diminished by the Defendant's failure to perform the covenants contained in the lease.

6. The claimant claims interest pursuant to section 35A of the Supreme Court Act 1981 for such period and at such rate as the court shall consider just and equitable.

AND the Claimant claims:

  (1) Damages;

  (2) Interest under paragraph 6 hereof.

Igor Counsel

Dated .... 20...

STATEMENT OF TRUTH

[I believe or The Claimant believes] that the facts stated in these **B5–03** Particulars of Claim are true.

[I am duly authorised by the Claimant to sign this Statement.]

Full name ....

(Signature)

(indicate in what capacity e.g. claimant or claimant's solicitor)

[Position or office held .... (if signing on behalf of firm or company)]

Address for receiving documents

(name and address of claimant's solicitors or as the case may be)

APPENDIX B6

SCOTT SCHEDULE

IN THE HIGH COURT OF JUSTICE
QUEEN'S BENCH DIVISION
TECHNOLOGY AND CONSTRUCTION COURT

<u>**Claim no. HT/01- …**</u>

Before His Honour Judge .... QC

<u>**Claimant**</u>

FRANK TOPPING

and

<u>**Defendant**</u>

ABC DILAPIDATION CLAIMS LIMITED

Scott Schedule served pursuant to the Order of His Honour Judge
.... QC
Dated .... 20…

DILAPIDATIONS

Item No.	Disrepair (include reference to clause in lease	Claimed cost of repair	Defendant's comments on disrepair	Defendant's cost of repair	Judge's column

Appendix B7

B7–01

IN THE HIGH COURT OF JUSTICE
QUEEN'S BENCH DIVISION
TECHNOLOGY AND CONSTRUCTION COURT

Claim No. [HC/HQ] …

Claimant

FRANK TOPPING

and

Defendant

ABC DILAPIDATION CLAIMS LIMITED

DEFENCE

1. The Defendant admits paragraphs 1 and 2 of the Particulars **B7–02** of Claim but denies that he is in breach of covenant as alleged or at all.

2. If, which is denied, the premises were in the condition alleged in the schedule of dilapidations referred to in paragraph 3 of the Particulars of Claim, that condition was due to an inherent defect in the construction of the premises, namely the absence of any or any adequate damp-proof course. Accordingly the Defendant is being asked to carry out [pay for as the case may be] an improvement not a repair. The Claimant will rely on expert evidence in support.

3. Further and in any event the Claimant has not suffered any damage to his reversion: he has demolished the premises, and would have done so on the termination of the Defendant's lease thereof in whatever condition they were in.

Robert Temple

Dated ……… 20…

STATEMENT OF TRUTH

B7–03 [I believe or The Defendant believes] that the facts stated in this Defence are true.

[I am duly authorised by the Defendant to sign this Statement.]

Full name ....

(Signature)

(indicate position or office held if signing on behalf of firm or company)

Address for receiving documents

(name and address of defendant's solicitors or as the case may be)

APPENDIX B8

<u>IN THE HIGH COURT OF JUSTICE</u>
<u>QUEEN'S BENCH DIVISION</u>
<u>TECHNOLOGY AND CONSTRUCTION COURT</u>

<u>Claim No. [HC/HQ] ...</u>

<u>**Claimant**</u>

FRANK TOPPING

and

<u>**Defendant**</u>

ABC DILAPIDATION CLAIMS LIMITED

REQUEST FOR INFORMATION

B8–02 Under paragraph

   1.   (identify any items that are insufficiently particularised and any details of the extent of the landlord's damaged reversion)

ROBERT TEMPLE

The defendant asks for a response to this request within 21 days
The address for serving the replies is:

Details of defendant's solicitors:

B8–03 Part 7 claim under the s.4 DPA 1972 and under section 11 of the LTA 1985 including claim for damages for personal injury

IN THE KINGSWAY ON SEA COUNTY COURT

Case No. KS101911

BETWEEN:-

PAUL ORELLY (1)

JOYCE LOFA (2)

Claimants

- and -

NORTH WAUDBY HOUSING ACTION TRUST

Defendant

PARTICULARS OF CLAIM

1. At all material times save as set out below the First and **B9–01** Second Claimants have been the secure tenants or otherwise the lawful occupiers of the house let to them by the Defendant at 111 Beethovenstrasse, North Hull, Hull ("the premises").

2. The Claimants temporarily vacated the premises between about December 1997 and early March 1998 while the Defendant carried out works of repair and improvement therein. Subsequently the Defendant transferred its freehold title in the premises to Kingsway City Council with effect from on or about 7th September 1998.

3. The tenancy agreement is subject to the implied covenant to repair set out at Section 11 of the Landlord and Tenant Act 1985. Additionally and alternatively, a covenant to a similar effect is an express term of the agreement.

4. Also, the said agreement is subject to an implied covenant that any works done to or at the premises by the Defendant, its servants or agents, would be carried out to a reasonably professional or workmanlike standard and in a reasonably professional or workmanlike manner.

5. Yet further and by virtue of the above, the Defendant owes the Claimants the duty of care set out at section 4 of the Defective Premises Act 1972.

6. The Defendant has been in breach of the above terms, obligations and duties.

Particulars

(i) Works had been carried out by the Defendant to the **B9–02** open fireplace and its flue in the premises' sitting room between about December 1997 and March 1998: alternatively, the Defendant had identified that work or further work needed to be done to the fireplace and flue during or about that same period.

(ii) The said works were either carried out defectively or were not carried out, whether in full or in part, as planned; the result was that the fireplace and flue were not left in proper working order.

(iii) Further to the sub-paragraphs above, the Claimants rely on the Statement of Leslie Dewdrop dated 17th

April 1999 (attached, as the First Schedule to the Particulars of Claim), and the Report of Bob Copper dated June 1999 (attached as the Second Schedule) in setting out particulars of the defects to the fireplace and flue.

(iv) The Defendant, its servants or agents, failed to install safely, and/or subsequently to check adequately or properly the safety of the fire, which from when it was first used upon the Claimants' return to the premises spilled noxious products of combustion into the room when alight: further or alternatively,

(v) The Defendant failed to arrange promptly or at all for the foregoing to be carried out, further or alternatively;

(vi) The Defendant, its servants or agents, failed in all the circumstances to ensure that the said fire was safe to use.

7. The Defendant, by its servants and/or agents, knew or in all the circumstances ought to have known of the defects set out above, by reason of the Claimants' reports to its local housing office of apparent problems with the fire from March 1998 onwards; from its own servants' and/or agents' attendances at the premises (particularly when inspecting and working upon the said fireplace and flue); and from its obligations under the repairing covenant.

8. By reason of the foregoing breaches of terms, duties and obligations by the Defendant, the Claimants have suffered loss and damage, discomfort, distress and inconvenience; and the value of the tenancy to the 1st and 2nd Claimants was diminished by an amount equivalent to 25% of the contractual rent from about March 1998 until about September 1998.

Particulars of Personal Injury

B9–03 The Claimants' dates of birth are as follows: 1st: 19/7/50, 2nd: 5/11/58. Both of the Claimants suffered from significant discomfort and ill-health as a result of persistent and frequent headaches, lethargy, and 'flu-like symptoms generally, caused by chronic low-level carbon monoxide poisoning over the period set out above, although with decreased use of the fire in summer their symptoms abated. The Claimants did seek medical advice at the time of their symptoms, but did not specifically relate their symptoms to their GP at the time. All the said symptoms cleared up completely after works were carried out to the fire in

September 1998. The Medical Reports of Mr P. Grout, Consultant in Accident & Emergency medicine, and both dated 31/7/98, are attached as the 3rd and 4th Schedules to the Particulars of Claim.

9. Further, the Claimants claim interest pursuant to Section 69 of the County Court Act 1984 for such periods and at such rates as the court thinks fit, on the sums found due to them.

AND the Claimants claim:

(i)   Damages exceeding £1,000 but not exceeding £5,000 for each Claimant

(ii)   Interest pursuant to statute

Simone Beavor

STATEMENT OF TRUTH

The Claimants believe that the facts stated in these particulars of **B9–04** claim are true. I am duly authorised by the Claimants to sign this statement.

Full name: [   ]

Name of Claimant's solicitor's firm: Nell Cudgell Solicitors

Signed: [   ]

Claimants' solicitor

Claimants' solicitors' address:

Neil Cudgell Solicitors, 530 Holders Road,   Humbler by Sea 3DT

DX: 1234321 Kingsway East

APPENDIX B10

B10–01 Defence to possession claim on grounds that tenant has failed to maintain in decorative repair and counterclaim that landlord in breach of section 11 LTA 1985

<u>**Case No. BYO911**</u>

IN THE BARNLEY COUNTY COURT

BETWEEN:-

BARNLEY METROPOLITAN DISTRICT COUNCIL

<u>**Claimant**</u>

and

DARREN HARDEN

<u>**First Defendant**</u>

and

KATRINA KNIGHT

<u>**Second Defendant**</u>

DEFENCE AND COUNTERCLAIM

DEFENCE

B10–02
1. To avoid repetition the Defendants plead to the Claimant's full Particulars of Claim and not to Form N119.
2. Save that it is denied that the Claimant is entitled to possession of the dwellinghouse, paragraph 1 of the Particulars of Claim is admitted.
3. Paragraph 2 of the Particulars of Claim is admitted.
4. Paragraph 3 of the Particulars of Claim is denied. The rent currently payable in respect of the said tenancy is £35.54 per week which the Defendants pay with the assistance of Housing Benefit.
5. Paragraph 4 of the Particulars of Claim is not admitted.
6. It is denied that the Claimant is entitled to possession on the grounds alleged in paragraph 5 of the Particulars of Claim or at all.
7. It is admitted that the Claimant's standard tenancy regulations contain Regulation No. 8 in the terms set out in paragraph 6 of the Particulars of Claim. It is denied that the Defendants

failed to maintain the interior decoration at the tenancy premises to an acceptable standard or that the majority of the rooms at the tenancy premises were in a poor state of decoration and cleanliness. In particular the Defendants aver:

a. that all rooms on the ground floor of the dwellinghouse are adequately decorated;

b. that the stairs and landing are adequately decorated;

c. that the rear left bedroom and the front bedroom on the first floor have cracking to plaster requiring repair by the Claimant which would disturb any decoration carried out beforehand;

d. the rear right bedroom to the first floor has antiquated electric wiring to the light fitting which is likely to require replacement with possible disturbance to decoration in the near future.

8. It is admitted that the Claimant's standard tenancy regulations contain a regulation in the terms set out in paragraph 7 of the Particulars of Claim.

9. It is denied that the Defendants have breached the said tenancy regulations alleged in paragraph 8 of the Particulars of Claim or at all.

10. Paragraph 9 of the Particulars of Claim is not admitted.

11. Paragraph 10 of the Particulars of Claim is denied.

12. Paragraph 11 of the Particulars of Claim is admitted.

13. It is denied that the Claimant is entitled to the relief claimed in paragraph 12 of the Particulars of Claim or any relief.

14. The Defendants aver that it would not be reasonable for the Court to make a possession order in all the circumstances of the case.

PARTICULARS

a. At the time of the commencement of the Defendants' tenancy **B10–03** the dwellinghouse required complete redecoration and the stripping of existing wallpaper. The Defendants' modest financial circumstances have made it necessary for them to carry out the redecoration in stages. The Defendants' circumstances were further reduced by the cost of installing necessary kitchen units (the kitchen containing only a sink unit at the time of the commencement of the tenancy) and painting the kitchen with fungicidal paint.

b. The Defendants' daughter Clarissa Harden, born on the 4th February 1993, suffers from glue ear and is very hard of hearing. At times the Defendants have to speak loudly or shout in order for Clarissa to hear them.

c.   Noise transmission between the dwellinghouse and the adjacent property occurs easily: the Defendants can hear their neighbours hoovering, using their washing machine, and speaking loudly.

d.   The Second Defendant suffers from hypertension which is exacerbated by stress: the making of a possession order would subject the Second Defendant to extreme stress and make it more difficult for her to cope with attempting to re-house herself and her family.

e.   The Defendants' daughter Kim Harden born on 4th January 1998 was born prematurely and has problems feeding: she would be particularly vulnerable if her family became homeless.

f.   The Defendants have no other accommodation available to them and do not have the means to put down a bond or deposit for accommodation in the private sector; if a possession order were made they would be at considerable risk of becoming homeless.

15.   Save as is hereinbefore expressly admitted the Defendants deny each and every allegation in the Particulars of Claim as if the same were herein set out and separately traversed.

16.   The Defendants further seek to set off against such sums, if any, as may become due from them to the claimant such sums as they may be awarded pursuant to their Counterclaim herein.

COUNTERCLAIM

B10–04   17. The Defendants' tenancy of the said dwellinghouse is subject to the following implied covenants on the part of the Claimant:

a.   To keep in repair the structure and exterior of the dwellinghouse, including drains, gutters and external pipes;

b.   To keep in repair and proper working order the installations in the dwellinghouse for the supply of water, gas and electricity, and for sanitation (including basins, sinks, baths and sanitary conveniences);

c.   To keep in repair and proper working order the installations in the dwellinghouse for space heating and heating water.

18.   Further at all material times the claimant has owed a duty to the Defendants their family and visitors to take such care as is reasonable in all the circumstances to see that they are safe from personal injury from damage to their property caused by any relevant defect which would, if the claimant had notice of it, constitute a breach of the Claimant's repairing obligations.

19. In breach of the said implied covenant and/or the said statutory duty the Claimant has allowed a state of disrepair to exist in the dwellinghouse.

PARTICULARS OF DISREPAIR

Full particulars of disrepair, which exceeds three folios, are **B10–05** contained in the First Schedule annexed hereto.

20. Notice of the said disrepair was given to the Claimant in the following manner:

a. by oral report made by the Defendants to the Claimant's servants or agents at the St. Edwin Area Housing Office at the time the Defendants signed the tenancy agreement for the dwellinghouse that the property suffered from dampness;

b. by further oral complaint made in or about 1997 to the Claimant's servant or agent at its Regent Street/St. Edwin office that the dwellinghouse was suffering from dampness;

c. by the Defendants permitting the Claimant's servant or agent one Sewell to visit the property on two occasions and inspect it;

d. by the Claimant's servants or agents carrying out inspection of the said dwellinghouse shortly before the commencement of the Defendant's tenancy thereof.

21. By reason of the matters aforesaid the Defendants have suffered loss and damage, inconvenience, discomfort and distress, and the value to them of their tenancy has been diminished.

PARTICULARS OF LOSS AND DAMAGE

Please refer to Second Schedule annexed hereto. **B10–06**

PARTICULARS OF INCONVENIENCE, DISCOMFORT AND DISTRESS

a. The dwellinghouse is cold, damp and uncomfortable;

b. The interior of the dwellinghouse, particularly the ground floor, is unsightly and provides a depressing environment in which to live;

c. The dwellinghouse is expensive to heat;

d. The Defendants have had to spend longer attempting to keep the dwellinghouse clean than they would have done if it were in repair;

e. The Defendants are embarrassed by conditions in the dwellinghouse and reluctant to entertain visitors there.

22. The Defendants further claim interest on such sums as may be awarded to them hereunder pursuant to section 69 of the County Courts Act 1984 at such rate and for such period as the Court shall think fit.

AND THE DEFENDANTS COUNTERCLAIM:

1. An order that the Claimant do cause to be carried out the works specified in a Schedule of Repairs to be served on or before discovery; alternatively
2. An order that the Claimant do pay to the Defendants the cost of carrying out the said works;
3. Damages limited to £5,000;
4. Interest as aforesaid.

S Dogboy

DATED this day of 1998

STATEMENT OF TRUTH

B10–07 I believe/the Defendant believes that the content of this Defence are true. I am duly authorised to make this statement on behalf of the Defendant.

Signed ....

Dated ....

Rallies,

40 Victoria Road,

Barnley,

B70 2BU.

Solicitors for the Defendants

Appendix B11

IN THE PARKSIDE COUNTY COURT

Claim No. 6LS58517

BETWEEN:-

DAVID STEPHEN BUCK

Claimant

and

ROYAL MAIL SLOW DELIVERY GROUP PLC

Defendant

DEFENCE

Mr Marmaduke Harmsworth

Pratt Partners

Josephs House

Hangover Walk

Parkside PP3 1NB

Your ref: ant and bee 123

Our ref: 160257

IN THE PARKSIDE COUNTY COURT

Claim No. 6LS58517

BETWEEN:

DAVID STEPHEN BUCK

Claimant

and

ROYAL MAIL SLOW DELIVERY GROUP PLC

Defendant

DEFENCE

B11–02 1. Paragraph 1 of the Particulars of Claim is admitted.

2. It is admitted that the Claimant suffered accidental injury during the course of his employment by the Defendant at the approximate time and on the date specified. No further admissions are made as to paragraph 2 of the Particulars of Claim.

3. The Defendant repeats paragraph 2 hereof. No further admissions are made as to paragraph 3 of the Particulars of Claim.

4. As to paragraph 4 of the Particulars of Claim, the Defendant believes that the Claimant's accident occurred in the Priority Service Locker, which was for sorting priority letters and parcels into required walks for collection by delivery personnel. The Claimant was also required to deal with dead letter mail. The Claimant was given a degree of freedom to arrange the said tasks and to arrange the system for performing the said tasks. It is averred that prior to the accident [Instructing Solicitors to insert the date if known] a proposal was made to the Claimant by Mr Peter Forrester , the Claimant's assistant line manager at the time of the accident, to remove a table from the Priority Service Locker to create more space. It was also suggested that a room known as the Disturber Locker would be utilised by the Claimant for sorting the priority mail before returning to the Priority Service Locker to deal with the dead letter mail. However, the Claimant declined to perform the said tasks in the suggested manner. It is admitted that the Claimant complained of space constraints, which were responded to in the manner described above. No further admissions are made as to paragraph 4 of the Particulars of Claim.

5. In the circumstances, it is averred that the Claimant had declined to implement the safe system for carrying out the said tasks which was proposed by the Defendant.

6. The Claimant admits paragraph 5 of the Particulars of Claim.

7. It is denied that the accidental injury the Claimant suffered was caused by the breach of statutory duty and/or negligence of the Defendant, its servants or agents.

8. In the circumstances, such injury, loss or damage as the Claimant may prove was caused wholly or in part by his own negligence.

Particulars of negligence

a.   failed to keep any or any proper look out;

b.   failed adequately or at all in time or at all to see, heed or act upon or avoid the said parcel, which he had placed on the floor;

c.   failed to pick up his feet or to step over or around the said parcel;

d.   failed to remove, clear, or otherwise render safe the part of the floor of which now makes complaint;

e.   (e) failed to take any or any adequate care for his own safety;

f.   failed to co-operate with the Defendant in implimenting the new system of work proposed by, inter alios, the Claimant's assistant line manager.

9.   The Defendant admits the alleged pain, injury, loss of amenity and damage referred to in paragraph 9. No admissions are made as to the alleged loss of earnings.

10. No admissions are made as to paragraph 10 the Particulars of Claim.

11. No admissions are made as to the claim for interest.

Marmaduke Harmsworth

DATED this   day of   2007

STATEMENT OF TRUTH

I believe/the Defendant believes that the content of this Defence are **B11–03** true. I am duly authorised to make this statement on behalf of the Defendant.

Signed ....

Dated ....

Pratt Partners

Josephs House

Hangover Walk

Parkside

PP3 ABC

Appendix B12

B12–01 Landlord's defence to disrepair claim by tenant in which specific performance and/or damages are sought based on there being no warranty of quality seeking to counterclaim/set-off arrears of rent

Case No. 6BED0323

IN THE BRADFORD ON AVON COUNTY COURT
BETWEEN:

SHARON KHAN

Claimant

and

SUNBERRY ON THAMES COMMUNITY HOUSING TRUST LIMITED

Defendant

DEFENCE

B12–02 Mr. William Bobsleigh

Sunberry on Thames Community Housing Trust Group

Legal Section

Trust House

5 New Augustus Street

Pompeigh

Berkshire BB1 4TT

Your Ref: LS/PN/00750

Our Ref: 154498

Case No. 6BD1234

IN THE BRADFORD ON AVON COUNTY COURT
BETWEEN:

SHARON KHAN

Claimant

and

SUNBERRY ON THAMES COMMUNITY HOUSING TRUST LIMITED

Defendant

DEFENCE

1. Save that the tenancy agreement of the premises was with **B12–03**
   the Claimant and Jason Lee Harper as joint tenants and not
   with the Claimant alone, paragraph 1 of the Particulars of
   Claim is admitted.

2. It is admitted that clause 2 contained a covenant on the part
   of the Defendant to keep the structure and exterior of the
   premises in good repair. In the alternative, section 11 of
   the Landlord and Tenant Act 1985 applied to the premises.
   It is denied that the Defendant was required to keep the
   structure and exterior of the premises in good repair at all
   times "irrespective of notice". The Claimant appears to have
   misconstrued the case of BRITISH TELECOM v SUN LIFE
   ASSURANCE SOCIETY. The Defendant is only in breach
   of its obligation to repair the structure and exterior of the
   premises when it has such information about the existence
   of the defect or defects alleged as would put a reasonable
   landlord on inquiry that works of repair are necessary and
   has failed to carry out the necessary works with reasonable
   expedition.

3. The presence of asbestos in the premises is admitted but
   it is denied that this constitutes any breach of the tenancy
   agreement. The Defendant covenanted to keep the structure
   and exterior of the premises in good repair but did not
   warrant that the premises had any particular quality nor that
   they were in good condition. Such minor cracks as existed
   in the premises were consistent with the age, character and
   prospective life of the premises and the locality in which
   they are situated.

4. Further, or alternatively, the Defendant has taken all necessary
   and reasonable steps to replace the asbestos in the property,
   which did not constitute an immediate hazard to health,
   by a series of improvements. In particular, the Claimant's
   property has now been fully refurbished so as to remove any
   asbestos within the premises.

5. The presence of cracks in the premises is admitted. The
   emission of dust therefrom is not admitted.

6. It is admitted that the Defendant was notified of defective
   plaster to the hallway at the premises on or about 15th August
   2001. The Defendant's surveyor inspected the premises on the
   15th August 2001 but was notified by the Claimant that her
   son was to plaster the door casing. It was therefore deemed
   appropriate to cancel any job order in relation to this item.

7. It is admitted that the Claimant reported a boiler leak. This was repaired on or about 31st December 2001.

8. It is admitted that on or about 6th February 2003 the Claimant notified the Defendant of condensation to a window at the premises and an inspection was carried out on the 18th February 2003 which revealed that there was no breach of any of the repairing obligations in the tenancy agreement and hence no requirement for action of any sort.

9. It is admitted that on the 10th June 2005 Mr. Garnier carried out an inspection of the premises on the Claimant's behalf. No copy of the said report accompanies the Particulars of Claim but the Defendant assumes it is in the same form as the report served with the letter before action dated 24th June 2005. By a letter dated 26th July 2005 it was pointed out to the Claimant's solicitors that the Housing Disrepair Protocol had not been complied with but indicated that the Defendant's Technical Liaison Manager would inspect the premises with a view to carrying out any repairs for which the Defendant was liable. However, no response was received from the Claimant's solicitors to this letter.

10. It is admitted and averred that the Defendant moved the Claimant into a replacement property on or about the 9th March 2006 to facilitate a number of improvements to the premises. The replacement premises were as good as her own and it is denied that compensation paid to other tenants on the estate in the factual circumstances which applied in their cases has any relevance to the Claimant's entitlement to "compensation for breach of the covenant for quiet enjoyment". For the avoidance of doubt, it is denied that there has been any breach of the covenant for quiet enjoyment and it is denied the Claimant is entitled to any loss or damage arising out of the need to move to alternative premises whilst the work was carried out, there being no breach of any of the obligations in the tenancy agreement. The removal of the Claimant from the premises was by her consent.

11. In relation to paragraph 11 of the Particulars of Claim, the rearrangement of the internal layout of the premises was chosen by the Claimant, who had the option of leaving that layout as it had been before the improvement work was carried out. In relation to the new floor covering the Claimant claims that she will need to purchase, these do not arise as a consequence of any breach of any of the obligations in the tenancy agreement. In any event, pursuant to clause 3.26 of the tenancy conditions which accompanied the tenancy

agreement, the Claimant is responsible for decorating the inside of the premises.

12. In relation to paragraph 12 of the Particulars of Claim, this is denied.

13. In relation to paragraph 13 of the Particulars of Claim, it is admitted that if the Claimant establishes actionable disrepair she will be entitled to damages for the diminution in value of the premises/her inconvenience. Otherwise, no admissions are made as to the said paragraph.

14. In relation to paragraph 14 of the Particulars of Claim:

    14.1 Asbestos at the premises has been removed by the Defendant at its expense and this sub-paragraph is therefore not understood.

    14.2 This sub-paragraph is denied. If, which is denied, there was at any stage actionable disrepair at the premises it is averred that the Defendant would only have become liable when it had both the information about the existence of the defect as would put it on reasonable enquiry as to whether works of repair were needed and had had a reasonable opportunity to effect the repair or repairs necessary. This does not apply in this case.

    14.3 Sub-paragraphs 14.3 and 14.4 of the Particulars of Claim are denied for the reasons given.

15. Paragraph 15 of the Particulars of Claim is denied. If, which is denied the Claimant has suffered any loss it is averred that she has failed in her duty to mitigate that loss by, for example, rejecting the opportunity of moving into suitable alternative accommodation to enable the Defendant to carry out the works of improvement to the premises referred to above. Specifically, the Claimant having agreed to move to suitable alternative accommodation changed her mind on the 13th June 2005 causing significant further delay.

16. Paragraph 16 of the Particulars of Claim is unsupported by any medical evidence contrary to 16PD.4 paragraph 4.3 CPR. The Defendant specifically denies that the Claimant has suffered any identifiable form of injury which would sound in damages.

17. Paragraph 17 of the Particulars of Claim is also denied.

18. It is denied that the Claimant is entitled to her costs even if she is successful in this claim for the following amongst other reasons:

    (i) her failure to follow the Housing Disrepair Protocol;

    (ii) the fact that her claim, based on her own expert evidence from Mr. Garner, has a value of less than

£1,000 and would be allocated to the Small Claims Track.

William Bobsleigh

DATED this day of 2006

Statement of Truth

B12–04 The Defendant believes that the facts stated in this Defence are true.

Signed...........................

Dated..............................

Sunberry on Thames Community Housing Trust Group,

Legal Section

Trust House

5 New Augustus Street

Pompeigh

Berkshire BB1 4TT

Your Ref: LS/PN/00750

Our Ref: 154498

APPENDIX C—Useful Websites

An A to Z of useful websites

A

Further detail of asbestos regulations and updated guidance may be found on the Health and Safety Executive website: *http://www.hse.gov.uk/campaigns/asbestos.*
Applied Energy Products, which provides guidance on the government's thermal efficiency and other standards with a view to achieving it's "Decent Homes Standard": *http://www.applied-energy.com.*
The Institute of Arbitrators provides much guidance on the selection of those qualified to sit and a list of members of the institute: *www.arbitrators.org.*

C

The Ministry for Communities and Local Government has information on its website about housing standards and related areas: *http://www.communities.gov.uk.*
Corgi direct for information on gas fires and safety including publications: *http://www.corgi-direct.com.*

D

Department of Trade and Industry which provides information on the enforcement of a wide range of safety regulations and the Impact of these on indicatory, now the Department for Business and Regulatory reform (BERR): *http://www.dti.gov.uk.*

H

Health and Safety Executive: *http://www.hse.gov.uk.*
HM Land Registry: *http://www.landregistry.gov.uk*
Housing disrepair protocol: A copy of this Protocol is available from the Dept of Justice website at: *http://www.justice.gov.uk/civil/procrules_fin/contents/protocols/prot_hou.htm.*
Her Majesty's Court Service:

http://www.hmcourts-service.gov.uk/.
Housing ombudsman:
http://www.ihos.org.uk/

J

Justice, Dept of: *http://www.justice.gov.uk*

N

NICEIC: *http://www.niceic.com*
National Mediation Helpline:
www.nationalmediahelpline.com

O

Office of Fair Trading for helpful guidance on the application of the
Unfair Terms in Consumer Contracts Regulations 1999:
http://www.oft.gov.uk.

P

Property Litigation Association: *http://www.pla.org.uk*
Parliament for all statutes and statutory instruments:
http://www.parliament.uk

R

Royal Institution of Chartered Surveyors:
http://www.RICS.org

S

Standing Conference of Mediation Advocates:
http://www.mediationadvocates.org.uk

T

Technology and Construction Bar Association (TECBAR), which
includes a list of mediator and arbitrator members:
http://www.tecbar.org.

Index

Act of God
liability and, 8–23
Agreements
lease,
before signing a, 1–03
Alternative dispute resolution
See **Dispute resolution**
Arbitration
appeal from, 19–15
award, 19–16
challenge to award, 19–14
clauses, 19–01
commercial disputes, 19–10
conduct of, 19–13
expert determination, 19–17,
19–18
scope of reference, 19–12
statutory rules, 19–11
Arthritis
damages for, 17–26
Assignee
position of, 1–10
Assurances
collateral,
before signing a lease,
1–03, 1–04
Asthma
damages for, 17–26
Builder
employer,
economic loss of, 9–09
excluded premises, 9–06
liability of,
common law, in, 9–02
limitation period, 9–08
purchaser,
economic loss of, 9–09
liability to, 9–02
repair work, 9–05
statutory duty of, 9–04, 9–07

Builder–landlord
liability of, 8–09, 9–03
tenant,
liability to, 8–09
tortious liability, 9–01
Building Act 1984
breach of duty, 11–04
building regulations,
breach of, 11–04
civil liability for breach,
11–05
economic loss, 11–05
status of, 11–03
building standards,
enforcement of, 11–02
local authority,
powers of, 11–02
negligence,
liability in, 11–02, 11–04
Building
dangerous, A6–02, A6–03
demolition, A6–01, A6-05
duty of care, A4–03
duty to build properly,
cases excluded, A4–02
generally, A4-01
supplementary points,
A4–05
landlord's duty of care, A4–04
neglected sites, A6–04
notices, A6–06, A6–07
ruinous and dilapidated, A6–04
Building regulations
breach of, 11–04
civil liability for breach, 11–05
economic loss, 11–05
status of, 11–03
Business lease
deed for, 1–04

Carbon monoxide
health and safety, 11–15
poisoning,
damages for, 17–26
Children
liability to, 10–10
Claims
amendments to, 18–26
bringing a, 18–01
cause of action accrues, 18–03
contractual, 18–03
contribution, for, 18–28
costs,
offers to settle and conduct,
18–41
part 36 offers, 18–40
dilapidations,
certification of, 18–13
landlord's claims, 18–12
pre–action protocol, 18–11
tenant's response, 18–15
timing of, 18–14
expert,
instructing a, 18–07
joint statements, 18–08
types of, 18–09
housing,
aims, 18–19
costs, 18–22
expert evidence, 18–21
non-compliance with
protocol, 18–23
protocol for, 18–17
scope of protocol, 18–18
steps under the protocol,
18–20
indemnity, for, 18–28
information,
requests for, 18–29
limitation on, 18–02, 18–05
nuisance, 18–05
particulars of, B3–01—B3–03,
B9–01—B9–04
parties to, 18–06
personal injury, 18–05, B9–

01—B9–04
pleadings, 18–24
pre–action protocols,
complying with, 18–10
service charges,
unpaid, 18–16
Scott schedules, 18–27, B6–
01—B6–02
statements,
case of, 18–25
joint, 18–08
truth, of, 18–30
summary judgment, 18–39
Technology and Construction
Court,
background, 18–35
litigation in, 18–36
procedure, 18–37
role of, 18–34
transfer to County Court,
18–38
tortuous, 18–04
track allocation, 18–31
unless orders, 18–33
Woolf reforms, 18–01
Collateral contract
warranties and, 1–04
Collateral warranty
argument for existence of,
1–04
tenants and, 1–04
third party, 1–02
Commercial leases
damages,
landlord's claim for, 17–07
Common parts of building
noise from, 6–07
nuisance from 8–16
repairs,
obligations to undertake,
5–11
self-help, 14–08
Contractors
liability to, 10–17

Contractual liability
principles of, 1–01
Contracts (Rights of Third Parties) Act 1999
effect of, 1–07
Costs
offers to settle and conduct, 18–41
part 36 offers, 18–40
Covenant
absolute, 6–06
application of, 6–03
assurance of, 6–02
breach of, 6–04, 6–07
defence, as, 6–08
derogation from grant of, consequences of, 6–04
nature of, 6–05
noise from common parts of building, 6–07
protection afforded by, 6–02
qualified, 6–06
quiet enjoyment,
defective premises and, 6–07
purpose of covenant, 6–05
repudiation of lease, 6–04
reserving powers, 6–03
right of entry, 6–08
Damages
aggravated, 17–22
alternative accommodation, 17–03
arthritis, 17–26
assessment for,
method of, 17–04
asthma, 17–25
betterment, 17–35
burden of proof, 17–10
carbon monoxide poisoning, 17–24
causation, 17–30, 17–31
claims for, 17–01
commercial dilapidations claim, 17–37

commercial leases, 17–07
consequential losses, 17–06
contractual claims, 17–37
contributory negligence, 17–28
covenant,
breach of, 17–08
damp housing conditions,
arthritis, 17–16
asthma from, 17–26
depression, 17–26
death,
liability for, 17–23
depression, 17–26
dilapidations,
breach of covenant, 17–08
diminution, 17–04
disrepair in residential leases, 17–02
employment,
future prospects of, 17–27
loss of, 17–27
exemplary, 17–22
first limb, 17–10
inconvenience, 17–03
interest, 17–36
judgment rate, 17–39
landlord,
design and build by, 17–21
little likelihood of repairs being done, 17–14
repairs undertaken by, 17–13
mitigate,
failure to, 17–30
loss and, 17–34
personal injury
claims, 17–38, B9–01—B9–04
liability for, 17–23
premises to be redeveloped, 17–15
profit,
loss of, 17–33
recoverable, 17–03
remoteness, 17–30, 17–32

repair costs, 17–06, 17–11
repairing obligation,
   breaches of, 17–09
repairs,
   arrangement to complete,
     17–17
reversion,
   diminution of, 17–18
residential leases at a ground
   rent, 17–05
second limb, 17–19
sub–tenancy,
   presence of, 17–16
tenant,
   claim of, 17–20
tort, in, 17–21
value figure,
   diminution in, 17–12

Death
liability for, 17–23

Decent Homes Standard
energy efficiency standards,
   powers to enforce, 12–19
enforcement of, 12–20

Defective Premises Act 1972
landlord,
   liability of, 9–13—9–23
licensees,
   position of, 9–26
remedies, 9–24
tenancies,
   assured, 9–25
   secured, 9–25
tenants,
   duty to, 9–13
third parties,
   duty to, 9–13

Definitions
dwelling house, 5–09
exterior, 5–08
good and substantial repair,
   2–07
good condition, 2–10
good tenantable repair, 2–10
habitable repair, 2–10

keep in repair, 5–08
long lease, 2–16
main structures of property,
   2–10
occupier, 10–05
premises, 10–04
structure, 5–08
take reasonable steps, 2–10
visitors, 10–07
waiver, 15–05
well and sufficiently lit, 2–10

Depression
damages for, 17–26

Dilapidations
breach of covenant, 17–08
certification of, 18–13
claim for, B5–01—B5–03
defence to, B7–01—B7–03
information,
   request for, B8–
     01—B8–03
landlord's claims, 18–12
pre–action protocol, 18–11
tenant's response, 18–15
timing of, 18–14

Dispute resolution
alternative dispute resolution
   schemes, 19–02
arbitration,
   appeal from, 19–15
   award, 19–16
   challenge to award, 19–14
   clauses, 19–01
   commercial disputes,
     19–10
   conduct of, 19–13
   expert determination,
     19–17, 19–18
   scope of reference, 19–12
   statutory rules, 19–11
early neutral evaluation, 19–09
Housing Ombudsman, 19–03
mediation,
   conduct of, 19–05
   costs of, 19–08

court based schemes,
19–04
generally, 19–02
non-government schemes,
19–04
without prejudice, 19–07
mediator,
choice of, 19–06
methods of, 19–01
proportionate dispute
resolution, 19–03
Economic loss
building regulations, 11–05
claim for,
employer, by, 9-09
purchaser, by, 9-09
recovery of, 8–10, 9–09
Emergency workers
liability to, 10–11
Employer
economic loss, 9-09
Employment
future prospects of, 17–27
loss of, 17–27
Energy efficiency
standards,
powers to enforce, 12–19
Equitable intervention
effect of, 1–06
Expert witness
instructing a, 18–07
joint statements, 18–08
types of, 18–09
Fire regulations
liability, 11–09
Forfeiture
breaches,
remedy of, 15–08
costs,
recovery of, 15–19
decorative repairs, 15–20
defence to, B4–01—B4–03
disrepair to premises, 15–01
landlord, right to,

leave granted to continue,
15–11
negotiating and, 15–22
restrictions on, 15–06
Leasehold Property Repairs
Act 1938,
avoiding provisions of,
15–13
introduction of, 15–09
requirements of, 15–10
workings of, 15–12
long leases and, 15–09
method of, 15–03
notice,
service of, 15–07
reform of law on, 15–23
relief,
against forfeiture, 15–14
applying for, 15–21
grant of, 15–17
payment of landlord's
costs, 15–19
statutory provisions, 15–15
sub–tenant and, 15–18
terms on which granted,
15–16
right to, 15–02
statutory jurisdiction,
grant of relief, 15–15
provisions of LPA 1925,
15–15
waiver,
disrepair and, 15–05
meaning of, 15–05
successful argument for,
15–04
Gas
See also **Energy efficiency**
appliances, 11–11
installations, 11–10
safety regulations, 11–12—11–
14, A10–01
Gypsies
possession order against,
13–01

Habitation
fitness for, 8–01
Health and Safety
access, 11–17
asbestos, 11–08
carbon monoxide, 11–15
disability discrimination,
11–22
duties, 11–07
electrical installations, 11–18
energy efficiency standards,
11–19
factories, 11–20
gas appliances, 11–11
gas installations, 11–10
gas safety regulations, 11–
12—11–14
home information pack, 11–19
liability, 11–06
offices, 11–21
personal injury,
safe from, 11–16
railway premises, 11–21
shops, 11–21
statutory offences, 11–07
Home information pack
health and safety and, 11–19
Housing Protocol
aims, 18–19
costs, 18–22
expert evidence, 18–21
non-compliance with, 18–23
protocol for, 18–17
scope of, 18–18
steps under, 18–20
Housing standards
assessing, A11–03
enforcement, A11–01
multiple occupation, A11–04
Human rights
challenges,
principal ways of making,
13–04
to date, 13–05
Convention rights, 13–02

decisions to date, 13–06
defences under, 13–01
future challenges, 13–07
gypsies,
possession order against,
13–01
liability under the Act, 13–03
Implied obligations
See Repair and maintenance
Implied terms
See Leases and agreements
Information
requests for, 18–29, B8–
01—B8–03
Landlord
See also **Builder-Landlord;
Forfeiture; Nuisance;
Repair and
maintenance**
adjoining occupier,
liability to, 8–03
right to sue, 8–06
damages,
design and build by, 17–21
little likelihood of repairs
being done, 17–14
repairs undertaken by,
17–13
liability of, 8–01, 9–13—9–23
tenants,
duty to, 9–13
third parties,
duty to, 9–13
**Landlord and Tenant
(Covenants) Act 1995**
effect of, 1-08
Law Commission
Renting Homes: the final
report, 5–17
**Law of Property
(Miscellaneous
Provisions) Act 1989**
compliance with, 1–05

Leasehold Property Repairs Act 1938
avoiding provisions of, 15–13
claims under, B2–01—B2–03
introduction of, 15–09
requirements of, 15–10
workings of, 15–12
Leasehold Valuation Tribunal
appeal before, 2–16
role of, 2–16
Leaseholders
long leases,
termination, 5–16
Leases and agreements
business efficacy test, 4–02
demised premises,
obligation to maintain,
4–06
furnished lets, 4–08
implied terms in,
decline to recognise, 4–07
generally, 4–02—4–05
repair and, 4–06
right of access to effect
repairs, 4–10
terminal dilapidations,
4–09
terminations, 4–09
inequality of bargaining power,
4–06
long leases,
termination of, 5–16
standing of, 1–01
variation of, A8–01
written, 1–04
Liability
landlord, of, 8–01, 9–13
occupier,
adjoining, 8–03
tortious, 8–01
Licensees
position of, 9–26
Local authority
Building Act 1984, 12–04

dangerous and defective
buildings,
power to control, 12–01
decent homes standard, 12–20
energy efficiency standards,
powers to enforce, 12–19
Environmental Protection Act
1990, 12–06
houses in multiple occupation,
duties and powers, 12–14
enforcement measures,
12–12
hazards covered, 12–11
health and safety rating,
12–10
licensing, 12–08, 12–09
new scheme, 12–13
Housing Act 1985, 12–05
Housing Act 2004,
enforcement measures,
12–12
hazards covered, 12–11
health and safety rating
regime, 12–10
licensing houses, 12–09
multiple occupation, 12–08
new scheme, 12–13
Housing Grants Construction
and Regeneration Act
1996, 12–07
powers of, 11–02, 12–04
public health, 12–02—12–03
renting homes, 12–21
statutory nuisances,
power to control, 12–15,
12–18
prejudice to health, 12–17
Mandatory injunction
See also **Specific performance**
Mediation
See **Dispute resolution**
Multiple occupation
houses in,
duties and powers, 12–14
enforcement measures,

12–12

hazards covered, 12–11

health and safety rating,
    12–10

licensing, 12–08, 12–09

new scheme, 12–13

standards, A11–04

statutory powers, 11–08

Negligence

categories of, 8–02

landlord and, 8–01

Neighbours

rights of support, 8–04

Nuisance

See also Rylands v Fletcher

abatement notice, A9–03

clean air and, A9–01

common parts of a building,
    8–16

entry to abate, 8–21

landlord,

acts of tenant, 8–19—8–21

liability of, 8–01, 8–11,
        8–14, 8–17, 8–18

rights of, 8–14

nature of, 8–12

retained parts of a building,
    8–16

statutory, A9–02, A9–07

tenant,

acts of, 8–19

liability of, 8–11, 8–13,
        8–19

rights of, 8–13

third party,

liability to, 8–11, 8–13,
        8–17

Occupier

adjoining,

landlord's liability to, 8–03

landlord's right to sue,
        8–06

tenant's liability to, 8–07

tenant's right to sue, 8–08

children,

liability to, 10–10

contributory negligence, 10–14

defences,

claim under act, B11–
        01—B11–04

voluntary assumed risk,
        10–22

warnings and exclusions,
        10–21

definition of, 10–05

duty to person other than
        visitors, A5–01

emergency workers,

liability to, 10–11

guests, 10–16

independent contractors,

liability for, 10–17

liability of,

excluding, 10–15

restricting, 10–15

tort, in, 10–01

negligence of, 8–05

trespassers,

duty to, 10–18, 10–20

intentions of, 10–19

standard of care, 10–20

trustees, 10–06

unincorporated associations,
    10–06

violenti non-fit injuria, 10–22

visitors,

assumption of risk, 10–13

children, 10–10

definition of, 10–07

duty to, 10–02, 10–03,
        10–09

legal rights, exercise of,
        10–08

obvious dangers, 10–12

Office accommodation

housekeeper,

provision of, 4–04

**Office, shops and railway
    premises**

health and safety, 11–21

Oral agreements
See **Leases and agreements**
Personal injury
claims for, 17–38, 18–05,
 B9–01—B9–04
liability for, 17–23
safety from, 11–16
Premises
definition of, 10–04
Profit
loss of, 17–33
Propriatory estoppel
doctrine of, 1–06
Privity rule
principle of, 1-02
Purchaser
economic loss of, 9-09
Quiet enjoyment
covenant, 6–01—6–08
defective premises and, 6–07
noise from common parts of
 building, 6–07
principle of, 6–01
purpose of covenant, 6–05
repudiation of lease, 6–04
reserving powers, 6–03
right of entry, 6–08
Quick v Taff–Ely
decision in, 2–02, 2–05
Repair and maintenance
See also **Damages**
access,
 statutory right of, 5–15
builder, by, 9–05
construction,
 approach to, 2–09
covenants to, A1–01
decorative repair, B10–01—
 10–07
disrepair,
 concept of, 2–02—2–05
 defence to claim, B12–
  01—B12–04
fit to live in,

meaning, 2–10
good and substantial repair,
 meaning, 2–07
good condition,
 meaning, 2–10
good tenantable repair,
 meaning, 2–10
habitable repair,
 meaning, 2–10
implied obligations on tenants,
 consequences of breach,
  7–05
 expectations of the tenant,
  7–04
 generally, 7–01
 inspection, to permit, 7–16
 limitation, 7–06
 occupy in a tenant–like
  manner, 7–02
 permissive waste, 7–12
 reform of, 7–17
 relevance of obligations,
  7-03
 remedies for breach, 7–11,
  7–13
 repairs, carry out, 7–16
 voluntary waste, 7–08
 waste, not to commit, 7–07
 watertight premises, 7–14,
  7–15
 wear and tear, 7–10
 wind tight premises, 7–14,
  7–15
improvement versus, 2–06
installations,
 generally, 5–13
 in proper working order,
  5–14
landlord,
 gas safety, A10–01
 implied obligations, 4–01,
  4–02
 obligations on, 2–01
lease,
 application to court to vary,

2–16
varying of, 2–16
Leasehold Valuation Tribunal,
appeal before, 2–16
role of, 2–16
long lease,
meaning, 2–16
licence to undertake,
granting of, 2–07
main structures of property,
meaning, 2–10
notice,
clauses, 2–14
communication of, 2–15
exceptions to requirement
for, 2–13
requirement for, 2–11
tenant, from, 2–12
reform,
proposals for, 2–17
repairing covenants, 2–01,
A2–01
repairing obligations,
application of, A7–03
contracting out, A7–02
courts and, A7–05
exceptions, A7-04
generally, A7–01
specific performance,
A7–07
residential accommodation,
minimum standard of,
4–01
section 11 obligations,
common parts, 5–11
disrepair, 5–10
dwelling house, 5–09
exterior, 5–08
keep in repair, 5–08
structure, 5–08
standard of repair, 5–12
statutory obligations on
landlords,
additional obligations,
5–06,

contracting out, 5–05
exceptions, 5–03
fit for habitation, 5–01,
5–03
freedom of contract and,
5–02
implied obligations, 5-07
keep in repair, 5–08
older leases, 5-06
repairing obligations, 5–04
structure and exterior,
5–07, 5–08
take reasonable steps,
meaning, 2–10
well and sufficiently lit
meaning, 2–10

Representation
standing of, 1–04

Right of entry
access to adjoining land,
freehold owners, 14–02
common law rights, 14–03
easement, establishing a,
14–04
nuisance, right to abate,
14–05
statutory intervention to
establish, 14–06
health and safety, 11–17
implied, 4–04
quiet enjoyment, 6–08
nuisance,
entry to abatement, 8–21
repairs,
to effect, 4–10, 5–15

Rylands v Fletcher
acts of God, 8–23
rule in, 8–01, 8–22
scope of, 8–24

**Sale of Goods and Services
Act 1992**
goods,
provision of, 9–12
seller/builder, 9–11
warranty under, 9–10

Scott schedules
claims under, 18–27, B6–
01—B6–02
Section 146 notice
precedent, B1–01
Self help
access to adjoining land,
freehold owners, 14–02
common law rights, 14–03
easement, establishing a,
14–04
nuisance, right to abate,
14–05
statutory intervention to
establish, 14–06
common parts,
defects to, 14–08
counterclaim,
ability to, 14–11
improvements,
right to carry out, 14–15
landlord,
compelled to carry out
repairs, 14–14
leaseholders, long,
rights of, 14–16
licensees,
position of, 14–13
methods of, 14–01
repair costs,
set–off following
assignment, 14–11
setting off, 14–10
withholding against rent,
14–09
right of, 14–01
set–off,
attempts to limit right of,
14–12
tenant's right to,
carrying out works, 14–07
compelling landlords to
undertake repairs,
14–14
deducting costs of repairs,

14–07
Service charges
unpaid, 18–16
Specific performance
See also **Damages**
basis for the award, 16–06
claims for, 16–08
court,
powers of, 16–09
damages in lieu, 16–11
delay, 16–04
enforcement, 16–10
general principles, 16–02
grant of order for, 16–01
interim prohibitory injunction,
16–07
interim relief, 16–07
refusal of, 16–03
schedule of work, 16–05
Sub-tenancy
damages, 17–16
**Technology and Construction
Court**
background, 18–35
litigation in, 18–36
procedure, 18–37
role of, 18–34
transfer to County Court,
18–38
Tenancy
See also **Leases and
agreements; Repair and
maintenance**
1995 Act,
operation of, 1–16
assignee,
default of, 1–11
liability of, 1–15
position of, 1–10
assignment,
tenant by, 1–14
landlord,
position of, 1–12
successor to, 1–13
original tenant and, 1–09

post–January 1996, 1–10
  original tenant, 1–11
  tenancies, 1–10
pre–January 1996,
  original tenant, 1–09
  successors, 1–10
surrender of, 1–04

Tenants
See also **Occupier; Repair
  and maintenance**
adjoining occupier,
  liability to, 8–07
  right to sue, 8–08
disrepair,
  claim for, B12–
      01—B12–04
nuisance,
  acts of, 8–19
liability of, 8–11, 8–13, 8–19
rights of, 8–13

Third party
See also **Occupier; Sub-
  tenancy; Trespassers;
  Visitors**
rights of, 1-02
nuisance and, 8–11
unlawful acts of, 8–05

Tort
liability in, A3-01

Trespassers
duty to, 10–18, 10–20

intentions of, 10–19
standard of care, 10–20

Trustees
liability to, 10-06

Unfair terms
Act of 1977, 3–02
leases in, 3–01
liability,
  restricting, 3–01
OFT Guidance, 3–07
power to vary terms, 3–06
reasonableness,
  concept of, 3–02
regulations,
  consumer, 3–03
  future challenges to, 3–07
  scope of, 3–04
  test of unfairness, 3–05
unreasonable terms,
  striking out of, 3–06

Unincorporated associations
liability to, 10-06

Visitors
assumption of risk, 10–13
children, 10–10
definition of, 10–07
duty to, 10–02, 10–03, 10–09
legal rights, exercise of, 10–08
obvious dangers, 10–12

Waiver
See **Forfeiture**